AUDIBLE
EMPIRE

REFIGURING AMERICAN MUSIC · A series edited by Ronald Radano and Josh Kun
Charles McGovern, contributing editor

Duke University Press · Durham and London · 2016

AUDIBLE EMPIRE

Music, Global Politics, Critique

RONALD RADANO AND TEJUMOLA OLANIYAN, EDITORS

Designed by Courtney Leigh Baker
Typeset in Minion Pro by Westchester Publishing Services

Library of Congress Cataloging-in-Publication Data
Audible empire : music, global politics, critique / Ronald Radano and Tejumola
Olaniyan, editors.
pages cm — (Refiguring American music)
Includes bibliographical references and index.
ISBN 978-0-8223-5986-9 (hardcover : alk. paper)
ISBN 978-0-8223-6012-4 (pbk. : alk. paper)
ISBN 978-0-8223-7494-7 (e-book)
1. World music—Social aspects—History.   2. Imperialism—Social aspects—History.3.
World music—Political aspects—History.   I. Radano, Ronald Michael, editor.
II. Olaniyan, Tejumola, editor.   III. Series: Refiguring American music.
ML3916.A925 2015
780.9—dc23   2015024232

Cover art: Detail of photo by Boulevard de la Photo. © Creative Market.

Duke University Press gratefully acknowledges the support of Global Studies,
a member of the Institute for Regional and International Studies of the University of
Wisconsin–Madison, which provided funds toward the publication of this book.

CONTENTS

ACKNOWLEDGMENTS

Audible Empire: Music, Global Politics, Critique emerged from the activities of the interdisciplinary Music-Race-Empire (MRE) Research Circle, which we organized at the University of Wisconsin–Madison in 2009. The Research Circle was made possible through the generous funding of UW's Institute for Regional and International Studies (formerly International Institute) and its Global Studies program, which supported the Circle from 2009 to 2012. We wish to thank Amy Stambach, the former Director of Global Studies, who originally approached us with the idea of organizing the Research Circle, and Gilles Bousquet and Guido Podestá, the former and current vice provost and dean of the Division of International Studies, for making it possible. Over the course of its institutional life, the Research Circle benefited from the unflagging support given by a number of UW staff. We'd like to single out here, in particular, Steve Smith, former associate director of Global Studies, who not only provided unremitting guidance, but also enabled us to begin a major, public research project that will ultimately document the production and global circulation of popular music between 1890 and 1940. We are similarly indebted to Scott Carter, the Circle's project coordinator, who worked with diligence and distinction in managing communications and programming activities and who played an important role in compiling the manuscript. Caitlin Tyler-Richards prepared the final, revised manuscript for submission and publication.

During the initial months of the Circle, we hosted a series of workshops and invited speakers, which culminated in a one-day event staged in collaboration with colleagues at the University of Chicago. Tim Brennan was generous in his participation at our inaugural event. We are also grateful to the UW Circle members Toma Longinović and Morgan Luker and to our Chicago colleagues Philip V. Bohlman, Melvin Butler, Travis Jackson, and Kaley Mason for their participation in Madison and Chicago. Phil was generous in taking the lead in organizing the event at Chicago's Franke Institute.

The present volume grew out of the Circle's 2011 symposium, "Music-Race-Empire," which focused on the transnational production of race through musical form and practices. The symposium brought together nearly two dozen scholars from across the United States, who presented for discussion and critique early versions of the essays compiled here. (Kofi Agawu and Michael Denning served as keynote speakers at the symposium.) Over the course of the event and in follow-up correspondence and revision, the topics broadened beyond the particularities of race to involve a series of subjects relating to global politics (hence, the more encompassing subtitle of the present volume). We extend our profound gratitude to all the participants, many of whom contributed to *Audible Empire*. (Olivia Bloechl, Ian Condry, and John Nimis were among those who congregated in Madison but could not join us in the publication.) There would have been no book at all without the contributors' unwavering commitment. The perceptive insights that all the symposium participants brought to the project's particular focus were unfailingly inspiring, and the authors responded to requests for clarifications and revisions with understanding and admirable good cheer. The symposium, moreover, would not have been possible without the dedicated hard work of all members of the Circle. Thanks especially go to Florence Bernault, B. Venkat Mani, Rubén Medina, Lalita du Perron, and the visiting guest Travis Jackson, who served as chairs and commentators. Additional support came from several UW units: the School of Music, Department of English, Department of African Languages and Literature, the African Diaspora and Atlantic World Research Circle, and the Institute for Research in the Humanities.

We are, finally, very grateful to Ken Wissoker, our editor at Duke University Press, for taking on the book and for his expert guidance all through the peer-review process. He ably selected two excellent anonymous reviewers whose reports were engaging, detailed, and meticulous. We had the added benefit of an extended conversation with one of them, Steve Feld, who revealed his role prior to a visit to Madison, which allowed us to engage in a valuable follow-up discussion during his stay. Two contributors, Jairo Moreno and

Phil Bohlman, generously provided astute readings of the introduction, for which we are also grateful.

We greatly appreciate the efforts of all those involved in helping us to draw out the significance of *Audible Empire* and for recognizing the timeliness and importance of the volume. Publication of this book was made possible in part by a subvention from the University of Wisconsin–Madison's Institute for Regional and International Studies and its office of Global Studies as part of the initial Research Circle grant.

Ronald Radano and Tejumola Olaniyan

INTRODUCTION   Hearing Empire—Imperial Listening

RONALD RADANO AND TEJUMOLA OLANIYAN

"Empire" is one of those wandering melodies of contemporary social and cultural analysis, a key word that seems to show up again and again, in any number of circumstances and settings. So oft-repeated and overrehearsed is "empire" that the term itself can appear, at times, imperial in character, and in its incessant display and repetition, it begins to take on qualities of abstraction. The obsessive iteration of empire (as with a related term, neoliberalism) leads to a loss of significance; its meaning comes to seem ambiguous, its power diminished. To propose now that empire be understood within the sensory realm of the auditory might seem to risk perpetuating an already problematic tendency. For if the concept of empire has become too abstract in its excessive usage, it would now appear, as a referent of the sonorous, to draw further into the ether, aligning with immaterial forms and bringing imperial action and history into that which we cannot touch, feel, or see. This is why, perhaps, historical studies of empire since, for example, Walter LaFeber, William Appleman Williams, and Eduardo Galeano have remained so materially grounded, having focused on legacies of militarism and economy;[1] why Marxian studies of historical materialism have centered on the visible and haptic; why Foucauldian interrogations of governmentality have targeted the apparatuses of security and law and conceptions of sovereignty; why even the critical turn bringing about British cultural, subaltern, and postcolonial studies have all typically asked the realms of human sound making to stay quiet. This is work for the big boys. Matters of superstructure, stand to the rear!

And yet if we simply pay attention or, better, give a listen—our metaphors of knowledge are fundamentally ocularcentric—we can begin to comprehend how the emergences of European imperial orders and the concomitant rise of political democracies have also been matters of the ear. Sound studies have heightened our attention to what we might call auditory significance, to the power and effect of sound's production and its reception in the formation of social and political orders. In a foundational historical work, for example, Alain Corbin demonstrates how village bells in nineteenth-century France had an ordering effect on the feel and character of town living. The audible clarity of a bell's tone became the source of contests over Roman Catholic and New Republic definitions of time, identifying the focus of debates about sound's sacral and secular symbolism, as well as its ownership under law.[2] As a colonizing force in the rise of empire, moreover, sound productions became a key tool in imposing other forms of discipline and order. At the outset, sound's presence was anything but orderly. Occupations were inherently noisy and chaotic, involving massive interventions of people, animals, materials, and things; of assembling, working, training, and discoursing; of violence, negotiation, and engagement. In its participation in social order, however, sound production quickly assumed a role in organizing human behavior. The Portuguese, British, and French empires were notorious for their ability to translate, mangle, and otherwise appropriate the local terms of places and people—"fetish," "caste," "griot," "Bombay," "Peking"—to the point of re-structuring terminological references of identification and self-knowing. Such discursive representations, in turn, informed the emerging orders of vernacular musical knowledge beyond the church and court. The second voyage of James Cook and the eighteenth-century tours of

Europe by music writers such as Charles Burney, for example, contributed to the aggregation of contested discourses of alterity in which music stood centrally. In a seminal essay on the anthropology of the senses, moreover, Constance Classen reports how auditory conquest succeeded in re-orienting the self-understanding of modern Andeans, who today "look nostalgically back on the pre-Conquest period as a golden aural/oral age when the world was animated by sound." From South Africa to Australia, as Mark M. Smith has observed, British colonizers expanded the regulating power of outdoor sound devices, employing them to structure work among aboriginal people and to introduce temporal orders according to newly industrial impositions of labor time.[3]

As the audibility of imperial presence resonated outward, reaching into the interstices of everyday social living and the structures of the economic, it simultaneously inhabited and reoriented the character of domestic spaces at home, turning its developments in science and technology inward, affecting the sound and feel of those who were otherwise largely oblivious to goings-on in the wider reaches of the world. Friedrich Kittler shows how nineteenth-century explorations of frequency rendered western musical practices into forms of abstraction dislodged from their historical moorings, obscuring the contextual specificity of European orderings of "music." Jonathan Sterne's important work on methods of listening and the shaping of hearing demonstrates how the new science of audibility served to discipline medical practices at this same historical moment, as it would later reorganize, through the advances of various mediating devices, from the telephone to the MP3, the very character of modern perceptions of sound. With these disciplines of listening, audition technologies begin to structure a peculiar, auditory phenomenology, a world in which, according to Georg Simmel, "the calculative exactness of practical life which the money economy has brought about corresponds to the ideal of natural science to transform the world into an arithmetic problem." These early twentieth-century anxieties would famously draw the concern of Theodor Adorno, in his pessimistic theorizing of regressive tendencies in composition and aesthetic judgment, a world suffused and inoculated by banality and repetition.[4]

More sanguine portrayals of the condition of metropolitan listening show how the force of cold war–era technologies, from the transistor to computer-generated sound, have offered a healthy measure of the sense of liveliness and pleasure in our listening lives, and together they have also inspired a reasonable skepticism about all the negativity of a "culture industry" and its deleterious effects. The proliferation of important recent studies, from Michael Bull's critical ethnography of radios and iPods to Kate Crawford's investigation into social-media listening, has shed new light on the profound effects of sound's possibilities of pleasure and affect and has exposed the weariness of some of the older claims about false consciousness. At the same time, however, there is a tendency in this same literature to lean toward celebration and, in the name of a new (yet very old) kind of elite cosmopolitanism, to broadcast claims of value according to a rich lexicon of subversive hipness. In this, Adorno has become a convenient scapegoat in popular music studies writ large, as we witness a seemingly magical world of metropolitan youth listening somehow cordoned off from the greater forces of global politics and political economy that instantiate it and distribute value, affect, and distinction worldwide. What might a critique of the imperial cast of global-metropolitan club culture look like? We'll have to wait and see. Meanwhile, since 9/11, a new generation of scholars has turned its attention to the violent effects of sound production in acts of militarism and, of equal importance, to the ways in which domestic productions of popular music, in their interaction with discursive regimes of mass media, reveal a spectral resonance of symbolic violence—what Matthew Sumera aptly calls "war's audiovisions."[5]

Our concerns about some of the problematic trajectories in what might be called the neoliberal turn in sound and popular-music studies have inspired here a moment of reassessment and taking stock. In this collection we want to turn down the volume in the celebration of modern technologies of sound, driven as much by a tolerance for capitalism's inexorable climb as by the playfulness of social media and MP3. We want to draw attention once more to fundamentally cultural matters of musical creativity. That is, we aim to highlight specifically human and, most typically, historical modes of auditory action—of people performing and making "music." While working from the important accomplishments of sound studies outlined above, we are also proposing in this volume a move away from what we perceive as the excessive tendencies in post–cold war cultural studies of sound production in an effort to find again material priority in the cultural and local. We are attempting to locate the historicity of empire's audible conditions that have carried forth as resonances into the present.

Looking back, the narratives of modern western empires are tales in which audibility conspicuously involved musical interventions carrying real consequence in social and cultural activity. Military occupations, for example, were not only noisy, but also often musical, whether appearing as part of the religious exercises of indoctrination that sounded among seventeenth-century Portuguese clerics in Central Africa or inside and outside the Spanish cathedrals of early-modern Latin America. Geoffrey Baker outlines in a fascinating study of colonial Cuzco, Peru, the many ways in which imperial musical practices of Spanish colonizers transformed the Andean auditory environment as it recast orders of musical knowledge and practice among indigenous musicians.[6] Beginning in the eighteenth century, moreover, military advances by the British and then, a century later, by the French under Napoleon (who brought with his colonizing assembly into Egypt a music scholar and transcriber, Guillaume-André Villoteau) employed newly developed brass instruments in the repertories of the march. Appearing against the background of a long tradition of musical militarism—for example, the Janissary bands of the Ottoman Turks—these newer, modern forms of plangent blaring and blasting organized the behavior of marching and fighting men as marches arose symbolically as an index of a newly constituted imperial sound. As Emily I. Dolan observes, musical militarism played an important role in the reorientation of instrumental practices of the classical and romantic orchestras, as European composers introduced a range of crowd-pleasing techniques highlighting noisy displays and celebrating the glories of empires of the past (e.g., Gaspare Spontini's *La Vestale*, an opera set in ancient Rome) and foreign wanderings in the present (Rossini's *L'Italiana in Algeri* [1813]). These audible, imperial legacies, in turn, became absorbed aesthetically in the taste preferences of the listening public and in the new practices of orchestration. Hector Berlioz's highly influential theory of orchestration, its conception of the orchestra as machine, and its hierarchical ordering of the "race of instruments," replete with personality traits, proposed the musician as a new form of alienated labor servicing a dominant composer. "There was certainly a new concept of orchestration," Hugh Macdonald observes, "manipulating the allocation of notes to create an effect unperceived by the players themselves."[7]

Across the nineteenth century and into the modern, the imperial character of musical creativity expanded across the fields of public culture, giving sensible form to varieties of popular entertainment. In a literal and direct way, the military brass band established the formative basis for the instrumental ensembles of nineteenth-century popular style, its duple metric patterns encouraging, in the new fashions of dance, conformity to regular, repetitious stepping. By the turn of the twentieth century, march-based instrumental conventions had defined the international sound of the West—together with local performance styles in colonial settings from Nairobi to Mumbai to Manila—its appeal increasingly attached to U.S. black musical practices translated and incorporated into Tin Pan Alley song, which was circulated globally via mass-produced sheet music, player-piano rolls, and a new labor class of professional entertainers. The widespread appeal of the bands led by John Philip Sousa propose him as the first imperial musician of modern popular culture, whose performances and recordings of black-based "ragtime song" and strains of imperialist nostalgia in the form of a frivolous two-step, "Hiawatha" (1903), and other tunes of the exotic broadcast to the newly colonized in East Asia and South America an audible signature of "America," cast in the spectral voices of those once enslaved or recently conquered.[8]

Such frivolity also engendered critique. Adorno's familiar rendering of early forms of Tin Pan Alley as part of a cultural "machine which rejects anything untried as a risk" acquires a more profitable interpretation in Peter Szendy's provocative reading of the pop song's alluring banality. For Szendy, these "ear worms" (harkening back not only to Mark Twain, but also to Charles Ives's "ear-stretching" exercises and a famous episode of *The Twilight Zone*) seem so wondrous because they brought forth a sense of mass-produced sound as a colonizing force. What is diverting about the hit is the sense that here, now, we encounter the commodity that speaks; it "speaks" to a population colonized and governed by a naggingly compelling turn of phrase that "comes to you just like that, without thinking about it, without wanting to, sometimes without even knowing or recognizing what it is." We can, finally, trace such a conception of imperial sound across the modern and into the present, appearing today in the global indoctrination in U.S.-based forms of racial authenticity that have appealed to popular musicians and audiences worldwide, whether in the form of the power ballads of Celine Dion still dominating contemporary Lagos; in the song contests of Europe, the United States, Korea, Japan, India, and elsewhere whose "voting rights" celebrate as they call into question the efficacy of democratic governance; or the mimetic circulation of black-infused club-culture beats and comedic practices such as "gangnam style," replete with self-mocking figurations of a spectral minstrelsy.[9]

Fair enough. What we've outlined thus far is part and parcel of the condition of auditory culture, a necessary observation that, on its own, might give too much emphasis to qualities of dominance. It is too simple to merely claim for empire a new sensory measure of audibility, as if in sound we will gain a fuller sense of the character and complexity of the imperial past. What is audible about empire is part of a larger working logic: it is not only the audibility of dominance; it is not simply the pernicious vibrations of rapacious capitalists, the sound of bad men. Nor do we want to suggest that empire's audibility identifies an exclusive, sonorous domain, as if this book discovers in the past and present previously unrecognized forms of sonic autonomy—a sociopolitical "absolute sound." Such a clear-cut separation from the ocular and haptic risks perpetuating false dichotomies distinguishing the oral and written, which have troubled music scholarship for decades and have been vigorously critiqued in the new sense studies literature. By "audible empire," we do not mean to suggest a discrete realm of sound to be observed separately from other territories of the imperial. Rather we seek to call attention to the discernible qualities of the heard—that which one hears and listens to—that condition imperial structurations and that reveal themselves as part and parcel of the regimes of knowledge, understanding, and subjectivity key to the constitution of both belonging and unevenness in the making of the modern. We seek, in turn, to flip it the other way around: to inquire into ways in which imperial structures help to modify and produce qualities of hearing and to make a "music" discernible in the first place. In this, we seek to recognize multiple qualities and characteristics of the audible and to do so dialectically, relationally. What we want to situate at the center of this volume are the many activities of humanly organized, performed sound that generate and reflect the ordering project of European thought and its conception of "music."

Euro-western musical knowledge itself conveys imperial power and intent. It does so because its very conception and form belong to the epistemological orders and historical localities of its various emergences. As Brian Hyer outlines in his magisterial essay "Tonality," in the belletristic tradition of European art music, theorists in the late eighteenth and nineteenth centuries conceived of tonality—the grammar and workings of modern, musical practice—according to a metaphorical language consistent with their frames of reference and positions as subjects of the state.[10] Rameau spoke metaphorically of the hierarchical relations between tonic and dominant (the first and fifth scale-degrees of the diatonic scale) as a force of nature abiding by laws of gravity outlined by Newton; d'Alembert understood that same fundamental relation according to olfactory metaphors of sourness and sweetness. It is, perhaps, no surprise, then, that other writers would frame their conceptions of tonal music according to metaphorical images of feudalism and imperial rule, as in Momigny's tonic "queen," "the purpose of all purposes, the end of all ends, for it is to her that the sceptre of the musical empire is entrusted." Beyond matters of tonality and syntax, the presumptions of value attached to European art music would also interact with common conceptions of world evolution, as in François-Joseph Fétis's racial hierarchy of musical ability (inverting stereotypes of Africans as "natural musicians"), which traces in a curious fashion to Alan Lomax's cantometric theories of vocal quality, geographic locale, and emotional character in the mid-twentieth century. As Hyer writes, "Despite the intended comparisons with natural laws, then, these 'Gesetze der Tonalität' [laws of tonality] were social in basis: there is in fact a strong correlation between tonal theories and conservative ideologies."[11]

As a civilized and civilizing cultural form, then, "music" turns away from its opposite, noise. In the self-fashioning of Enlightenment thought, music's sonorous logic, complexity, and formal symmetries replicate classical ideals: "a harmony of the spheres that established the ratios between planetary orbits (later human souls) equaled those between sounds."[12] Tonality brought into audible form a naturalized, iconic civility, which, in turn, rendered that which sounded different as many calamities of noise in need of discipline, muting, silence. The command to silence grew from an effort to contain the din—the noise of the "Negro," "Chinaman," and "lazy native"—commonly portrayed in European travelogues over four centuries, together with those interior, domestic forms of irrationality and difference within emerging empires: the hysteria of women; the clatter of the rabble. (It is no coincidence that the piano player in Marx's *Grundrisse* is compared with the madman.)[13] But it is even more than that. As Veit Erlmann argues in his book *Reason and Resonance*, the very idea of the rational, which Europe would hold up to itself as the height of civilization, would be constituted not in contrast but in relation to the auditory. In this rendering, reason and resonance identify twin trajectories in the emergence of modernity, calling into question easy binaries of ocular- and logocentrism. Idea and the ear form in relation: what harmony would achieve as a civilizing force, bringing aural conceptions of native otherness into the auditory range of listeners in Vienna, Paris, and London, developed from an internal sense of difference, from a musical version of the exteriority-of-nationalism constituted within the interiority-of-racism that Étienne Balibar has proposed as a fundamental pattern in modern societies of the West. "Reason," the titular mark of European supremacy, grew as a cohabitation and negotiation with resonance, an unreasonable auditory phenomenon nonetheless central to modern society's constitution. This positioning of music is akin to what Jean-Luc Nancy names *sens*, a politically enabling listening, which has been re-fashioned by the contemporary music theorists Jairo Moreno, Gavin Steingo, and Barry Shank as constitutive of an audible making of the political, of, after Chantal Mouffe and Jacques Rancière, a radically democratic "agonistic pluralism."[14]

The audibility of reason—sonorous tonality assuming a place alongside Enlightenment's key figure of "light"—helps to explain why musical practices became so consequential in the many forms of struggle recorded under the name "resistance" over the course of the modern era of western empire. The organizing force of song served to center group commitments during the French Revolution and the rise of British labor; musical practices forged the social constitution of black subjects in the Americas as a racially identifiable "people," and as an oppositional force coalescing in highly charged political settings, from the rise of "yellow music" in 1930s Shanghai to the claims of jazz as "Degenerate Art" in Nazi Germany. For decades, observers have analyzed the power of music as an organizing political force in a range of settings, from Rabindranath Tagore's *The Home and the World* (1919) to Alejo Carpentier's *La Música en Cuba* (1946) to Nelson Mandela's *Long Walk to Freedom: The Autobiography of Nelson Mandela* (2008). The importance of music making in political struggle has been subjected to critical scrutiny, first in a scattering of texts, from the pioneering studies of jazz by Sidney Finkelstein, Eric Hobsbawm, and Amiri Baraka, to what has become a flurry of publication since British cultural studies and African American studies helped to lead the shift away from formal analytical studies and open up a new kind of criticism focusing on music's influence in the constitution of public culture. We need not rehearse the many important investigations that have characterized this important historical turn; they have become the critical literature of a new, culturally based music studies crossing multiple disciplines. We might underscore once more, however, that these musical practices were as forceful as forms of discipline as they were in organizing resistance. Critical musical practices (and, indeed, the very activity of critical listening to radical art) are never simply and merely oppositional. What Richard Middleton names "the voice of the people" was and is "*constitutive* of modernity itself (modernity as it actually developed), its role not only reactive but also productive, not only responsible to but also responsible for (that is, dialectically implicated in) its own apparent negation."[15]

The field of ethnomusicology stands at the forefront among academic music disciplines in its enduring commitment to representing the broad range of human musicality. Since its inception in the 1950s, it has sought to "assuage the traumas of three centuries of colonialism" and provide representation to the range of world traditions beyond the monuments of European classical art. In its ambitions, ethnomusicology also aspired to a position of musicological leadership; it was, in its heyday, as one of its leading scholars put it, "a field of study caught up in fascination with itself."[16] And yet in its ambitions toward progressive leadership, the discipline has sometimes appeared naïvely oblivious to its own culpability in imperial projects, reflecting a curiously unironic (and, perhaps, distinctively American) sense of virtue and righteousness.

Ethnomusicology's origins are commonly traced to the turn of the twentieth century and identified with an intellectually diverse group of scholars based in Berlin (with parallel initiatives appearing in the United States, Britain, and elsewhere), who, through comparative methods grounded in social evolutionary theory, worked together in pursuit of "questions about music that are founded in the concept of music as a cultural phenomenon, as a domain of human thought and behavior rather than as 'art.'"[17] Although these comparative procedures were "unquestionably Eurocentric," founded on Europe's colonial conquests (Germans in the Pacific Islands, the French and Belgians in Africa, the British in India, the Dutch in the East Indies, etc.), and enabled by a massive repository of recorded "specimens" of musical foreignness (most notably, the Berlin Phonogramm-Archiv), they also developed from a shared ambition among a group of German intellectuals representing a range of disciplines who aspired to learn how modes of musical practice informed the character of a complex, global hierarchy. In ways consistent with the historical moment, these early scholars appealed "for rendering evolution audible," as Eric Ames aptly put it. "The empire is proud of its colonies and does everything in its power to exploit them materially," observed Carl Stumpf, one of the leaders of the Berlin School, in 1906. As a matter of course, "Phonographic records should not be lacking. . . . Such an [archive] is a necessary corollary of our colonial aspirations in the highest sense."[18]

After World War II, as the center of western political power shifted more securely to the United States, a diverse body of U.S. scholarship developed, sharing an ideological resemblance in its commitments to Boasian cultural relativism and an empirically based scientism informed by German precedents. Viewed together, the U.S. initiatives proposed a shift away from the comparative methods of the Berlin School in the name of a pluralistic musical democracy curiously consistent with the "end of ideology" posture orienting a broad range of 1960s-era scholarship, as it advocated ethnographic and performance-based methods for studying primarily nonwestern traditional musics that had been neglected by musicology's belletristic commitments. It is interesting to observe, therefore, how at the same time that ethnomusicology posed a challenge to European classicism and aestheticism, it also established its own aesthetic-based hierarchies and musical canon—"the best in all the world's music," as a leader in the field put it—thus perpetuating an imperial form of knowledge that it had explicitly sought to critique.[19]

Ethnomusicology's rise to prominence was fueled in large part by a cold war–era infusion of federal and private-foundation funding (Ford, Carnegie, Rockefeller), which supported ethnographic research on world music as part of an overarching mapping and analysis of global geographies, what famously became known as area studies. The discipline's foreign investigations tended to follow U.S. geopolitical involvements and social movements, while at the same time perpetuating the needs and expectations of college and university music departments, where ethnomusicology programs were typically housed. While research was highly varied, curricula typically favored musical traditions with well-documented theoretical traditions that could be compared with those of Europe: the notated, classical traditions of India, China, Japan, Java, and the Middle East. African music studies also received considerable attention in the context of black liberationist politics and efforts documenting African traditions, its teachings frequently represented by scholars with a grounding in jazz and blues (Alan Merriam, Richard Waterman, Charles Keil); Latin America, and particularly Cuba, was for a long time largely neglected by English-language researchers. What might have taken shape according to a myriad of approaches frequently conformed to interpretive models grounded in the study of European art music.[20] In many departments, "world music" would be conceived as a kind of alternative to the classical musical repertory. In place of the five-hundred-year historical development of European style, students could take a sequence of classes similarly focused on formal matters and, in the more established programs, acquire musical "fluency" in a foreign music, modeled after foreign-language study. In this way, the theoretical emphasis inherent to the field's first emergence, which would be pursued by a handful of radical scholars, would be largely redirected to foreground the acquisition of musical knowledge. The imperial conditions of European art music study and practice—repertoire as focus of analysis; value and significance determined by complexities of form—also established the character of how ethnomusicology would play out as an academic discipline.

The rise of Indonesian music studies offers a particularly conspicuous demonstration of how the alignment of western political-economic interests and enduring high-cultural commitments to aestheticism and art led to a voluminous body of scholarship dedicated to a seemingly unlikely cultural territory. Scholarship on gamelan developed against the background of seminal anthropological research in Southeast Asia and Oceania and in large part through the pioneering efforts of Jaap Kunst, a Dutch musician who, under the employ of the Netherlands' colonial government, undertook a series of studies of Indonesian music and musical instruments. The Dutch presence in Southeast Asia reached back to the seventeenth century, but it was the discovery of a massive body of natural resources two hundred years later that drove the colonizing mission of the Dutch East Indies. The Dutch colonial presence would affect and realign indigenous musical practices, its changes developing "in inverse proportion to the King's power—power that was, of course, rapidly decreasing under Dutch colonial rule." Of particular interest to Europeans were the traditions of gamelan orchestras, so much so that an early British official, Sir Thomas Stamford Raffles (who founded Singapore), brought back to England an ensemble specially tuned to accommodate European temperament and scales.[21] But scholars such as Kunst (and composers such as Claude Debussy and Colin McPhee) were drawn to the gamelan for its inherent properties, leading to another kind of imperial reordering, particularly after World War II, in the distribution of these grand ensembles of bronze percussion instruments to the forums of the western conservatory and concert hall. At the same time that indigenous populations wrested political control from a recalcitrant Dutch government and sought, through decades of domestic contest, to shape a sovereign Indonesia, western students of Javanese and Balinese art music undertook scrupulously detailed investigations of indigenous musical systems, whose scholastic representations often appeared dislocated from the political tumult inhabiting the region. In college classrooms in the United States, moreover, as interest in gamelan blossomed during the 1960s and 1970s, leading exponents with keen awareness of Indonesia's political struggles (exacerbated by western involvements) faced their own struggles of teaching traditional practices at the risk of "encouraging simple-minded pseudo-mysticism on the part of one's students."[22] Such a graphic disconnect between on-the-ground political realities and lofty, academic extractions of "art" continues to trouble the wider field of ethnomusicology into the present, identifying an enduring imperial tendency characterizing the discipline as a whole.

The point of this overarching critique is not to denounce the good intentions of a progressively minded music discipline and its many contributions to knowledge. Nor do we want to downplay the critical force of the field as a whole, which, through the many inspirational studies across the century— from the foundational work of the Berlin School to the influential studies of David McAllester, Bruno Nettl, John Blacking, Judith Becker, Anthony Seeger, Steven Feld, Martin Stokes, Louise Meintjes, Ana María Ochoa Gautier, and Timothy Taylor, to name just a few—has made possible the study of music beyond European art in the first place. Our aim, instead, is to call attention to the depth and pervasiveness of imperial tendencies. The audibility of empire is hardly limited to colonizing influences and realms of the foreign. We can hear empire in the familiar orders of the here and now—in epistemologies that structure and constitute our forms of knowledge acquisition; in our curricula and modes of pedagogy in the teaching of "world music"; in the recordings of global pop; in the concert performances of difference that draw our curiosity and attention. So can we recognize the force of the imperial in the many gestures to "inclusion" that inform recent historical musicological investigations, which, in their attempts to acknowledge difference—as in the creation of veritable global histories of music—reinscribe and reinforce traditional center/periphery distinctions. Once again, it would seem, musicology has the world by its tail, and in its enduring commitment to Eurocentric conceptions of musical "art," it stands forever tall.[23] Just as we seek to give presence to those sounding practices and musicalities previously silenced, so can we also pay attention to the forces of empire that are constitutive of musical conceptions and productions even in their most vociferous forms of critique.

Audible Empire: Music, Global Politics, Critique thus proposes music as a means of comprehending empire as an audible formation, whose very audibility draws the listener (and even the hearer) into a vast network of language, supra-linguistic sensory fields, regimes of knowledge, and new modes of subjectivity. Empire's audible formation was constituted, in its loud and voluble origins, by cultures of sound making, hearing, and listening that are dizzying in their categorical diversities and spread. Self-reflexively, we must acknowledge that this latter claim could be made at all only because the "diversity" and the spread became so widely available and could be known and perceived as such. We know that was not always the case in the history of music till the age of empire and the Industrial Revolution. This same historical process that made possible for the first time in history the greatest aggregation and speediest circulation of different kinds of knowledge about the most diverse peoples, subjects, and places also wrought epochal changes on the organization of music that still endure—stoutly, dynamically—two centuries later.

IF THERE IS A central sonic story to our modern time, finally, it is about the profound transformations, and there is hardly a more evocative and energetic teller than Jacques Attali. In his *Noise: The Political Economy of*

Music—especially the fourth chapter, which is devoted to repetition as the third stage in the history of music as a commodity form—he details how, at the end of the nineteenth century, the technological inventions of duplication and repetition rapidly became the preeminent mode of experiencing music—the "consumption of replications."[24] With recording, music became a commodity, an object of exchange across vast spaces, "music without a market" because the locally anchored use value it used to have was now replaced by anonymous exchange over unknown borders of a transnational market: what Steven Feld has famously dubbed "schizophonia."[25] In the resulting global mass circulation and exchange of music, musicians had become a symbol of a "nonideological multinationalism: esteemed in all of the most cosmopolitan places of power, financed by the institutions of the East and West, they are the image of an art and science common to all of the great monologuing organizations."[26] Put sound repetition, mass circulation, and monologue together and the result is a tame and tamed music, aesthetically and politically. "Popular music and rock," Attali says baldly, "have been recuperated, colonized, sanitized."[27] Music in the age of repetition became a most potent means of subjectification on an unprecedented scale; repetition in all its ever self-refining forms and speed remains the entrenched, distinctive mode of music under the empire of industrial capitalism and its transformations so far.

It is hardly possible to understand the modern subject and subjectivity outside of this vast soundscape. The scholars whose essays we have collected in this book astutely survey and interrogate the decidedly multivocal and multidirectional circulations between and among sound, voices, bodies, machines, and institutions that the empire of political economy and its sonic face, the empire of musical repetition, engendered. Of course, the vast range of historically grounded national and transnational explorations collected here can only be faintly gestured in Attali. More substantively, Attali was too quick and too predictable to seek a way outside the economy of mass circulation to rescue music and restore its meaning. Indeed, mass music has been a potent catalyst in "consumer integration . . . cultural homogenization . . . cultural normalization, and the disappearance of distinctive cultures."[28] If it is hard to countenance how therefore a way out of the dystopia has to resemble an earlier noncommercial, use-value stage of culturally distinctive musics, it is not because of a failure of imagination but of a well-considered refusal to indulge in prophetic fancies serving only the formalist functions of theoretical symmetry and completeness. What if the dystopia occasioned by the empire of music as commodity demands a different conception of "distinctive," "difference," and "culture"? What if we re-estrange ambiguity so that we can discover some of its productivity that we have forgotten or have always missed? The empire of the musically audible, the essays here tell us, calls for critical arsenals for *situated* readings that are both historically anchored and conceptually daring, readings that, while being historically well informed, do not assume the sanctity of already well-known conceptual directions of exploration.

We have provided, within four broad categories, one excellent handle to begin engaging the problematics that the essays centrally explore. Neither the categories nor the essays are in any inviolable order, so they reward entrance from any point; forward or backward, there are enriching and mutually illuminating overlaps between and among them. Musical repetition and its global distribution, we have noted, are distinctive to the age of empire. We conceive the enabling means of that transmission, the "technologies of circulation," very broadly, as the essays in part I show. From Michael Denning's masterly survey of the advent of electrical recordings in the early decades of the twentieth century to Nan Enstad's meticulous mapping of the itineraries of jazz and cigarettes in interwar Shanghai and Andrew F. Jones's close exploration of the transmission powers of genre and generic labels in 1960s Chinese-language musicals in Hong Kong and Taiwan, technologies of musical circulation are not just materials or commodities but also conceptual categories. The relationship is not one-sided: the technologies help circulate the music, but music too was indispensable in the creation and dissemination of technologies, commodities, ideas, styles, and cultures of aurality, affect, and politics.

The vast transnational ecology of musical creation, exchange, circulation, and consumption thus created meant, however, that music could not but have a most problematic relationship to space. After all, this was an age also of remorseless boundaries, physical and social, between, among, and within nations and peoples. Abrasive "audible displacements," discussed in part II, are what results from empire's dramatic impact on what Philip V. Bohlman describes as the earlier recognized metaphysics of music's mobility—the fact that it could move and be moved, be "spatially malleable and mobile." His tracings of the triangulations of race, music, and empire in diverse places, from the crowded slums of India to Romani borders, Brazilian favelas, and imperial Basra in Iraq, are as poignant as they are insightful about that crucial power of empire that has endured in its transformations: the capacity to impose silence in a variety of ways, where there should be raucous noise and the registration of its many labors and the corporeal and social garbs it bears.

In the disciplined silence we hear echoes of a certain kind of "listening" that Jairo Moreno thoughtfully maps out: an aurality, a kind of listening and hearing that U.S. imperialism, its racialized nationalism and cultural insularity (not just in popular attitudes but also in artistic and analytical discourses), has instituted in the understanding of jazz since the last century. Highly discriminatory in the kind of inaudibility (and, indeed, invisibility) it engenders (not just about others but also about itself), this "imperial aurality" conscripts listening in the service of the nation, marshals a "worldliness" that is in reality undergirded by U.S. particularities and interests and that sustains powerful myths of national self-sufficiency and creative autonomy that are part and parcel of U.S. exceptionalism.

The challenge for us as scholars and researchers is to sharpen our listening and hearing abilities. Both Micol Seigel and Josh Kun provide for us richly layered instances of doing just that. Their accounts of two exemplary musical lives—respectively, the Brazilian singer Elsie Houston and Arnulfo Aguilar, the Mexican creator of Sonido Condor—graphically register the audible displacements that occur when musical creators and their musics cross borders. Houston in her time performed across continents, in an entertainment industry that was acutely gendered and racialized and full of both "possibilities and limits for Afro-diasporic solidarity across the Americas." The narrowly fragmented and fragmentary ways through which she has been appropriated by diverse constituencies over the years have been most revealing of the stakes of audible displacements, as Seigel revealingly makes clear. Kun distills from his examination of the musical practice of the Mexican *sonideros* (sound makers) across the borders of Mexico and the United States an aesthetics of *allá*, a complicated gesture to a visionary place of potentially in the now but yet unreached, a way of using recorded sound and audio technology "to engage with spatial politics in the age of asymmetrical economic globalization, naturalized systems of deportation and border militarization, and intensive global migration and displacement."

Over the past three and a half decades, those asymmetries of economic globalization have become so systemic that their context and circumstances of generation and reproduction demanded a new naming or specification. The efforts of Antonio Negri and Michael Hardt proved evocative. "Empire" before was imperialism, the era of the dispersal abroad of basically European national territorial boundaries with various forms of sovereignty shouldered by a more or less unidirectional economic power and political influence between the colony and the metropole. In the new meaning, "empire" is the name for the era of declining national sovereignty and the rule instead of "national and supranational organisms" that progressively envelop "the entire global realm within its open, expanding frontiers."[29] Audible displacement in the context of *this* empire, Gavin Steingo perceptively argues, is even more insidious, and the scholar's "listening and hearing" challenge becomes infinitely more complicated. In his multisided examination of the production, distribution, and consumption of contemporary South African kwaito music under the broad umbrella of empire's transformations in labor and labor relations, he shows how empire is indeed audible in the music—we don't have to listen hard—but not in the songs themselves. How does one inside empire critically listen when empire itself "'composes listening' . . . structures and organizes the relations through which kwaito becomes audible in the first place"? The maw of the market is cavernous and its jaws are ever ready to crush but this is hardly a write-off of enabling cultural politics, just a clearheaded, knife-edge accounting of what is possible and the limitations and outright indeterminacies in what are, from some perspectives, gains. This is the tough critical outlook we learn from both Penny Von Eschen's examination of the poetics and politics of the dub poet Linton Kwesi Johnson and his "contrapuntal bassline to the hegemonic global dogma of privatization" in the context of the end of the cold war and from Morgan Luker's investigations of the contradictory (re)erasure that often inevitably accompanies various official and scholarly affirmation and recognition of this or that racial origin of tango in late nineteenth-century Argentina. This is also seen in Marc Perry's perceptive examination of the contemporary hip hop scene and specifically during the Hip Hop Festival in Cuba in 2000. The chastening but by no means dispiriting question he poses on "the elusive nature of both empire and the promise of revolutionary alterities at the millennial turn" is this: "Where indeed in the antipodal end might empire and revolution reside in the current age of neoliberal capital?"

The distinctive feature of the sound of empire—the sound that creates and is created by empire—is its constitutive *productivity*, its multiple transformations and effects across vast and diverse boundaries. But, conceptually speaking, this is so because of its other feature that is also constitutive: its untamable susceptibility to relativization. This is a good thing, especially for those in subordinate positions under its rule. As Brent Hayes Edwards astutely shows, the intimidatingly vast nature of Hugh Tracey's archive of colonial recording notwithstanding, his edifice wobbles in logic at critical points. And, in any case, that vastness did not obviously intimidate anticolonial theorists and writers who later on, by omission or commission, polemically ignored him in their figurations of African music and African anticolonialism. In another context and focusing on another genre, prose fiction, Amanda Weidman cogently demonstrates a similar contestatory relationship between competing visions of sound in colonial India. She identifies the central sonic tropes of the "anthem" and the "echo" in, respectively, Rabindranath Tagore's *The Home and the World* (1919) and E. M. Forster's *A Passage to India* (1924). The "anthem" is the nationalist's dream of the "controlled, intentional, collective" voice of the nation coming into being, while Forster's "echo" speaks the "uncontrolled, unintentional," and imponderable colonized India in the colonizer's imagination. But imperial sound's susceptibility to relativization is not to be taken for granted at all. A supple and flexible empire is also, after all, most likely to be an enduring one, burdens, warts, and all. Since the ground of resistance is veritably impure—it must of necessity work within the terrain it is resisting against—only the hard *work* of conscious counteridentification and misidentification can harvest the possibilities of a susceptible hegemony. A deft articulation of this challenge is seen in Nitasha Sharma's consideration of post-9/11 desi and Arab rappers caught between being co-opted and "never fully co-opted" by "corporate colonization." Most productively foundational in his exploration is Kofi Agawu's account of the colonization of Africa by the institution of European tonal thinking and practice since the 1840s. *Institutions*, as entrenched, codified ways of ordering practices and relationships in society, are inescapable. They enable. They could be quite unobtrusive and invisible when they are not embodied in physical structures or not formally or conventionally so named. But they also define and circumscribe and are conserving and conservative. When their substantive content is affect-laden such as music, the issue of forming and reforming institutions of that affective content becomes even more challenging. Tonal thinking and practice as an *institution* was part of the colonizers' "civilizing mission," but the colonized, after a while, found some voice and agency within it. Because many scholars today, far less bold, would stop at this "balancing" in their examinations of the aftereffects of colonialism (their accounts of historical, unequal encounters are always in the end balanced!), Agawu's considered statement on the loss column of the balance sheet is worth quoting at some length:

> More tragically perhaps, we have overlooked or undervalued the creative potential of a number of musical resources, resources that have been consigned to the margins at various schools of music since tonality took center stage as the desired modern language. Various uses of nontempered scales, the possibilities opened up by overtone singing, echo-chamber effects associated with water drumming, subtle

explorations of the boundaries between speech and song . . . and the achievement of closure not through stepwise motion or a juvenile slowing down but by the use of melodic leaps and the injection of rhythmic life: these and numerous others constitute a rich set of stylistic opportunities for the modern composer. We await an Africa-originated resistance to the easy victories that tonal harmony has won on the continent since the 1840s.

"Audible" empire affirms that empire constituted as much as it was constituted by sound. To open up the audibility of empire as a problematic is to call for a more capacious rethinking of the constitutive processes of empire as well as of modern sound and its study. We invite readers to share in the wealth of insights and sounds offered by our contributors.

NOTES

1. Walter LaFeber, *The New Empire: An Interpretation of American Expansion, 1860–1898* (Ithaca, NY: Cornell University Press, 1963); William Appleman Williams, *The Tragedy of American Diplomacy* (New York: W. W. Norton, 1959); Eduardo Galeano, *Open Veins of Latin America*, trans. Cedric Belfrage (1971; repr., New York: Monthly Review, 1973).

2. Alain Corbin, *Village Bells: Sound and Meaning in the 19th-Century French Countryside*, trans. Martin Thom (New York: Columbia University Press, 1998).

3. Vanessa Agnew, *Enlightenment Orpheus: The Power of Music in Other Worlds* (New York: Oxford University Press, 2008); Constance Classen, "Sweet Colors, Fragrant Songs: Sensory Models of the Andes and the Amazon," *American Ethnologist* 17, no. 4 (November 1990): 724; Mark M. Smith, *Sensing the Past: Seeing, Hearing, Smelling, Tasting, and Touching in History* (Berkeley: University of California Press, 2007), 46.

4. Friedrich Kittler, *Gramophone-Film-Typewriter*, trans. Geoffrey Winthrop-Young and Michael Wutz (1986; repr., Stanford, CA: Stanford University Press, 1999), 24; Jonathan Sterne, *The Auditory Past: Cultural Origins of Sound Reproduction* (Durham: Duke University Press, 2003); Sterne, *MP3* (Durham: Duke University Press, 2012); Georg Simmel, "The Metropolis and Mental Life," in *The Sociology of Georg Simmel*, trans. Kurt H. Wolff (1902–3; repr., Glencoe, IL: Free Press, 1950), 412. Among the most famous of Adorno's commentaries is "On the Fetish Character of Music and the Regression in Listening" (1938). The best compilation of Adorno's music writings is Adorno, *Essays on Music*, ed. Richard Leppert (Berkeley: University of California Press, 2002). "On the Fetish Character" appears on pages 288–317.

5. Matthew Sumera, "War's Audiovisions: Music, Affect, and the Representation of Contemporary Conflict" (PhD diss., University of Wisconsin, 2013). See also Steve Goodman, *Sonic Warfare: Sound, Affect, and the Ecology of Fear* (Cambridge: MIT Press, 2012); and Juliette Volcler, *Extremely Loud: Sound as a Weapon*, trans. Carol Volk

(2011; repr., New York: New Press, 2013). For a useful collection focused largely on domestic representations, see Jonathan Ritter and J. Martin Daughtry, eds., *Music in the Post-9/11 World* (New York: Routledge, 2007).

6. Geoffrey Baker, *Imposing Harmony: Music and Society in Colonial Cuzco* (Durham: Duke University Press, 2008).

7. Emily I. Dolan, *The Orchestral Revolution: Haydn and the Technologies of Timbre* (Cambridge: Cambridge University Press, 2013), 232. Dolan writes, "Music history has found it easy to overlook how much this militaristic style dominated the sound of early romantic music, ignoring its overt political associations in order to create the familiar story of the emergence of 'absolute music'" (228–29). Hugh Macdonald, *Berlioz's Orchestration Treatise: A Translation and Commentary* (Cambridge: Cambridge University Press, 2002), xxx–xxxi ("race of instruments" appears on page 296). For Berlioz's fascinatingly ambiguous portrait of Chinese music, in which he famously dismisses its aesthetic qualities while praising China's commitment to musical traditions, see "Moeurs musicales de la Chine (Musical Customs of China)," in *The Art of Music and Other Essays*, trans. Elizabeth Csicsery-Rónay (Bloomington: Indiana University Press, 1994), 176–79.

8. Frederick Schenker, "Navigating Musical Latitudes: Hearing Empire in the Global Circuits of Early Twentieth-Century Popular Music" (paper presented at the International Association of the Study of Popular Music, Chapel Hill, NC, March 13–16, 2014).

9. Max Horkheimer and Theodor W. Adorno, *Dialectic of Enlightenment: Philosophical Fragments*, ed. Gunzelin Schmid Noerr, trans. Edmund Jephcott (1947; repr., Stanford, CA: Stanford University Press, 2002), 106; Peter Szendy, *Hits: Philosophy in the Jukebox*, trans. Will Bishop (2008; repr., New York: Fordham University Press, 2012), 5. We might also think of these forms, cut loose from copyright and ownership, as a kind of immaterial, formless form: organized sound giving cast to a new, auditory "second nature." For Ives's "ear stretching," see James Peter Burkholder, *Charles Ives and His World* (Princeton, NJ: Princeton University Press, 1996), 18; Juliet A. Williams, "On the Popular Vote," *Political Research Quarterly* 58, no. 4 (December 2005): 637–46; and Limor Shifman, *Memes in Digital Culture* (Cambridge: MIT Press, 2014).

10. Brian Hyer, "Tonality," in *Cambridge History of Western Music Theory*, ed. Thomas Christensen (Cambridge: Cambridge University Press, 2006), 726–52; Timothy Taylor, *Beyond Exoticism: Western Music and the World* (Durham: Duke University Press, 2007).

11. Katharine Ellis, *The New Grove Dictionary of Music and Musicians*, 2nd ed., s.v. "Fétis" (Oxford: Oxford University Press, 2001); Alan Lomax, "Folk Song Style," *American Anthropologist* 61 (1959): 927–54; Hyer, "Tonality." See also Bennett Zon, *Representing Non-Western Music in Nineteenth-Century Britain* (Rochester, NY: University of Rochester Press, 2007); Julie Brown, ed., *Western Music and Race* (Cambridge: Cambridge University Press, 2007).

12. Kittler, *Gramophone-Film-Typewriter*, 24.

13. Syed Hussein Alatas, *The Myth of the Lazy Native* (London: Frank Cass, 1979); Karl Marx, *Grundrisse: Foundations of the Critique of Political Economy*, trans. Martin Nicolaus (1939; repr., London: Penguin, 1993), 305.

14. Veit Erlmann, *Reason and Resonance: A History of Modern Aurality* (London: Zone, 2010); Étienne Balibar, "Racism as Universalism," in *Masses, Classes, Ideas: Studies on Politics and Philosophy before and after Marx* (New York: Routledge, 1994), 191–204; Barry Shank, *The Political Force of Musical Beauty* (Durham: Duke University Press, 2014); Jairo Moreno and Gavin Steingo, "Rancière's Equal Music," *Contemporary Music Review* 31, nos. 5–6 (2012): 487–505.

15. Richard Middleton, *Voicing the Popular: On the Subjects of Popular Music* (London: Routledge, 2006), 23. His emphasis.

16. David McAllester, "The Astonished Ethno-muse," *Ethnomusicology* 23, no. 2 (May 1979): 180; Alan Merriam, *The Anthropology of Music* (Evanston, IL: Northwestern University Press, 1964), 3.

17. Dieter Christensen, "Berlin Phonogramm-Archiv: The First 100 Years," in *Music Archiving in the World: Papers Presented at the Conference on the Occasion of the 100th Anniversary of the Berlin Phonogramm-Archiv*, ed. Gabriele Berlin and Artur Simon (Berlin: Verlag für Wissenschaft und Bildung, 2002), 22–23.

18. For "unquestionably Eurocentric," see ibid.; Lars-Christian Koch, "Images of Sound: Erich M. von Hornbostel and the Berlin Phonogram Archive," in *The Cambridge History of World Music*, ed. Philip V. Bohlman (Cambridge: Cambridge University Press, 2013), 475–97; Carole Pegg, Helen Myers, Philip V. Bohlman, and Martin Stokes, "Ethnomusicology," in *The New Grove Dictionary of Music and Musicians*, 2nd ed., ed. Stanley Sadie (New York: Grove, 2001); Eric Ames, "The Sound of Evolution," *Modernism/Modernity* 10, no. 2 (2003): 320n21.

19. McAllester, "The Astonished Ethno-muse," 180. Philip V. Bohlman argues that ethnomusicology's canon was less specifically aestheticist than it was canonical in its commitment to the study of cultural significance. See his essay "Ethnomusicology's Challenge to the Canon; the Canon's Challenge to Ethnomusicology," in *Disciplining Music: Musicology and Its Canons*, ed. Katherine Bergeron and Philip V. Bohlman (Chicago: University of Chicago Press, 1992), 116–36.

20. The musicological tendency was for a time so pervasive that one of the leading anthropologists in the discipline, Alan Merriam, prepared a study of the Flathead Indians in which music analysis stood central. Merriam, *Ethnomusicology of the Flathead Indians* (Chicago: Aldine, 1967).

21. John Pemberton, "Musical Politics in Central Java (or How Not to Listen to Javanese Gamelan)," *Indonesia* 44 (October 1987): 23; Maria Mendonça, *The New Grove Dictionary of Music and Musicians*, s.v. "Gamelan: II: Outside South-east Asia."

22. Judith Becker, "One Perspective on Gamelan in America," *Asian Music* 15, no. 1 (1983): 85. Maria Mendonça reports that there were more than 150 gamelans housed at U.S. institutions by the end of the twentieth century (Mendonça, "Gamelan: II").

23. Equally troubling is the tendency to attempt drawing together the fields of historical musicology, ethnomusicology, and music theory in the name of a singularly committed, object-oriented discipline of "Music" studies. These efforts still drive training and hiring practices in most contemporary music departments.

24. Jacques Attali, *Noise: The Political Economy of Music*, trans. Brian Massumi (1977; repr., Minneapolis: University of Minnesota Press, 1985), 88. See Attali's summary of the

chapter on repetition: "The third network, that of repetition, appears at the end of the nineteenth century with the advent of recording. This technology, conceived as a way of storing representation, created in fifty years' time, with the phonograph record, a new organizational network for the economy of music. In this network, each spectator has a solitary relation with a material object; the consumption of music is individualized, a simulacrum of ritual sacrifice, a blind spectacle. The network is no longer a form of sociality, an opportunity for spectators to meet and communicate, but rather a tool making the individualized stockpiling of music possible on a huge scale. Here again, the new network first appears in music as the herald of a new stage in the organization of capitalism, that of the repetitive mass production of all social relations" (32).

25. Ibid., 116. See also Steven Feld, "From Schizophonia to Schismogenesis: On the Discourses and Commodification Practices of 'World Music' and 'World Beat,'" in *Music Grooves: Essays and Dialogues*, ed. Charles Keil and Steven Feld (Chicago: University of Chicago Press, 1994).

26. Attali, *Noise*, 116.

27. Ibid., 109.

28. Ibid., 111.

29. Michael Hardt and Antonio Negri, *Empire* (Cambridge: Harvard University Press, 2000), xii. Hardt and Negri's large structure-based reading of empire continues to be foundationally apt and useful. It already and more suggestively incorporates the concerns of content-based readers more immediately concerned about the subordination of different and local practices and epistemologies and the need for their recuperation and refurbishing. One interesting recent example of the latter is the "decolonial" movement, borrowing strands from the long tradition of anticolonial and postcolonial thinking but especially focused on Latin America. See Walter D. Mignolo, *The Darker Side of the Renaissance: Literacy, Territoriality, and Colonization*, 2nd ed. (Ann Arbor: University of Michigan Press, 2014), and Walter Mignolo and Arturo Escobar, eds., *Globalization and the Decolonial Option* (New York: Routledge, 2010). But "empire" was and is not against difference as such, conceived as local, regional, racial, or ethnic; it was, and remains, in fact, the core engine for the manufacture, dissemination, and exploitation of difference.

PART I · **TECHNOLOGIES OF CIRCULATION**

1 · DECOLONIZING THE EAR The Transcolonial
Reverberations of Vernacular Phonograph Music

MICHAEL DENNING

In a handful of years between the development of electrical recording in 1925 and the outset of the Great Depression in the early 1930s, a new soundscape was created in a series of recording sessions around the world. In late October of 1925 in the Caribbean port of Havana, Victor recorded the pioneering Cuban son sexteto, Sexteto Habanero, with its three string players (*tres* [the four-stringed Cuban treble guitar], guitar, and bass) and three percussionists (*bongó*, *clave*, and *maracas*). Within the next five years, hundreds of recordings of son sextetos and septetos appeared (the septeto added a trumpet), and Afro-Cuban music echoed around the world under the name "rumba." About two weeks later, in early November 1925, OKeh Records recorded, in Chicago, a young trumpet player from the Mississippi Delta city of New Orleans, Louis Armstrong, together with his Hot Five, a jazz quintet of trumpet, trombone, clarinet, piano, and banjo. There had been a number of earlier recordings of African American jazz musicians, going back at least to the 1922 recording of Kid Ory's band, and Armstrong himself had been recorded anonymously as a side man, but the ninety or so "race records" made by Armstrong with his Hot Five and Hot Seven (which added tuba and drums) between 1925 and 1929 became the embodiment of "hot jazz."

The following spring—in May 1926—a young singer from another cotton-growing Delta, that of the Nile, Umm Kulthūm, recorded ten double-sided 78s for Gramophone in Cairo. Though she may have recorded a few tracks for Odeon earlier, the Gramophone recordings of 1926 marked a key turning point in her career, with a new ensemble (qānūn/kanun [zither], violin, 'ūd/oud, riqq [hand percussion—Arabic tambourine]) and a new repertoire based on the colloquial poetry of Ahmad Rāmī. The recording of "In Kunt Asaamih" (If I were to forgive), probably released in 1928, "sold unprecedented numbers of copies."[1] In November 1926 from the rural towns of Jalisco, mariachi music, which had come to prominence after the revolution, was recorded in Mexico City by the pioneering band named Mariachi Coculense of Cirilo Marmeolejo. In the wake of Victor's trip, many Mexican artists traveled to the United States to record popular *corridos*, which are topical ballads, often of revolutionary heroes and battles, sung by duets accompanied by guitar. "This period from 1928 to the mid-1930s" is, as the record producer Chris Strachwitz notes, "the 'Golden Era' for the commercially recorded corrido."[2] That same month, in Batavia (Jakarta), a young Eurasian singer and dancer of the city's *bangsawan* theater, Miss Riboet, recorded a number of kroncong tunes for the German label Beka, and she became the first great recording star of the Dutch East Indies, soon to be the new nation of Indonesia. She was so successful that Beka issued a special series of Miss Riboet records for tunes like "Krontjong Dardanella." In December 1926, the tango sextet of Julio de Caro recorded the first "modern tango," "Recuerdo."[3] Though tango has a slightly different recording history, thanks to the pioneering work of Max Glucksmann's Discos Nacional (the landmark recording is usually taken to be Carlos Gardel's 1917 recording of the tango song "Mi Noche Triste" [My sad night]), "Recuerdo" became one of the fundamental instrumental tangos of the electric era, helping to establish the sextet (two bandoneons, two violins, piano, and bass) as the characteristic tango ensemble. In August of the following summer, 1927, the Trinidadian calypsonian Wilmoth

Houdini recorded three *paseos* with a New York–based Trinidadian string band (guitar, piano, violin, and *cuatro*) for Victor. Houdini was a seaman who had played in Port of Spain's calypso tents in the years after World War I before migrating to New York in the mid-1920s. He was the first of the postwar calypsonians to record, and he eventually became the "most recorded calypsonian of his generation."[4] During that same August, the Victor recording scout Ralph Peer set up a temporary recording studio in the Piedmont mill town of Bristol, Tennessee, to record local singers of "old-time" music. In what has been called the "big bang of country music," Peer made the earliest recordings of the first great stars of U.S. country music, the Carter Family and Jimmie Rodgers.[5] The Carter Family recorded only a half dozen numbers those first two days, but one of them, "Single Girl, Married Girl," a brief but eloquent narrative of the economy of gender, took off when it was released in 1928 and made their initial reputation. If the Carter Family captured one half of the ideological doubleness of country music (a vision of rural domesticity and family music making, closely tied to hymns and religious music), Jimmie Rodgers, the singing brakeman, captured the other half: country music as a road music of lone male singers on the rails. The son of a Mississippi railroad worker, he had worked for years as a brakeman and flagman, before beginning to work medicine shows as a blackface entertainer. Between 1927 and his death of tuberculosis in 1933, he was the most popular country performer. Later in the fall of 1927, Victor recorded the *cai luong* actress Dào Nha in Hanoi in French Indochina. Cai luong was the modern vernacular theater, "the most popular theatrical entertainment in Vietnam."[6]

At the end of 1927, Kalama's Quartet, a Hawaiian ensemble featuring the steel guitarist and falsetto singer Mike Hanapi, recorded a medley of hulas and "Inikiniki Malie" (Gentle pinches of wind) for OKeh Records in New York. Though the international popularity of Hawaiian music had been triggered a decade earlier, much of what was heard as "Hawaiian" music was simply Tin Pan Alley tunes with mock Hawaiian lyrics. The recordings of Kalama's Quartet, together with Columbia's recordings of Hawaiian songs by the steel guitar virtuoso Sol Hoʻopiʻi in Los Angeles that same fall, led to the international circulation of recordings by Hawaiian artists. A few months later, Brunswick made the first major commercial recordings in Honolulu.

In January 1928, the first major commercial series of West African records (the Zonophone EZ series) was released in Gold Coast towns like Accra; one of the tunes recorded by the Kumasi Trio was "Amponsah," which was to become a standard of Ghanaian highlife. The following spring, March 1928, a young *taarab* singer from the East African port of Zanzibar, Siti binti

Saad, traveled with her group to Bombay to make the first commercial recordings in Swahili for Gramophone, the first of hundreds of recordings she made in Bombay and Mombasa over the next three years, songs that were to make her the "most widely praised and revered taarab performer" in East Africa.[7] Her given name, Mtumwa, translates literally as slave or servant; trained as a potter, she had migrated to the city and had learned to recite the Koran; she was given the name Siti (lady), not unlike Billie Holiday's Lady Day, by a patron.[8] Only a handful of her recordings remain in circulation, but ethnomusicologists have found that her songs remained central to the taarab repertoire in postcolonial Tanzania at the end of the twentieth century.[9]

In June 1928, the eighteen-year-old gypsy virtuoso Django Reinhardt, who had become well known in the dance halls of working-class Paris while playing banjo-guitar in the accordion-fronted bands of Parisian musette, was first recorded by the Compagnie Gramophone du Française in Paris's Pigalle, accompanying the musette accordionist Jean Vaissade on ten dance tracks. In December 1928, Parlophone used the new electrical process to record the great Brazilian choro composer and flutist Pixinguinha, together with veterans of his Batutas, who had returned to Rio following their success in Argentina and Paris. Within a year, Victor had recruited him as its house arranger and bandleader in Rio; by 1932 he was also the bandleader for Brazilian radio's first program to feature samba.

In 1929, the twenty-year-old silent film star Li Minghui recorded "Maomao Yu" (Drizzle), written by her father, the pioneering songwriter Li Jinhui, for Pathé. Li Minghui was, as Andrew Jones wrote, "among the first women to break the Qing dynasty taboo against public performances by women in the mid-1920s," and "Maomao Yu" became the first "standard" of *shidaiqu* (modern song), the popular "yellow music" of Shanghai's cabarets in the 1930s and 1940s in the wake of the May Fourth New Culture movement and the Shanghai uprising of 1927.[10] In September 1929, Odeon first recorded the pioneering Martinican dance band of Alexandre Stellio. Beguine had become a popular dance in Parisian music halls, and Stellio's Antillean Orchestra would perform at the 1931 Colonial Exhibition outside Paris.

Though there had been a handful of recordings of the bedoui songs of Oran, in western Algeria just before World War I, it was the June 1930 recordings of Cheikh Hamada that triggered the wide recording and circulation of the songs of the cheikhs and cheikhas that have come to be called *roots rai*. And in October 1930 Griffiths Motsieloa arrived in London from South Africa to organize a pioneering session of recordings of South African *marabi* and vaudeville tunes for the South African market, beginning with his own

"Aubuti Nkikho" (Brother Nkikho), with its yodels and Hawaiian guitar. It was the first record on Eric Gallo's Singer label. Motsieloa went on to become Gallo's musical director, and his own band, the Merry Blackbirds, would be a leading black South African band, playing dances and fundraisers for the African National Congress and the black trade unions in the 1930s and helping to define the township jive of the black townships.

THESE RECORDING SESSIONS, which rendered a musical revolution on disks of shellac, took place alongside the first stirrings of anticolonial activism and thought. In February 1927 nearly two hundred pioneering anticolonial activists from Asia and Africa met in Brussels to form the League against Imperialism. They were members of a host of anticolonial organizations: the Etoile Nord-Africain, the Destour, the South African National Congress, the Indian National Congress, and the Comité de Défense de la Race Nègre. The Brussels conference was just one of a series of such meetings that took place in various imperial cities in the decade after World War I: there were the three Pan-African Congresses in Paris, London, and Brussels between 1919 and 1923, initiated by W. E. B. Du Bois among others; the Baku Congress of the Peoples of the East in 1920, which marked the anticolonial turn in Communist theory and practice; and the congress of the Union Intercoloniale in Paris in 1921, which brought together activists from the French colonies, including a young Ho Chi Minh. These meetings of young intellectuals and activists were themselves reverberations of the protest and unrest that ranged from the massive Chinese student demonstrations that became known as the May Fourth movement, to the noncooperation campaigns in India that brought Gandhi to international attention, to the Egyptian uprising of 1919, and to the strikes of black miners in South Africa.

However, these recording sessions also coincided with a wave of primitivism and exoticism among the modernist countercultures of the imperial capitals. Dance "crazes" broke like waves in the cabarets of Paris, New York, and Berlin, beginning with the tango just before World War I and followed by the Charleston, the rumba, and the beguine in the decade after the war. The modern "night club" assumed a colonial shape from New York's Cotton Club to Paris's Bal Coloniale. Empire was displayed and performed for metropolitan audiences in a series of world's fairs and colonial expositions, which featured the "exotic" musics of the colonies. The Panama-Pacific International Exposition in San Francisco in 1915 triggered the vogue of Hawaiian music; the Ibero-American Exposition in Seville in 1929 brought Cuba's Septeto Nacional to

Europe to perform and record, helping to trigger the "rhumba craze"; and the 1931 Paris International Colonial Exposition not only featured Stellio's Antilles orchestra, but also was the occasion for the recording of musicians from Algeria to Madagascar to Indochina.

So how do we understand these recording sessions? Are they instances of colonial mimicry, a derivative discourse, a commercial exploitation of the exotic? Or might they be akin to the fugitive meetings of anticolonial intellectuals, imagined leagues against imperialism? I want to suggest that vernacular gramophone music was a fundamental part of the cultural revolution that was decolonization. The links between print and anticolonialism are often noted: Ngugi wa Thiong'o's classic *Decolonizing the Mind* addressed the politics of language in African literature. Frantz Fanon famously pointed to the role of the radio in the anticolonial struggle in Algeria. Perhaps the gramophone or phonograph was equally, if not more, important to "decolonization."

These vernacular phonograph musics not only captured the timbres of decolonization: the emergence of these musics—hula, rumba, beguine, tango, jazz, samba, marabi, kroncong, taraab, chaabi—*was* decolonization. It was not simply a cultural activity that *contributed* to the political struggle (though there are cases of musicians taking political stances and actions); it was somatic decolonization, the decolonization of the ear and the dancing body. Decolonization, I will suggest, was a musical event. Moreover, this decolonization of the ear preceded and made possible the subsequent decolonization of legislatures and literatures, schools and armies. The global soundscape was decolonized by the guerrilla insurgency of these new musics before the global statescape was reshaped.

It is difficult to hear these vernacular phonograph musics as a decolonization of the ear for two reasons. First, there was often a profound gap between decolonization as a political revolution—the winning of formal political independence and the indigenization of state apparatuses from legislatures and schools to armies and police—and decolonization as a cultural revolution—the iconoclasm that smashed the aesthetic and philosophical idols of everyday life, the ordinary hierarchies and inequalities that depended on common-sense ideologies of "race," "color," and "civilization." For every brief moment of convergence between the political and cultural revolutions, there are long stretches where they seem completely separate. Antagonism and mutual suspicion were perhaps more characteristic than solidarity and alliance between the forces of political and cultural decolonization; anticolonial political activists and thinkers were often tone-deaf when hearing these new musics. So a history must rely more on analogies between the two nonsynchronous processes than on relations of cause and effect. Second, there is a gap between the biographical time of individual musicians making recordings—and the remarkably brief window in time when the recording industry was open to these vernacular musics—and the *longue durée* of cultural revolution, a remaking of the very structure of feeling, as new sensibilities and new aesthetics become new ways of living. If, over generations, these musics did decolonize the ear, it remains difficult to register this in particular recordings by particular musicians. It was never self-evident what the decolonization of music would sound like or what musics were or were not part of the colonial order. But this gap is not different in kind than the parallel one between the longue durée of political decolonization and the biographical time of political actors; the debates over figures like Umm Kulthūm, Louis Armstrong, Rita Montaner, and Carmen Miranda are not dissimilar to those over Gandhi and Bose, Nkrumah and Senghor, Mao and Ho Chi Minh, who struggled among themselves over the strategies and ideologies of anticolonialism.

It is a mark of these discontinuities that those who forged the very notion that decolonization was a cultural as well as a political revolution had a profound ambivalence about these musics, as one can see in the fraught reflections, asides really, that occur in the writing of the figures—Fanon and Édouard Glissant—who came of age in the era of vernacular gramophone music and particularly in writings about beguine, the dance-band music of Martinique. Fanon enjoyed the beguine of Stellio, but the only reference to the music in his writing comes in the 1955 essay "West Indians and Africans," where two periods in West Indian consciousness are delineated in an almost autobiographical sketch: "Before 1939, the West Indian claimed to be happy, or at least thought of himself as being so. He voted, went to school when he could, took part in the processions, and drank rum and danced the beguine."[11] This sense of music as part of an unreflective colonial daily life returns when he writes that the French radio station in Algeria, Radio-Alger, was "listened to only because it broadcast typically Algerian music, national music."[12]

Glissant, Fanon's contemporary, directly juxtaposed beguine to "the prestigious history of jazz" in a critique of national culture as withering in its way as that of Fanon. As jazz accompanied the migration of blacks within the United States to "the great sprawling cities," Glissant writes, "black music is reborn." "This music progressively records the history of the community, its confrontation with reality, the gaps into which it inserts itself, the walls which it too often comes up against. The universalization of jazz arises from the fact that at no point is it an abstract music, but the expression of a specific situation." In contrast, the beguine represents the suspended state of Martinique where the plantation system collapsed and "nothing replaces it." "The 'beguine' is the true voice of Martinique, from the plantations to the intense activity of the town of St.-Pierre. But from 1902 . . . it no longer develops." "Musical creativity, cut off from the imperatives of reality, becomes folkloric (in the worst sense). . . . You must 'do things' in your country to be able to sing about it. If not, musical creativity is reduced to a numbing, neurotic practice that contains nothing but the capacity for disintegration."[13] For Glissant, as for Fanon, beguine remains caught in colonial stasis, folkloric in the worst sense.

How do we understand the profound ambivalence of these reflections? Or the continuing ambivalence of postcolonial critics? When Brent Hayes Edwards discusses the emergence of beguine in the music halls of Paris, he revisits the music and dance through the writings of the black internationalist intellectuals living there, and he distinguishes between the dance venues, noting that the second Bal Nègre "became a means for the Antillean community to evade the throngs of European spectators who were overwhelming the first Bal Nègre." Nonetheless, when considering Odeon's marketing of beguine for the gramophone, he concludes that "the commodification of recorded beguine is simultaneously the commodification of the colonies."[14]

However, unlike the live performances of beguine in the dance halls of the imperial metropolises, the phonograph records of these musics were made almost entirely for export to the "local" market. Though there is no doubt that the metropolitan music industry was appropriating the labor of colonial musicians, they existed more in the fashion of the second Bal Nègre (aimed at the Antillean community) than the first (aimed at the European spectators). One can see this both on an anecdotal level and in export statistics. On the anecdotal level, Rodney Gallop, one of the earliest European reviewers of vernacular phonograph records in the late 1920s and early 1930s, regularly noted that, although the records he was reviewing were manufactured in Britain, they were difficult to acquire in Britain: they were immediately exported to the local market and were assumed to have no wider interest.

This is also registered in export statistics, because record-pressing capacity remained concentrated in the large factories of Britain, Germany, and the United States. Exports soared between 1925 and 1929, particularly to areas where the new vernacular gramophone musics were being recorded and marketed. The rise of popular Arabic song, figured by Umm Kulthūm, paralleled a six-fold increase in British exports to Egypt; the twenty-fold increase in exports to Turkey, providing recordings of Greek, Turkish, Arabic, Armenian, and Jewish musics, was a sign of Istanbul's musical cosmopolitanism. In

British West Africa, where the Zonophone African series was marketed, record imports grew seven-fold from 1925 to 1928; the popularity of kroncong accompanied a similar four-fold growth in exports to Java and the Straits Settlements.[15]

German record exports grew even more dramatically: not only had German exports to Egypt grown more than six-fold, but two East Asian markets—the Dutch East Indies and China—which were not even enumerated in 1925 were almost as large as the total exports of 1925.[16] What was the meaning of these shellac disks being sold in colonial ports and mill towns around the world? They were a different musical culture than the live performances in Parisian music halls and colonial exhibitions. In what ways and under what circumstances did these gramophone musics decolonize the ear?

The most striking—but atypical—examples of the gramophone's decolonization of the ear appear in the places where the electrical revolution in sound coincided directly with anticolonial struggle. Here the links are so direct as to be misleading, as both anticolonial militants and colonial authorities connected the circulation of records and the circulation of opposition. In southern India, for example, as the historian S. Theodore Baskaran noted, the Civil Disobedience campaign of 1930–31 led the local branch of the Odeon Company to produce records by popular Tamil artists who supported the campaign. A celebrated example was the popular vernacular singer K. B. Sundarambal who "campaigned actively for Congress": when, in 1931, Gandhi was released from prison and invited to the Second Round Table talks in London, Sundarambal released a record celebrating the event: "Gandhi has reached London / Let Us Honor Him."[17] In his discussion of the place of song in the Indian anticolonial movement, Baskaran accents two particular significances of gramophone records as opposed to printed song booklets. First, the "coming of the gramophone to Tamilnadu in the early 1920s was," he argues, "something in the nature of a revolution. It was the first time that music was accessible to all, irrespective of caste or class. . . . Through the gramophone, even people in interior villages without electricity could listen to famous musicians." Second, colonial authorities did not immediately recognize the influence of gramophone records. "Only towards the end of the Civil Disobedience Movement, by which time there were already hundreds of gramophone records of patriotic songs in circulation, did the government seem to wake up to their importance," Baskaran writes. In contrast to the popular song booklets that were proscribed under press censorship laws, "there was," he notes, "no specific law which could be used against gramophone records," and few were banned.[18]

The ubiquity of gramophone records and their evasion of colonial control are echoed in Rebecca Scales's recent research in French colonial archives. In 1937, an Algerian police agent produced a study of Arabic-language records and Algerian listening habits, reporting that "there is hardly a *café maure* or family—however modest their condition—that does not have a phonograph and a collection of popular songs." It was more difficult to monitor and censor gramophone records than print or film. When a record of a "piano solo" issued by a local North African label was found to contain no piano solo but rather a singer calling on Algerians to join Messali Hadj's recently formed Algerian People's Party, the colonial authorities tracked the distribution of the record from Algiers to cafés, markets stalls, and brothels in tiny villages, leading them to seize records and close cafés.[19] In Shanghai, as Andrew Jones has shown, popular "yellow music" and left-wing nationalist music were intertwined. Li Minghui was, according to one of her contemporaries, at "the front lines of the New Culture Movement; . . . the more they [conservative critics] loudly and cruelly cursed her [public appearances], the more youth who had been influenced by the New Culture Movement supported her."[20]

In some cases, particular events or figures in anticolonial struggles became the subjects of popular recordings. Baskaran says that the execution of Bhagat Singh in Lahore in March 1931 provoked the largest number of songs, including one recorded by Sundarambal.[21] A parallel instance can be seen in Trinidad where a number of calypsos were recorded about Uriah Butler and the Butler "riots," part of the massive Caribbean strike wave that hit the British Empire in 1937 and led to a major colonial investigation. In early 1938, the calypso singer Atilla the Hun (Raymond Quevedo), who had become the voice of ordinary Trinidadians, not only in the annual competitions among bands in the carnival tents, but also on recordings made in New York and shipped back to Trinidad for carnival season, took up the strikes in several famous songs. The first, a critique of the colonial commission's report, was banned in Trinidad—there is at least one report that Atilla was himself briefly arrested—but he responded with two songs that couched the story of the strike in praise songs for the two colonial figures who had been dismissed or transferred, as well as an ostensibly neutral narrative of the strike.[22]

Nevertheless, the political stances taken by musicians and their lyric commentaries on the politics of anticolonialism are the least significant part of the cultural revolution worked by these musics. We can't deduce the anticolonial meaning of a record from the politics of the musician or even from its lyrics; often the most innocuous songs carried anticolonial and nationalist connotations in the eyes of the authorities or the population. This is particularly true of one of the most common song forms, the romantic lyric tribute to the land, often built on the simple musicality of place names. Such songs make up much of the repertoire of commercial Hawaiian music and are usually interpreted as innocuous appeals to tourists. However, given the centrality of land in colonial dispossession, and given the unambiguous association of many of those Hawaiian lyrics, including the oft-recorded "Aloha 'Oe" written by Queen Lili'uokalani, deposed and imprisoned by the colonialists, the reclaiming, in the Hawaiian language, of the winds, waters, and rains of Minnehaha and Hanalei, may have been heard as an anticolonial lament as powerful as Atilla's humorous calypsos about Butler.

However, it is unpersuasive simply to reverse the poles, de-exoticize the musics, and celebrate the role of the gramophone musics in the struggle for national liberation. For this misses the fact that, as nationalist critics recognized early on, these musics don't easily fit into nationalist garb; they were creolized, mixed-race musics from the start. The canonizing gestures of post-revolutionary and postcolonial regimes to mobilize these musics as nationalist "audiotopias," often taking particular regional musics as metonymies of the whole nation, created a complex process, and, when successful, often ended up succumbing to an official state nationalism. As Pramoedya Toer later wrote about Indonesia's kroncong, "Kroncong still had some power before independence, it still contained a vitality—the vitality of a nation that was not yet free. As the Revolution erupted and passed, kroncong remained just a kind of narcissism, a posy of empty words, a culture of masturbation. Equal to the culture of great speeches, and of puppet shadow theater."[23]

These musics and records shared the ambiguity of the colonial ports and railway towns in which they took shape; they were two-faced musics, objects of suspicion, intimate with both colonial and indigenous forms and instruments. There were four elements to this suspicion, though different critics accented different elements. First, the musics were entwined with colonial musics. Empire, as Kofi Agawu argues in his essay within this volume, was a musical event: the conquest and colonization of territories was "accompanied" by the musical occupation of the space, and the projection of a new colonial order in sound. The vernacular phonograph musics were as deeply indebted to key transcolonial practices—hymn singing and military brass bands—as to the street-parading ensembles that marked turn-of-the-century ports: the second line of New Orleans, the *comparsas* of Havana, the calypso tents of Port of Spain. The remarkable missionary energy put into the propagation of Christian hymn singing leads one to suggest that musical conversion is a necessary condition for religious conversion: to learn to sing is to learn to pray and to "believe" in a new way. Similarly, the building of colonial forces of order—colonial police and armies—depended on the musical "auxiliaries"—the military brass bands and police bands that were developed around the globe. Many of the musicians who recorded in the late 1920s got their training in military bands.

Almost all of the vernacular phonograph musics adopted the mass-produced musical instruments of the European and American metal-working factories, combining them with artisan-crafted local instruments in unique new ensembles. A striking example was the new music theater of 1920s Vietnam, cai luong, which featured, as Jason Gibbs has shown, two ensembles: one with Vietnamese instruments playing pentatonic melodies on plucked and bowed stringed instruments, and a second with western military band instruments, playing "fanfare music."[24]

Thus colonial musical practice instituted new disciplines of the body—new ways of singing, of dancing, of marching, of playing instruments. To speak of the colonization of the "ear" is thus a metonymy: for the reshaping of the musical subject is not only a reshaping of the individual's musical muscles—the articulated flesh and bones that make up the singing voice, the instrument-playing hands and lips, the dancing feet and hips. It is also the reshaping of the order of the group—the creation of marching bands and church choirs: a colonization not only of the body, but also of articulated bodies.

Gandhi himself gives a good example of this when, in his *Autobiography*, he writes that his youthful attempt to become an "English gentleman" was as much about music and dance as language and elocution: "I thought I should learn to play the violin in order to cultivate an ear for Western music. So I invested £ 3 in a violin and something more in fees." He also "decided to take dancing lessons"; it was, he writes, "beyond me to achieve anything like rhythmic motion. I could not follow the piano and hence found it impossible to keep time." Though he gives up this attempt to cultivate a colonial ear and to keep colonial time, he later recalls that "the National Anthem used to be sung at every meeting that I attended in Natal," and he felt that he "must also join in the singing": "With careful perseverance I learnt the tune of the 'national anthem' and joined in the singing whenever it was sung." He "likewise taught the National Anthem to the children of [his] family" and "to students of the local Training College." Only later did the text begin "to jar on" him: "As my conception of *ahimsa* [nonviolence or nonharming] went on maturing, I became more vigilant about my thought and speech."[25] There is no question that this musical colonization was an unfinished project, not least in the eyes of the colonizers. Musical cultures around the world remained a battleground between different musical codes, and the musical codes of European colonialism took root mainly in the official musicking of schools, armies, and churches and in the urban ports and colonial capitals. But it was precisely in the shadows of urban schools, armies, and churches that the vernacular phonograph musics took shape.

The second suspicion lay in the commercial nature of these musics; they emerged out of the unrespectable world of popular theater and dance, with their links to illicit sexuality and intoxication. Many of the early phonograph stars came out of the vernacular vaudeville performance, which combined melodramatic theater, comic sketches, puppet shows, and lyric song, all accompanied by small orchestras that combined European and indigenous instruments. In Java, kroncong grew up, performed by mixed-race Eurasian performers, out of the bangsawan theater. In the Philippines, one finds a similar theater, linked to memories of the liberation struggles; in South India, the early Tamil recording stars are figures in the popular theater; and the Cantonese opera of the early twentieth century, which became a staple of gramophone recordings, is a similar formation. In Cuba and the United States, this vaudeville theater is overdetermined by a tradition of minstrelsy and blackface performances. So there was always an ambiguous relation between these theater musics and the nightlife of the colonial ports and subsequent anticolonial nationalist and communist movements. At times, the vernacular stage was a vehicle for anticolonial sentiment; more often it was a stage for ethnic and racial caricature.

The third suspicion was that these musics were imitative, rather than original. There was a famous controversy in 1920s Brazil when the choro composer and bandleader Pixinguinha was accused of giving up Brazilian forms for those of American jazz.[26] Filipino musicians were regularly characterized as particularly able practitioners of these musics—from jazz to Hawaiian—but without an original music.[27] And, finally, these musics fell between both the established aristocratic learned musics and the traditional folk practices of rural agricultural communities, and thus they faced the suspicion both from nationalists constructing a classical tradition and from folklorists and colonial ethnomusicologists seeking to capture and preserve traditional musics.

Thus these musics often appeared as absurd as the colonially educated anticolonial activists themselves, "trousered Africans" as they were dubbed. Indeed, the underlying framework for thinking about these musics was not the discourse of folk music, nor even the discourse about the African American spirituals, but the discourse about gypsy music. For Roma musicians, like

African American enslaved musicians, had long been characterized in nineteenth-century European discourse not as a rural national peasantry with a folk music, but as outcast urban entertainers, virtuoso improvisers on other people's music. This ideology explicitly reappears in writings about the *tzigane* dance bands of this era and in Béla Bartók's 1931 essay "Gypsy Music or Hungarian Music?," which argued that "what people . . . call 'gypsy music' is not gypsy music . . . not old folk music but a fairly recent type of Hungarian popular art music," played "'for money' by urban gypsy bands."[28] The suspicion of these musics has never lifted; after all, how can an entertainment music, played for money, imitating the latest musical fashions, linked to the vice district and the tourist cabaret, trigger the central musical revolution of the twentieth century and, in the process, decolonize the ear?

In large part this was accomplished through the travels of these musics, not to Paris and Berlin, but to Rio, Kinshasa, and Shanghai. The antinomies that haunt the debates over these musics—their initial appearance as an exotic "craze" abroad and a disreputable "noise" at home, and their subsequent vindication as a music both "national" and "popular"—depend on a too-simple geography that reads home as the nation and abroad as the imperial metropolis. I suggest that the recent rethinkings of the space of decolonization allow us to recast our understanding of these musics.

If one reads the conjuncture of mid-twentieth-century decolonization less in the light of the nation-states that resulted from it and more in the light of the uneven history that produced it, we see the crucial importance of Frederick Cooper's insistence that "the success of anticolonial movements . . . cannot be explained on a colony-by-colony basis"; rather it depended on "territory-crossing politics" like the pan-Arab and pan-African movements.[29] This is particularly true of the hinge decade after the crisis of World War I. "Black internationalism," Brent Hayes Edwards writes of this moment when the term is coined, "is not a supplement to revolutionary nationalism, the 'next level' of anti-colonial agitation. On the contrary, black radicalism necessarily emerges through boundary crossing—black radicalism *is* an internationalization."[30]

We need a parallel reconceptualization of these vernacular phonograph musics. For if these musics figured anticolonial opposition, they did not necessarily figure anticolonial space—home rule, *swaraj*, the Negro World—as national space. Rather, like the forms of black and anticolonial internationalism, these vernacular phonograph musics took shape in an archipelago of colonial ports and mill towns, within an imperial commodity chain whose links were not only banana boats and coal trains, but also gramophone records and steel guitars. And, as with anticolonial thought itself, we shouldn't see the musical cultures of this archipelago through a model of center and periphery, source and echo. It was commonly thought at the time that these musics were simply echoes of U.S. jazz. But this is no more accurate than the analogous idea that anticolonial movements and theories were simply echoes of Soviet revolution. Jazz was a central instance of the new vernaculars, but the fact that contemporaries heard the new musics as forms of "jazz" is really more akin to the equally common perception that every anticolonial activist—even Gandhi in the eyes of some British colonial officials—was a "bolshevik."

Rather than this image of jazz echoing around the planet, in various delayed repetitions, one might adopt Ronald Radano's use of "resonance": resonance, he writes, is "the sounding after an unlocatable origin . . . the 'afterlife' of a negative sonic inception."[31] However, in the era of electrical recording, the gramophone seems less like a resonant instrument, sympathetically vibrating, than a reverb unit. Reverberation—the "acoustic context of a sound" consti-tuted by the multiple and overlapping repercussions from the surrounding surfaces of the sound's space—suggests the timbral chaos and sheer noise of the gramophone boom.[32]

Just as different spaces amplify certain frequencies and deaden others, so the transcolonial soundscape amplified some musics over others. There is no necessary or direct relation between the size and resources of a colonial territory and the influence of its music. Glissant may have been accurate in his sense that beguine did not develop as richly as jazz, but his oddly direct sense of the relation between communities and musics is misleading. Just as a handful of Caribbean intellectuals from George Padmore and C. L. R. James to Aimé Césaire and Fanon had a disproportionate impact on anticolo-nial thought, so particular musics from Cuban son to Hawaiian steel guitar seem to have disproportionately long reverberation times.

Almost all of these musics reverberated because they were constituted by movement, as musicians traveled to perform and to record and as disks were imported and exported around the world. The musicians were inter-colonial migrants not unlike the early anticolonial militants and intellectu-als; indeed the South African communist Albert Nzula managed to travel from Cape Town to Moscow in 1931 by "posing as one of Griffiths Motsie-loa's singing group going to London for recording."[33] Consider the guitarist Oscar Alemán. Born in Argentina in 1909, but orphaned in Santos, Brazil, he started by playing the Brazilian cavaquinho. He then formed a Hawaiian duo, Les Loups, with Gastón Bueno Lobo while also recording tangos for Argentine Victor. They went to Europe in 1929 as a Hawaiian music duo, but he went on to lead a swing quintet, recording sambas; he was also in the band that backed Josephine Baker.[34] Alemán might be seen as a marginal figure to each of these musics, neither jazz nor Hawaiian, neither samba nor tango; alternately, he might be taken as a quintessential figure of the new music, mediating between the exotic and the vernacular, Paris and Rio by way of Honolulu and Harlem.

The records circulated like Garvey's *Negro World*, carried by sailors and maritime workers and imported by a commodity chain of music stores. A number of critics have commented that the European reception of jazz was inflected by the fact that the race records of, for example, Louis Armstrong were not available and that jazz came to mean Paul Whiteman. In Brazil, by contrast, the Parlophon catalog of 1928–29, which is dominated by Brazilian records, features not only Armstrong's "West End Blues" but also Kalama's Quartet as "Discos de Dança, New-York." Similarly, a regionwide market in Arabic-language records (often referred to as "Egyptian music") developed, just as movements for independence emerged across North Africa in the wake of World War I. Noting that the imported Baidaphone records circulated "the official and unofficial songs of the different Muslim countries," the Algerian agent in the Bureau of Native Affairs wrote, "While this might appear anodyne, in fact they inculcate in the native the idea that there exist in the world peoples having his faith . . . who have kept more or less the façade of Arab states and who proclaim their desire for liberty in their maternal language and not in that of a foreign *Marseillaise*."[35]

The popularity of "El Manisero" (The peanut vendor) has long served as a figure for the impact that Cuban music made on Europe and North America, an exotic sound packaged as "rumba": the English lyrics even recast the song as exotic local color. But "El Manisero" had an equal if not greater resonance across Africa, where it was the first of hundreds of recordings of Cuban music released in Africa when Gramophone repackaged Victor's Cuban recordings as the GV series in 1933. In the Congo, these recordings of Cuban soneros triggered the emergence of a Lingala rumba. As a Congolese musician recalled, "South American music, the records we had here, especially on the GV label, distributed works that Congolese people picked up on right away."[36] There are stories of musicians calling out the songs by their GV numbers, rather than by their Spanish titles.

Perhaps the most remarkable transcolonial influence in this era was the music of Hawaii, and no music had more ambiguous relation to decolonization. The international vogue for Hawaiian music seems the perfect example of the expropriation of a music for the tourist exotic. Hawaiian music came to international attention through its presentation at the Panama-Pacific Exposition in San Francisco, which celebrated the United States' recently acquired Pacific empire. A traveling Broadway show, *Bird of Paradise*, and the allure of the sexualized Hawaiian women dancing the hula—which had been attacked by missionaries throughout the nineteenth century as an obscene dance—echoed the cult of Josephine Baker in Paris. Several scholars, including Adria Imada, have persuasively analyzed the orientalism of the vogue for Hawaiian music.[37] Moreover, the commercial Hawaiian music of Kalama's Quartet and Sol Ho'opi'i with its steel guitars and ukeleles seemed far from the traditional *meles* and chants that were being collected and recorded at the same time by the folklorist Helen Roberts: her books and recordings of the ancient chants for the Bishop Museum in the mid-1920s lie in the ethnographic tradition of folk music recording between Francis Densmore's recordings of the musics of the Utes and Alan Lomax's recording of the musics of the Mississippi Delta.

Indeed, one of the characteristic timbres and sounds of the commercial Hawaiian music of the 1920s—that of the steel guitar—was almost immediately adopted by U.S. country musicians, not least by Jimmie Rodgers who hired Hawaiian musicians to accompany him. As a result, contemporary ears have a hard time hearing it as Hawaiian music. But the reach of commercial Hawaiian music—the product of a colonial plantation economy that forced together Asian, Pacific, and Atlantic peoples and cultures—was as wide and influential as that of Cuban son or U.S. jazz. It was heard throughout the archipelago of colonial ports: there were Hawaiian musical groups in Shanghai, and it was central to the formation of kroncong in Indonesia. Hawaiian music became an element of Hindi film music, and the influence of Hawaiian guitar styles in South Africa led to the adoption of the term Hawaiian—*hauyaii*—in Bantu languages.[38]

As these phonograph records reverberated from port to port, they figured a model of the postcolonial world; they projected a new harmony, a new rhythm, a new dance. But they also prefigured the contradictions of the decolonizing movements and states: the divide between a democracy of improvisation, and a cult of populist stars and band leaders; a divide between male instrumentalists, inheriting the craft ideologies of artisan music making, and the now open, and openly sexualized, ambivalence toward the woman singing star; the emergence of particular regional musics as emblems of the nation's people.

Music constitutes subjects as social subjects: the rhythms of songs, dances, and marches merge bodies and voices. Thus one might say that a people or movement must be constituted musically before they can be constituted politically. If, as Benedict Anderson suggested three decades ago, the nationalisms of the eighteenth and nineteenth centuries depended on the books and newspapers of "print capitalism," one might argue that the popular movements of the era of decolonization depended, ironically, on the electrical acoustics of a "sound capitalism" and on the new urban plebeian musics they circulated around the world. The decolonization of the ear made possible the decolonization of the territory.

NOTES

This essay draws from my forthcoming book, *Noise Uprising: The Audiopolitics of a World Musical Revolution* (London: Verso, 2015).

1. Virginia Danielson, *The Voice of Egypt: Umm Kulthūm, Arabic Song, and Egyptian Society in the Twentieth Century* (Chicago: University of Chicago Press, 1997), 73.

2. Chris Strachwitz, "A History of Commercial Recordings of Corridos," liner booklet for *The Mexican Revolution; Corridos about the Heroes and Events 1910–1920 and Beyond* (Arhoolie Folkloric ARHCD 7041–7044, 1996).

3. Robert Farris Thompson, *Tango: The Art History of Love* (New York: Vintage, 2005), 201.

4. John Cowley, liner notes to Wilmoth Houdini, *Poor but Ambitious: Calypso Classics from Trinidad, 1928–1940* (Arhoolie Folkloric ARHCD-7010, 1993), 2.

5. Charles K. Wolfe and Ted Olson, eds., *The Bristol Sessions: Writings about the Big Bang of Country Music* (Jefferson, NC: McFarland and Company, 2005).

6. Jason Gibbs, "Spoken Theater, La Scène Tonkinoise, and the First Modern Vietnamese Songs," *Asian Music* 31, no. 2 (2000): 1.

7. Laura Fair, *Pastimes and Politics: Culture, Community, and Identity in Post-Abolition Urban Zanzibar, 1890–1945* (Athens: Ohio University Press, 2001), 1.

8. Ibid., 179–82.

9. Kelly M. Askew, *Performing the Nation: Swahili Music and Cultural Politics in Tanzania* (Chicago: University of Chicago Press, 2002), 109–12.

10. Andrew F. Jones, *Yellow Music: Media Culture and Colonial Modernity in the Chinese Jazz Age* (Durham: Duke University Press, 2001), 113.

11. David Macey, *Frantz Fanon: A Biography* (New York: Picador, 2001), 123–24; Frantz Fanon, *Toward the African Revolution: Political Essays*, trans. Haakon Chevalier (New York: Grove, 1967), 19.

12. Frantz Fanon, *A Dying Colonialism* (New York: Grove, 1967), 74.

13. Édouard Glissant, *Caribbean Discourse: Selected Essays* (Charlottesville: University Press of Virginia, 1989), 110–12.

14. Brent Hayes Edwards, *The Practice of Diaspora: Literature, Translation, and the Rise of Black Internationalism* (Cambridge: Harvard University Press, 2003), 146.

15. United Kingdom Statistical Office of the Customs and Excise Department, *Annual Statement of the Trade of the United Kingdom with Foreign Countries and British*

Countries 1929 Compared with the Years 1925–1928, vol. 3 (London: His Majesty's Stationery Office, 1930), 340–41.

16. Herausgegeben vom Statistischen Reichsamt, *Monatliche Nachweise über den auswärtigen Handel Deutschlands* 1 (December 1925): 159; Herausgegeben vom Statistischen Reichsamt, *Monatliche Nachweise über den auswärtigen Handel Deutschlands* 2 (December 1929): 177.

17. S. Theodore Baskaran, *The Message Bearers: The Nationalist Politics and the Entertainment Media in South India 1880–1945* (Madras, India: Cre-A, 1981), 55, 57.

18. Ibid., 56, 57, 60.

19. Rebecca P. Scales, "Subversive Sound: Transnational Radio, Arabic Recordings, and the Dangers of Listening in French Colonial Algeria, 1934–1939," *Comparative Studies in Society and History* 52, no. 2 (2010): 399, 403–4.

20. Quoted in Jones, *Yellow Music*, 91.

21. Baskaran, *The Message Bearers*, 54.

22. For a detailed account, see Dick Spottswood, "Who Was Butler?," in *The Classic Calypso Collective, West Indian Rhythm: Trinidad Calypsos on World and Local Events Featuring the Censored Recordings 1938–1940* (Bear Family Records/BCD 16623 JM, 2006), 53.

23. Quoted in Rudolf Mrázek, *Engineers of a Happy Land: Technology and Nationalism in a Colony* (Princeton, NJ: Princeton University Press, 2002), 196.

24. Jason Gibbs, "The West's Songs, Our Songs: The Introduction and Adaptation of Western Popular Song in Vietnam before 1940," *Asian Music* 35, no. 1 (Autumn 2003/Winter 2004): 58.

25. Mohandas K. Gandhi, *An Autobiography: The Story of My Experiments with Truth* (Boston: Beacon, 1993), 50–51, 172–73.

26. See Rafael José de Menezes Bastos, "Brazil in France, 1922: An Anthropological Study of the Congenital International Nexus of Popular Music," *Latin American Music Review* 29, no. 1 (2008): 1–28; and Micol Seigel, *Uneven Encounters: Making Race and Nation in Brazil and the United States* (Durham: Duke University Press, 2009), 95–135.

27. Lee Watkins, "Minstrelsy and Mimesis in the South China Sea: Filipino Migrant Musicians, Chinese Hosts, and the Disciplining of Relations in Hong Kong," *Asian Music* 40, no. 2 (2009): 89.

28. Béla Bartók, "Gypsy Music or Hungarian Music?" *Musical Quarterly* 33, no. 2 (1947): 240–41.

29. Frederick Cooper, *Colonialism in Question: Theory, Knowledge, History* (Berkeley: University of California Press, 2005), 200, 24.

30. Edwards, *The Practice of Diaspora*, 243.

31. Ronald Radano, *Lying Up a Nation: Race and Black Music* (Chicago: University of Chicago Press, 2003), 11.

32. Albin J. Zak III, *The Poetics of Rock: Cutting Tracks, Making Records* (Berkeley: University of California Press, 2001), 76.

33. Jonathan Derrick, *Africa's "Agitators": Militant Anti-Colonialism in Africa and the West, 1918–1939* (New York: Columbia University Press, 2008), 277.

34. Michael Dregni, *Django: The Life and Music of a Gypsy Legend* (New York: Oxford University Press, 2004), 99–103.

35. Scales, "Subversive Sound," 400.

36. Gary Stewart, *Rumba on the River: A History of the Popular Music of the Two Congos* (London: Verso, 2000), 13.

37. Adria Imada, *Aloha America: Hula Circuits through the U.S. Empire* (Durham: Duke University Press, 2012).

38. Martin Clayton, "Rock to Raga: The Many Lives of the Indian Guitar," in *Guitar Cultures*, ed. Andy Bennett and Kevin Dawe (Oxford: Berg, 2001), 187–88, 204n19.

2 · SMOKING HOT Cigarettes, Jazz, and the Production of Global Imaginaries in Interwar Shanghai

NAN ENSTAD

Jazz and cigarettes: the pairing still has an affective resonance. I picture the jazz clubs of the 1940s and '50s, when musicians and fans alike pursued the art in a haze of smoke that only enhanced the ambiance of the setting. Though I was not yet born during this period, this image of the smoky jazz club is reiterated in countless films and photographs of this lost era, and it is integral to nostalgic longing for it.[1] But the origin of the association of jazz and cigarettes is older than this: it dates to the international dance craze of the 1920s and '30s, when jazz and cigarettes circled the globe, triumphant together in their unprecedented popularity. In the 1920s, jazz referred to popular dance music that included a wide variety of styles, typically carrying black racial inflection. In the same years that jazz fever hit, cigarette sales boomed, astounding even their promoters with their new renown. From New York to Shanghai, the economies and affects of cigarettes and jazz intertwined in a dance as intimate and seductive as the fox-trot or the lindy hop.

We could turn our spotlight of exploration of jazz and cigarettes on any number of cities—New York, Berlin, Paris, Singapore, Manila, Tokyo, Shanghai—but Shanghai holds special analytical appeal. The British American Tobacco Company (BAT), the largest cigarette company in the world, had its largest branch in China, with its headquarters in Shanghai. BAT epitomized the urge for global dominance among emerging multinational corporations, and it gravitated to Shanghai because the city had become a corporate mecca. China evaded outright colonization by a western power, but nineteenth-century wars with Great Britain and Japan had forced treaties that opened cities like Shanghai to foreign businesses, giving those companies enormous advantages. By 1918, just before the dance craze hit, seven thousand foreign companies had established a presence in China.[2] The Shanghai jazz scene quickly became especially diverse and elaborate as musicians and dancers migrated there from many countries in order to entertain the burgeoning foreign capitalist elite. Cigarettes and jazz were big business in Shanghai and they spun to the fast beats of global capitalism and imperialism.

Cigarettes and jazz joined forces in Shanghai and elsewhere by both accident and design. Offering cigarettes for sale at cabarets was an innovation that probably seemed obvious to cigarette salesmen and cabaret owners alike. The cabaret soon became a scene of an affective experience of smoking, jazz music, and dance. Linked by atmosphere and movement, the experiences of jazz and cigarettes literally entwined. Tobacco companies seized upon this synergy and made it part of their explicit marketing strategies. They sponsored jazz radio shows in Shanghai, much as they did in the United States, tying cigarette branding to the aura of jazz and selecting the kind of jazz that filled the airways. In a real way, then, each product helped shape what the other came to be.

Exploring cigarettes as part of a study of jazz highlights jazz's complex status simultaneously as a function of capitalist, imperial projects and as something that produces expressive and participatory cultures. Jazz's artistry can deflect attention from its status as a commodity; cigarettes' reputation as heavily marketed and branded corporate products draws attention to the forces of promotion and distribution that shaped jazz and cigarettes both. At the same time, cigarettes can remind us that the artistry of jazz was not simply, perhaps not even primarily, about individual musical genius but took place as part of scenes of performance, dance, intimacies, and style. Scholars have attributed jazz's participatory performance style to African American cultural traditions that closely link music and dance as co-evolving art forms.[3] Despite acknowledging this fact, jazz scholarship continues to profoundly neglect dance in the participatory scene of early jazz and focuses instead on musicians and the music itself in relative isolation. Attention to cigarettes returns us to the scene of jazz. How one holds a cigarette, the method of exhale, and the smoky atmosphere that results were variously part of the jazz experience for musicians and dancers.

In this essay, I explore the ways that cigarettes and jazz became linked economically and affectively in Shanghai cabarets. I explore the ways that cigarettes and jazz dance circulated in that space, producing the atmosphere and interior geography of the cabarets while accruing affective power. I follow theorists who argue that affect does not reside in a person or thing but is produced through the circulation of things.[4] What theorists mean by circulation is often vaguely defined. Here I am interested in the economic and social circulation that brought cigarettes, jazz music, and the cabarets themselves to Shanghai as well as a closer view of the physical and intimate circulation of cigarettes and jazz within the cabarets and how this process transformed bodies and spaces, creating a highly charged yet unstable cabaret experience.

The first part of this essay thus explores the economy and phenomenology of globally circulating jazz and cigarettes in Shanghai cabarets. This inquiry tells us much about the transformative power of jazz and cigarettes but little about how that power materialized in social relations. The remainder of the essay shows the articulation of jazz and cigarettes to the practices of specific producers/consumers—BAT foreign employees who were clients at the cabarets and African American musicians who produced jazz music on the bandstands—within the cabarets. That is, I examine the ways that particular kinds of subjects emerged in dynamic response to the economic and affective potentials of jazz and cigarettes in an imperial context. Cigarette employees gained investments in imperial processes through their consumption of cigarettes and jazz, while African American musicians found their position as subjects far more contradictory, exposed to both the pleasures and pains of imperialism.

SHANGHAI'S FIRST CABARETS opened soon after World War I and catered to foreign businessmen, both stimulating and profiting from foreigners' desire for opulent places to socialize and celebrate the fruits of western imperialism. Western businessmen built most of the cabarets in the early 1920s.[5] Owners hired live jazz bands and dance hostesses, or taxi dancers, who danced with the overwhelmingly male clientele for a fee. An English-language guidebook conveyed the centrality of cabarets in the wide array of amusements the city offered, particularly to foreign residents and visitors:

> Shanghai has its own distinctive night life, and what a life! Dog races and cabarets, hai-alai and cabarets, formal tea and dinner dances and cabarets, the sophisticated and cosmopolitan French club and cabarets, prize fights and cabarets, amateur dramatics and cabarets, treatres [sic], movies and cabarets, and cabarets—everywhere, in both extremities of Frenchtown (French Concession), uptown and downtown in the International Settlement, in Hongkew, and out of bounds in Chinese territory, are cabarets. Hundreds of 'em![6]

The division between the international settlements, where foreigners resided and largely recreated, and the rest of the city is captured by the guidebook's reference to the Chinese city as "out of bounds." This colonial geographic imaginary is also exemplified in a comment made by a BAT employee, Irwin Smith, who thought that Shanghai "was just like any other foreign city except the Chinese were there."[7] Cabarets initially replicated the logics of imperialism, placing the needs of foreign elites at the center of the experience.

Because of the lucrative cabaret scene, Shanghai became a very important place for jazz music in Asia. The music scene was profoundly international: musicians from the United States, the Philippines, China, Russia, and Japan all competed for gigs. The most successful obtained extended contracts in Shanghai, but many traveled a circuit that included cities like Singapore, Hong Kong, Manila, and Calcutta, along with Shanghai. African American musicians became particularly popular on this circuit because, as the "originators of jazz," they promised an authentic sound for those longing to dance.[8] Like musicians, taxi dancers converged in Shanghai from near and distant places, including China, the Philippines, Russia, Korea, Greece, and Japan. The jazz scene in Shanghai was so elaborated that Japanese musicians went to Shanghai to learn "authentic" or "American" jazz. While Shanghai's cabarets began as a foreign institution, owned by and catering to foreign elites, by the late 1920s competition for clientele was fierce and some owners began to woo wealthy Chinese customers. At the same time, Chinese entrepreneurs entered the business. As Andrew Jones notes, the resulting heterogeneous music scene generated innovations and hybrids, including a mix of jazz,

Hollywood film music, and Chinese folk song called "yellow music," in Chinese-dominated venues.[9]

Shanghai was equally significant as a site of cigarette production and consumption. By the 1920s, the BAT and the (Chinese) Nayang Brothers Tobacco Company were two of the largest industries in Shanghai, and their massive local factories produced billions of cigarettes for the growing market of foreign and Chinese urbanites. BAT was one of the largest employers in the Shanghai area.[10] Cigarette smoking, like jazz performance, was especially an urban phenomenon during these years in China, a fact that accentuated cigarettes' association with urbanity and modernity. Cigarette consumption in the city was high: 5.09 cigarettes per capita per day by 1935.[11] Cigarette marketers directed money, talent, and new printing technologies into finding ways to entice people to smoke, and cigarette advertising was ubiquitous in the city.

Both jazz music and cigarette smoke became integral to the interior geography and distinctive atmosphere of the cabarets. A BAT employee, James Hutchinson, noted that when he entered the Cercle Sportif Français in 1930 the music was "deafening" and the cigarette smoke so thick it took his eyes several minutes to adjust so he could discern faces.[12] Sound and smoke both altered the atmosphere of a space and how it looked and felt to be there. The organization of the cabaret space in both Shanghai and the United States reserved a large central area for dance, with a periphery of tables for clients who wished to smoke cigarettes, drink alcohol, and talk.[13] At the Canidrome in Shanghai, for example, a very large space in front of the bandstand encouraged dancing couples to fill the center of the room, circled by a narrow band of small, intimate tables. (See figure 2.1.) At some clubs, dance hostesses occupied one side of the dance floor while clients eyed them from the other before inviting one to dance or join their table. Cigarettes and jazz thus functioned in a symbiotic way to shape the interior of cabarets.

Cigarettes and jazz also shared a unique capacity to structure the leisure experience at cabarets. Unlike other commodities present or even required at the cabaret, such as cosmetics or fashionable clothing, cigarettes and jazz dance had particular temporal qualities. Both could be used to mark time: one more cigarette, one more dance. Both also could motivate the body through space: to the center of the dance floor or to the periphery to a table. As jazz dance charged the body in movement, cigarettes animated the body at rest. Cigarette smoking and jazz dance thus were the media through which the body became part of, even constituted by, the cabaret.

Furthermore, the activities of jazz music and cigarette smoking carried distinct powers to transform bodily and emotive sensations in ways that not

FIGURE 2.1. The Canidrome dance floor. Courtesy of Institute for Jazz Studies, Rutgers University.

only facilitated eroticism but also came widely to serve as signs of the erotic. Both cigarette smoking and jazz dance allowed physical intimacy between cabaret customers. The one-step, the fox-trot, the lindy hop: the point for fans of this era of jazz was an expressive capacity to embody the music in dance. "Listening" was a full-body experience. Spinning together on the cabarets' large dance floors allowed strangers to touch each other's bodies in ways otherwise forbidden. Dancing to jazz music combined precision and skill in executing set dance steps with personal improvisation and expression. "Hot" syncopated rhythms favored dances that moved the hips and could require considerable physicality, in contrast to nineteenth-century European ballroom dances that held the body more stiffly erect.[14] Likewise, physically lighting one's own or another's cigarette, sharing cigarettes, and breathing the smoke of another's cigarette all engaged the mouth, hand, and breath in a sensuous and intimate activity. Jazz dancing and smoking carried expressive capacities that were at once shared and distinguished by personal signatures. The space of cabarets became widely celebrated and decried for this eroticism, a defining element of the jazz craze.

The eroticism of the cabaret experience carried a racially transgressive element for many foreigners in Shanghai. Consider this scene of intoxication from an English-language guidebook to Shanghai in the 1930s, under the heading "Dancing and Music": "The throb of the jungle tom-tom; the symphony of lust; the music of a hundred orchestras; the shuffling of feet; the swaying of bodies; the rhythm of abandon; the hot smoke of desire—desire under the floodlights; it's all fun; it's life. . . . There's nothing puritanical about Shanghai."[15] The "throb of the jungle tom-tom" efficiently references notions of primitive African rhythm at the heart of the racialization of jazz. Pointedly containing "nothing puritanical," jazz according to this view was sexually passionate, primitive, and black, in contrast to rational, civilized whiteness. Jazz's racial status was ambiguous in Shanghai, as elsewhere. Many white musicians played in Shanghai cabarets (and resented competition from Filipinos and Russians). Paul Whiteman achieved early and uproarious fame in Japan and elsewhere in Asia. As David Suisman notes, U.S. recording companies discriminated against African Americans, a fact with international consequences because jazz recordings were a key way in which jazz first circulated in Asia.[16] Still, notions that African Americans offered a more authentic jazz sound clearly circulated among the foreign elite in Asian ports of the 1920s.

Chinese people in Shanghai also came to see jazz as originally or in essence black. In 1933, the celebrated fiction author Mu Shiying reflected these sensibilities in his story titled after a popular brand of cigarettes, "Craven A." His main female character, Lin Taili, was a sexually adventurous taxi dancer who favored Craven A cigarettes and danced "like a daughter of Africa" to the rhumba at a Shanghai cabaret, by which Mu meant that she was a particularly seductive dancer.[17] Thus, the transgressive eroticism of the cabaret experience engaged and fueled the racialization of jazz, making possible new investments in racism through a wide range of racially inflected pleasures.[18]

As the story "Craven A" indicated, cigarettes only added to the sexual charge of the cabaret atmosphere. Taxi dancers very typically smoked cigarettes and drank alcohol with their clients. An anticigarette campaign in the turn-of-the-century United States and England had linked cigarettes to alcohol as intoxicating substances and associated both with moral and physical ill health. Considered a masculine prerogative in these countries, women's cigarette smoking held particularly transgressive and sexual connotations. Though cigarette smoking itself held no shame for women in Chinese culture, smoking in public did mark a woman as transgressive.[19] Thus, the guidebook writer's phrase the "hot smoke of desire" uses the word "hot," associated both with jazz rhythm ("the rhythm of abandon") and an exhaled breath, to merge the effects of jazz and cigarettes with "desire."

Explicit cigarette marketing and branding efforts soon sought to reinforce the association between cigarettes and jazz occasioned by their synchronicity in the cabarets. In 1928, Jinyue cigarettes sponsored an early evening "tea dance" at Shanghai's New Carlton Ballroom, offering free cigarettes to attendees.[20] This move at once used free cigarettes to entice new dancers to the New Carlton and sought new smokers among jazz enthusiasts. Soon after, the BAT sponsored a recorded jazz radio show in Shanghai that broadcast several nights each week. James Hutchinson created the programs:

> An English advertising house opened a broadcasting station. The company decided to try it out on a high-grade cigarette and I spent the best part of a week selecting records from the vast stocks imported by the four leading music houses. Then the company presented me with a small receiving set to check up on our tri-weekly programs, and from six in the evening until eleven I listened to . . . American jazz.[21]

Hutchinson, a white man from North Carolina, gained significant power to shape the kind of jazz that hit the Shanghai airwaves on one station. Given that the company designated a "high-grade" cigarette as the sponsor, the intended audience was elite foreigners. No doubt, the announcer made sure that listeners heard the brand name of the sponsoring cigarette between each and every number.

While local BAT employees must have weighed in on the decision to engage in radio advertising, they also certainly drew on their knowledge of cigarette-sponsored radio shows in the United States. In 1928, the American Tobacco Company created a sensation by sponsoring the *Lucky Strike Radio Hour*, a show that became so popular that it shaped the sound and economy of jazz on the radio. Other companies followed suit and a barrage of shows soon followed, including the *Old Gold Hour*, the *Camel Caravan*, the *Chesterfield Show*, and the *Raleigh-Kool Program*.[22] When a cigarette company sponsored a radio show in both the United States and China, it produced the entire show rather than simply commissioning commercials. Regulations stipulated that U.S. radio shows could not use recordings, so cigarette-sponsored shows became a primary means of exposure for bands in the United States. In both the United States and China, the company carefully chose the jazz played on the show. The cigarette shows did not simply transmit jazz, they shaped and, especially in the United States, standardized a jazz product, making jazz part of the branding of cigarettes.

Cigarettes and jazz together became more than the sum of their parts. In the context of the cabaret or the radio show, they promised to transport and transform their consumers. But transform to where? Transform into what? How did the affective experience of cigarettes and jazz shape the meaning of imperialism in daily life? The answer depended on who one was. The remainder of this essay considers how cigarette company employees and African American musicians took up residence in the world of Shanghai's cabarets.

HUNDREDS OF YOUNG white men came to interwar Shanghai in the service of cigarettes. Southerner James B. Duke formed BAT by merging his American Tobacco Company with the British Imperial Tobacco Company in 1902. Duke hired a fellow North Carolinian, James A. Thomas, to head the China branch, which Thomas grew to be BAT's largest. Thomas tapped tobacco networks in North Carolina when hiring men to work in China, not only because such men had experience in tobacco but also because the southern economy was weak and young men were desperate for opportunity. Most of the men who arrived at BAT headquarters in Shanghai were young, unmarried, from rural areas or small towns, and away from home for the first time. Shanghai was the biggest city most had ever seen. Many reported feeling bewildered upon arrival and were patently afraid of Chinese people because of their prior exposure to racist Fu Manchu films and the like. They clung to their coworkers, especially at first, as they took on new subjectivities as representatives of a global corporation.

The cabarets became a key transformative site for BAT employees as they gained new imaginaries of themselves in the larger world of global capitalism. Indeed, the cabarets' initial purpose had been precisely this imperial function for foreigners; BAT employees joined many other representatives of foreign businesses in rooting their corporate culture in the cabarets. Irwin Smith gained his footing in BAT on the cabaret dance floor. He recalled attending the cabarets with coworkers:

> Well, you know Mr. RH Gregory, he was out there. He always thought a lot of the young fellows. . . . He was a fine old gentleman and there wasn't anything stuck up about him. He'd take you to the cabarets. He'd buy the tickets and put them on the table and say, "Boys, let's have some fun," and you'd dance all you wanted to. He'd sit there, he wouldn't do any dancing, but he'd sit there and have a lot of fun. He and this Joe Honeycutt used to go cabareting quite a bit.[23]

By hosting the event and buying the dance tickets, Gregory made the cabarets an integral part of the pleasures and social privileges of employment with BAT, as well as the creation of social cohesion in BAT's business culture.

Dancing to jazz music was integral to this process of building global imaginaries and corporate identities. Many BAT employees commented on the international composition of the dance hostess workforce. In 1930 Hutchinson recalled that "along the dimly lighted criss-crossing streets behind the Astor House were dozens of international dance halls and cafés, some with Chinese dance partners, some with Japanese, some with Russian and some with a mixture of the three, including sensual mixed-breeds."[24] In Hutchinson's erotic imagination, "mixed-breeds" were more "sensual," a view rooted in the socially constructed fears and attractions of racial crossing. The nationality and race of dancers gave a cabaret its character and became a commodity for clients' consumption. Frank Canaday recalled that in 1923 he "went to some dance and cabaret place and danced with some Russian, French and Greek girls there till about 2am." He also recalled another night when they hopped to various places, drinking beer and "kidding the girls—Koreans—Russians—Lord knows what."[25] Many taxi dancers enhanced their cabaret pay with sex work after hours. Though foreign BAT employees did not record such exchanges, James N. Joyner took a Chinese taxi dancer as a mistress for several years.[26] No doubt their romance began with a turn on the dance floor and a shared cigarette.

Canaday's phrase "Lord knows what" to refer to the range of nationalities of taxi dancers aptly expressed the imperial privilege he experienced at the cabaret. The economy of the cabaret prompted and drew on globalized movements of women, erased their stories, and offered them as a leisure commodity for the pleasure of foreign businessmen so that nationality became a kind of flavor in a smorgasbord of global options: Russian, French, Chinese, Korean, Greek, "Lord knows what." Thus did the privileges of the assemblage for BAT employees blend an ability to know and have with an erasure and an unknowing so characteristic of imperialism in general. Foreign BAT employees' public intimacy with dance hostesses gave an erotic charge to their new position as representatives of a transnational corporation in the global city of Shanghai, as they enacted investment in relations of inequality on the dance floor.

Foreign BAT employees seemed entirely unaware, for example, that some Chinese taxi dancers in cabarets catering to a Chinese clientele had achieved a starlike status, becoming well known and celebrated in the tabloid press for their beauty, style, and dancing ability. David Field notes that this fame was two sided, winning taxi dancers censure in much of Chinese society as taxi dancers became a lightning rod for debate about the relationship between foreign companies, changing Chinese cultures and emerging national sensibilities.[27] Thus, the cabarets were not static places of fixed social relations but shifted with ownership, employees, and clientele. Jazz and cigarettes, however, remained.

Like other clients, BAT employees smoked cigarettes between dances, but in their case they consumed the products they promoted during the day. Smoking the company product could produce a proprietary identification with the company and the product, despite the low-level positions that most of them held. Though this typically went without explicit comment, Canaday noted that when BAT rented a cabaret for a party, his "main amusement [came] from watching [his coworker] Stanley Grey's efforts to thwart the 'squeeze' of too many cigarettes and cigars by the Chinese boys employed to sell the companies products from table to table."[28] Chinese workers typically increased their meager wages through the moral economy of the "squeeze," a surcharge of cash or products. Grey must have been unsuccessful if his efforts were entertaining enough to distract Canaday from other pleasures. For Chinese workers, cigarettes and cigars were valuable items that they could smoke themselves, use as gifts or barter, or sell for cash. Cigarettes linked both Chinese workers and foreign BAT employees to economies and affects of global capital.

BAT employees tended to hop from club to club in ways that emphasized male homosocial bonding, strengthening ties within the company and with other foreigners. Canaday recorded a night's festivities in his diary in 1923. He began the evening with drinks at the American club (men only) with a few friends. There they met a few more men and the group went by car to the Western Tavern in Hongkew, where they heard an "American jazz band" and two more men joined them. "Our party of eight was now having too good a time looking and talking to give any time to the Russian girls across the room who seemed interested. None of us deserted the table to dance." Canaday knew that the expected behavior, and the one that turned the greatest profit for cabaret owners and dancers, was the male-female dance, and he took pleasure in his group's refusal of that script. At 1:30 AM, all eight took a car to the Del Monte. He utilizes a feminine gendered image to describe his group's appearance and spirit of togetherness: "There two more men joined us and we began to look like the front row of a glee club as we occupied a row of tables across one end of the dance floor." Soon a portion of this crowd ("six men still 'with us' when we counted noses in the car") went to Mumm's Café, ate ham and eggs, and "took . . . turns dancing with a Russian girl." At 4:00 AM, Canaday finally went home to get "a few hours sleep before office time."[29] From the men's-only club at the beginning of the evening, to "taking . . . turns" with a professional dancer, the practice of club hopping opened up a space for public intimacies between men to be as or more intense than the male-female couples on the dance floor. Normative corporate culture, thus, carried possibilities for homoerotic experience in excess of the intended imperial script.

The cabaret and its articulation of jazz and cigarettes thus was a site of transformation for BAT employees from the United States who were adapting to their new role as representatives of a transnational corporation. BAT employees gained erotic and affective relationships to the commodity they promoted during the day as well as to jazz and the company culture. Not least, they took up residence in the global city of Shanghai through physically intimate dances to jazz music with women from multiple nations, echoing an imperial position of capturing the world's resources. At the same time, the intimacies of jazz and cigarettes were not fully predictable. Just as cabarets became sites of queer culture in the United States and Paris, so did the conditions exist within the assemblage for same-sex eroticism and pleasure.

THOUGH ENTREPRENEURS BUILT Shanghai's cabarets explicitly and exclusively to serve the foreign elite, after only a few years the economy of the cabaret scene shifted, creating new room for Chinese entrepreneurs and, incidentally, African American musicians. According to Field, the cabaret scene was so hot in the immediate post–World War I era that it quickly became overbuilt and, by the mid-1920s, some owners wished to sell. Two Chinese entrepreneurs, known only by their surnames Tong and Vung, became major players in the Shanghai cabaret business. They soon bought several cabarets in Shanghai, including the large and famous Canidrome Ballroom.[30] Tong and Vung contracted with scores of African American musicians and bands to work in Shanghai. At the same time, some foreign and Chinese cabaret owners wooed an elite Chinese clientele to the cabarets.

Tong and Vung's contracts with African Americans shifted the kind of transnational flow occasioned by the Shanghai cabarets. Rather than the cabaret economy being in the hands of the western elites that controlled the foreign settlements, some economic agency now rested in the hands of Chinese entrepreneurs and African American booking agents. Françoise Lionnet and Shu-mei Shih call this kind of formation "minor transnationalism," that is, transnational exchange between colonized or formerly colonized people that circumvented the imperial powers.[31] Apparently, most foreign-owned cabarets had worked with the booking agency Hamilton House. S. James Staley, a white musician in Shanghai, claimed that R. T. Hamilton of Hamilton House, Shanghai, was "in charge of most of the theatrical, music and entertainment bookings throughout the Far East"; in contrast, no African American musician mentions this agency. In 1924, Canaday noted with great surprise and delight, after coming upon an American jazz band in a Shanghai cabaret, "the traps man an American nigger!"[32] Canaday's use of the derogatory term combined with his enthusiasm captures the ambiguous place of African American musicians on the foreign cabaret bandstand, while his surprise indicates that their presence was still rare.

Teddy Weatherford, a Chicago piano player, became a booking agent for Tong and Vung in the early 1930s, building on a pipeline between the U.S. jazz scene and Shanghai. Weatherford had made many connections and a name for himself through six prior years on the Asian circuit. Weatherford got his start in Asia with the Jack Carter Band, among the first African American bands to travel the Asian jazz circuit. In 1924, Carter, originally from Columbus, Ohio, traveled from Shanghai to Singapore to Calcutta. He brought with him a band, including Weatherford on piano; a singer, Valeida Snow, who had performed with him in Chicago; and a professional dance troupe.[33] The dance troupe was crucial for it introduced new steps to eager dancing audiences. When Jack Carter's orchestra performed in Singapore in 1928, the *Straits Times* celebrated that a "real 'colored cabaret' [has] reached Singapore at last."[34]

Weatherford stayed in Asia for the rest of his life and did much to expand opportunities for African American musicians along the circuit, including in Shanghai, through his musicianship, personality, and business savvy. He became famous at the Winter Garden at the Grand Hotel in Calcutta, and he played regularly in Manila, where an African American named Tom Prichard owned a cabaret and expressly sought to book African American bands. Langston Hughes recalled, "A big, genial, dark man, something of a clown, Teddy could walk into any public place in the Orient and folks would break into applause." By the mid-1930s, Weatherford was so famous that when he was in Shanghai, he'd play with four bands in four different places nightly, spending only about thirty minutes with each band but bringing home four paychecks.[35]

It is not clear exactly when Weatherford's association with Tong and Vung began, but the *Pittsburgh Courier* claimed that Tong and Vung began hiring African American bands in the 1920s and continued in the mid-1930s "to encourage the migration of the American Negro to the Far East." Weatherford directly booked Buck Clayton's band to play at Tong and Vung's Canidrome

Ballroom. In 1934, Weatherford traveled to Los Angeles in search of a band, offering one-way passage and guaranteed paychecks. The *Chicago Defender*'s West Coast music reporter wrote, "China! China! The favorite topic of conversation and conjecture at present among the profesh [profession] on the coast. . . . This is . . . since Teddy Weatherford arrived here last winter from Shanghai on the lookout for a band and entertainers to take back." Buck Clayton's band played in the Central Avenue scene but struggled to find work in the midst of the Depression. "We were pretty desperate," recalled Clayton. "We even went to a couple of hot-dog stands to try to influence the owners to use jazz. One of these owners says, 'Are you crazy? Just how in hell do you think I can use a fourteen-piece band in a hot-dog stand?' "[36] The band changed its name to Buck Clayton and His Harlem Gentlemen, to emphasize the African American membership of the band, though none of the members were from Harlem, further indication that being African American musicians was a selling point in Shanghai. Clayton's trumpet player, Happy Johnson, extended the pipeline: he eventually started his own band and traveled back to the United States to recruit members.

African American musicians noted that their employment by Tong and Vung in the Shanghai cabaret scene was different in both economy and affect than playing in U.S. elite cabarets or hotels. Clayton recounted the businessmen treating them to a banquet, a customary Chinese business practice: "We were met by the bosses of the Canidrome Ballroom, Mr. Tong and Mr. Vung. They were two very rich Chinese, one fat and the other skinny, but both were very nice people. They greeted us with a huge welcoming committee and soon we were at a banquet that was really something else. I didn't know what I was eating and I couldn't eat with chopsticks but I was happy."[37] Happy Johnson recounted that Tong and Vung treated them to "a real Chinese fashionable dinner of about seventy-five courses. Gee I never saw so many different foods in all my life." Tong and Vung might have viewed African Americans as an inferior race, but by extending business courtesies to the musicians they stood in stark contrast to whites in the United States. The customs of Jim Crow segregation rested on withholding courtesies and titles from African Americans, even in business exchanges. Two years before Jack Carter went to China, for example, a white hotel proprietor in Florida hired his band to play in his white-only ballroom but assured the white public that he did his best to "segregate the men while they were with me and to make [them] feel like servants." In Shanghai, in contrast, jazz musicians were treated like "the Emperor of China."[38]

Black musicians often described their work in Shanghai as free from racism because they could get high-class gigs and enjoyed wide popularity. Happy Johnson reported, "This was the break of our lives for over here is a real golden opportunity for our profesh. China is the last resort for the colored musicians. We are the talk of the Far East and the Orient, and it seems too good to be true, and it is true." "There is absolutely no color line over there," Johnson told a reporter when stateside to hire more musicians. "All Negroes need to do is produce." Clayton later recalled, "I still say today that the two years I spent in China were the happiest two years of my life." Noting the impact on his subjectivity, he continued, "My life seemed to begin in Shanghai. We were recognized for a change and treated with so much respect." Perhaps the strongest testimony comes from musicians who chose to stay in East Asia. Reginald Jones, the bass player in Clayton's band, married a Filipina woman and settled in Shanghai. Ernest (Slick) Clark, a trombone player, went to Shanghai in 1935 and stayed. Weatherford married an Indian woman and lived in Shanghai and Calcutta until his death. Irene West, the manager of the MacKay Twins in Asia, wrote in the *Baltimore Afro-American,* "Do you wonder why so many of your race who make good abroad never wish to return to this Jim-crow America! Would you? The Chinese, Filipinos and Indians look upon the colored American with admiration and respect. He is somebody in the lands of color."[39]

Though African American musicians found relief from U.S. racism, Shanghai's foreign settlements were imperial, segregated spaces that imposed their own racist practices. African Americans found themselves barred from entering most public places unless they were working. U.S. marines stationed in Shanghai, U.S. businessmen, and white U.S. musicians all resented the prestige that African American musicians enjoyed. Marines picked fights with bands on more than one occasion by hurling racial slurs. In one case, Clayton lost his gig at the Canidrome because he became embroiled in a fight on the cabaret floor with a marine who objected to his presence on the stage with a white female dance troupe from California. U.S. southern businessmen, possibly some from BAT, then called for Clayton's band to be fired and Tong and Vung complied. Clayton suspected that white musicians had staged the entire conflict in order to get his band ousted from the cabaret.[40] If Clayton was correct, racial solidarity among U.S. residents of Shanghai reasserted white supremacy in treaty port relations. Shanghai's cabaret economy thus brought particular potential pleasures and dangers for African American musicians. They did not escape the imperial context but took up an ambivalent place within it.

As for African American musicians' experience of jazz dance and cigarettes, the evidence is spotty but compelling. Clearly, as producers of the music, African Americans had a different relationship to the space and to dance than clients, just as BAT employees had a particular experience of cigarettes. Many bands at this time incorporated dance steps into their performance and appreciated and responded to enthusiastic or skilled dancers on the floor, fostering a creative relationship between dancers and musicians. Like customers, musicians formed relationships with taxi dancers, but these relationships carried a unique range of potentials. For some, the ready and inexpensive sex with taxi dancers was an exciting privilege and they responded much as did young white men who worked for BAT. Hughes traveled in Shanghai at this time and recalled Irene West asking him to speak to the young MacKay Twins, a tap dance duo from Los Angeles' Central Avenue, about slowing down in their sexual exploits. According to Hughes, the young men "were both feeling their oats—and sowing them. Between the White Russian women and the Japanese girls, the boys almost never got back to their hotel at night."[41] Clayton recalled his entire band going as a group in rickshaws to the doctor to receive treatment for sexually transmitted diseases they contracted in the treaty port. African American musicians could tap imperial pleasures, despite the fact that those pleasures had not been assembled with them in mind.

At the same time, something happened at the cabarets that also made relationships possible between African American musicians and taxi dancers. Hughes noted that he went for breakfast to Weatherford's home in the Chinese city with the band. The location itself was significant: virtually all BAT employees lived in the international settlements, and some reported fear of traveling through the Chinese city. African Americans, in contrast, encountered discrimination in the settlements and typically rented places in Chinese neighborhoods. At Weatherford's apartment, the band members' wives and girlfriends made a southern-style breakfast; the diverse group of Russian and Japanese girlfriends or wives followed the instructions of the African American wife who had traveled with one band member from Harlem.[42] James Joyner, a BAT employee, took a Chinese taxi dancer as a mistress as well, and the particular contours of these relationships are ultimately impossible to judge. However, African American musicians shared a position as cabaret workers with taxi dancers, which might have been what enabled them to create relationships and integrate them into their social scene, so that Hughes referred to them as girlfriends rather than as mistresses.

The specific place of cigarettes in African Americans' Shanghai cabaret experiences is not mentioned in the rare remaining remembrances, but cigarettes' powers are on display in a posed photograph of Clayton with a rickshaw driver on a street in the International Settlement of Shanghai (see figure 2.2). The cigarette and white suit mark Clayton as a jazz musician, while the rickshaw and driver establish him as a foreign elite in the imperial setting. The rickshaw picture was a genre among colonial travelers to China and many of the BAT employees sent such a picture home to family members. It established the westerner as imperial and leisured in relation to the rickshaw driver, a menial, "primitive" laborer. In Clayton's picture he stands in the foreground, dressed in a fine, white suit, and is conspicuously holding a cigarette and white derby hat. In contrast, the rickshaw driver is off to the side, dressed in simple pants and shirt, hat, and bamboo shoes. His shirt is open to the waist, revealing his body and indicating his physical labor.

Clayton explained that his own clothes were a benefit of the favorable exchange rate experienced by all westerners, and they were acquired specifically for jazz performance:

> As soon as we hit Shanghai we were smothered with tailors who made suits, hand-made suits, for such ridiculous prices that we were ordering them like millionaires. . . . I wouldn't be exaggerating if I said that I believe we had more uniforms than Duke Ellington. We had tuxedos of different colors, we had full dress suits both in black and in gray colors, we had many white suits of different materials.[43]

The cigarette and the suit serve as props from the cabaret that allow Clayton to extend his claim on celebrity onto the public street. The white suit, bought for performance, and the cigarette's central placement mark his special status. The cigarette, held centrally before his chest, helps create a contrast with the Chinese rickshaw runner. While Clayton is at leisure and holding a cigarette, the rickshaw runner's hands are occupied by holding the rickshaw handles. At the same time, Clayton is posed in the International Settlement, the part of the city where he was most likely to face racial discrimination. Clayton's status as a jazz musician is rendered here as a resolute claim to imperial power, reaping and representing the benefits of western privilege in Shanghai.

The assemblage of jazz and cigarettes, then, created opportunities for African Americans in Shanghai and generated a contradictory global imaginary. On the one hand, the distance from the U.S. system of racism and the dynamics of minor transnationalism allowed them to have cooperative, if not egalitarian, relationships with Chinese businessmen and dance hostesses from many nations, with possibilities for anticolonial pleasures. On the other hand, imperial relations in Shanghai meant that the assemblage refracted

FIGURE 2.2. Buck Clayton in the International Settlement. Courtesy of Institute for Jazz Studies, Rutgers University.

many inequities. The musicians could end up on either end of power relations, victims of imperial racism in the foreign settlements or privileged as relatively well-off foreigners in relationship to Chinese workers.

SHANGHAI CABARETS BROUGHT CIGARETTES and jazz into an intimate relationship: two commodities, two elements of expressive culture entwined in their economic, cultural, and bodily circulation to become a mechanism for producing experience. Shanghai cabarets emerged as a particularly imperial institution, designed to cater to the fantasies of grandeur held by the western representatives of foreign companies in Shanghai. Cigarettes and jazz materialized those fantasies in breath and beat, the flick of an ash and the flair of an intricate dance step. Ephemeral though they were, we can learn more about the range of investments in empire by examining the two products together. Indeed, music in the era of globalization rarely circulates in an isolated way but carries attendant commodities and styles that constitute music as a powerful, complex experience, shared yet deeply personal. The sensational phenomenon of the Shanghai cabaret soon exceeded its original, imperial function and incorporated new entrepreneurs, clients, and musicians, but the centrality of cigarette smoking and jazz dance remained. Thus, the actions of cigarettes and jazz were not mechanistic but intertwined with the social history of the treaty port that governed pathways of entry to the space. Jazz and cigarettes ultimately ask us to confront the doubleness of commodity culture and empire itself: they were at once a site of promotional capitalist culture as well as of quotidian creativity, conducive to surprises, innovations, and resistance.

NOTES

For helpful comments on earlier drafts of this essay, I thank Finn Enke, Dave Gilbert, Fritz Schenker, Ron Radano, Teju Olaniyan, and the History and Theory Group at the University of Toronto, especially Elspeth Brown, Michelle Murphy, and Ritu Birla.
1. Stephen Cottrell, "Smoking and All That Jazz," in *Smoke: A Global History of Smoking*, ed. Sander L. Gilman and Zhou Xun (London: Reaktion, 2004), 154–59.
2. Sherman Cochran, *Big Business in China: Sino-Foreign Rivalry in the Cigarette Industry, 1890–1930* (Cambridge: Harvard University Press, 1980); Andrew F. Jones, *Yellow Music: Media Culture and Colonial Modernity in the Chinese Jazz Age* (Durham: Duke University Press, 2001), 65.
3. Brenda Dixon Gottschild, *The Black Dancing Body: A Geography from Coon to Cool* (New York: Palgrave Macmillan, 2005).

4. Sara Ahmed, "Affective Economies," *Social Text* 79, no. 2 (Summer 2004): 117–39; Melissa Gregg and Gregory J. Seigworth, eds., *The Affect Studies Reader* (Durham: Duke University Press, 2010), 1–25; Kathleen Stewart, *Ordinary Affects* (Durham: Duke University Press, 2007), 1–2.

5. Andrew David Field, *Shanghai's Dancing World: Cabaret Culture and Urban Politics, 1919–1954* (Hong Kong: Chinese University Press, 2010), 21–25.

6. H. J. Lethbridge, *All about Shanghai: A Standard Guidebook* (1935; repr., Hong Kong: Oxford University Press, 1983), 73.

7. Irwin S. Smith Oral History, July 28, 1982, East Carolina Manuscript Collection, J. Y. Joyner Library, East Carolina University (hereafter, Smith Oral History).

8. African American newspapers document the travels of musicians in Asia. Quote is from *Straits Times*, November 30, 1928, 10. Frederick Schenker's dissertation in progress, "Performing Empire: Music and Race in Colonial Asia's Jazz Age" (PhD diss., University of Wisconsin–Madison), will further illuminate the contours of this circuit.

9. Field, *Shanghai's Dancing World*, 19–52; E. Taylor Atkins, *Blue Nippon: Authenticating Jazz in Japan* (Durham: Duke University Press, 2001), 19–44; Jones, *Yellow Music*, 73–104.

10. Cochran, *Big Business in China*, 16, 129, 164, 137; Elizabeth J. Perry, *Shanghai on Strike: The Politics of Chinese Labor* (Stanford, CA: Stanford University Press, 1993), 135–36.

11. Carol Benedict, *Golden Silk Smoke: A History of Tobacco in China, 1550–2010* (Berkeley: University of California Press, 2011), 152–53.

12. James Lafayette Hutchinson, *China Hand* (Boston: Lothrop, Lee and Shepard, 1936), 314.

13. See Shane Vogel, *The Scene of Harlem Cabaret: Race, Sexuality, Performance* (Chicago: University of Chicago Press, 2009), 62–73.

14. Gottschild, *The Black Dancing Body*, 12–40.

15. Lethbridge, *All about Shanghai*, 76.

16. Atkins, *Blue Nippon*, 19–44; David Suisman, *Selling Sounds: The Commercial Revolution in American Music* (Cambridge: Harvard University Press, 2009), 207–9.

17. Mu Shiying, "Craven 'A,'" in *Mu Shiying Dai Biao Zuo* [Mu Shiying's representative work], trans. Wang Haochen (Beijing: Huaxia Chubanshe, 1998), 85. See also Shumei Shi, *The Lure of the Modern: Writing Modernism in Semicolonial China, 1917–1937* (Berkeley: University of California Press, 2001), 317–22.

18. See Ronald Radano, *Lying Up a Nation: Race and Black Music* (Chicago: University of Chicago Press, 2003), 234–37; Susan Cook, "Passionless Dancing and Passionate Reform: Respectability, Modernism, and the Social Dancing of Irene and Vernon Castle," in *The Passion of Music and Dance: Body, Gender and Sexuality*, ed. William Washbaugh (New York: Berg, 1998), 133–37.

19. Matthew Hilton, *Smoking in British Popular Culture 1880–2000* (Manchester, UK: Manchester University Press, 2000), 138–50; Claudia Tate, *Cigarette Wars: The Triumph of "the Little White Slaver"* (New York: Oxford University Press, 1999), 93–118; Benedict, *Golden Silk Smoke*, 12–13, 200, 210.

20. Field, *Shanghai's Dancing World*, 78–80.

21. Hutchinson, *China Hand*, 377–78.

22. Philip K. Eberly, *Music in the Air: America's Changing Tastes in Popular Music, 1920–1980* (New York: Hastings House, 1982), 32–33, 114–17; Jim Cox, *Music Radio: The Great Performers and Programs of the 1920s through Early 1960s* (Jefferson, NC: McFarland and Company, 2005), 25–26, 35, 39, 48, 50.

23. Smith Oral History.

24. Hutchinson, *China Hand*, 351.

25. Frank Canaday Papers, Diary, June 26, 1923, July 18, 1923, Yenching Library, Harvard University (hereafter, Canaday Papers).

26. James N. Joyner Papers, Special Collections Department, J. Y. Joyner Library, East Carolina University.

27. Field, *Shanghai's Dancing World*, 8–12.

28. Canaday, unpublished memoir, Canaday Papers.

29. Canaday, Diary, August 18, 1923, Canaday Papers.

30. Field discusses Tong and Vung (Dong and Feng) on pages 92–96 of *Shanghai's Dancing World*.

31. Françoise Lionnet and Shu-mei Shih, eds., *Minor Transnationalism* (Durham: Duke University Press, 2005), 1–21.

32. S. James Staley, "Is It True What They Say about China?" *Metronome* (December 1936): 47; Diary, January 7, 1924, Canaday Papers.

33. *Chicago Defender*, July 31, 1926, 6; Bradley Shope, "They Treat Us White Folks Fine," *South Asian Popular Culture* 5, no. 2 (2007): 105; Langston Hughes, *I Wonder as I Wander: An Autobiographical Journey* (New York: Rinehart, 1956), 251.

34. *Straits Times*, April 22, 1937, 13.

35. Hughes, *I Wonder as I Wander*, 251–52; *Chicago Defender*, August 23, 1930, 5; Buck Clayton, *Buck Clayton's Jazz World*, assisted by Nancy Miller Elliott (New York: Oxford University Press, 1987).

36. *Pittsburgh Courier*, August 17, 1935, A7; *Chicago Defender*, September 1, 1934, 9; Clayton, *Buck Clayton's Jazz World*, 60.

37. Clayton, *Buck Clayton's Jazz World*, 67.

38. *Chicago Defender*, July 14, 1934, 8; *Chicago Defender*, February 4, 1922, 15; *Chicago Defender*, April 28, 1934, 8. See Jones, *Yellow Music*, 103, for Chinese views of jazz.

39. *Chicago Defender*, July 14, 1934, 8; *Pittsburgh Courier*, August 17, 1935, A7; *New York Amsterdam News*, December 11, 1943, 1A; Clayton, *Buck Clayton's Jazz World*, 70, 78; *New York Amsterdam News*, July 14, 1945; *Baltimore Afro-American*, October 21, 1944, 12.

40. Clayton, *Buck Clayton's Jazz World*, 75–76.

41. Hughes, *I Wonder as I Wander*, 252–53.

42. Ibid., 257–59.

43. Clayton, *Buck Clayton's Jazz World*, 70.

3 · CIRCUIT LISTENING Grace Chang and the Dawn of the Chinese 1960s

ANDREW F. JONES

This essay listens to Chinese-language musicals from Hong Kong and Taiwan, produced on the front lines of the cold war in the early 1960s and emerging from a moment in which these regions were poised for takeoff into the upper strata of the global manufacturing economy. Known throughout the Chinese-speaking world yet largely unheard in the metropolitan West, their soundtracks partake fully and creatively in globally circulating popular cultures, engaging in particular with Afro-Caribbean-derived genres such as mambo and calypso. I contend here that they may help us to think our way into, if not out of, two key questions in popular music criticism.

The first is the question of historicism. What allows us to say that a song or a style is "of its time"? Conversely, is it possible to bring sounds of radically different provenance into critical conjunction just because they happened to have been produced at the same time? In other words, what might we gain from listening synchronically to music made at the same time in different social or geographical locales? Can a certain year or a particular decade serve as a meaningful framing device in narratives of musical historiography? More specifically, I am interested in the question of whether we can usefully identify something like a global 1960s in music. To what extent would such a formulation need to rely on an account, deterministic or otherwise, of technological change, from the emergence of the jet plane and the concomitant boom in civil aviation, to the worldwide dissemination of television and transistorized electronics? I try to open up these questions by way of engaging the emergence of a distinctive "period style" at the dawn of the Chinese 1960s. How did this music sound, why did it sound that way, and what can it tell us about the 1960s we thought we already knew?

A second and closely related question has to do with the question of genre in recorded music—or, more precisely, the kinds of ideological work we perform when we attempt to name, identify, or substantiate generic divisions, particularly when they get mixed up with troublesome and ideologically freighted categories such as folk versus popular music. I am interested in thinking not about how a particular genre can be described in a constative sense, but about what genre formations can *do* and what sorts of transactions they began to enable, especially with the increasingly global reach of mass media in the postwar period. How are genres launched into global circulation? Is "genre" itself a kind of "portmanteau" or shipping container that allows music to become globally portable? Can we think of genres not as essences or even as particular repertoires, but as vernacular modulations of globally circulating forms, resonating within migratory and mass-mediated circuits? How do we listen for and trace the architecture of such circuits, and what might they tell us about the mobility of musical forms in an era of recorded and increasingly portable sound? Might it be that the increasingly globalized diffusion of certain genres—and thus their fungibility as mass-mediated commodities—is an important harbinger of the musical 1960s?

My inquiry into these questions takes off from the music of Grace Chang (known as Ge Lan in Chinese), who was Hong Kong's celebrated pop diva, movie actress, and "mambo girl" in the 1960s. But I will also take a circuitous detour into the somewhat lesser-known and far less high-flying world of Taiwanese dialect musicals of the same era, before coming to a hard landing at the end. Along the way, we will hear how various genres—from Afro-Caribbean-derived musics such as mambo, cha-cha, and calypso, to rhythm and blues and country and western, as well as Japanese *enka*—circulate within the musicals of the period and how these musicals serve as vehicles for the circulation and re-articulation of these forms well beyond their putative places of origin. How do those sounds travel, what happens to them in the process, and how might the routes they take help us map the hard contours and lingering musical aftereffects of empire in East Asia, be it British, American, or Japanese?

Let's begin with a scene from Chang's 1963 star vehicle, *Because of Her* (*Jiao wo ruhe bu xiang ta*), produced like all of her late '50s and early '60s musicals by the chief competitor of Hong Kong's famed Shaw Brothers film studios, the ambitiously multinational Singapore-based Cathay Organisation. Owned by Loke Wan Tho (Lu Yuntao), a dashing and determinedly modern scion of a Malaysian mining, rubber, and real estate magnate, Cathay had by 1963 parlayed its real estate holdings into a circuit of first-run cinemas throughout Southeast Asia.[1] Its subsidiary, the Hong Kong–based Motion Picture and General Investment (MP&GI, or *Dianmao*) studio, in turn, supplied Cathay's theaters with feature films. Both MP&GI and the Shaw Brothers, finally, maintained a cozy and mutually profitable relationship with EMI's Hong Kong subsidiary, Pathé Records, hence the prevalence in this era of musical pictures based primarily around the performances of songstresses in the Pathé stable.[2]

In the case of *Because of Her*, the title song comes early on in the picture, when Chang's character, devastated that her musician boyfriend has departed from Hong Kong's Kai Tak Airport to study in Japan, decides to try out for a role in a musical. Accompanied by an older pianist, and dressed rather primly in a blue frock, Grace's figure is tightly framed by the camera as she begins what appears to be a rather staid recital of a *lied*-like song. After a few measures, however, with an infectiously mischievous grin and an irreverent snap of her fingers, she and the song are utterly transformed. The camera pulls back to reveal a room full of brightly clad bobbysoxers in miniskirts. A young man with pomaded hair holding a solid-body electric guitar suddenly starts to play a crude rock and roll riff, and Grace's body begins to sway and twist to the rhythm. With a portable tape recorder placed conspicuously in the foreground, the directors of the troupe watch in amazement as Chang belts out the rest of the song's lyrics (see figure 3.1).

It is an astonishing performance, not only because of Chang's newfangled dance steps, but also because it quite literally stages what we might call a

FIGURE 3.1. Grace Chang in *Because of Her*.

musical great leap forward. It would not have been lost on contemporary audiences that the title song is one of the monuments of the early assimilation of western musical forms into a new modern Chinese art-song vernacular: the great linguist and May Fourth–era scholar Y. R. Chao's 1926 composition "How Could I Not Miss Her" (Jiao wo ruhe bu xiang ta). Chao's use of parallel fifths to sound out on the piano what he called "sinified harmonies"— even within the realm of what he called "world music" (by which he meant what appeared to his generation as an unquestionably "universal" western music)—is matched by the deliberate delicacy with which the melody is made to mirror the tonality of the mandarin Chinese lyrics.[3] These delicacies are precisely what are lost in the leap from vocal art song to rock and roll, from the high-minded literary youth culture of the May Fourth movement of the 1920s and its efforts to forge a modern Chinese vernacular, to the cold war–era ascendancy of U.S. mass culture to the status of a global vernacular. And yet, despite this disjunction, both the original composition and its makeover represent self-consciously localized inflections of globally circulating musical idioms.

The scene also plugs into what was still an emergent mode of musical production in the early 1960s: the new availability of portable, relatively inexpensive means of musical production and reproduction enabled by transistorized solid-state electronics, as exemplified by mass-produced and mass-marketed electric guitars, transistor radios, tape recorders, and eventually televisions, many of which had already begun to be made in Japan for global consumers.[4] The ability of such music to fly free of generational and geographical moorings seems to be figured in the film by the effortless riffing of the guitarist, who barely seems to be plugged in at all. As the scene progresses, the increasing disparity between the soundtrack (which begins with piano and voice but finishes with the brassy flourishes of a fully orchestrated yet invisible big band) and the diegetic space of the rehearsal room on-screen might well remind us of the extent to which this mobility was largely a cinematic fantasy.

GRACE CHANG WAS HERSELF the most celebrated cinematic embodiment of mobility in the Hong Kong cinema of the early 1960s. She was famed for her prowess as a dancer and performer in a range of different styles, from the mambo to more traditional modes such as Peking opera. Her life story, as reported in newspapers and glossy magazines such as MP&GI's own *International Screen* (*Guoji Dianying*), reflected the dislocations of the postwar period. Her father, an official in the Ministry of Transport in Nanjing under Nationalist (KMT) rule, educated her in a Catholic school in Shanghai, before the family emigrated to Hong Kong in advance of the communist victory in 1949.[5] Chang's own path followed that of the prerevolutionary Shanghai music and film industries to Hong Kong. It is thus no accident that she recorded for Pathé, one of the most important corporate refugees from the colonial era in Shanghai, and that many of her biggest hits were penned by prominent popular composers from the heyday of Shanghai modern songs (*shidai qu*), such as Yao Min and the Japanese film composer Hattori Ryuichi.[6] Chang's star image, as several critics have noted, was also deeply entwined with the projection of an ideal of postwar social and class mobility, as even a cursory look at the titles of some of her films reveals, from *Our Dream Car* (*Xiangche meiren*; 1959) to *Air Hostess* (*Kongzhong xiaojie*; directed by Evan Yang and Yi Wen, also from 1959), of which more later.[7]

The same year Chang made these films, she herself took flight, visiting the studios of NBC in Los Angeles in late October to appear on a "Pacific Festival" edition of the *Dinah Shore Show*, alongside the Japanese diva Yukiji Asaoka as well as dance revues from the Philippines and Korea.[8] (See figure 3.2.) In addition to performing an adaptation of a Shanghai-era piece penned by Yao

FIGURE 3.2.
Grace Chang on
the *Dinah Shore
Show*. *International
Screen* 49 (1959).
Courtesy of soft-
film.blogspot.com.

Min, "The Autumn Song" (Qiu zhi ge), Chang joined Asaoka and Shore in singing a version of "Getting to Know You" from the 1957 Rodgers and Hammerstein blockbuster *The King and I*—an apt choice given the orientalist and pedagogical overtones of the original musical.[9]

This appearance on U.S. television—a first in the annals of Chinese popular music history, as the breathless coverage in the Chinese-language press emphasized time and again—also led to the release in 1961 of a long-playing record in Capitol Records' "Capitol of the World" series.[10] This series was one of the ways in which Capitol took advantage of the global reach of its parent company, EMI, which had purchased the upstart West Coast label in 1955.[11] The producer, Dave Dexter Jr., who would go on to notoriety as the man who supervised the Beatles' introduction into the U.S. market, should be seen as a crucial figure in the invention *avant la lettre* of "world music" as a marketing category in the United States. Dexter spent the late 1950s traveling the globe (including Hong Kong) in search of acts that could be repackaged for U.S. audiences. Dexter's greatest, albeit more or less accidental, triumph was his

FIGURE 3.3. Cover
art for Grace Chang's
Capitol Records
release.

FIGURE 3.3. Cover
art for Grace Chang's
Capitol Records
release.

decision to repackage and release the Japanese crooner Kyu Sakamoto's 1963
hit "Ue o muite arukō," retitled for the U.S. market as "Sukiyaki."[12]

In this light, the song "Because of Her" might be seen as a recapitulation of
a leap Grace Chang had already achieved, moving from Y. R. Chao's conception of "world music" as a universal idiom to a very different sort of "world
music," one ethnically marked yet manufactured by the far-reaching recording and televisual networks of corporate giants like EMI and NBC. In her
brief yet charming segment on the *Dinah Shore Show*, Chang is introduced
(in a characteristically cold war circumlocution) as "China's loveliest motion
picture star." The cover of the Capitol long-player record bills her as "Hong
Kong's Grace Chang" and "The Nightingale of the Orient" (see figure 3.3).
What I hope to suggest here, however, is that these attempts to *locate* Chang
and her music (which can veer from swing to cha-cha to calypso to Shanghai
"modern songs" and from ersatz orchestral Chinese folk to operatic torch
songs to rhythm and blues within the space of a single record, or even a
single cinematic sequence) obscure the fact that Chang cannot be adequately
understood as the product of a singular place. Instead, we might well listen
to her work as embedded in a complex and multiply mediated circuit, one
that (to name just the most important coordinates) stretches from colonial
Shanghai to Hong Kong, from Hong Kong to diasporic Chinese settlements
in Southeast Asia and in Taiwan, across the Pacific to Hollywood and Tin

Pan Alley, and from New York City to Caribbean islands such as Cuba, Trinidad, and Jamaica from which so much of the material for her music was drawn. And from the Anglophone Caribbean, of course, we might even circle back to London, the headquarters of EMI, and of the proprietors of the British Crown colony of Hong Kong.

What kinds of analytical gains might come of this kind of "circuit listening"? All local musics—particularly in the modern era of commercial sound recording—are constituted by (and need to be historicized in terms of) the particular circuits of media and migration in which they are embedded. Circuit listening may help us to avoid falling into models of musical interpretation that rely on vague attributions of one-sided and seemingly inevitable influence, while at the same time opening our ears to the agency, irreducible dynamism, and complexity of any local mediation of "global" cultures. It is not so much that Chang successfully mimics an originary mambo in her 1957 blockbuster *Mambo Girl* (*Manbo nülang*), for instance, but rather that she and her collaborators participate in a circuit, routed by way of Havana, Mexico City, New York, and Hollywood to Tokyo, Seoul, and Hong Kong, that reproduces "mambo" as a global vernacular.

We also need to be able to differentiate between different sorts of musical circuits. There are old, "slow," and vastly consequential circuits, such as the enduring musical pathways linking the west coast of Africa with the islands of the Caribbean and with Brazil, connected in turn to metropoles such as New Orleans, New York, London, and Lisbon, tracing a "black Atlantic" network that has left an indelible imprint on global popular musical practices.[13] There are also short circuits, flashes in the pan like Kyu Sakamoto's "Sukiyaki," novelty acts that cross over and blow up but never come to constitute a real musical system. There are rural circuits in which musical performance and reception remain largely if not entirely local. This is perhaps the realm of what we think of as "indigenous music" or "folk music." Most indigenous musics, however, tend to emerge from out of long historical circuits and migratory movements, and many have been brought into regional, national, and even global circuits in the twentieth century. The Mississippi Delta blues and the *huangmeidiao*, or "yellow plum," opera of Anhui province in China are two such examples of local forms that entered into transnational circulation in the 1960s.

There are open circuits characterized by a high degree of circulation and turnover, as well as closed circuits bound by topographical, ethnolinguistic, political, economic, infrastructural, and other sorts of constraints. It should go without saying that not all circuits are born equal, nor are they able to run on the same power sources. Their routes have been traced by histories of colonial domination and reflect unequal global, national, and regional divisions of labor. Indeed, we need to understand circuits not merely as routes that enable circulation, but also (and often simultaneously) as containment structures put in place so as to segregate socio-musical space, protect markets, or prevent unsanctioned movement(s). Different musical locales, finally, may be mapped in terms of the multiple musical circuits in which they are simultaneously embedded, and those maps will give us a sense not only of their distinctive historical pathways, but also of the ways in which any given historical moment is a palimpsest of overlapping, but not always contiguous or contemporaneous, circuits. The sort of "circuit listening" I am proposing, then, is inevitably also a kind of historical cartography, a reconstruction of the mediated spaces and sedimented temporalities out of which musical sounds emerge.

IN SOME WAYS, Grace Chang's "Capitol of the World" release might seem like a failed attempt to leap from one circuit—Mandarin popular music—to the global entertainment circuit that bears the shorthand designation of "Hollywood." The record failed to chart in the United States, and Chang never became a crossover success.[14] Barriers (linguistic and otherwise) were still in place, despite the optimistic take of the record's liner notes, which tout Hong Kong as a desirable destination for musical tourism and as an open switch on a global circuit: "The colorful port of Hong Kong, one of the busiest in the world, is a melting pot of music from all over the world. Businessmen, travelers, immigrants, students, sailors—everybody brings his music (or musical preferences) when he comes to Hong Kong—and the result is a free exchange unmatched anywhere else."

This is also the sort of promotional rhetoric that helped to sell Chang's MP&GI musicals. In fact, I would argue that films such as *Because of Her* and *Air Hostess* are profoundly self-reflexive productions. Their primary object of representation is precisely the circuit along which Chang, her music, and the cinema itself as a commodity are imagined to travel. *Because of Her* features a particularly bravura example. After Chang's character joins the song and dance revue for which she has auditioned, we are treated to a lengthy musical-stage sequence documenting—or perhaps merely envisioning—a triumphal world tour. (It is not clear if the troupe ever leaves Hong Kong.) The sequence begins as Chang sings a big band cha-cha number called "Muchacha" (penned by Hattori) in front of a pastoral "Chinese" backdrop, complete with

FIGURE 3.4. Grace Chang's world map in *Because of Her*.

a painted pagoda. Suddenly, and in tandem with the lyrics of the song, Chang is foregrounded against a map of the world, with each country depicted as a bordered two-dimensional plane—not unlike a series of blank television screens—into which Chang is able to enter and through which she and the stage itself are transported someplace else (see figure 3.4). What ensues is a whirlwind fantasia of international stereotypes, from Hawaiian hula dancers to Japanese geishas to New York swing dancers to Venetian gondoliers and Latin boleros, each with generically correct music and scenery to match. The sequence concludes with a triumphant mise en scène in which all of the dancers are united in front of what appears to be a giant roulette wheel, as if to emphasize the circular logic of the sequence and its circumnavigation of what the film scholar Brian Hu has termed the "world stage" of MP&GI's backstage musicals.[15]

In *Air Hostess* as well, the plot is largely a pretext for the cinematic staging of Chang's peregrinations. Filmed on location in Taiwan, Singapore, and Thailand in Eastman color, the film follows the trials and trajectory of a character named Lin Kepin, as she learns how to be an effective airline stewardess while at the same time falling for her taciturn pilot, played by Roy Chiao. Kepin's gendered desire for a modernity and mobility beyond the constraints of the bourgeois family is figured by the opening musical sequence, "I Want to Fly in the Blue Sky" (Wo yao feishang qingtian). Yet as more than a few critics complained at the time of its release, the film often seems less like a story of emancipation than an advertisement for the fledgling civil aviation and tourism industries. As Poshek Fu has pointed out, the film foregrounds "the airline business as an incubator for a new transnational capitalist corporate culture."[16] This agenda hardly seems surprising given that Loke Wan Tho doubled as chairman of the board at Malaysian Airways. Closer to home, Cathay Pacific (whose facilities are on display in the film) had in July 1959 swallowed its closest competitor, Hong Kong Airways, and was poised to enter a period of annual growth in the double digits throughout the 1960s.[17]

The film's narrative itinerary traces a Southeast Asia–bound, Chinese diasporic (Nanyang) circuit that of necessity excludes "Red China." Chang's ports of call are, in fact, exactly coterminous with the territories and terminals along Cathay Pacific's route map, the Cathay Organisation's exhibition circuit, and Pathé's principal markets for Mandarin pop records. By the late 1950s, the Cathay Organisation had already affiliated with fifty-seven movie theaters in Taiwan alone, added to a network of more than two hundred venues in Singapore, Malaysia, and Borneo. In addition, the organization boasted of distribution agents in Hong Kong, Taiwan, the Philippines, Vietnam, Thailand, Cambodia, and Burma.[18] Not surprisingly, given Loke Wan Tho's avowedly anticommunist politics, as well as the manifest importance of its market, Taiwan rates an extended sequence, during which Chang goes sightseeing around Taipei.[19] Her day ends with a performance in the ballroom of the Grand Hotel (Yuanshan Fandian)—a landmark high-rise constructed by the KMT government in high-orientalist imitation of the palaces of the Forbidden City—of an ersatz folk number called "Taiwan Melody" (Taiwan diao), composed by Yao Min, with no reference to local musical traditions, and set to a swaying, mock-mambo beat.[20] The lyrics extol the beauty, bounty, strategic military position, social harmony, and infrastructural accessibility of the island nation:

I love to sing a Taiwan song
It's where the coast is long and the mountains high
With glorious harbors everywhere and roads in every direction
Railroad lines running from the north to the south
It's the frontline of the Pacific Ocean, Taiwan, the treasure island!
A wonderland with harvests all year round
The villages are full of joy, profiting from sugar and tea

Every household has plenty to eat

Pineapples, watermelons, and bananas are our special treats

Everyone praises the island, from long-term locals to new arrivals.[21]

A contemporary review of the film in Hong Kong's pro-communist daily, the *Ta Kung Pao*, took issue with these claims, arguing that MP&GI was merely in the business of whitewashing U.S. clientelism in Taiwan. Nor does this particular critic miss the fact that the film is "less a story, than a documentary" designed to prime the pump of the tourist economy.[22] *Air Hostess* is, in other words, an advertisement for itself, promoting both the musical numbers that are performed at each stop along MP&GI's and EMI's distribution networks, and the developmental aspirations and diasporic circuits of capital that constituted "free China" at the dawn of the 1960s.

We are told in great detail how Chang moves across this space: the movie includes what now seem quite superfluous primers on subjects like passport control, customs regulations, catering arrangements, and the like. What is left unspoken but everywhere assumed, however, is the ease with which global pop genres are translated into Chinese and reproduced in each of Chang's tropical ports of call. What sort of medium allows for this movement, in addition to material substrates such as celluloid and vinyl? Perhaps the most crucial passport for Chang's music is that it functions as a *vernacular*, both linguistically and musically.

Chang's use of Mandarin Chinese allows her music to fly free of the patchwork of dialects (Cantonese, Toishan, Hokkien, Hakka, Wu, and many variants) that divide Chinese diasporic space. My argument here rests on the notion that a vernacular (or what is referred to as *baihua* in Chinese) is always an intermediary form, located above a panoply of local languages, but still subsidiary to a cosmopolitan or imperial language such as English.[23] The vernacular Chinese promoted by Y. R. Chao and the May Fourth generation of Chinese intellectuals, in this view, did not so much vernacularize classical Chinese as re-create Chinese as a vernacular in the image of cosmopolitan national languages such as English and French—languages that were themselves once vernaculars of Latin. Vernaculars, in other words, are precisely those languages that circulate widely enough to be appropriated for local use. And for that reason, somewhat counterintuitively, they also open up the possibility of local inflections of what had seemed to be a universal standard. In this sense, the Hong Kong Mandarin musical itself is an example of what the late, great film scholar Miriam Hansen referred to as a "vernacular modernism": a globally circulating form, able to technologically mediate the pleasures and terrors of a universal modernity, yet also subject to local conditions and articulations.[24]

Globally circulating genres such as mambo and calypso arguably function in a similar register. They are musical vernaculars, emerging from particular (and often marginalized) cultural circuits, and they serve as a common language between an imperial dominant and local particulars. Yet as Gustavo Pérez Firmat, writing about the history of the mambo, brings to our attention, this process of "vernacularization" often involves a kind of hollowing out of the history of a musical form, the elimination of those aspects of the music's particularity that cannot easily be translated.[25] Mambo, itself a fusion (or perhaps a reduction in the culinary sense) of bop with the rhythmic breakdown of the Cuban *charanga*, traveled so well, Pérez Firmat argues, because it was "logoclassic," reducing lyrics to sonorous fragments and articulate speech to rhythmic bursts of sound, as in Perez Prado's trademark grunts.[26]

Typically, the world-beating mambos of the mid-1950s by Perez Prado and Tito Puente laconically announced themselves as mambos ("Que rico el mambo"; "Mambo No. 8"; Puente's "Hong Kong Mambo," likely inspired by his 1962 concert tour to Asia).[27] These titles are performatives, linguistic packages that turn each song into a kind of container for the genre, before the needle ever lands in the groove. This musical cargo was distributed not only through records, but also by Hollywood films such as RKO's 1955 *Underwater!*, which brought Prado's "Cherry Pink and Apple Blossom White" to acclaim in Japan and throughout East Asia, spawning numerous local adaptations and articulations of the mambo rhythm.[28] Sometimes these cinematic routes were even more circuitous, bypassing Hollywood altogether. The popularity of Perez Prado's music in South Korea, for instance, is usually attributed to the screening in Seoul of the Mexican *cabaretera* films for which Perez had provided his signature sound, as well as the subsequent borrowing of the mambo for Han Hyung-mo's blockbuster melodrama *Madame Freedom* (1956).[29] In the case of Grace Chang's own breakout performance in *Mambo Girl*, inspiration was taken from a 1954 Italian American coproduction, *Mambo* (directed by Robert Rossen), as well as Rosemary Clooney's number one hit of the same year, "Mambo Italiano," as taught to Chang by a Filipino percussionist and dance instructor named Ollie Delfino.[30]

A similar hollowing takes place in the case of calypso, which, according to contemporary accounts, reached Hong Kong largely on the wings of Harry Belafonte's appropriation of the form for his eponymous 1956 gold record for RCA-Victor. Local film buffs were made aware of the early roots of the form in Trinidad and Afro-Caribbean culture, as indicated by a capsule history provided in Chinese and English by MP&GI's house publication, *International Screen*, from 1957:

> Calypso craze is sweeping the entire world like a full-force hurricane brushing aside the once popular Rock and Roll and Cha Cha. Calypso is by no means a new dance or music. According to the dictionary, the definition of Calypso is: lively, rhythmic, topical ballad improvised and sung by natives of Trinidad. It is characterized by wrenched syllabic stress and loose rhythms.
>
> Its history dates back to the 18th century when slavery was still in practice in Trinidad of the British West Indies. The negro slaves, after a day's work, amused themselves by singing songs and executing dances. This kind of dance and music is called calypso.
>
> Its revival today is attributed to American negroes.
>
> Calypso dance is easy to learn. Anyone who knows Latin American dance will be able to learn in half an hour.[31]

In practice, however, the form was appropriated almost entirely as a rhythm and as a dance step through which the company (and Chang) might perform their own familiarity with global trends. Chang's performance of "I Love Calypso" (Wo ai kalisao; also composed by Yao Min), set in an appropriately tropical nightclub setting in Singapore, reduces the rich verbal humor and caustic commentary for which the genre was originally known to an almost incantatory and self-reflexive refrain: "Oh calypso, oh calypso, I love swaying back and forth to the calypso." The orchestration itself bears little relation to the music of Trinidadian calypsonians, and the film's mise en scène allows for but a single musical instrument, despite the off-screen presence of a big band: a close-up of the bongos, focusing our visual attention on the rhythmic pulse assumed to be the fundamental syntax of the genre. This is calypso in name only perhaps, but "calypso" is as calypso does, and the packaging simultaneously puts the music in place and allows it to fly free of its provenance.

IF HONG KONG in the early 1960s appeared to be an open switch, linked directly if slightly belatedly to the latest dance crazes in the United States and elsewhere, Taiwan seemed to belong to a subsidiary circuit. The mambo, or so the legend goes, was transmitted to Taiwan by Grace Chang herself, when she sparked a craze for the unfamiliar genre after a command performance for Nationalist troops during a promotional visit to the KMT-controlled island in the late 1950s. There may be some truth to these stories. One of the earliest songs to self-consciously take on the "mambo" mantle in Taiwan and first recorded in 1960, "Shandong Mambo" (Shandong manbo), was written by a soldier named Wang Fei in 1957 as a result of his exposure to Chang's performances. The tune was subsequently cut in at least one other version in the mid-1960s and was covered many years later by the legendary performer Teresa Teng. Wang, referencing his own origins in China by parodically playing up the "down-home" Shandong accent typical of many mainlander refugees who fled to Taiwan in the wake of the KMT's defeat in 1949, also folds into its lyrics an ingenious, and disingenuously naïve, linguistic commentary on the assimilation of a foreign genre to local tastes:

> Speaking of "mambo," talking about "mambo"
> We [Shandong people] don't really know what's "mambo"
> Is it "*mantou*" [Chinese steamed buns]?
> Or is it "*mianbao*" [Western bread]?
> Can anyone tell us what you know?[32]

Wang Fei's recording is for the most part a mambo in name only, constructed around a standard 4/4 "go-go" beat, punctuated by an elementary electric guitar riff, with only the vaguely "Latin" opening fanfare on the trumpet alluding to its supposed Caribbean origins.

Listening to mambo in Taiwan may also suggest some of the complexities of Taiwan's unique position within global musical circuits. While the story of Grace Chang carrying the mambo torch to Taiwan has a compelling narrative clarity, the trajectory of Taiwanese popular music cannot be reduced to a unidirectional movement in which Shanghai's Mandarin pop music tradition is transmitted, via Hong Kong, to the cabarets of Taipei. Instead, as C. S. Stone Shih reminds us, there has been a rich history of reciprocal musical flows between Taipei, Hong Kong, and Shanghai since at least the interwar period, as well as a complex interpenetration of local Hokkien-dialect popular balladry (*geyao*) with Japanese, American, and various regional Chinese musical cultures.[33]

The presence of Latin music in postwar Taipei, dating to well before Chang's star turn, is a case in point. As early as 1949, members of Shanghai's Peace Hotel jazz band had arrived on the island, bringing with them a working knowledge of prewar rumbas.[34] Even more significantly, a local textile manufacturer and amateur musician named Hsieh Teng-hui founded in 1953 a Latin-tinged big band called the Taiwan Cuban Boys. Working from swing and rumba charts he had learned in Thailand, Hsieh and his collaborators also studied with Filipino musicians headlining at nightclubs and cabarets in Taipei, as well as cribbing compositions from visiting U.S. and Japanese tourists and functionaries. While the band was asked to efface its Cuban inspiration by no less a personage than President Chiang Kai-shek after Castro's revolution in 1959, the renamed Kupa Boys (*Guba Yuedui*, literally the "Drum Kings") went on to become the house band at Taipei's Ambassador Hotel for over a quarter of a century.[35] Indeed, it was in the early 1960s, with the civil aviation boom and concomitant growth of Taiwan's tourist trade, that the Kupa Boys really hit its stride, with four offshoots working various hotels and, after 1962, regular appearances on the newly established TTV television station.[36]

It was also in 1962, seven years after the height of Perez Prado's popularity, and five years after Chang's "Mambo Girl" had lit up screens across the Chinese-speaking world, that the legendary Hokkien-dialect singer Hong Yifeng released a now-classic emblem of a bygone era in Taiwanese dialect popular music called "Formosa Mambo."[37] The very rhetoric of the song's title seems to indicate the ease with which adjectivally modified "mambos" circulate as a kind of global vernacular, serving simultaneously as a signifier of local identity and as a token of transnational engagement. But the smoothness with which this cross-border transaction is linguistically effected masks a rather more complicated story about the Chinese 1960s. Hong Yifeng hailed originally from the southern city of Tainan, led a successful touring revue beginning in the 1950s, and recorded for Taiwan's most successful purveyor of Hokkien-language ballads, the Tainan-based Asia Records. By the early 1960s, Hong Yifeng, like Grace Chang, had come to rely on the musical cinema for his popularity. Unlike Chang, who had the wind of Cathay's considerable market capitalization in her sails, Hong had access to a far more limited production and exhibition circuit. Even more crucially, he lacked as a Hokkien speaker the linguistic "passport" that would allow his work to travel fluidly across national borders. While the production of Amoy-dialect cinema (Amoy is a variant of Hokkien spoken in the Fujianese city of Xiamen, across the strait from Taiwan) had emerged as early as the 1950s to cater to audiences in Hong Kong, Southeast Asia, and Taiwan, the films were burdened by a reputation for "shoddiness" and for being baldly derivative of their Mandarin and Cantonese counterparts.[38] Hokkien, in short, inhabited an altogether different circuit, marginalized with respect to the Mandarin vernacular, and permanently restricted to a regional (if also transnational), rather than nominally national ambit. For Hong to represent "Free China" to American audiences on the *Dinah Shore Show* would have been unthinkable.

By the early 1960s, with Fujian province behind the bamboo curtain, and Hokkien speakers a minority market in Hong Kong and Singapore, most production shifted to what was by far the largest Hokkien-speaking market in the world: Taiwan. As a result, Hokkien films and popular music became "increasingly local" in character.[39] After 1962, with the burgeoning importance of television as a conduit for popular music promotion, Hokkien music was further marginalized by strict KMT restrictions on broadcasting in "dialect," rather than in Mandarin Chinese.[40] These restrictions did not apply to live performance, records, or theatrical screenings, and Hokkien cultural production continued to survive and to thrive in these venues until the late 1960s, albeit within an increasingly narrow and undercapitalized sector. Many films, funded by fly-by-night production companies, have been lost, in part because so few prints were struck in the first place.[41]

What have come to be called *Taiyu* or "Taiwanese-language" musicals had at least two more strikes against them. Within Taiwan, they were often associated, especially by mainlander émigrés, with all that was local, low-class, and lumpen. They were at the same time ideologically tainted in the eyes of the Nationalist government by what Guo-Juin Hong has called their "unclean severance" from the specter of Japan's half century of colonial rule in Taiwan, as well as its lingering linguistic and cultural influence.[42]

Indeed, Taiwanese ballads and Taiyu musicals throughout the 1960s situated themselves quite squarely within a circuit in which Japan remained a crucial point of reference. The "mixed-blood" (*hunxie gequ*) songs of Hong Yifeng and performers like Wen Xia, pressed in local plants in the industrial Taipei suburb of Sanchong where migrant workers from the rural south tended to cluster, often directly adapted the melodies of the latest Japanese *enka*, updated with Taiwanese lyrics.[43] Even local compositions by composers such as Hong, while keen to incorporate some of the rhythm and blues and country western styles emanating from U.S. Armed Forces radio in Taiwan and Japan, tended to adopt vocal styles and melodic profiles reminiscent of enka and other Japanese pop styles. In some cases, these "mixed-blood songs" represented a compensatory measure, in that the direct importation of Japanese records, for which there remained an enthusiastic following among Taiwanese who had been educated during the colonial era, had been restricted since the 1950s. The link to Japan, moreover, was not only a question of listening to smuggled or pirated enka records. As part of his apprenticeship in the entertainment business, for example, Hong spent a year in Japan, learning his craft at Toho Studios before returning to Taiwan in the early 1960s. For

Hokkien speakers, "mixed-blood" music was, to all intents and purposes, the Taiwanese mainstream.

Yet there may have been a foreboding sense, even in 1962, that the Taiwanese musical cinema was a dead end, a closed circuit. The runaway success of Hong Kong's Shaw Brothers' Technicolor production of the operatic story of star-crossed and cross-dressed lovers in *Love Eterne* (*Liang shanbo yu zhu yingtai*; 1962) that same year heralded the emergence of a glossy pop aesthetic predicated on standard vernacular Chinese. Indeed, Shaw's huangmeidiao musicals, loosely based on a folk form from Anhui province but colorfully packaged with the aid of Pathé Records as a linguistically standardized cross-platform media spectacle, came to dominate pan-Chinese screens and air-waves for the rest of the decade. By the mid-1960s, as a result of KMT direct investment in the development of what was dubbed a cinema of "healthy realism" at its Central Motion Picture Company (CMPC) studio, the monochrome products of the Hokkien-dialect cinema began to sputter, and by the early 1970s, it had essentially succumbed, a victim of strict political controls on television broadcasting (which banned Japanese imports and suppressed non-Mandarin programming), as well as of market forces.

For these reasons, the Taiyu films of the early 1960s—black and white in an era in which MP&GI had already begun to film in Eastman color—seem to cast a lingering look back toward an idealized rural and Japanese colonial past, while registering the parallel anxieties of Taiwan's rapid urbanization. Hong Yifeng's first (and only extant) feature is typical in this regard. Titled *Lingering Lost Love* (*Jiuqing mianmian*), the film tells the melodramatic tale of a schoolteacher and amateur composer named Hong Yifeng who is assigned to work in a rural area in the agricultural heartland of southern Taiwan. Hong quickly falls in love with a local betel-nut farming beauty, but her father, who has already arranged for her to be given to his boss in return for a better position, objects. The two lovers elope, fleeing to a mountain retreat in Alishan but are separated once more by gangsters dispatched by her father to bring her back home. Our heroine is eventually forced into a loveless marriage in Taipei. Hong, heartbroken, also moves to Taipei, becoming a renowned balladeer. In a scene that reflects on the ascendancy of the novel technology of television, Hong's lover chances to tune in to a radio broadcast of the title song. Tearfully, she watches as a spectral image of Hong is superimposed over the speaker of the old-fashioned tabletop wireless (see figure 3.5), as if to compensate for the device's lack of televisual presence, and the radio announcer finishes the broadcast by promoting an upcoming

FIGURE 3.5. Hong Yifeng in *Lingering Lost Love.*

concert appearance at a local dancehall. She and their illegitimate daughter
(who had for a time fended for herself as a street urchin lost in the big city)
are reunited when Hong appears onstage.

What is fascinating about the film, and others of its kind, is the extent
to which its narrative is structured around the north-south railway network
constructed under Japanese colonial rule (and mentioned approvingly in
Chang's "Taiwan Melody"). In films like *Lingering Lost Love*, however, the
railway figures not so much Taiwan's infrastructural advantages, as the powerful and ongoing cultural and economic disparities between urban Taipei,
with its high concentrations of mainlander émigrés and its links to global
capitalism, and the agricultural supply regions to the south. This topographical divide is traversed over and over again in these films, providing a frame
for their melodramatic plots of country lovers rent apart in the crucible of
the capitalist city, and it is even inscribed in their titles, redolent of missed
opportunities and fateful separations, from the *The Last Train from Kaohsiung*
(*Gaoxiong fa de weibanche*; 1963) to *The Early Train from Taipei* (*Taibei fa de
zaoche*; 1964). Both the title sequence and the climactic sequence of *Lingering
Lost Love*, set to the title track and filmed along the outmoded narrow-gauge

FIGURE 3.6. Title sequence of *Lingering Lost Love.*

colonial railway constructed by Japan to log the giant cypresses that used to cover the slopes of Alishan, seem to present a highly kinetic and cinematographic vision of the machinations and forking paths of fate, of the belated and backward circuit in which both the characters and the film itself are trapped. In a series of mesmerizing tracking shots, the camera repeatedly casts its gaze backward at the rails, as the train itself glides steadily forward, across precipitous bridges, through dark tunnels, and across railroad switches (see figure 3.6). Meanwhile, the music, a distinctive fusion of enka melody and jazz instrumentation, anchored by Hong's baritone vocals, tracks the movement of the train by way of the steady blues-style comping of a piano.[44]

When airplanes, the figure of modern mobility par excellence in the MP&GI musicals, come up at all in the films of this era, they appear as harbingers of a terrifying accident of fate. A sequence from a 1968 melodrama called *Hot Meat Rolls (Shao rouzong*, meaning a kind of Taiwanese tamale wrapped in banana leaves) is a salient example. Focused on a middle-class father who has lost everything as a result of his own extramarital folly, the film serves as a reminder of the precariousness of Taiwan's economic development. In an early scene, the father figure, having finally located a job as a sign painter and

FIGURE 3.7. The roar of the jet plane in *Hot Meat Rolls*.

settled down in humble working-class lodgings in Taipei, delivers a homily over the dinner table about class mobility to his two children. Suddenly, we cut to an image of a massive jet plane, its engines screaming directly overhead (see figure 3.7). This shatteringly loud and seemingly unmotivated interruption is followed by a shot in which we learn from the family's kindly neighbors that the father has tumbled from his perch atop a signboard that he was in the process of painting and has shattered his arm. Perhaps the appearance here of a jet airplane was an accident, an artifact of the film being made just underneath the approach to Taipei's Songshan Airport. But it is quite deliberately retained as a means of signifying the shock of the father's own catastrophic accident. The tumble leaves him permanently disabled, and his daughter is left to fend for herself and the family by selling the shao rouzong of the film's title on the streets of Taipei.

The contrast with a film like *Air Hostess* could not be clearer—one film presents the view from above, the other resolutely from below, as modernity leaves a disenfranchised working class behind. And yet, even as *Air Hostess* shows off its mastery of the global vernacular, emblematizing the free flow of people, capital, cultures, and goods, its narrative is also haunted by the specter of the hollowness of its own aspirations and the dangers of unfettered circulation. For as part of Kepin's induction into her role as a stewardess, she is convinced by a customer to carry, unbeknownst to her, what turns out to be a parcel containing smuggled counterfeit jewelry. It is a minor subplot but one that I think is quite significant within the overall narrative and ideological economy of the film. Might the musical genres Chang delivers so blithely across national borders also be mere packages, even counterfeit goods?

This parallel between the film's plot and the transnational traffic in music is not so outlandish as it may seem. In fact, Taiwan's substantial production of pirated LPs of both western and Hong Kong–produced Mandarin popular music thrived in tandem with commercial aviation. By the mid-1960s, Taiwanese factories were churning out at least 35,000 (and by some estimates many more) pirated records per month, catering to U.S. GIs on "rest and relaxation" leave from the escalating conflict in Vietnam, budget-conscious music fans in Hong Kong and Southeast Asia, as well as local aficionados of U.S. and U.K. chart hits, referred to in Taiwan as "hot music" (*remen yinyue*).[45] This trade in counterfeit pressings was lucrative, fetching up to ten times their original price in Hong Kong, and its primary victims were, according to one contemporary report, "the Shaw Brothers' stable of stars . . . and England's the Beatles."[46] A newspaper report from 1968 about a young Hong Kong man detained at customs in Taipei for attempting to smuggle more than nine hundred such records on his flight home hints at the scale of this sort of illegal traffic, as well as its modal reliance on civil aviation and the tourist trade.[47] Even more interestingly, industry insiders attest that Taiwanese record companies often pressed stewardesses flying routes between Taipei, Hong Kong, and the West Coast of the United States into service as couriers for the latest LPs, which were delivered to Taiwanese factories and quickly reproduced as pirated discs.[48]

Perhaps a still more uncanny parallel with real-life events is presented in the denouement of the film with which I began the essay, *Because of Her*. When we left Chang last, she was triumphantly touring the world in the wake of the departure of her boyfriend for Japan. She is soon forced to reveal that she is pregnant with his child—a condition with dire economic consequences for the troupe, which is entirely reliant on her star power.[49] The manager of the troupe agrees to marry her and to pretend that the child is his own. But just when their act is reestablished at a high-class nightclub and the couple have settled into a comfortable bourgeois existence, the prodigal boyfriend touches down once again at Kai Tak Airport and is hired by the troupe. At the climax of an elaborate restaging of Y. R. Chao's title song in a classic Hollywood mode, Chang is compelled to perform along with her ex-lover, elevated together by means of a stage pulley into the cloud-dappled empyrean of an ersatz blue sky, as her husband conducts the band from the orchestra below the stage. As her erstwhile leading man leans in to kiss her, Chang glances anxiously toward the orchestra and her husband, who is utterly absorbed in the performance. This moment of misgiving proves fatal. Suddenly losing her footing on the narrow, pulley-suspended platform atop which she is perched, she plummets into the pit below the stage. The film ends with an aerial shot of her limp body, a deep red trickle of Technicolor blood running across her white dress. This terrifying fall from grace, of course, is the stuff of bad dreams and bad melodrama, but is also a reminder of the gravity with which even entertainment films represented the developmental aspirations of the Chinese 1960s.

The scene also proved to be one of Chang's last appearances onscreen. Just months after the film's premiere, she announced her final departure from the world of filmmaking in favor of married life, and in doing so, she dealt a serious blow to MP&GI's hopes of competing with its rival in the film business, the Shaw Brothers. In June 1964, the Cathay Organisation's owner and principal impresario, Loke Wan Tho, traveled to Taiwan to attend the Asian Film Festival, explore the possibility of expanding the company's extensive film exhibition circuit in Taiwan, and indulge his passion for bird-watching.[50] On a lark, Loke arranged an afternoon sight-seeing trip to the city of Taichung on a chartered C-46 transport.[51] The flight foundered en route, and all fifty-nine passengers perished in the crash.

NOTES

1. An important English-language source for Cathay and MP&GI is Ain-ling Wong, ed., *The Cathay Story*, rev. ed. (Hong Kong: Hong Kong Film Archive, 1992). See also Lim Kay Tong, *Cathay: 55 Years of Cinema* (Singapore: Landmark, 1991).

2. See, for instance, "Baidai changpian wangluo Dianmao qunxing" [Pathé Records nets MP&GI's flock of stars], *International Screen* 33 (July 1958): 50–51.

3. See Y. R. Chao, *Xin shige ji* [New poetic song collection] (Shanghai: Commercial Press, 1928), 8–11. The collection and its introductory essays on the question of Chinese and Western music have been translated by Kaelyn Lowmaster with John A. Crespi and published online by the MCLC Resource Center as "Y. R. Chao and the *New Poetic Songbook*," accessed February 3, 2012, http://mclc.osu.edu/rc/pubs/chao.htm.

4. For the history of the transistor radio and other portable radio receivers in American life, see Michael B. Schiffer, *The Portable Radio in American Life* (Tucson: University of Arizona Press, 1992). For a sense of the Japanese contribution to transistor radio production and design, see Roger Handy et al., *Made in Japan: Transistor Radios of the 1950s and 1960s* (San Francisco: Chronicle, 1993).

5. For a sketch of Chang's life story, see Guo Shu, "Bu jin yinhe gungun lai—Zhongguo yingxing lishi hua lang" [The silver river rolls on and on: A historical gallery of Chinese film stars], *Dianying Huakan*, no. 4 (2004): 58–59.

6. On the emergence of modern Chinese popular music in the Shanghai of the interwar period and its relation to the transnational recording industry, see my *Yellow Music: Media Culture and Colonial Modernity in the Chinese Jazz Age* (Durham: Duke University Press, 2001). Hattori began working in the Shanghai film industry during the occupation of that city by Japanese forces during the war, and he went on to collaborate with Shaw Brothers and MP&GI until the late 1960s.

7. See, for instance, Poshek Fu, "Modernity, Diasporic Capital, and 1950s Hong Kong Mandarin Cinema," *Jump Cut*, no. 49 (Spring 2007), www.ejumpcut.org/archive/jc49.2007/Poshek/text.htm; and Mary Wong, "Women Who Cross Borders: MP&GI's Modernity Program," in Ain-ling Wong, *The Cathay Story*, 85–93.

8. The *New York Times* gives a brief account of her appearance. See John B. Shanley, "Bayanihan Troupe," *New York Times*, October 26, 1959, 59.

9. The performance is available online at www.youtube.com/watch?v=Ibo_rJeDZjw. Many thanks to Durian Dave, author of a Hong Kong and Chinese film history blog, softfilm.blogspot.com/, for locating the footage.

10. See, for instance, the series of five articles covering her visit to the United States in Taiwan's *Lianhe Bao* [United daily news] from September 24, 1959, to November 21, 1959. Interestingly, her performance in the United States was also rebroadcast in Taiwan by the U.S. Information Service.

11. For an in-house introduction to Capitol Records and its corporate history, see Paul Grein, *Capitol Records: Fiftieth Anniversary, 1942–1992* (Hollywood, CA: Capitol Records, 1992).

12. For Dave Dexter's life and work, see his *Playback: A Newsman-Record Producer's Hits and Misses from the Thirties to the Seventies* (New York: Billboard, 1976).

13. Steven Feld's work on the complex musical, material, and intellectual interactions among musicians in Ghana, the Caribbean, the United Kingdom, and the United States is an eloquent exposition of this circuit. See *Jazz Cosmopolitanism in Accra: Five Musical Years in Ghana* (Durham: Duke University Press, 2012). For a classic formulation of the pan-Atlantic circulation of a black musical modernism, see Paul Gilroy, *The Black Atlantic: Modernity and Double Consciousness* (Cambridge: Harvard University Press, 1993). Timothy Brennan has also written persuasively of the webs of cultural and spiritual affiliation linking the musics of West Africa and Cuba to those of the United States and beyond in his *Secular Devotion: Afro-Latin Music and Imperial Jazz* (London: Verso, 2008).

14. While there were reports in the Chinese press that the first pressing of the record had "sold out," there is no evidence that the record entered the Billboard charts, and Capitol Records did not opt to release a follow-up. See " 'Ge Lan zhi ge' zai Mei da shou huanying" [Hong Kong's "Grace Chang" warmly received in the US], *Lianhe Bao*, May 2, 1961.

15. See Brian Hu, "Star Discourse and the Cosmopolitan Chinese: Linda Lin Dai Takes on the World" *Journal of Chinese Cinemas* 4, no. 3 (November 2010): 185–86.

16. Poshek Fu, "Modernity, Cold War, and Hong Kong Mandarin Cinema," in Ain-ling Wong, *The Cathay Story*, 28.

17. See "Cathay Pacific," accessed February 15, 2012, http://en.wikipedia.org/wiki/Cathay_Pacific.

18. See Lim Kay Tong, *Cathay*, 44, 152.

19. Interestingly, Cathay was hit by serious labor unrest in 1961 and by a concerted strike led by "leftist activists" in 1963. See ibid., 57–58.

20. Reputedly based on the melody of a Cantonese popular song, the song's bright pentatonic melody and orchestration are also a "playful" response to Hollywood *chinoiserie*, according to Wong Kee-chee. See his "Yao Min's 'MP&GI Style,'" in Ain-ling Wong, *The Cathay Story*, 148.

21. This last line is a not-so-veiled sop to the social and economic tensions on the island between the largely Hokkien-speaking Taiwanese and the nearly two million refugees from the Chinese mainland who fled to the island in the wake of the defeat of the KMT by the Chinese Communist Party in 1949.

22. See Gao Shanyue, "*Kongzhong xiaojie* bie you yongxin" [The other agenda of *Air Hostess*], *Ta Kung Pao*, June 10, 1959, 6.

23. For discussions of the vernacular in history, see Sheldon Pollock, "The Cosmopolitan Vernacular," *Journal of Asian Studies* 57, no. 1 (February 1998): 6–37; and "Cosmopolitan and Vernacular in History," *Public Culture* 12, no. 3 (2000): 591–625.

24. See Miriam Bratu Hansen, "Vernacular Modernism: Tracking Cinema on a Global Scale," in *World Cinemas, Transnational Perspectives*, ed. Nataša Ďurovičová and Kathleen Newman (London: Routledge, 2007), 295. This is one of a series of essays in which Hansen articulated the scope and heuristic consequences of "vernacular modernism." See also "The Mass Production of the Senses: Classical Cinema as Vernacular Modernism," *Modernism/Modernity* 6, no. 2 (1999): 59–77.

25. See Gustavo Pérez Firmat, *Life on the Hyphen: The Cuban-American Way* (Austin: University of Texas Press, 1994), 87–88.

26. Ibid., 88.

27. For Puente's tour in Hong Kong, see Carl Myatt, "Tito Puente Dates Boost Latin Music," *Billboard*, November 7, 1962, 33.

28. For contemporary coverage of the mambo craze in Japan and elsewhere in East Asia, see "Music: Mambo-San," *Time*, July 25, 1955. See also Hui, "Pailameng faxing diyi bu manbo yingpian" [Paramount distributes its first mambo movie], *Lianhe Fukan*, May 10, 1955, 6.

29. See Kathleen McHugh, "South Korean Film Melodrama: State, Nation, Woman, and the Transnational Familiar," in *South Korean Golden Age Melodrama: Gender, Genre, and National Cinema*, ed. Kathleen McHugh and Nancy Abelmann (Detroit, MI: Wayne State University Press, 2005), 32–33.

30. Sek Kei, "One Big Happy Family: Grace Chang's MP&GI Story," in Ain-ling Wong, *The Cathay Story*, 192. *Mambo Girl*, on an initial investment of $144,842 Hong Kong dollars, brought Cathay box office receipts of $300,748 from screens in Singapore, Malaya, Thailand, Vietnam, the Philippines, and Indonesia. See Lim Kay Tong, *Cathay*, 148. Delfino, an important figure in the dissemination of Latin music in Hong Kong, is also featured in *Mambo Girl*.

31. "Kalisao xianhua" [Calypso enjoys worldwide popularity], *International Screen* 23 (September 1957). In fairness, the Chinese text of the piece is both more detailed and somewhat more sophisticated than the English summary, acknowledging both the

modernity of Trinidadian calypsonians, as well as their "literary" and "harmonic" talent. A nearly verbatim English-language description of the new dance step also appears in a second Hong Kong film journal, *Southern Screen*. See "Gelisao yu qiaqia" [Calypso and cha cha], *Nanguo* 3 (October 1958). Thanks to Jean Ma for sharing these materials with me. The notion that calypso was a successor to, or even a threat to displace, rock and roll was common at the time. See Ray Funk and Donald R. Hill, "'Will Calypso Doom Rock 'n' Roll?': The U.S. Calypso Craze of 1957," in *Trinidad Carnival: The Cultural Politics of a Transnational Festival*, ed. Garth L. Green and Philip W. Scher (Bloomington: Indiana University Press, 2007), 178–97. For contemporary efforts to define the calypso, see Daniel J. Crowley, "Towards a Definition of the Calypso," *Ethnomusicology* 3, no. 2 (1959): 57–66.

32. Wang Fei's original recording is available on youtube.com, albeit without any discographic information, accessed February 8, 2012, www.youtube.com/watch?v=Ts1WrdMO1Es&feature=related. I have located a subsequent 33 1/3 LP record from the Black Cat Record (Heimao Changpian) label in Taiwan with a cover of the song, unattributed to any particular artist but featuring a rudimentary "Latin" beat played on the bongos. The record (BCL 66 A) can be roughly dated from between 1963, when LPs were first produced in Taiwan, and 1968, when government agencies first required records to be labeled with their dates of production. My gratitude to Xu Guolong (K'ho) of Wien Records, Tainan, for his assistance in dating the record. The following blog entry also contains a useful history of the song: http://blog.roodo.com/muzikland/archives/15634765.html (accessed February 8, 2012).

33. For C. S. Stone Shih's illuminating intervention into prevailing pop musical historiography, see "Taiwan geyao zuowei yizhong 'shidai shengxing qu': Yinyue Taibei de Shanghai ji zhu hunxue meiying" [Taiwan ballads as a form of mainstream popular music: Shanghai and other mixed-blood influences in musical Taipei, 1930–1960], *Taiwan Shehui Xuekan* 47 (September 2011): 94–141.

34. C. S. Stone Shih, personal interview, December 30, 2011.

35. See David Frazier, "Kupa Big Band: That Old Style Hoklo Swing," *Fountain: Arts and Living* 4 (2010): 30.

36. For an account of the band's origins and activities, see the composer Huang Guolong's *Zhongwai gujin yinyue chaoliu* [Musical currents: Chinese and foreign, ancient and contemporary] (Taipei: Wuzhou Chubanshe, 1970), 261–63.

37. Hokkien is a general term for the Minnan dialects, deriving from the Zhangzhou and Quanzhou regions of southern Fujian province, widely spoken in Taiwan and across the diaspora.

38. See Jeremy Taylor's groundbreaking critique of nation-centered approaches to Chinese cultural production in "From Transnationalism to Nativism? The Rise, Decline, and Reinvention of a Regional Hokkien Entertainment Industry," *Inter-Asian Cultural Studies* 9, no. 1 (2008): 66. For a comprehensive study of Hokkien-dialect cinema, see Taylor's *Rethinking Transnational Chinese Cinemas: The Amoy-Dialect Film Industry in Cold War Asia* (London: Routledge, 2011).

39. Taylor, "From Transnationalism to Nativism?," 69.

40. Ibid. Huang Guolong also cites the years between 1962 and 1967 as the "age of television" in Taiwanese popular musical history, as televised broadcasts eclipsed live

performances in cabarets and other venues as the primary means of securing promotional notice and recording contracts. See Huang, *Zhongwai gujin yinyue chaoliu*, 80.

41. Of ten films starring the Hokkien star Wen Xia, for instance, only his last, *Goodbye, Taipei* (*Zaijian Taibei*, 1969), survives in the Taipei Film Archives. Similarly, only Hong Yifeng's most popular film, *Lingering Last Love*, is still extant.

42. See Guo-Juin Hong, *Taiwan Cinema: A Contested Nation Onscreen* (New York: Palgrave Macmillan, 2011), 7, 60–62.

43. For an excellent musical analysis of Hong's work and its fashioning of a new "bass" aesthetic in Taiwanese balladry, see Wan-Ting Chiu, *Baodao diyin gewang: Hong Yifeng zhuixun zhi lu* [Formosan baritone king: Hong Yifeng's journey of discovery] (Taipei: Tonsan, 2013).

44. Elsewhere in the film, Hong's music harks back not only to doowop and early rock and roll, but also to the yodeling of Jimmie Rodgers.

45. This figure derives from a 1965 article by He Fan, "Taiwan daoyin changpian" [Taiwan's fake label records], *Lianhe Bao*, October 27, 1965. Carl Myatt, writing in *Billboard*, reports that the monthly figure for Taiwanese pirate records is much higher: "150,000 LPS . . . leave Taiwan every month," according to an EMI Hong Kong representative. See Carl Myatt, "Pirates Capturing Business," *Billboard*, August 31, 1963, 30.

46. He, "Taiwan daoyin changpian." As quoted in Ye Longyan, *Taiwan changpian sixiang qi, 1895–1999* [Remembering the Taiwanese recording industry, 1895–1999] (Luzhou: Boyang Wenhua, 2001), 201–2.

47. See Ye, *Taiwan changpian sixiang qi*, 146–47.

48. Personal interview with the Taiwanese music scholar and collector Xu Guolong (Kho), Wien Records, Tainan, Taiwan, July 10, 2011.

49. This is also a plot that reflects Chang's real-life marriage to a wealthy businessman and her maternity leave in 1961, circumstances that led her to retire from filmmaking in 1963.

50. On Cathay's ties with Taiwan, see Emilie Yueh-yu Yeh, "Taiwan: The Transnational Battlefield of Cathay and Shaws," in Ain-ling Wong, *The Cathay Story*, 72–76.

51. Loke's ornithological research was published in a monograph entitled *The Company of Birds*, and he enjoyed recording birdsong with a portable Nagra and a parabolic reflector. See Lim Kay Tong, *Cathay*, 6, 17.

PART II · **AUDIBLE DISPLACEMENTS**

4 · THE AESTHETICS OF ALLÁ Listening Like a Sonidero

JOSH KUN

A boundary is not that at which something stops, but . . . that from which something begins its presencing.—MARTIN HEIDEGGER, "Building, Dwelling, Thinking"

It is said that music knows no boundaries; it is more accurate to say that it redefines them.
—JODY BERLAND, "Locating Listening"

God of heaven and earth, I am disillusioned and dispirited because I was not able to arrive at my destination. . . . They arrested me for crossing a line that has been designated a border. I beg that you give me the serenity to accept these obstacles of life and the strength to transcend them.
—"PRAYER FOR IMPRISONMENT OR DEPORTATION," *Migrant Prayerbook*

In February 2011, Arnulfo Aguilar was pulled over by police on an Iowa highway on suspicion of drug trafficking. After calling for backup, the police detained him for hours while they searched the three semi-trailers that he was traveling with. No drugs were found, no traffic citation was issued, no public apology offered. The cops were obviously not fans of *cumbia sonidera*, or else instead of racially profiling a middle-aged man from Mexico City with a legitimate work visa as a drug trafficker they would have profiled him for what he actually is, a dangerous DJ carrying three truck rigs full of spectacular sonic contraband: speaker towers, mixers, CDJ decks, amps, monitors, microphones, and crates of light gear that, when assembled and plugged in, produce undocumented music full of clandestine codes that moves across borders without stopping at checkpoints.

Aguilar is the creator of Sonido Condor, which, since its beginning in 1980 as a small neighborhood sound system blasting *cumbias* for local dances in Mexico City's Colonia Argentina, has grown into arguably the biggest, most successful, most tireless, and most elaborate of all Mexican *sonideros* (literally sound makers or sound men). When he performed in Mexico City for his twenty-fifth anniversary show in 2005, he performed for more than thirteen hours straight for at least three hundred thousand people. Dubbing himself *el hijo del pueblo* (the son of the people), Aguilar is constantly on tour playing for Mexican audiences on both sides of the border—from towns and cities across Mexico to states throughout the United States. When he was pulled over in Iowa, he was in the midst of a semiannual U.S. tour that took him through California, Oregon, Texas, Illinois, and Wisconsin.

While the majority of his success comes from the live and in-person encounters of his dances, Aguilar has also built an impressive online presence. The majority of his *bailes*, or dances, end up as fan-shot videos on YouTube that can typically rack up more than 200,000 views each; his website is packed with flash animation, voluminous personal histories and reflections, photos, tour info, and downloads; and he promotes his frequent webcasts of social and political commentary (which he shoots himself in his home office) on his Twitter feed. It's all part of Aguilar's careful self-fashioning as a neo-revolutionary DJ defined by *orgullo Mexicano* (Mexican pride) and the motto *solo viven aquellos que luchan* (those that fight are the only ones who survive), a liberationist sonidero fighting for the rights and dignity of the people who come alive through the music he mixes. In his official logo, the "O" of "Condor" is the face of Che Guevara.

The night after the Iowa incident, Aguilar performed in Milwaukee's Buddhist Temple Hall, where he used his detention by the police as an opportunity to critique anti-immigrant xenophobia and the policed free movement of Mexican migrants through the spaces of the United States. He reminded the crowd of what they all already knew: in the world of *sonideros*, music is a performance of migrant politics, and the DJs mix an enactment of the mix of the worlds and cultures that his dancers embody. Sonideros like Aguilar are mobile architects of what Ron Radano calls "the poetics of the musically social," and their CDs, mixes, and performances are dynamic cross-border demonstrations of "the ways in which the social occupies musical experience and conversely how musical creation and listening inform the feel and affect of social being."[1]

El Sonido es Cultura

Mexican *sonidos,* or mobile sound systems, play a meaningful, and increasingly popular, role in cross-border Mexican music culture. In their basic structure, sonidos are similar to the sound systems that have prospered across the world, from Jamaica to Colombia, from the South Bronx to the Congo to anywhere else there is music, a few loudspeakers, and a public space available for technological hijacking, sound customizing, and communal ritual. Like with the pioneering reggae sound systems of Kingston, Jamaica, Mexican sonidos are based on the grassroots customization of sound technologies as mobile, community PA units: stacks of speakers, walls of mammoth amplifiers, and a DJ who mixes prerecorded songs and dub-plates into new sonic combinations for dancing crowds. Operating through what Julian Henriques calls "sonic dominance," sound systems go beyond a strictly technological function and become musical instruments, technological media, and cultural apparatuses, "microcosms of the social, cultural, and economic sonic relationships in which they partake."[2] They traffic, as Henriques puts it, in both *base* and *bass*—grassroots, bottom-up, working-class technologies of sound and culture shaped into listening communities by the vibrational low-end force of high-volume bass frequencies.[3] Or, as Graham St. John has argued of sound systems in Australia, the sound-system emphasis on excessive sound amplification is really about the amplification of community ideas, values, and debates so that they can be heard—so loud they are impossible to ignore—in the alternative public spheres their sounds make possible.[4]

Condor and other leading Mexican sound systems, like Sonido La Conga, Sonido Changa, and Sonoramico, are all digital DJs, mixing CDs and MP3s of mostly Mexican and Colombian cumbia alongside blasts of salsa and classic rock en español, but in the 1960s, DJs and record collectors began the sonidero tradition by spinning *discos* and acetates of Colombian hits of the past decade and nascent Mexican singles ("La Pollerá Colorá" [the red skirt] for example) at neighborhood dances through modest mobile sound systems often consisting of turntables, a speaker "trumpet" cone, a microphone, and the back of a flatbed truck for a stage. The original sonidero loudspeakers would be tied to tree branches and were often dubbed *tomateras,* because they were the same speakers used to sell tomatoes from the backs of trucks as they moved through neighborhoods.[5] In the early days, sonideros playing gritty *vallenato-* and *guacaracha-*style cumbias were often written off as minor entertainment—"And now, to keep the party going, we leave you with your home stereo"—but now they function more as architects of a mobile, binational sonic community.[6] It's just one more chapter in the global history

FIGURE 4.1. Livia Radwanski, from the series *Cultura Sonidera*, 2008.

of cumbia as a genre of unending flexibility, able to shape-shift and transform as it adapts to various local, regional, and national musical traditions.[7]

"Technologies offer new futures for our pasts," Diana Taylor has rightly suggested, but they also offer new futures for our presents, and at bailes throughout Mexico and the United States, the sonidero show goes far beyond a standard musical performance and becomes what we might call a transfrontera audio communicational event.[8] Bailes are as much for dancing as they are for dialogic messaging, with fans inserting pointed personal messages, prayers, and dedications of love into the DJ's live mix (see figure 4.1). Using scraps of papers, the sides of Styrofoam cups, cell phones, and sidekicks, party attendees hand the sonidero DJs personalized messages and requests—many of them addressed to family members living far away—in the hopes that the DJ speaks the message into the mix.[9]

"Some people may not like the fact that we talk the whole time, but those people are probably not from Mexico," says the New York sonidero Fausto Salazar, who performs as Potencia Latina (Latin Power). "We are here to cheer people up. To have a good time, you just have to go to the sonidero station and ask for a shout-out, and you will feel nice." Or as another sonidero put it, "You want people to say, 'With the power of Sonido Dragon's voice, this message will reach all the way to Mexico.'"[10] Unlike Jamaican sound systems, which are intensive sonic interventions into the politics of local place (the yard, the dancehall), Mexican sound systems tend to emphasize the opposite—the dancehall, the community center, the parking lot—as a place that leads to a place beyond (Mexico, United States), a locale that is amplified to be heard beyond its limits. Mexican sound systems, while making local interventions, are increasingly transnational and global in their approach to sonic mobility, whether it be the physical travels of a sound system throughout the United States and Mexico, the cross-border distribution of sonidero mix CDs, sonidero websites and digital networks, or the global dissemination of sonido music, concert promotion, and social messaging on YouTube and file-sharing sites.

The sonidero party itself becomes a site of offline, site-specific, live-in-the-mix participatory culture, where to be present is to become part of the mix itself, using the music as an interpersonal messaging platform. After hours of broadcasting shoutouts and reading notes over shuffling cumbias, the DJs then burn the CDs on site, sell them to the dancers after the show, and the CDs are then sent back home to Mexico (or to the United States) to family, friends, and loved ones.[11] They are examples of what Jody Berland has called "teletopographic" cultural practices, in that, for sonideros and their fans, "distance is simultaneously inscribed in and overcome by mediating technologies."[12]

For so many millions of migrant Mexicans, forced to leave their home country to work in the United States, the border becomes a marker of distance, separation, and death, and the sonidero mix becomes a coping tool—a kind of musical suture, a cross-border sonic network that communicates through distance and heals the wounds of separation, creating digital sonic spaces where identity can be negotiated and rehearsed and social justice can be imagined and voiced. The musical collages of sonideros certainly fit within Nicolas Bourriaud's paradigm of "the art of postproduction" in that they create new cultural objects—continuous talk-over cumbia mixes blasted with sound effects—out of preexisting cultural objects (individual cumbia songs) and thereby invent "paths through culture."[13] Yet I want to stress that the paths followed and invented by sonideros, while shaped through technologies of sound, are also rooted in the paths and lines of cross-border migrant traffic and movement—the paths their music creates are responses to the paths of physical cross-border migrancy. This means that their postproduction paths are not one-way trips or straight-shot highways: their paths are loops and circuits, sonic networks that move across mobile nodes along the maps of the extended U.S.-Mexico borderlands.

Sonido Condor has even uploaded a series of YouTube videos entitled "Llegando a . . ." consisting of nothing more than shots of Aguilar's trucks moving down a road and "arriving" at various towns and cities throughout Mexico in preparation for a show. Each video stops before the event itself begins, highlighting the centrality of mobility and arrival—and all of their violence, pain, and fear—to the social and geographic horizon of the migrant trip, as well as the subsequent centrality of mobility and arrival to sound systems that increasingly exist to perform for and with migrant audiences by continually arriving in new sites along the binational map of Greater Mexico. In this way, the mobile consciousness of sonideros helps give voice to "the world-making aspirations of Mexican border crossers" that Alicia Schmidt Camacho has written about as "migrant imaginaries," symbolic and cultural fields that sustain the precarious subjectivity and "fragile agency" of migrants living and working on the margins of national sovereignty and in the heart of Homeland Security cultures of surveillance, security, and detention. "Cultural forms are not a reflection of the social," she writes, "or merely a detached 'set of ideas,' but rather the means by which subjects work through their connections to a larger totality and communicate a sense of relatedness to a particular time, place, and tradition."[14]

Precisely because of this nuanced attention to the spatial politics of mobility, of the ragged, sun-beaten, surveilled, and often deadly roads that connect the "here" and the "there," sonideros are shaping what I've come to call an *aesthetics of allá*, a way of using the arts—specifically here recorded sound and audio technology—to engage with spatial politics in the age of asymmetrical economic globalization, naturalized systems of deportation and border militarization, and intensive global migration and displacement. In Spanish, *allá* is neither the here we can see and know (*aquí*) nor the there we can see and know (*allí*). Allá can refer to both an over there that is visible but at a distance, or an over there that is not yet visible, a "beyond" space we know is there but is not currently occupied or realized, a there that is still a destination or a departure—a there that may be still over there but that can be imagined from the right here. Sonideros are remapping the cultural, sonic, and political geographies of Mexico and what Los Tigres del Norte once sang about as *el otro México*—the Mexico being re-created by Mexican migrants and immigrants north of the borderline—by using the crossfader and the mix to blend the here of the baile, the here of the site of listening, with an allá that can't be easily seen but can be conjured and imagined through sound and music.[15] Or to use the geographer Susan J. Smith's helpful framework, allá is an example of "space as a listening," a geography beyond the visible.[16] As a critique of the present—of the here and now—allá's there that is not quite here can be Mexico for Mexicans in the United States, can be the United States for

Mexicans in Mexico, and can also function as a more symbolic and affective space of political and cultural relief and hope and promise for both.[17] The Mexican musical allá is in that sense also a Mexi-furist "space is the place," a sonically speculative "browntopia," to echo Graham Lock, where music becomes a momentary audio home of rescue and belonging that is always bound (as the "blutopias" of African American music are always linked to the history of slavery) to the dangers that produce it: the struggles and violences of U.S.-Mexico immigration and U.S.-Mexico economic and political realities under global capitalism.

Using cultural and political futurism to respond to past and present violence can also be seen in the frequent use of science fiction and interstellar imagery in sonidero advertising and self-branding. Sonido Condor's flyer for a 2007 party in Houston, Texas, for example, pictured Aguilar's signature Che Guevara–emblazoned semi-trailers as soaring cosmic space ships docking into a large doomed mothership, and sonidero sound effects typically include futuristic sci-fi sound effects that portray the sound systems themselves as interstellar space crafts fueled by the musical mixes of the DJ that fly across space and time. A recent mix by a Puebla sonidero, Alexx Perez, begins with a voiceover declaring "De Puebla para todo el mundo" (from Puebla to the whole world) followed by the zapped blips and bleeps of laser beams, as if the sonidero was a musical astronaut traveling through space through the mixes of his sound system (there was a particularly sonidero sensibility to the 2009 pro-immigrant outer-space tweeting of the Mexican astronaut Juan Hernández, the son of Mexican migrant workers in California, when he wrote "what surprised me is when I saw the world as one. There were no borders. You couldn't distinguish between the United States and Mexico"). Most sonideros also begin their baile performances with *presentaciónes*, long and often theatrical introductions that typically cast the sound system as a space shuttle counting down for takeoff, ready to transport the audience to another place through music. Here is how Cathy Ragland, the leading U.S. scholar of Mexican sonideros, has memorably described it:

> The sonidero reminds attendees at the baile that the "disco mobil" (the mobile disco of the sonidero) is always "ready for travel." Frequently reiterating his stage name, such as "Potencia Latina" (Latin Power) or "El Condor," he boasts of his powerful system and unique music selection: "el señal mas potente" (the most powerful signal) or "música electrónica inteligente" (intelligent electronic music); throughout he reiterates his boastful tagline, such as "la maxima autoridad del sonido"

("the maximum authority of the sound system"), or "el destructor de leyendas" ("the destroyer of legends").[18]

The practice at the heart of the aesthetics of allá is crossfading, the DJ practice of managing at least two separate audio input channels by using the cross-fader toggle switch of a mixing board. Each input line represents its own distinct set of sonic information and ideas, and the crossfader allows the DJ to move between each channel without silencing either. The art of the crossfader is not only moving between two worlds but also moving between them seamlessly and strategically, finding common beats, tempos, melodic moments—points of convergence that allow new mixes to be born. Crossfading mixes while preserving difference, and it slides between worlds without fully erasing one in the pursuit of another.

Sonideros are crossfader specialists, both literally in their use of the cross-fader to slide between cumbias but also figuratively in their use of the crossfader to inhabit (as the poet Stanley Plumly might have put it) "the abrupt edge" of uneven globalization, juggling geographic spaces, homelands, territories, and spaces of belonging with the skillful, careful dance of a horizontal toggle. The DJ mix, even at its most seamless, is made of cuts, scratches, and fade-outs; it is built on an aesthetic of bordering and excising, a surgery of sound that, even when corrective and successful, is marked by wounds. The crossfade of allá, then, becomes a migrant strategy for emergency living in the age of what T. J. Demos has called "crisis globalization," where the contradiction of the free flow of ideas, culture, commerce, and money coexisting alongside the po-liced flow of bodies and individual freedoms—boundless possible life in one lane riding alongside boundless possible death in another—is constitutive of, and not an anomaly of, the very condition of neoliberal globalism itself.[19] As Mary Louise Pratt and others have reminded us, it is the unflows, not the flows, of globalization that are its primary characteristics (the waits, not the accelerations; the hierarchization, not the flattening), and the mobilities, spatialities, and networks it can produce always have material causes, im-pacts, and inequities on the ground of everyday social experience. As a mu-sical aesthetics, then, allá is about imagining and enacting social possibility but always in the face of extreme social risk and geographical dislocation.[20] Its networks of sound and culture are born of displacement and tinged with loss, and its aquí/allá "transnationalism"—as utopian and hopeful as it can feel in the space of a song or a DJ mix—is always linked to the forced move-ments and ruptures of empire across the extended spaces of the U.S.-Mexico borderlands.

Thus, we might say that sonideros transcend the standard dual input channel model of the crossfader and practice a kind of triple crossfading: sonic, spatial, and heterochronic. They crossfade one cumbia into the next, crossfade homelands and communities, and crossfade one temporality into another, creating mobile communication and musical networks that travel in the space of the compressed, burned, bounced, and downloaded mix, interpersonal communication and national and regional history and memory that lives in the slide of the crossfader. To listen like a sonidero, then, is to listen for culture's mobility (coerced and witting), to hear local spaces as nodes of global connection and resettlement, to use music and the technology of the DJ mix to create spaces of communication and connection across uneven and often perilous U.S.-Mexico geographies that are shaped and formed in the space of the musical mix itself. To listen like a sonidero is to respond to social and political emergencies with emergency music, to crossfade cultural and national experiences, to juggle spaces of belonging, to remap space and time, to know that you might be playing a gig in Puebla but you will be heard in galaxies far, far away, whether across the border or across the universe.

Sonideros emphasize travel and transport precisely because they participate in a cross-border network and entertainment culture of migrant music making and because their mixes and bailes are directly addressed to Mexican populations with high-risk relationships to the freedoms and dangers of movement across a heavily policed geopolitical border. Aguilar's brief detainment in Iowa was just a small trace of the border's dialectics of freedom and unfreedom—its unhomely home for what Demos has called "the impossibility of sitedness"—and of the territorial control and spatial fragmentation that continue to be tactics of enforcement that fortify the border as a site of what Achille Mbembe has dubbed "necro-power."[21] The mixes of sonideros are part of a larger Mexican music culture that is continually responding—through sound, lyrics, and public activism—to new security regimes of deportation, border militarization, and "illegal" profiling. They recognize that, as Saskia Sassen has written, the state is a mix of regimes, and the border wall or fence or line is increasingly a territorial maker of a de-territorial condition—what she calls "the border function."[22]

The criminalization of movement continuously faced by so many migrants working and living north of the line has grown all the more intensive and manic as nation-states use the brutalizing political theater of border militarization to compensate for a loss of sovereign power. As Wendy Brown has argued, the walls and fences of the U.S.-Mexico border might be intended as proof that national divisions can indeed be sealed, but in truth those same walls and fences are evidence of the opposite: the erosion of sovereignty and the blurring of easily marked divisions.[23] In their live party crossfades and transnational CD burns, sonideros face those flows and barriers, those movements and detainments, and turn them into musical mixes sensitive to the struggles of migrancy and celebratory of the will to live through them.

The Songbook of Migrancy

What are the songs and sounds of an imaginary and imagined freedom of movement along the border? How has U.S. empire along the Mexican border shaped the evolution of its popular music and how has music responded to the imperial histories and imperial presents that continue to structure social and political life across the border's policed territories? In the spaces of the border's various acoustic communities, what does an emancipatory, or at the very least ethical, migrant critical listening sound like?

These are questions that lie at the heart of sonidero practice and popularity, and they have been vital questions ever since the border was created in 1848 to end the Mexican-American War in Manifest Destiny's most infamous real estate deal. Yet they have become especially urgent and vital in a contemporary political and economic moment when the border increasingly bears the weight of the social, political, and economic asymmetries of free-trade capitalism, intense anti-immigrant xenophobia, and the rising death toll of a vicious binational drug war. Precisely because of their central role in filtering and managing the flows of economic globalization, Alejandro Lugo has called for an end to the common belief in borders as places of crossing, insisting instead that borders are primarily places of inspection characterized by the "pervasive pattern of cultural surveillance" and ought to be redefined as "ethnographic objects that are mainly characterized by supervision and scrutiny."[24]

In 2001, Los Tigres del Norte, the most prominent architects of Mexican migrant music, recorded "Paisano a Paisano" and imagined themselves in the middle of the Sonoran desert, surrounded by the freedom of expanses and distances, the desert's limitless horizons and vistas, while singing about their limits in a time of border war:

I have spent my life exploring other lands to give a better future to my children. . . . Because we've wanted to work, they have declared war on us, they are patrolling the borders, but they cannot tame us. . . . The nation hurts so much when my people cry—this is an international cry. From countryman to countryman, before I go on singing I ask the boss, who picks the harvest? Who cleans the hotels and restaurants and who kills themselves working construction while the boss scolds us while knitting in his luxurious mansion?

The song's video emphasized the border's convergence of transnational territory, state power, and cultural performance by cutting between the band performing alone against a sun-bleached desertscape with images of Mexicans working and living on urban U.S. streets.

That the song would so openly engage in a rhetoric of war and battle is but one example of how central music has always been to the broadcasting and negotiating of cultural and political conflict between the United States and Mexico. As scholars of the Mexican *corrido*—that durable ballad of border and migrant experience since the nineteenth century—have long noted and as Américo Paredes made the centerpiece of his landmark 1958 study *With His Pistol in His Hand*, the music of the Mexican borderlands and by extension the music of migrant Mexico on the move is its own system of countermedia, its own musical information network, necessarily tuned to political upheaval and clashes over territorial belonging. While the wars of the border are not exclusively fought through acoustic and musical strategies, Mexican migrant music—from corridos and norteño to cumbia sonidera—has long been driven by a particular spatial imagination and spatial politics, a commitment to envisioning and enacting a freedom of movement across political geographies that might very well be designed to restrict and police that freedom of movement.

In the Mexican anthropologist Manuel Gamio's pioneering 1927 migration study of two thousand Mexican immigrants returning from the United States he found that 20 percent of them brought back phonographs. For every 100 immigrants, 118 records returned to Mexico.[25] Which is to say that moving back and forth across the border has always been, in part, a musical act, and migrancy is a sonic practice as much as a spatial one. Instead of treating the border—be it as line, monument, fence, wall—as a partition of silence where narrative does not exist, Mexican migrant music has treated the border as something that, to borrow the title of Paul Botello's East Los Angeles mural that dons the cover of the *De Paisano a Paisano* album, "sings, speaks, and shouts," full of stories and brimming with narrative; the border is a living musical witness to the injustices and triumphs of Mexican life. The Mexican scholar Gustavo López Castro has written extensively about Mexican corridos as forming a decades-spanning "songbook of migrancy," a mobile archive of everyday migrant life, of cross-border feelings and emotions that create communities of sentiment between Mexico and the United States and that lives in both formal and informal markets. The songbook of migrancy, he argues, will remain alive and valid as long it continues to function as "a cultural link between absences and anguish."[26]

We can hear this songbook at work from the very start of recorded Mexican music in the United States. The history of the recorded corrido in fact begins with songs of undocumented immigration, labor, anti-immigrant violence, and deportation; the style's first commercial U.S. heroes are *indocumentados*, deportees, and the unjustly convicted. One of the very first commercially recorded corridos in the United States, "Vida, Proceso, y Muerte de Aurelio Pompa," told the story of a Sonoran immigrant laborer, Aurelio Pompa, who comes to work in Los Angeles where he suffers constant abuse and harassment from an Anglo carpenter foreman who eventually beats him. After Pompa shoots him in self-defense, he is arrested and executed. The uncredited authors of the song give Pompa a voice from the dead and allow him to deliver a message to fellow immigrant workers: "Tell my race not to come here / For here they will suffer / There is no pity here." Six years later, also in Los Angeles, Los Hermanos Bañuelos' recorded "El Lavaplatos" (The dishwasher) and told the story of an undocumented immigrant who leaves Mexico hoping to make it as a Hollywood star and ends up first as a migrant field worker and then as a dishwasher in a restaurant not far from the Hollywood backlots he had once dreamt about. "Farewell dreams of my life," the migrant dishwasher sings, "Farewell movie stars / I return to my dear country / Poorer than when I came."

Fueled by the economic collapse of the Great Depression, the years between 1929 and 1939 led to the deportations and repatriations of more than five hundred thousand Mexicans living and working in the United States. As a result, the single most common topic for corridos submitted to U.S. record labels in the late '20s and early '30s was deportation, from "El Paisano Repatriado" and "Las Leyes de Inmigracion" to "Los Repatriados." Los Hermanos Bañuelos had one of the more popular deportee songs after they entered another L.A. recording studio to record "El Deportado" (The deportee), a song advertised by Vocalion Records as a "sentimental corrido" that "tells the story of many Mexican expatriates in the United States."[27] The song ends with a Dust Bowl saga that, in both subject and lyrical phrasing, presaged Woody Guthrie's classic 1948 protest song "Deportee," which angrily memorialized the plane-crash deaths of Mexican braceros: "Today comes a large cloud of dust and with no consideration, women, children and elders are being driven to the border. We are being kicked out of this country. Goodbye, beloved countrymen they are going to deport us. But we are not bandits we came to work hard."

El Más Allá

Allá is over there. It is beyond what's right here. But it's also el más allá, the beyond, the afterlife. The allá of migrant Mexican music is also connected to this other space, to what exists after living ends.[28]

Early in *De L'Autre Côté* (*From the Other Side*), Chantal Akerman's 2002 documentary about migrant deaths along the Arizona-Mexico border, she allows the camera to linger for more than three minutes on a side street in Agua Prieta, Sonora, a border city of nearly one hundred fifty thousand people that continues to be impacted by migrant arrivals and departures. Though Agua Prieta can be bustling, Ackerman asks us to focus on the effects of leaving by mostly portraying the city as vacant and full of solitude. The occasional truck guzzles along. A stray figure crosses the road. In the background, the faint traces of a norteño song can be heard echoing from a source we can't make out—a truck's radio, a bar's jukebox. "I'm leaving," a voice sings. "I'm leaving." The music becomes part of the town's expression of its emptiness as a site of departure with no guarantee of a safe return, a border landscape of leaving.

The scene recalls a musical tradition of migrant affect and longing that perhaps received its most canonical early statement in "Canción Mixteca," written back in 1934 by Jose López Alavez, a Mixtec Indian from Oaxaca who wrote the song after leaving Oaxaca to live and study in Mexico City. "How far I am from the land where I was born," the song begins. "Immense nostalgia invades my thoughts and seeing me so sad and alone like a leaf in the wind, I'd rather cry, I'd rather die from *sentimiento*, from these painful feelings." The song's melancholic evocation of the sadness of leaving home soon turned it into a kind of unofficial anthem of migrancy, of Mexico on the move—whether from rural pueblos to urban centers within Mexico or from rural pueblos to urban centers of the North. The song gives us the archetype of migrant aesthetics: distance from the homeland brought on by displacement, nostalgia that is immense and oceanic, lives marked by sentimiento produced by the distance that migrancy makes. In the music of migrant Mexico, Alavez's sentimiento, which translates literally as sentiment or feeling, becomes the affective glue of transnational community. In her writing on the border singer Lydia Mendoza, Yolanda Broyles-González defines Mendoza's "working-class sentimiento" as the sustenance of Mexican identity and cross-border community, "homeland constituted in song."[29]

Yet in recent decades that working-class sentimiento has also evolved into something else: a mourning over death and disappearance, a musical grieving over lost immigrant lives. Ever since the 2004 militarization legislation of Operation Gatekeeper sealed urban points of entry and pushed more and more migrants to head into the punishing deserts of Arizona to cross north, the desert borderlands have become synonymous with the dehydrations, hyperthermia, and body dumps of migrant death, with thousands perishing each year. Where early western desert explorers like Clarence King once remarked on the desert as an ecological graveyard, a cemetery of dried bones and skeletal plant life, now the desert discourse of death more often than not involves the bodies of Mexican migrants. As Los Tigres del Norte sang in 1985, the border is the tomb of the migrant. "The roses of Mexicali and the blood in the Rio Grande," they sang, "two different things, but they are brothers in color, and the borderline is the wetback's tomb." The white crosses tacked to border fences from Tijuana to Juarez that line swatches of desert sand are continual reminders of migrancy's perils and the disposability of human life. Death is increasingly a way of life in the borderlands spaces of Mexican migrancy, a surveilled and policed binational political landscape where, as Mbembe writes, "vast populations are subjected to conditions of life conferring upon them the status of the living dead."[30]

Through their CD mixes and their bailes, sonideros join this tradition of music as a negotiation of el más allá by reimagining musical performance as an act of *social presencing*. By sending a message through the mix, sonideros create Mexican presence out of Mexican invisibility, loss, and longing, and they use music to explore Thomas Dumm's notion of loneliness as "the experience of the pathos of disappearance." For Dumm, loneliness is a political experience in that it "is instrumental in the shaping and exercise of power, the meaning of individuality, and the ways in which justice is to be comprehended and realized in the world."[31] The sonidero message mix and its accompanying informal economy of CD copying and sales, in creating its own offline version of a "networked information economy" with its own "networked public sphere," make present those who are not physically there in the space of the party—those back home, those who have passed—but also give voice and name to those who are there whose daily lives as migrants in the United States too often render them as present absences, a precarious migrant subjectivity characterized by silences, invisibility, fear, and often perilous alterity. Or as Salazar, or Potencia Latina, so memorably explained it to Ragland:

> When I am performing in Mexico, people often end their salutations and dedications with "presente, cien por ciento." That is to say that they are here, with me, completely. Since I have traveled from New York, it is important for many people who have family and friends in the US to send their dedications and salutations through me and say that they are with me. Also, in the US it is the same for a sonidero who travels from Mexico to perform. They will want to be "presente" with him too. It is like you are "there" in Mexico, or with me you are "here" in New York.

Sonideros on both sides of the border have, like Salazar, been overt in connecting what they do to migrant activism and frequently use their sonido performances and CD mixes to launch political commentaries on immigrant justice, employing sound-system amplification as a form of migrant protest—decibels as politics.

In the wake of the landmark May 1, 2006, marches that filled the streets of states across the United States (from New York and California to Illinois, Georgia, Wisconsin, and Louisiana) with millions of marchers protesting against restrictive immigration laws, Sonido Condor collaborated with El Tigre Sonidero to weigh in by uploading a video to YouTube that mixed live performance footage, photo collage, original animation, and a cumbia soundtrack. It opened with a dedication: "For the immigrants of the United States. The 1st of May is the Day of the Immigrant. Immigrants are essential for this country because it gets rich off our sacrifices." Then as a Condor cumbia mix plays, the screen fills with images of giant white crosses in the desert sand labeled *no olvidado* (not forgotten), home-made monuments to lost migrant lives in the "death-worlds"—what the video calls "the dangerous desert roads"—of the militarized borderlands. The video, which has garnered more than four hundred thousand views, then cuts to a Condor performance, which he begins with a speech about the urgency of immigrant protest. "This is for all of those who on May 1 did not go to work," he says, "and took to the streets to march peacefully to show the United States that we are not criminals. We are workers in search of immigration reform." He asks the crowd to cheer in their honor as the video moves through shots of immigration protests, Latino corner grocery stores, and white crosses. As the cumbia mix plays, we hear a sample of Aguilar saying "immigration reform" on continual loop.

As powerful as much of the Sonido Condor video is, I do not want to suggest that the aesthetics of allá or the aesthetics of migrant politics are somehow seamless, automatic, or univocal. After Aguilar pays tribute to immigrants and marchers, he goes on to vigorously condemn as "traitors" (specifically, "Chinguen a su madre, traidores!") all those who decided not to march and go to work instead. The video ends with a series of targeted accusations of national treason: Mexican pop artists who make their money in Mexico and spend it in Miami "increasing insecurity in Mexico City"; Mexican politicians who rob their own people and then gamble their money away in Las Vegas; those who celebrate the flags of other countries without knowing and promoting their own history; those that get rich off Mexican poverty, invest their fortunes in dollars, keep their money in foreign banks, and cause devaluations back at home; *coyotes* who take money from fellow Mexicans and then leave them to die in the desert.

Aguilar's inclusion of a hypernationalist treatise into a musical mix on supporting immigrant rights created its own public forum of debate in the comments section, with the majority of the nearly three hundred responses taking vocal issue with his conflation of Mexican migrants who kept working with corrupt Mexican politicians. "It's easy for you to say this," one commenter argues in a sentiment echoed by many, "because you are not here having to work to feed your children and your family." Another argues that "the only traitor to Mexico here is the government, not immigrants." I mention the dispute between Aguilar and his online fans precisely to emphasize the extent to which the sonic amplification practices of Mexican sonidos produce not only the amplification of migrant politics as I have been suggesting, but also the amplification of public debate around immigrant politics, national identity, and economic necessity over an online digital platform of communication networks. Just as CDs from sonidero bailes offer a means of trans-spatial migrant communication through a combination of live event and recorded music, sonidero YouTube videos like this one splice recorded music, recordings of live performances, and social and political commentary to offer a means of trans-spatial discourse and intra-migrant talk-back on the very question of migrancy's impact on Mexicanness itself.

Speaker-man: A Closing Track for the Sonidero Mix

In 2009, the Tijuana-raised, now Arizona-based, conceptual artist Julio Cesar Morales debuted a watercolor painting he named "Undocumented Interventions #17" (see figure 4.2).[32]

FIGURE 4.2. Julio Cesar Morales, "Undocumented Interventions #17," 2009.

Part of a larger series of work exploring *contrabando* as an economic and aesthetic condition of contemporary globalization that includes paintings of Sponge Bob piñatas stuffed with people and faux-blueprints of narco drug-tunnel houses, "#17" details a Mexican man attempting to smuggle himself across the border by hiding inside a home stereo speaker.[33] Morales has created a number of different pieces that focus on sound and migrancy, including a "Sonido Pirata" installation in the street-front window of a Los Angeles gallery and a "Migrant Dubs" sonidero project that led him and his collaborator, Eamon Ore-Giron—a sonidero disciple himself, who also performs and records digitally inflected cumbias as DJ Lengua—to make a twenty-minute video of New York's Sonido La Conga performing at a baptism (the video features saludos read from the glowing screens of two-way pagers and cell phones). While the immediate reference of "#17" may be human trafficking and smuggling across the U.S.-Mexico border, the image of a man in a speaker—the man-as-speaker, the speaker-as-man—directly echoes the sound-man and sound-subject of the sonidero figure, and it is a powerful reminder of how central sound reproduction and sound technology are to migrant economics, survival, and identity across the borderlands. Through Morales's x-ray vision of the pirate economies of migrant life, the sonic subject is both absent and present at once, in transit between a here and an allá that is left behind and on the horizon.

NOTES

A previous version of this chapter appeared in *Public Culture* 27, no. 3 (September 2015). Both versions have benefited greatly from conversations with Cathy Ragland, Eamon Ore-Giron, Jace Clayton, Julio Cesar Morales, Toy Selectah, Julia Palacios, and Elizabeth Villa.

1. Ronald Radano, "Introduction," *Musical Quarterly* 89, no. 4 (Winter 2006): 3.

2. Julian Henriques, "Sonic Dominance and the Reggae Sound System Session," in *Auditory Culture Reader*, ed. M. Bull and L. Back (Oxford: Berg, 2003), 452. See also Henriques, "Situating Sound: The Space and Time of the Dancehall Session," in *Sonic Interventions*, ed. Sylvia Mieszkowski, Joy Smith, and Marijke de Valck (New York: Rodopi, 2007), 287–310.

3. Julian Henriques, *Sonic Bodies: Reggae Sound Systems, Performance Techniques, and Ways of Knowing* (London: Continuum, 2011), 13.

4. Graham St. John, "Outback Vibes: Sound Systems on the Road to Legitimacy," *Postcolonial Studies* 8, no. 3 (2005): 321–36.

5. For a more complete history of cumbia in Mexico and of the early days of sonideros in Mexico City and Monterrey, see Dario Blanco Arboleda, "Los bailes sonideros: Identidad

y resistencia de los grupos populares Mexicanos ante los embates de la modernidad," and Marco Ramirez Cornejo, "Entre luces, cables, y bocinas: El movimiento sonidero," both included in the catalog published by the multinational collective of musicians, artists, historians, and critics, El Proyecto Sonidero, *Sonideros en las Aceras, Véngase la Gozadera* (Creative Commons: Tumbona, 2012). For more info, visit elproyectosonidero.org.

6. Helmer G. Morales, "Sonideros, sobreviventes del desdén," *El Universal*, February 20, 2008.

7. This is the point driven home by Héctor Fernández L'Hoeste and Pablo Vila in the introduction to their edited volume *Cumbia! Scenes of a Migrant Latin American Music Genre* (Durham: Duke University Press, 2013).

8. Diana Taylor, "Save as . . . Knowledge and Transmission in the Age of Digital Technologies," *Foreseeable Futures #10: Position Papers from Imagining America* (Imagining America, 2011), 2, http://imaginingamerica.org/wp-content/uploads/2011/05/Foreseeable -Futures-10-Taylor.pdf.

9. The Mexico City–based photographer Livia Radwanski has documented this messaging in her remarkable series from 2008 to 2012, *Cultura Sonidera*, http:// liviaradwanski.com/site/archives/portfolio/cultura-sonidera.

10. Tripti Lahiri, "Under the Musical Spell of the Sonidero," *New York Times*, November 22, 2003.

11. The spoken saludo that reaches across national borders is, of course, not unique to sonideros. It's a regular feature on Mexican radio stations, especially those that now use digital online streaming, such as La Más Perrona (1410 AM in Mexico City) and XEBU La Norteñita (620 AM in Chihuahua), and remains a staple of the English-language oldies show that is still hosted out of Los Angeles by Art Laboe.

12. Jody Berland, *North of Empire: Essays on the Cultural Technologies of Space* (Durham: Duke University Press, 2009), 5.

13. Nicolas Bourriaud, *Postproduction: Culture as Screenplay: How Art Reprograms the World* (New York: Lukas and Sternberg, 2002).

14. Alicia R. Schmidt Camacho, *Migrant Imaginaries: Latino Cultural Politics in the U.S.-Mexico Borderlands* (New York: New York University Press, 2008), 5.

15. As I explore in the larger project from which this essay is drawn, songs about allá are nothing new to Mexican music and have in fact been a central part of the Mexican popular musical archive, whether it's songs about *el otro lado* (the other side) or about specifically being neither *aquí* nor *allá*, like Chavela Vargas's version of Fernando Cabral's "No Soy de Aqui ni Soy de Allá" and Los Tigres del Norte's "Ni Aqui ni Allá." Yet such spatial formations are typically seen as examples of a migrant state of nonbelonging, a limbo, a state of being caught between countries and cultures. For me, the aesthetics of allá are up to something different; they are less about limbo and division, more about suture and bridging. For a good example of aquí/allá thinking, see Patricia Zavella, *I'm Neither Here nor There: Mexicans' Quotidian Struggles with Mexican Migration and Poverty* (Durham: Duke University Press, 2011).

16. Susan J. Smith, "Performing the (Sound) World," *Environment and Planning: Society and Space* 18, no. 5: 615, and "Beyond Geography's Visible Worlds: A Cultural Politics of Music," *Progress in Human Geography* 21, no. 4 (August 1997): 502–29.

17. Inspired by José Muñoz's recent work on queer futurity, allá is as much a possibility as it is a potentiality, "a thing that is present but not actually existing in the present tense . . . a then that disrupts the tyranny of the now." José Muñoz, *Cruising Utopia: The Then and There of Queer Futurity* (New York: New York University Press, 2009), 9.

18. Cathy Ragland, "Mexican Deejays and the Transnational Space of Youth Dances in New York and New Jersey," *Ethnomusicology* 47, no. 3 (Autumn 2003): 338–54. See also Ragland's updated version of this article as "Communicating the Collective Imagination: The Sociospatial World of the Mexican Sonidero in Puebla, New York, and New Jersey," in Fernández L'Hoeste and Vila, *Cumbia!*, 119–37.

19. T. J. Demos, *The Migrant Image: The Art and Politics of Documentary during Global Crisis* (Durham: Duke University Press, 2013).

20. See, for example, Mary Louise Pratt, "Why the Virgin of Zapopan Went to Los Angeles: Reflections on Mobility and Globality" (keynote address presented at the Third Annual Encuentro of the Hemispheric Institute, Lima, Peru, July 8, 2002), http://hemi.nyu.edu/eng/seminar/peru/call/mlpratt.shtml; David Featherstone, Richard Phillips, and Johanna Waters, "Introduction: Spatialities of Transnational Networks," *Global Networks* 7, no. 4 (2007): 383–91; Alejandro Portes, Luis E. Guarnizo, and Patricia Landolt, "The Study of Transnationalism: Pitfalls and Promise of an Emergent Research Field," *Ethnic and Racial Studies* 22, no. 2 (1999): 217–37.

21. Achille Mbembe, "Necropolitics," in *The Unhomely: Phantom Scenes in Global Society*, ed. Okwui Enwezor (Barcelona: Biacs, 2006), 32–51.

22. Saskia Sassen, "Weaponized Fences and Novel Borderings: The Beginnings of a New History," in *Beyond la Frontera: The History of U.S.-Mexico Migration*, ed. Mark Overmeyer-Velázquez (New York: Oxford University Press, 2011). See also Nicholas de Genova, "The Deportation Regime: Sovereignty, Space, and the Freedom of Movement," in *The Deportation Regime: Sovereignty, Space, and the Freedom of Movement*, ed. Nicholas de Genova and Nathalie Peutz (Durham: Duke University Press, 2010), 33–68.

23. Wendy Brown, *Walled States, Waning Sovereignty* (New York: Zone, 2010).

24. Alejandro Lugo, *Fragmented Lives, Assembled Parts: Culture, Capitalism and Conquest at the U.S.-Mexico Border* (Austin: University of Texas Press, 2008), 118.

25. Manuel Gamio, *Mexican Immigration to the United States: A Study of Human Migration and Adjustment* (Chicago: University of Chicago Press, 1930).

26. Gustavo López Castro, *El Río Bravo es charco: Cancionero del migrante* (Zamora: Colegio de Michoacán, 1995).

27. Nellie Foster, "The Corrido: A Mexican Culture Trait Persisting in Southern California" (M.A. thesis: University of Southern California, 1939), 24.

28. There is a vast, well-established literature on the role of death in the Mexican cultural, social, folk, and spiritual imagination. A nearly exhaustive introduction can be found in Claudio Lomnitz's *Death and the Idea of Mexico* (Cambridge: MIT Press, 2005). In my larger project from which this essay is taken, I explore musical death in the context of *narcocorridos* and what I call *necrocorridos*. For a sample, see Josh Kun, "Death Rattle," *American Prospect*, January 5, 2012, http://prospect.org/article/death-rattle.

29. Yolanda Broyles-González, *Lydia Mendoza's Life in Music/La Historia de Lydia Mendoza: Norteño Tejano Legacies* (New York: Oxford University Press, 2001), 181–82.

30. Achille Mbembe, "Necropolitics," 51.

31. Thomas Dumm, *Loneliness as a Way of Life* (Cambridge: Harvard University Press, 2008).

32. For more on this work and Morales's entire *Contrabando* series, see Josh Kun, "Arts of Contraband: On Julio Cesar Morales' Contrabando at Frey Norris," in *Contrabando: Julio Cesar Morales*, April 2–May 28, 2011 (San Francisco: Wendy Norris Gallery, 2011), 3–4.

33. The longer version of this essay in my forthcoming project follows the sonidero impulse and the aesthetics of allá through other contemporary visual, sonic, and conceptual artists such as Gary Garay, Pedro Lasch, and Jace Clayton/DJ Rupture.

5 · SOUND LEGACY Elsie Houston

MICOL SEIGEL

Radio fans who tuned in to NBC Chicago round about 9:00 PM on a Monday night in the mid-1950s were treated to the silky voice of Etta Moten Barnett. In her weekly show *I Remember When*, Moten's aristocratic inflection and gorgeous bell tones pulled her guests into an intimacy evocative of a drawing-room tea. She turned advertisements into genteel advice, offered memories of people as if you, gentle listener, surely knew them too, and sang or played recordings of varied tunes. Moten's aim was not merely to entertain; she was a subtle cultural worker, weaving musical filaments into political messages about the beauty and value of African and African American culture, the advances black people were making worldwide, and the unity of humankind that ought to mitigate against racism in the United States. Moten was one of many such people in the United States and elsewhere who have placed hope in culture—and in music in particular—as a resource for political contestation.[1]

The relationship between music and politics is enormously important and complex. Music is a potent site of social engagement, but because the message of the medium is always contested—no one ever succeeds in defining, for all listeners and for all time, what a given piece or genre of music *means*—music can lend itself to a great range of projects. One can learn a great deal about activists or movements by looking at the ways they project their goals into the limpid mirror pools of music. One can also discern, by looking at the ways people use music to stake political claims, the contours of the contexts that make certain interventions possible on the one hand and needed on the other.

Etta Moten's radio program featured her travels throughout the Americas, and it occasionally played music by some of the musicians she encountered along the way. In her discussions of a Brazilian musician named Elsie Houston, an intriguing politics of memory emerges. Moten's citation of Houston reveals some underappreciated aspects of the possibilities and limits for Afro-diasporic solidarity across the Americas by allowing us to ask a series of questions about the musicians and musics that traveled across the Americas in the twentieth century. What conditions make it possible for musicians to cross national borders, visit other countries, and play, listen, and live abroad? How do the factors of race, nation, and empire intersect—here overlapping, there countervailing—to constrain travel for some and speed others along their way? If travel, as mobility, indexes other forms of privilege, what can travel tell us about the complex interweave of privileges structured by race, nation, and empire? Finally, at a scale that can see subjects working as conscious agents rather than passive objects of grand, anonymous webs, how do musicians actively use travel and music to intervene in the power relations of race, nation, and empire?

Following Moten to Houston leads us to and through these questions to Houston herself. The problem, and the fertile potential of arriving there, is that it offers no stopping point. Houston is a preternaturally kaleidoscopic figure, appearing one way here, another there. She was able to sidestep the categories projected onto her, occupy the liminal spaces in between, and negotiate possibilities with impressive skill. Ultimately, alas, Houston was unable to fulfill the ambitions she harbored for herself, and the end of her life story is tragic. That must remain in mind while we honor her accomplishments, lest we peer through over-rosy lenses. Thus qualified, following the ways Houston was represented in her day or memorialized after her death can reveal both the utility of music for political struggles and the stakes of those campaigns: the hopes for racial uplift and unity that inspired Etta Moten to play Houston's songs; the routes of empire that had earlier, in the 1920s and '30s, sent Houston to Paris and New York; and the currents of race and nation that made a group of Afro-Brazilians return to her work at the turn to the twentieth century. This essay winds through these sets of cultural politics, tracing the claims they staked on Houston's music and the contours of historical contexts they reveal.

Etta Remembers When

In her fifties in the '50s, when she created the radio show *I Remember When*, Moten played the mature doyenne, looking back and summing up the wisdom of her years. Although she would live another half century, Moten already had much to draw on from her limelit life: stage success on Broadway; roles written by Zora Neale Hurston, Langston Hughes, and George Gershwin (e.g., five years of knockout performances as the title female role in *Porgy and Bess*); tours across the United States and South America; concerts for presidents; a film career. She could reflect on travels to Africa with her husband, the Associated Negro Press founder Claude Barnett, where she met dignitaries and politicians of many newly independent nations. Increasingly activist as her fame grew, Moten played African instruments, lectured about the virtues of African and Afro-descended people, and imported their arts and crafts to her Harlem gallery.[2] Contributing to the New Negro cultural tapestry, Moten wove all this into an unquestionably political message about race and racism.

Some of the nuances of Moten's cultural politics emerge in her discussion of her 1936 tour to South America. Rio de Janeiro, she rhapsodized, was paradisiac. "If it were possible, all thoughts of home are almost blotted from your mind when you step off the boat in Rio de Janeiro, that beautiful, beautiful city," Moten thrilled. She adored the lights in the harbor, Corcovado, Sugarloaf, the sidewalks. Everywhere, she reported, "you walk on beauty, your eyes take in beauty, you breathe beauty."[3]

Rio was paradise with a purpose, of course. Moten's comfort in Brazil had as much to do with history as aesthetics: "You feel a kinship. I did. And you learn why. They have the same sort of history as ours, that is of the American Negro, the American of African descent. You have a feeling of being at home there, and I learned why. They too are of African descent, they were brought there by the Portuguese. They were emancipated a little bit after the American Negro was emancipated."[4] A shared past and common heritage, Moten offered, could ground a sense of identity; Moten invited her listeners to imagine the community of what we now call the African diaspora.

Moten's object in this transnational community building was domestic, of course, because she was speaking to U.S. lecture and radio listeners. She was arguing against racism at home by calling attention to the supposed lack of race hatred abroad. As she continued regarding the history of slavery in Brazil, "The only difference is that when they were emancipated, they became Brazilians. Period. No hyphenation or anything, just Brazilians." Moten offered a time-tested argument about the relative lack of racism in other countries: similarly constituted populations had yielded nonracist systems. Racism was neither natural nor necessary.[5]

Moten often avoided direct mention of "race" or "racism" in a curtsy to the codes of politeness that structured her genteel world. She dwelled instead on human "similarities and differences," often using these terms without naming any actual qualities people might share.[6] Moten developed this pointed yet vague strategy by discussing music, and its paradox is nowhere more clear than in her citation of a Brazilian artist who had died in 1943 and whom Moten invoked as a sister spirit: Elsie Houston. Houston and Moten had never met or even communicated directly. Houston by then had faded from prominence, making her all the more available for reframing.

Moten played Houston's recordings in order to compare "the spirituals of the American negro" with Brazilian folk genres. She introduced the South American musician as "one of the best exponents of Brazilian music, Elsie Houston, the Brazilian soprano." Despite the raceless descriptor, Moten made things clear to those who could hear such a message. She promised that Houston's recordings would show "the similarities" with African American musical forms, and she kindly requested her audience just to "see if you see some of these similarities." Moten sang "Nobody Knows [the Trouble I've Seen]" in her mellow, educated voice and then let Houston's voice fill the airwaves, singing Jaime Ovalle's "Aruanda."[7] "Did you see what I mean," Moten insists? "That was so similar."[8]

Perhaps. Equally mellow and nuanced, Houston's voice did have much in common with Moten's. Born one year apart, the two singers were both formally educated, classically trained, and keenly interested in what both called the "folk music" of their respective nations. The songs sound alike simply by virtue of their being performed by similar voices with minimal accompaniment.

Beyond that, Moten never specified what about the music one might find similar: meter, harmonic progressions, melodic range, instrumentation, rhythm, tonal alphabet? Moten was content to leave the substance of the similarity unclear while taking care to specify its source: "In most of the Brazilian music, similar to the Afro-American music, there is that blending of the fetish ritual of Africa with the Christian doctrine. In other words, you find a primitive beat underneath, and then the western feeling sometime in the melody or maybe with the text."[9] The difference Moten heard, and offered to her listeners to hear along with her, was less in the music than the social world that produced it.

Moten relied, for her alluring claims, on music's infinite openness to interpretation. Music is an eloquent form of communication, all the more because nowhere is there a single, agreed-upon, formalized, and codified syntax or grammar. No one controls musical interpretation, though many try. Musicologists define genres, but music as a whole exceeds and disobeys all strictures placed on it; it is constantly in flux. No sooner does "jazz" appear and seem coherent but it morphs into "hot," "Chicago," "bebop," "cool," "hard," and so on. Or polka, habanera, maxixe, tango, samba. Music evolves faster than language because it evades codification. Notational systems developed for one set of instruments or one tonal lexicon fail when applied to another. This "failure" is felicitous, ultimately: while no one would get much out of a long lecture in a language one did not understand, there is definite pleasure and gain in listening to music from distant places, peoples, or periods.

The apparent accessibility of music is misleading, however. Consider how difficult it is to translate from concepts to language, how wide the gap between the object signified and its signifier. Now consider how difficult it is to translate between the even more distant worlds of language and music. Music has no direct relationship to objects or concepts; it is untethered and impossible to secure. Perhaps that is as close to a definition of "the aesthetic" as we ever need to get. But continue: the sign-object gap doubles when you add in a foreign language; translation between languages is notorious as an endeavor fraught with projection and approximation. How enormous, how yawning, then, is the abyss between the set of signs-signifieds of one language and a musical system from a distant place with different cultural texture and an entirely unlike set of musical practices and forms. No equivalences can be drawn. There is only a wide-open field for interpretation. Music from somewhere else offers a Rorschach blot of the highest order.

No wonder, then, that there is so much interest in music as evidence. It can support any case one might like to make. Music is particularly favored stuff for the illustration of racial and national essences.[10] It is a form that has long seemed to offer lessons about these social categories. Musicians are particularly good objects for projection—and subjects of their own representation, if they are agile. Houston was one such subject, burdened with projections from the moment of her emergence during the 1920s jazz age, all the way up to today, and also fantastically strategic in her negotiation of the possibilities this projection offered up to her.

Moten's deployment of Houston to suggest commonalities across the African diaspora is justified in some ways and misleading in others. Certainly Brazil and the United States do share certain cultural threads thanks to the influx of African people during slavery and since. Music is undeniably one of the most important sites of this sharing. Elsie Houston did enjoy some elements of background and upbringing in common with Etta Moten, including some unquantifiable measure of African descent. Moreover, there is justification, regardless of "truth," in Moten's just motives and worthy intent. Yet to conflate the two artists in identifications, intentions, or the ways they lived (and died) is not simply to miss the singularity and genius of each. It is also to miss the important differences in their respective contexts, including the ways race and nation functioned to structure their experiences and possibilities. Moten survived to a rare, hearty old age while Houston left us too young; Moten found venues for the kinds of performances she wanted to offer while Houston was forced into unbearable compromises; Moten is widely and fondly remembered while Houston has a tiny, if devoted, coterie.[11]

For the Record

Elsie Houston was born in 1902 in Rio de Janeiro. Her father, a dentist from Tennessee, was one of the disaffected confederates who fled to Brazil after the Civil War. He married a Brazilian woman and settled with her in Rio to practice dentistry, joining the city's cultural elite.[12] As befit the child of an august family, Elsie Houston traveled to Europe in her twenties for classical music training and the Parisian finish so highly valued by her class compatriots.[13] There she performed, socialized, or trained with high-powered intellectuals and artists including the Brazilian composers Luciano Gallet and Heitor Villa-Lobos, the German soprano Lilli Lehmann, the Brazilian modernist writer Mário de Andrade, the French actor-director Lugné Poe, the French soprano Ninon Vallin, the Polish pianist Artur Rubinstein, and the French surrealist writer Benjamin Péret, whom Houston married in 1927.

Like other elite Brazilians with modernist leanings in the '20s, Houston encountered futurism, surrealism, and the "Negro Vogue," and she found her attention directed to the folkloric forms of Brazil, including Afro-Brazilian traditions.[14] These she treated with enthusiastic distance and clear elitist inflection.[15] Although Houston's views and politics are difficult to discern exactly, she seems to have shared the hopes vested in primitive and modern art in that era.[16] After World War I, many people yearned to entrust cultural approximation with the task of diminishing the hatred that had ignited that devastating conflict. Modernists in Europe and the Americas set this hope to music and prose, producing art with a politicized message of cultural relativism and tolerance.[17]

If the '20s were a heady time for Houston, the '30s seem to have been less joyous. Houston's relationship with Péret was rocky, according to friends. Her sister remembered that "Benjamin didn't like music. He got in the way of her studies."[18] In 1933, after the birth of their son, Houston left Péret. She was back and forth between Brazil and Paris over the next few years and then in 1937 she headed to New York, where she would spend most of the rest of her numbered days.[19]

In the United States, Houston led a very different sort of life than she had in Paris. She still ran with a crowd of left, transnational intellectuals, such as the writer Jane Bowles and the composer Paul Bowles, and Carl Van Vechten, the writer and photographer, who produced several photographic portraits of her.[20] The Bowleses and Van Vechten were part of New York's Greenwich Village bohemian scene, and Van Vechten, author of a controversial novel about black New York, enjoyed many connections to Harlem Renaissance figures whom he befriended and photographed. Van Vechten, the Bowleses, and the composer Virgil Thomson, a great fan of Houston's, were members of Kirk Askew's Harlem-oriented salon, a probable route of introduction for Houston to New York avant-garde art spaces, including the outer ripples of New Negro or Harlem Renaissance circles.[21]

Still, it is important not to assume that Houston identified herself as Negro or that others identified her as such. Houston did not simply become black under the aegis of the one-drop rule. Her racial position, already complex, shifted newly when she arrived in the Empire City. Her national and class positions shaped the interpretation of her racial self, and all those social categories shifted in tandem with gender.

In New York, forgoing the authorial stance of composer or intellectual, Houston became primarily a performer. If this was a role more feminized than those she had previously been interested to play, it was not necessarily more passive: Houston was an energetic and dedicated stage presence, sustaining a calendar impressive for its intensity and the range of types of programs offered.[22] She appeared in formal, classical-music concert halls in solo recital and with elite orchestras, for charity benefits, live on the radio, and in New York's lush nightclubs, such as the Rainbow Room or the "chichi" Upper East Side Le Ruban Bleu.[23] Houston became a favorite ingredient in the saucy pan-American programs that crossed high/low cultural divides, from the Brazilian Music Festival at the Museum of Modern Art, to the Pan-American Union's free outdoor concerts in Washington, DC, to the New York World's Fair.[24]

This last category of performance is the most revealing of the context for Houston's U.S. stay. As the deep shadows of the Depression, the Third Reich, and increasingly rigid Jim Crow segregation lengthened, the United States worked to bolster its place in the hemisphere with the Good Neighbor policy, a "passionate courtship of Latin America" by the U.S. federal government, which translated trade pacts into "the universal language of the conga drums."[25] In this political-ideological context, Houston's expertise in Brazilian folklore no longer granted her the status of vanguard intellectual. Instead it framed her as a native informant, an "authentic" representative of a fascinatingly exotic form.[26] Drawn into the cultural field of U.S. imperialism, Houston resisted in some ways, and in others she worked doggedly to make it her own. In the glare of Good Neighbor footlights, Houston performed an "authentic" Brazil.

In Houston's first year in the United States, she usually programmed both French and Brazilian songs. North American audiences quickly demonstrated their preferences. In a 1938 solo recital, "particularly in the songs of her own land, Miss Houston's singing was cordially received."[27] A month later at Le Ruban Bleu, Houston's fans knew what they wanted to hear from her. "In Paris and New York she has quite a following which is not shy in asking for its favorites, including her unusual Brazilian incantation."[28]

Houston adapted her repertoire to highlight the quasi-religious "incantation," and reviewers began to praise what they called her "voodoo songs." In an otherwise biting review of a 1940 multiartist show, a critic found "the one bright spot" in Houston; "her Voodoo songs supplied the only pleasurable event of the series. They had definite musical interest, and she sang them with her familiar but unforgettable magic."[29] Another dour critic found an entire Museum of Modern Art (MOMA) concert series lifeless, "except for one inspired moment . . . when Elsie Houston went into her Voodoo act by candle light."[30] Upon her death, newspapers would call her specialty "Brazilian folksongs of the voodoo variety."[31] Houston must have grimaced and sung loudly to drown out her own highly precise understanding of distinctions among the various popular forms she had studied.[32]

As Houston put "voodoo songs" in her programs, the word "exotic" began to appear to describe her. She programmed such songs for her solo appearance with the prestigious National Symphony in Washington, DC, in 1941, and in a radio interview there a year later, the host advertised her as the "exotic Brazilian soprano and voodoo singer, soloist with the National Symphony Orchestra at the Watergate Pan-American program."[33] One reviewer called her *intervals* exotic; another described a colleague, Olga Coelho, as "less exotic, less colorful" than Houston and "a singer of subtlety and grace."[34] As one might imagine, Coelho's looks tended to the fair, spare, angular end of the spectrum.

Houston's sexuality was significant to her U.S. reception. Rarely did she smile for the camera. In photo after photo, she peers out from heavily kohled lids with lips pressed firmly together, as if immobilized by the weight of the jewels in her ears and the wisdom of the ages. Houston was not asexual—not at all. In her candlelit "voodoo act," drumming to accompany her own singing, Houston smoldered with the self-aware maturity of the priestess, long past the stage of the virginal novice. What a striking contrast Houston's gender expression offers to Etta Moten's chaste, gracious womanliness defined by the careful propriety of her class aspirations. Houston well understood that the Good Neighbor policy relied on and fed a vision of nations as sexed and as engaging in lubriciously anthropomorphic "relations," but she deftly sidestepped the full weight of the resultant expectations.

Along with her refusal of the infantilization of a conventional femininity, Houston refused to be treated as a social inferior. As a deeply aristocratic person, she may have been unprepared for the social reevaluation her "voodoo act" imposed, but she quickly grasped its effect and responded. By 1941 Houston was no longer content to describe her father as a dentist of the Tennessee Houstons and her mother as "a Brazilian girl" he married. Modifiers in captions and press coverage began to ratchet up her class position: "Elsie Houston, singer ambassadress between the Americas, is a Brazilian by birth, Baroness Marcel de Courbon in private life and a great-great-grandniece of Sam Houston, first president of Texas."[35] The Sam Houston affiliation began to crop up regularly, and her mother became a member of "a distinguished Spanish family" or from "Portuguese aristocrats who settled in Brazil 300 years ago."[36]

Houston's deepest refusal to conform to expectations was a refusal to be any single thing at all. Houston was literally a changeling. A writer who likened her to "an African queen" also characterized her features as "Mayan" (any American indigenous group in a pinch) and described her skin as "oily and watery," combining two things that notoriously do not mix. Then again, he remembered her appearance with difficulty. It "changed from time to time," he observed, flagging Houston's fluid self-presentation.[37] She often earned oxymoronic accolades, such as the praise of one reviewer for her "familiar but unforgettable magic."[38] Another reporter sounded similar notes in a 1940 review: "One cannot discuss Miss Houston's songs in detail, though they were very striking in most instances. Nor is her remarkable delivery of them easy to describe."[39] Houston defied description.

Importantly, Houston was not locked into the social category one might expect from "an African queen" in the interwar United States. Houston surely understood the social and professional consequences of the label "Negro." Most of the time, Houston succeeded in keeping it off her back by performing a quality ("Brazil") that could elude U.S. racial categories. Reviewing Le Ruban Bleu, a critic listed "Elsie Houston, Brazilian singer; Marie Eve, Swiss mimic, and Jimmy Daniels, Negro, singer, late of Paris."[40] Something about Houston—perhaps simply the "Brazilian" taking up the space where another adjective might have fit—held the reviewer's pen. There were, however, telling exceptions. On the occasion of the 1940 Festival of Brazilian Music at MOMA, José Ramos Tinhorão, a nationalist Euro-Brazilian music critic, denounced her as "the American mulatta Elsie Houston, born in Brazil by chance."[41] This little bullet of vitriol, intended primarily to insult, parts the curtains of the codes of politeness that kept the blackness of this daughter of the elite unspoken. It would be fascinating to know what prompted it, beyond resentment of Houston's transcendence of national boundaries, which Tinhorão devoted his life to reinforcing.

In one sense, Tinhorão's ill-intended caption was correct: Houston made her career by performing, for elite North American and European audiences, "authentic" Brazilian folklore, when her claims to authenticity were threadbare. She was born in her nation's capital, a most urban locale from which to launch an exploration of the rural forms of folklore, and it was Houston's experience of Paris in the 1920s that catalyzed her turn to Brazilian popular forms: her Brazilianness was mediated by Europe. What is more, Houston had U.S. nationality through her father and probably French through Péret.[42] Still, it would be difficult to imagine a more faithful or expert elite exponent of these forms. Houston's "inauthenticity" proves primarily the impossibility and irrelevance of authenticity itself.

Houston's determined fluidity refused, overall, to fit expectations dumped onto the shoulders of dark-skinned women associated with exotic else-wheres. She knew perfectly well what those expectations were, all her careful self-presentation confirms, though she kept it under wraps. "She has some very sharp opinions on foreign affairs which she wouldn't divulge," the *Washington Post* once complained.[43] Houston chided U.S. musicians for failing to appreciate their folk form, "Negro music,"[44] but did not identify herself with it. As she told another reporter, "Jazz has done much to help South Americans understand people here, and South American music played in the United States is helping you to know us."[45] Houston praised jazz and "Negro" music while claiming for herself the broadest possible speaking position, a collective "us" not just from Brazil but from all of South America.

Houston's broad and mobile identifications seem to have left her no solid ground. As one of her fans wrote, when Houston left Paris for New York, "she turned back to her hemisphere, not wholly home."[46] For Elsie Houston, there *was* no place called "home." In early 1943, with a brace of concerts re-cently completed and more in the works, Houston took her own life. Friends blamed financial concerns and the "humiliations" of nightclub work, ways of noting that conditions in New York during the war ultimately prohibited Houston from carving out the elite concert space she wanted for her folkloric interpretations. Houston's death reveals the pain of her position in a foreign culture industry that did not fully appreciate her talents, the strains of contesting gender conventions, and the foundering of Houston's own elite expectations on the shoals of New York's particular racializations. How bewildering, how exhausting it must have been, even for this dynamo, to navigate two imperial formations, multiple nationalisms, and the shifting valence of race across time (the '20s to the '30s) and space (Rio, Paris, New York). How unfair that some of the misrecognitions that plagued her during her life survive in the ways Houston is remembered.

Etta Moten's memory of Houston extends some of these misrecognitions and reveals one set of guiding lines. Moten suffered the racial constraints that also penned in Elsie Houston, but she negotiated them differently, in part due to her metropolitan location. From her (relatively) secure position Moten was able to lean out, reaching over U.S. borders to borrow examples from afar. While she worked with the best of intentions and to much excel-lent effect, Moten's imperial posture inadvertently reproduced some of the ideological conditions that contribute to antiblackness, for imperialism and racism are irrevocably intertwined. The effect was worse for those on the receiving ends of both, where Houston stood, though Moten never intended to hurt people such as Houston. She would have been horrified at the thought, as Moten thought of herself as profoundly *like* Houston.

Why, Moten had even played a Brazilian—an Afro-Brazilian, at that—on the big screen. In 1933, singing the "Carioca" for the big dance number in *Flying Down to Rio*, filmed in Hollywood, Moten swayed with a basket of fruit on her head. She anticipated Carmen Miranda's U.S. appearance by a half decade, delighting Brazilian fans (she later learned). That was the source of her invitation to South America, where she learned that she had played "something called a Baiana." Bahia, she explained on the radio, was a state in "the north of Brazil, which is similar to the south of the United States, in that the folk music of Brazil comes from the north."[47] When Moten said "folk," she meant "black," whereas Houston, who also sang Brazilian folk music on U.S. stages, defined the category like the professional musicologist she was. Houston's "folk" was not a racially specific euphemism. It was also not a category she embraced as part of her own identity. Yet she was unable to prevent U.S. audiences from seeing her that way, or Moten from tapping her posthumously as such.

If Moten insisted on Houston's blackness, projecting a quality Houston would not have recognized, she refused another that Houston would have preferred her to see: Moten failed to divulge to her radio audiences that Houston was her cosmopolitan peer. Moten never mentioned that Houston was highly educated, had studied in Paris, had lived in New York. These details would have cast doubt on Houston's native-folk authenticity, so key to the argument Moten wanted to make (and believe) about New World Africanisms in art.

Moten did not—could not—realize that Houston too was playing an Afro-Brazilian. When Houston appeared as such on stage or on the air, she was obscuring her French and North American citizenship and wide class-mitigated leeway in racial definition. Houston understood the changing spectacularity of her self-presentation, and she milked her appeal and authority as a citizen of Brazil with claims on North America, a foot in the African diaspora, knowledge of "civilized Europe," and an authentic and expert vehicle for the vicarious experience of the exotic. As a result she was always (Afro-)Brazilian as excess: in superfluous and highly contrived, performative ways; in stunningly convincing and compelling ways. Houston's various Brazilian, Afro-Brazilian, even *uber*-Brazilian personae confirm not the particulars of her given identities but instead that "all race identity is . . . the product of passing"; Houston's acts of life, like deliberate drag, reveal not only "the imitative structure of gender" but also that of race and nation.[48]

Rerelease

In 2003, the Brazilian record label Atração Fonográfica rereleased fourteen of Elsie Houston's recordings under the title *A Feminilidade do Canto* (*The Femininity of Song*).[49] The CD coincided with a huge government- and corporate-sponsored exposition of Afro-Brazilian history and culture originally curated for the Museu Afro Brasil. "The show rescues the heritage of slavery and the Luso-Afro-Brazilian imagination," proclaimed one of the museums that received the traveling exhibition; its "nearly 600 sculptures, paintings, photographs, films, [and] silver and gold objects, show the saga of Africans and their descendants in Brazil from the early 16th century to the present day."[50] Houston's "rescue" from obscurity was a small part of this massive labor of revindication and ideological resituation; Houston's memory in this forum shows once again somewhat more about the platform her music provided for cultural politics than some revelation of the "truth" of her life.

The CD title, *The Femininity of Song*, is quite odd, given Houston's highly unconventional femininity. The essays in the book published along with the CD invoke gender only secondarily, focusing instead on Houston's devotion to Brazilian national culture. Illustrative is the introductory essay to the collection by the artist Emanoel Araújo, director of the São Paulo Museu Afro Brasil. Araújo's essay sandwiches statements about Houston's blackness between mitigating gestures to nation and the transnational sphere, all heavily inflected by gender. It places Houston in the movement "to recuperate and revalorize all things *national*" focused on "pure Brazilian subjects" (*temas de pura brasilidade*) via folklore. Her "profound and concerned search for our roots" worked to promote "the art of the people." Araújo praised Houston in telling terms. She "impregnate[d] into the legitimately popular songs which she incorporated into her repertoire, many of which she collected herself, the coyness and cunning that only her mestiza voice managed to stamp on the limpid, clear modulations of the extraordinary singing of this Brazilian soprano, acclaimed in Europe and the U.S. between the 1920s and the early '40s." Houston's originality, Araújo concluded, "carries the mark of the ancestry and the magic of Africa which is within us all."[51]

For Araújo, Houston's musical value hinges on race. He situates Houston, via her music, as that quintessential agent of racial mixture, the mixed-race woman. He ends with an unusually explicit statement marking Houston as Afro-descended, circumscribing that possibly off-putting identification by ascribing African heritage to every reader willing to enter the final, generous "us." The other pieces in the volume toe the same fine line between naming Houston's African ancestry but then insisting on her patriotism, touching the question of race but then retreating to the promise of nation, with cordiality and access to all. Nothing confirms the irony of this position more than the involvement of Tinhorão, the music critic who hated Houston in her lifetime. Tinhorão, it turned out, owned some of the only surviving copies of Houston's songs, and he lent them to the organizers for remastering; they thank him in the text with no sense of paradox.

A Feminilidade do Canto features Houston in the service of the contemporary project of situating Afro-Brazilian figures as national heroes, a brick in the edifice of the neo-racial democracy that has brought notions of Brazilian racial harmony back to the fore in academic as well as popular circles. This version of Houston, dedicated to a quiescent, reactionary nationalism, must ignore her foreign parentage and marriage and her several willing exiles, first in Paris and then in New York.

For these curators, Houston is the patriot who confirms the Brazilianness of blackness. For New York nightclub audiences in the 1930s and '40s, Houston was the delicious exotic, available for their delectation. For Parisian modernists, her quintessential Brazilian roots incarnated surrealist politics. For Etta Moten and her New Negro listeners, she personified the changing same of a blackness allied in the drive for racial peace. Houston was all of these things and none, conscripted for service to other people's cultural politics thanks to her eminently interpretable categorical liminality and the illusory lucidity of music. The work Houston's persona as symbol performed also reveals the political currents shaping those projects, because activists cited her music to combat imperialism or racism or to support certain strains of nationalism. Some of those currents lifted Houston's sails, namely the imperial trade winds that sent her first to Paris, then to New York, but in other ways Houston was cruelly buffeted by those same streams, in the form of the racist exoticism that barred her from full professional expression on U.S. stages. Likewise Etta Moten drew on imperial currents for her travels, exercising some of the privileges of empire even as she fought its racist matrix, and the Museu Afro Brasil drew on the transnational contexts shaping Brazilian nationalism to argue against racism within the borders of their struggle as they saw it. Houston's gift to social analysis is this set of insights regarding the interlaced and overlapping projects of U.S. and European empire, U.S. black cultural politics, and Brazilian neoracial democracy, and, more abstractly, the political valence of music itself.

NOTES

1. Thanks to the organizers of the Music-Race-Empire conference in Madison, Teju Olaniyan, Ronald Radano, and Scott Carter, as well as all the participants in that wonderfully fruitful workshop; the knowledgeable archivists of the Schomburg Center for Research in Black Culture; and to Peter Oehlkers, whose erudite fandom of Elsie Houston is inspiring. Also thanks for support for this article to Libby Ginway, Davarian Baldwin, Minkah Makalani, and Sarah Zanti.

2. Nora Holt, "Music," *New York New Amsterdam News* (*NYNAN*), April 3, 1948, 4; "Etta Moten Talks on African Trip," *NYNAN*, November 4, 1950, 7; "Etta Moten to Speak in Queens," *NYNAN*, April 26, 1958, 24; "New Program Eyes Women in Nigeria," *NYNAN*, April 16, 1961, 19; Sara Slack, "Sara Speaking," *NYNAN*, February 13, 1971, 6; "800 Admired, Many Bought at 4-Day Show," *NYNAN*, August 12, 1950, 16.

3. "Orchids in the Moonlight," side 2, no. 1 of *Etta Moten Barnett's Return to the United States* (Chicago: WMAQ Radio, 1955), sound recording, New York Public Library, Schomburg Branch, Recorded Sound Division. The second phrase, "your eyes take in beauty," is a slight paraphrase necessary due to conditions in the archive. The other quotes are accurate.

4. Ibid.

5. North American antiracists, from abolitionists to Black Power theorists, have made this point using Brazil as counterpoint, and Brazil is only one of many locations that have served this logic. David J. Hellwig, ed., *African-American Reflections on Brazil's Racial Paradise* (Philadelphia: Temple University Press, 1992); Micol Seigel, "Beyond Compare: Historical Method after the Transnational Turn," *Radical History Review* 91 (Winter 2005): 62–90; Seigel, *Uneven Encounters: Making Race and Nation in Brazil and the United States* (Durham: Duke University Press, 2009).

6. "Orchids in the Moonlight"; see also "With the Art Van Dam Quintet," side 2, no. 2, of *Etta Moten Barnett's Return to the United States.*

7. "Aruanda," on *Elsie Houston Sings Brazilian Songs* (New York: RCA Victor, 1954). For this match, thanks to Peter Oehlkers, electronic communication, June 10, 2011. On Ovalle, an erudite, bohemian Rio de Janeiro composer, see *Dicionário Cravo Albin da música popular Brasileira*, s.v. "Jaime Ovalle" (Rio de Janeiro: Instituto Cultural Cravo Albin, 2002–11), accessed June 10, 2011, www.dicionariompb.com.br/jaime-ovalle.

8. "With the Art Van Dam Quintet."

9. Ibid.

10. Micol Seigel, "The Disappearing Dance: Maxixe's Imperial Erasure," *Black Music Research Journal* 25, nos. 1/2 (Spring/Fall 2005): 93–117.

11. Here I reiterate thanks to Peter Oehlkers (Robert Porter), curator of a wonderful annotated web biography of Houston, *The Annotated "Ends Her Life: Elsie Houston,"* accessed June 11, 2011, http://home.comcast.net/~gullcity/elsiehouston/Houston.html.

See also Oehlkers, *Robert's Basement,* http://robertsbasement.blogspot.com. Deep thanks to Oehlkers for sharing his careful and minute research.

12. "Notes from My Talk with Captain Geyser Péret," interview by M. Elizabeth Ginway, São Paulo, June 9, 1983, 3. Many thanks to Ginway for invaluable assistance on this material, including sharing her research and interview notes.

13. Jeffrey D. Needell, *A Tropical Belle Epoque: The Elite Culture of Turn-of-the-Century Rio de Janeiro* (New York: Cambridge University Press, 1987); "Conversa com Mary Houston Pedrosa," interview by M. Elizabeth Ginway, Rio de Janeiro, March 17, 1983, 1. On Elsie's place among Brazilian artistic elites, see Aracy A. Amaral, *Tarsila: Sua vida, sua obra* (São Paulo: Perspectiva, 1975), 327n25; and with Patrícia Galvão (Pagu) in K. David Jackson, "Alienation and Ideology in *A Famosa Revista* (1945)," *Hispania* 74, no. 2 (May 1991): 298–304.

14. Jody Blake, *Le tumulte noir: Modernist Art and Popular Entertainment in Jazz-Age Paris, 1900–1930* (University Park: Pennsylvania State University Press, 1999); Karen C. C. Dalton and Henry Louis Gates Jr., "Josephine Baker and Paul Colin: African American Dance Seen through Parisian Eyes," *Critical Inquiry* 24, no. 4 (Summer 1998): 903–34; Tyler Stovall, *Paris Noir: African Americans in the City of Light* (Boston: Houghton Mifflin, 1996); Michel Fabre, *From Harlem to Paris: Black American Writers in France, 1840–1980* (Urbana: University of Illinois Press, 1991); Mariana Torgovnick, *Gone Primitive: Savage Intellects, Modern Lives* (Chicago: University of Chicago Press, 1990); Philippe Dewitte, *Les mouvements nègres en France pendant les entre-deux-guerres* (Paris: Harmattan, 1985); Mário da Silva Brito, *História do modernismo Brasileiro,* vol. 1 of *Antecendentes da semana de Arte Moderna,* 6th ed. (1978; repr., Rio de Janeiro: Civilização Brasileira, 1997); Amaral, *Tarsila;* Aracy A. Amaral, *Blaise Cendrars no Brasil e os modernistas* (Rio de Janeiro: Livraria Martins Editora, 1970); Blaise Cendrars, *Etc., etc.,* . . . *um livro 100% Brasileiro* (São Paulo: Editora Perspectiva, 1976); Blaise Cendrars, *Histoires Vraies* (Paris: Bernard Grasset, 1927); Darius Milhaud, *Notes without Music* (1952; repr., New York: Knopf, 1953); Wilson Martins, *O Modernismo (1916–1945),* vol. 6 of *A Literatura Brasileira,* 4th ed. (São Paulo: Editora Cultrix, 1973).

15. Elsie Houston, "La musique, la danse et les cérémonies populaires du Brésil," in *Art populaire: Travaux artistiques et scientifiques du 1er Congrès international des arts populaires, Prague, 1928* (Paris: Duchartre, 1931), 162–64; Elsie Houston, *Chants Populaires du Brésil,* 1ère série (Paris: Librairie Orientaliste Paul Geuthner, 1930). Houston expressed a similar elitism in "Na civilisáda Europa os rythmos da musica Negra, provocam enthusiasmo e reclamam applausos," *Progresso,* March 24, 1929, 1.

16. Earl Warner, "Cavalcade of Songs Tells Story of America's Past," *Daily Worker,* June 7, 1941; "Programs of the Week," *New York Times* (*NYT*), April 28, 1940, 122; "Benefit Takes Form of a Bassinet Dance," *NYT,* November 20, 1938, 46. In 1941, a *Washington Post* reporter complained that Houston would not share her political opinions: "Brazilian Diva Says Music'll Unite Americas," *Washington Post,* July 24, 1941, 17. Paul Bowles claimed Houston avoided talking politics because she was a Trotskyist: Bowles, *Without Stopping: An Autobiography* (New York: Ecco, 1985), 211, cited in Peter Oehlkers (Robert Porter), "Paul Bowles and Elsie Houston," *Robert's Basement,*

accessed June 9, 2011, http://robertsbasement.blogspot.com/2005/11/paul-bowles-and
-elsie-houston.html.

17. Elizabeth M. Ginway, "Surrealist Benjamin Péret and Brazilian Modernism," *Hispania* 75, no. 3 (September 1992): 543–53; Jacqueline Chénieux-Gendron, "Surrealists in Exile: Another Kind of Resistance," *Poetics Today* 17, no. 3 (Fall 1996): 437–51; Mary Ann Caws, "Péret's 'Amour sublime'—Just Another 'Amour fou'?" *French Review* 40, no. 2 (November 1966): 204–12; Marie-Denise Shelton, "Le monde noir dans la littérature dadaiste et surréaliste," *French Review* 57, no. 3 (February 1984): 320–28; Robin D. G. Kelley, "A Poetics of Anticolonialism," *Monthly Review* (November 1999), www.monthlyreview
.org/1199kell.htm; Brent Hayes Edwards, *The Practice of Diaspora: Literature, Translation, and the Rise of Black Internationalism* (Cambridge: Harvard University Press, 2003); Sidra Stich, *Anxious Visions: Surrealist Art* (New York: University Art Museum; Abbeville, 1990).

18. "Conversa com Mary Houston Pedrosa," 2.

19. Tarsila mentions a concert by Elsie Houston that seems to have been in Brazil in 1933; see Amaral, *Tarsila*, 341n6. On the trip in 1939, see Gregóire de Villa-Franca and Maria Lucia Montes, eds., *Elsie Houston/A Feminilidade do Canto*, liner notes booklet to album of the same name (São Paulo: Grupo Takano, 2003), n.p. (unpaginated; my page count: 16, 22).

20. Oehlkers, *Annotated "Ends Her Life,"* accessed June 11, 2011. See also Oehlkers, *Robert's Basement*. Three of the portraits are Lot 12735, nos. 536, 537, and 538 in the Carl Van Vechten Collection of the Library of Congress Prints and Photographs Division.

21. Peter Oehlkers, electronic communication with author, June 14, 2011, citing in part Anthony Tommasini, *Virgil Thomson: Composer on the Aisle* (New York: W. W. Norton, 1997).

22. Houston's U.S. performances bridge two long gaps: for all of 1939 and then the second half of 1942, the U.S. press was silent about her. She was apparently in Brazil in 1939. The writer Patrícia Galvão (Pagu) included in her novel *A Famosa Revista* a lightly fictionalized account of a visit Houston paid Pagu in jail in 1939. See Jackson, "Alienation and Ideology," 301, 303n17.

23. "Music Notes," *NYT*, November 19, 1937, 26; "Latins Take Broadway by Storm," *WP*, April 27, 1941, L9; "Elsie Houston of Brazil Heard," in "Music in Review," *NYT*, February 7, 1938, 10; "Composers' Group in Concert Here," *NYT*, March 11, 1940, 17; "Spanish Program Heard at Stadium," *NYT*, July 15, 1940, 20; Arthur Cohn, "Philadelphia Story," *Modern Music* 19, no. 3 (March–April 1942): 187–89; Donald Fuller, "Forecast and Review: Americans to the Fore—New York, 1941–42," *Modern Music* 19, no. 2 (January–February 1942): 109–15; "Elsie Houston Soloist; Offers Latin-American Songs at Young People's Concert," *NYT*, January 17, 1943, 41; "Benefit Takes Form of a Bassinet Dance"; "Programs of the Week," *NYT*, April 28, 1940; "Radio Programs Scheduled for Broadcast This Week," *NYT*, January 2, 1938, 11; "Today on the Radio," *NYT*, January 6, 1938, 42; "Pan-American Talks Open," *NYT*, March 4, 1938, 6; Jack Gould, "News of the Night Clubs," *NYT*, January 2, 1938, 2; "News and Gossip of the Night Clubs," *NYT*, March 6, 1938, 150; "At the Night Clubs; Hotels," *NYT*, October 26, 1940, 18; "The Night Clubs during November," *NYT*, November 2, 1940, 18; "News of the Night Clubs," *NYT*, February 14, 1943, X2.

24. "Pan-American Talks Open"; "Festival of Brazilian Music" [at the MOMA], *NYT*, October 6, 1940, 138; "Villa-Lobos Music Heard at Festival; Works of a Brazilian Composer on Second Program of Fete at Museum of Modern Art; Elsie Houston a Soloist," *NYT*, October 19, 1940, 24; "Brazilian Music on the Air," *NYT*, November 10, 1940, 158, cited in Oehlkers, *Annotated "Ends Her Life"*; "Night of Americas Voices Unity Theme; Diplomacy and Arts Join in Hemisphere Program Here," *NYT*, February 15, 1943, 12; "Music of the Week," *NYT*, February 14, 1943, x6; "Americas Night Tomorrow," *NYT*, February 13, 1943, 8.

25. Davidson Taylor, "The Enduring Elsie Houston," *Saturday Review*, July 31, 1954, 55; "Latins Take Broadway."

26. Although Antônio Pedro Tota claims she was represented as a "more erudite" version of "the same sensuality" as other Latin Americans in New York: Tota, *O imperialismo sedutor: A americanização do Brasil na época da segunda guerra* (São Paulo: Companhia das Letras, 2000), quoted in Gisela Cramer, "How to Do Things with Waves," in *Media, Sound and Culture in Latin America and the Caribbean*, ed. Alejandra Bronfman and Andrew Grant Wood (Pittsburgh: University of Pittsburgh Press, 2012), 50.

27. "Elsie Houston of Brazil Heard," in "Music in Review: Segovia, Guitarist, Heard—Enesco Offers 'Emperor' Concerto—Modern Works Given—Other Programs," *NYT*, February 7, 1938, 10.

28. "News and Gossip of the Night Clubs." Villa-Franca and Montes also note this shift from erudite to folkloric music while in the United States: "Elsie Houston," 21.

29. Colin McPhee, "Jungles of Brazil," *Modern Music* 18, no. 1 (November–December 1940): 42.

30. Minna Lederman, "Museum Pieces," *Modern Music* 18, no. 4 (May–June 1941): 265. See also "News of the Night Clubs," *NYT*, February 14, 1943.

31. "Brazilian Soprano Is Found Dead Here," *NYT*, February 21, 1943, 20; "Elsie Houston: Noted Singer Dead; Listed as Suicide," *Washington Post*, February 21, 1943, 14.

32. On *voudun* and *candomblé* or *macumba*, see Melville J. Herskovits, "African Gods and Catholic Saints in New World Negro Belief," *American Anthropologist* 39 (1937): 635–43; and later, Roger Bastide, *Les Ameriques noires: Les civilisations africaines dans le nouveau monde* (Paris: Payot, 1967); and Pierre Verger, "Book Review of Alfred Metraux, *Voodoo in Haiti*," *Man* 60 (July 1960): 111–12.

33. "Brazilian Girl to Sing with National Symphony," *Christian Science Monitor*, July 16, 1941, 16; "Hearing Ahead," *Washington Post*, July 19, 1942, L4.

34. "Composers' Group in Concert Here"; Colin McPhee, "Scores and Records," *Modern Music* 22, no. 1 (November–December 1944): 59.

35. "Elsie Houston, Singer Ambassadress," photo (Marcus Blechman, photo credit), *Theatre Arts*, April 1942, 279. In Houston's *NYT* obituary, Marcel Courbon (no "de") was identified as a "friend."

36. "Brazilian Girl to Sing with National Symphony"; "Elsie Houston: Noted Singer Dead."

37. Taylor, "The Enduring Elsie Houston."

38. McPhee, "Scores and Records," 42.

39. "Composers' Group in Concert Here."

40. Gould, "News of the Night Clubs."

41. José Ramos Tinhorão, *O samba agora vai . . . a farsa da música popular no exterior* (Rio de Janeiro: JCM Editôres, 1969), 40.

42. Houston's death certificate listed her as a U.S. citizen. Borough of Manhattan death certificate no. 4387, Municipal Archives, 31 Chambers Street, New York City.

43. "Brazilian Diva Says Music'll Unite Americas."

44. "Brazilian Music on the Air."

45. "Brazilian Diva Says Music'll Unite Americas."

46. Taylor, "The Enduring Elsie Houston."

47. "With the Art Van Dam Quintet."

48. Samira Kawash, "*The Autobiography of an Ex-Coloured Man*: (Passing for) Black Passing for White," in *Passing and the Fictions of Identity*, ed. Elaine K. Ginsberg (Durham: Duke University Press, 1996), 70; Judith Butler, "Imitation and Gender Insubordination," in *The Lesbian and Gay Studies Reader*, ed. Henry Abelove, Michèle Aina Barale, and David M. Halperin (New York: Routledge, 1993), 307–20; Butler, *Bodies That Matter: On the Discursive Limits of "Sex"* (New York: Routledge, 1993); Butler, *Gender Trouble: Feminism and the Subversion of Identity* (New York: Routledge, 1990), 137; Harryette Mullen, "Optic White: Blackness and the Production of Whiteness," *diacritics* 24, nos. 2–3 (1994): 74–89.

49. Emanoel Araújo, *A Feminilidade do Canto* (São Paulo: Atração Fonográfica, 2003).

50. "Para nunca esquecer: Negras memórias, memórias de negros," Museu Oscar Niemeyer Online, accessed January 15, 2011, www.pr.gov.br/mon/exposicoes/negras.htm.

51. Emanoel Araújo, "Elsie x Abigail," in Villa-Franca and Montes, *Elsie Houston/A Feminilidade do Canto*, n.p. His emphasis.

6 · IMPERIAL AURALITY Jazz, the Archive, and U.S. Empire

JAIRO MORENO

U.S. Empire: Between Autarchy and Anarchy

Between 1789 and 1895, the United States intervened in foreign countries 103 times.[1] During the latter part of the long nineteenth century, the Caribbean and Latin America became its main imperial theater. A few highlights from that time frame follow:

- 1850–56: American soldiers protect the construction of a trans-isthmian railroad in Panama.
- 1856: William Walker, backed by a mercenary army, takes control of Nicaragua.

- 1885: As one of its first acts of "gunboat diplomacy," the USS *Wachusset* is sent to defend American lives and their property in Guatemala.
- 1898: The United States wins the Spanish-American War, liberating Cuba and taking possession of the islands of Puerto Rico.
- 1906–9: U.S. forces occupy Cuba.

These geopolitical interventions strengthened and consolidated the United States as both nation-state and imperial power.[2] The rest is history.

And music: as regiments went and came, so did their sounds. With a robust colonial tradition of military bands, music in the Spanish Caribbean provided a fertile, imperial, aural "contact zone."[3] W. C. Handy (1873–1958), the self-titled "father of the blues," remarked how the rhythmic pattern he used in the introduction and bridge sections of "St. Louis Blues" (1914) came from something he first heard during a 1900–1901 tour of Cuba with the Mahara's Minstrels.[4] The song became Handy's most popular, circulating widely as part of the U.S. music history canon; it has since been famously sung by Bessie Smith in 1929, featured in the eponymous 1958 movie starring Nat "King" Cole, stunningly rendered by Herbie Hancock (with Stevie Wonder) in 1998, and imaginatively re-created by the trombonist Wycliffe Gordon in 1998, among many others. The afterlife of the imperial "contact zone" has been economically profitable and materially pliable, its resonance enduring and showing no signs of falling silent; its imperial binds, however, have long faded from memory.

Given imperial contact, it stands to reason that U.S. music history could have been cast as being partially rooted in and routed through the wealth of transformations undergone by extraterritorial sonic materials.[5] Instead, nativist narratives free of imperial binds won over. Indeed, etymology reminds us that the word "empire" connotes both the power to birth itself (L. *parire*) and the capacity to "pare down" others (L. *parere*) in the process. Jazz may be paradigmatic. Despite the sonorous vitality of imperial contact, jazz will be cast as being exclusively the province of American creativity, ingenuity, and the will to experimentation of its musicians, ever ready to traverse cultural and geographic frontiers.[6] This narrative consolidates by century's end when, coinciding with unprecedented support by the state and civil society (i.e., cultural policy institutions and governmental, private, public, and corporate monies), jazz is declared a "national treasure."[7] Legislative and public institutionalization helped create a strong sense of national aesthetic autarchy grounded on the idea of jazz as an American creation and contribution to musical arts on the one hand, and, on the other, as the sonorous embodiment of the greatest sociocultural aspirations of human conviviality and the political ideals of participatory liberal democracy of U.S. society.[8] Empire couldn't be farther from this vision of jazz.

But can the nation's creative accomplishments and the state's and civil society's participation in them be separated from empire? Timothy Brennan doesn't believe so: "a national agenda[,] fed not only by generals but by artists and authors (both black and white), severed jazz from the rest of the world."[9] "Imperial jazz" constitutes a national reality, though not, however, simply for being the music of an imperial nation.[10] Brennan explains: "I am not saying that since jazz is from the United States and the United States runs an empire, that jazz is 'imperial,'" rather, "imperial jazz" constitutes "the ideological outlook that comes naturally to an imperial power [for] [t]here are demands made on researchers and the public in advance that this politically and symbolically potent music be considered officially (and only) the possession of one nation." Given the "huge cultural capital at stake," foreign labor or contribution must be in the end necessarily muted.[11] Imperial jazz fulfills the autarchic needs of a self-declared exceptional nation.

The effacement of imperial traces from domestic "cultural" phenomena is consonant with a long-standing practice of imperial denial by the United States.[12] As Amy Kaplan argues, "Cultural phenomena we think of as domestic or particularly national are forged in the crucible of foreign relations."[13] But lest we think this as a matter of repression of knowledge, we might consider questions of self-intelligibility, as imperial geopolitical coordinates become diffuse and even imperceptible at the center. "The location of the United States and Europe and their economic and discursive wealth, capital, and political power," Elizabeth Povinelli remarks, "was not self-evident and was certainly not anchored in their own borders."[14] None of this renders the foreign for peaceful subsumption. To the contrary, it creates what Kaplan, after W. E. B. Du Bois, calls "the anarchy of empire," namely, "ways of thinking about imperialism as a network of power relations that changes over space and time and is riddled with instability, ambiguity, and disorder."[15] Insecure about the strength of cultural borders to safeguard the properly domestic and to keep the world at bay, U.S. social institutions endeavor constantly to assert the autarchic character of its aesthetic and political accomplishments, but they do so, in the cases I detail, by repeatedly invoking the world while, paradoxically, ignoring it.

U.S. imperialism exists in dialectical tension with a state-nationalist rationality for which black-white racial dynamics are integral. I take as a point of departure Étienne Balibar's proposition that "racism is constantly emerging out of nationalism, not only towards the exterior but towards the interior," for, as he writes, "in the United States, the systematic institution of segregation . . . coincided with America's entry into world imperialist competition and with its subscribing to the idea that the Nordic races have a hegemonic mission."[16] The national anarchy embodied in ongoing racial tension finds in a peculiar ideology of imperial autarchy its counterpoint. I give this dialectic a further turn, with jazz as an axis: through historically shifting forms, the nexus between U.S. racial relations, empire, and jazz provides the conditions of possibility for perfectly justifiable positions on racial solidarity and historical participation from conservative and progressive actors (musicians, academics, critics) alike to adopt a hegemonic mission that reduces the world to a vast chronotopic archive where racial gains are obtained and in which they must be inscribed. I trace diverse configurations of a world (its places, spaces, and temporalities) both invoked and negated as a necessary condition for musical production but vigorously kept from depleting the "national treasure." I call this the "imperial archive."

The Imperial Archive and Aurality

Performing in Memphis in 1909, W. C. Handy had a powerful experience:

> I noticed something that struck me as a racial trait, and I immediately tucked it away for future use. It was the odd response of the dancers to Will H. Tyler's [sic] Maori. When we played this rhythm and came to the Habanera rhythm, containing the beat of the tango, I observed that there was a sudden, proud and graceful reaction to the rhythm. Was it an accident, or could the response be traced to a real but hidden cause? I wondered. White dancers, as I had observed them, took the number in stride. I began to suspect that perhaps there was something Negroid in that beat, something that quickened the blood of the Dixie Park dancers. [Dixie Park was an amusement park with a predominantly black clientele.] Well, there was a way to test it. If my suspicions were grounded, the same reaction should be manifest during the playing of La Paloma. We used that piece, and sure enough, there it was, that same calm yet ecstatic movement. I felt convinced. Later, because of this conviction, I introduced the rhythm into my own compositions. It may be noted in the introduction to the St. Louis Blues [1914], the

instrumental piano copy of *Memphis Blues* [1912], the chorus of *Beale Street Blues* [1916] and other compositions.[17]

"I . . . tucked it away for future use." This simple phrase goes to the heart of the archive in its basic capacity to save something for later retrieval. But this something—here a rhythmic configuration as the minimal unit of musical intelligibility—enters into a complex set of relations that constitutes the archive beyond a depository and instead as a dispositive for the production of affective intensities. Race-based difference and socialized forms of corporeal expression are cast in a particular language of affective distinction ("a sudden, proud and graceful reaction to the rhythm") and channeled through a cognitively comprehensible grid of music-stylistic taxonomies ("beat of the tango," "habanera rhythm"). Other relations emerge in connection to material networks of commercial exchange (the dance itself, the acquisition of musical resources overseas, its eventual distribution as commodities via the phonographic, film, and radio industries) and to emerging intertextual constellations ("La Paloma," "St. Louis Blues," "Beale Street Blues"). The archive is coterminous with the intersensory, affective, cognitive, discursive, material, perceptual, and rhetorical network I call *aurality*.[18] Though listening plays a central role in aurality, aurality cannot be reduced to it.

I propose that we conceive of the archive in the context of U.S. empire and Kaplan's and Du Bois's "anarchy of empire" as an "imperial archive."[19] This archive encompasses a set of permutations of the relation between remembering and forgetting (remembering; forgetting; remembering to remember; remembering to forget; forgetting to forget; forgetting to remember).[20] It constitutes a recursive and iterative mechanism for the imperial accumulation of time and space: its own and that of others.[21] It is that relation to time and space that both presents them and presents the contents of its holdings *as* that which is available as a result of imperial access to the world. It also presents the world *as* that which is possible to experience and understand from the perspective of empire's center; that is, it can be experienced and/ or understood as not being imperial at all. As a mechanism for accumulation, the imperial archive constitutes the empire as *potentia* (its power and capacity) and as *potestas* (the effective exercise of that power and capacity in relation to others and itself as well as the commanding authority to exercise that power and capacity).

In some sense, the imperial archive counts everything—the world— among its holdings. But because no archive could ever hold everything in consignment, two things must happen. First, some things require that they be forgotten, on condition that they remain in potentia. Second, some things require that they be inscribed, or *co-signed*. Once co-signed, these things become *consigned* in the more manageable aural archive, one that remembers and safeguards (Handy's "tucks") on the condition that much else be forgotten. It is this archive that figures forth nationally as well as individually. In it, co-signation and consignation are of a piece. Thus, for Handy, the "habanera rhythm" inscribes a place of origin. But the elision of other traces of its acquisition (the imperial situation, the local histories of other places) also constitutes a mode of inscription: it frees the sociocultural association he posits to emerge within local and national contingencies as possible and necessary under conditions of racial inequality and state-enforced separation at home.

By making available content possible, the archive gives intelligibility to national sociopolitical contingencies, dispersing and amplifying material content (here a rhythm) across the network of aurality. Several transformations enable the passage from the *available* to the *possible* and to what is actually experienced and understood. The private impressions and reflections of an individual mediate and are mediated by a public discourse about racial particularity and difference. This movement from the public space (a dance hall, the circuit of dance halls where Handy performed) to the public sphere demands the inscription of the sonic into a classificatory and interpretive framework, as well as a narrative that produces social meaning and value out of musical detail: a public concern, a *res publica*. The specifically musical public Handy imagines emerges as a corollary to the intractable but real problem of white-black racism in U.S. society; *this* public, in short, does not precede the problem, and neither does the "something Negroid" in the "habanera rhythm."[22]

The constitutive paradox of an archive that must constantly forget in order to constantly remember parallels the anarchy that sustains its claims to autarchy. Susceptible to endless configurations, the archive demands not only that some things circulate and others do not (because they are forgotten) but also that the modes of circulation of those that do be regulated. Imperial acquisitions move within a restricted economy redolent of what Igor Kopytoff identifies as the demarcation of "areas of homogeneity"; these afford a modicum of "cognitive order" to an empire "riddled with instability, ambiguity, and disorder," as Kaplan puts it.[23] Such order creates delimited domains (the cultural, the economic, the geopolitical, the political, the psychological) where particular "spheres of value" accrue whose function it is to allow or disallow specific forms of exchange and/or modes of circulation. For instance,

Handy's "habanera rhythm" owes its presence in St. Louis to a dense network of relations, in many of which the rhythm was fully embedded as a commodity. The inscription of this rhythm as a negroid phenomenon effects what Kopytoff calls its "singularization," a kind of decommodification that takes it outside of the market's sphere. Imbued with ethnoracial value, instead, this rhythm becomes a stable category within the holdings of an aural archive: this is how it is cognitively and affectively heard and corporeally understood. It is also how it is rendered intelligible—transformed and translated—to the nation. Singularization does not preclude the continuing circulation of the rhythm as commodity; to the contrary, archival singularization compels its exploitation, reproduction, distribution, and consumption in the marketplace. Overlapping spheres of value configure what is presumably the same material extracted from the imperial situation, each with its proper mode of transaction. The "negroid character" of the "habanera rhythm" may be only shared or generationally inherited within people of the same race and ethnicity, although potentially anyone can buy into it, but "St. Louis Blues" can be sold and bought, reproduced, re-mediated, and endlessly transformed within the circuitry of capitalism. For the institution of the archive, this constitutes a key element in the granting of immunity from the vagaries of exchange, commodification, and monetization to certain spheres (i.e., blackness as a cultural practice and property cannot itself be bought).

The archive operates at multiple and simultaneous registers. If empire makes of the world its holdings in potentia, it demands domiciles where to consign its contents across a distributed network anywhere from the private domain of Handy's reportedly prodigious musical memory, to genre categories of music that require public agreement in order to function, to the public sphere where musical configurations are heard as embodying ethnoracial preferences and/or proclivities (corporeal, cognitive, etc.). Singularization and the harnessing of particular aspects of music to specific modalities of exchange, commodification, materialization, and immaterialization occur alongside processes of domiciling. In the end, the ambiguity of autarchy and anarchy of the archive demands that it be sheltered. Consignation in a domicile and co-signation are the archive's main sheltering dispositives. But as Derrida proposed, the archive remains caught in the unresolved ambiguity of sheltering (the nation, in this case) and in need of shelter.[24]

The archive itself cannot be archived, Derrida argues, which complicates its temporalities. Rather than tracing a linear trajectory from imperial acquisition to domestic appropriation, assimilation, and integration, the imperial archive allows us to consider its paradoxical character as being an origin that, in order to commence, relies on authorities, inscriptions, and co-signatures that are not in themselves imperial. Handy is hardly the first such authority. This well-known quip by "Jelly Roll" Morton also demonstrates how to think of the archive:

> Now take *La Paloma*, which I transformed in New Orleans style.[25] You leave the left hand just the same. The difference comes in the right hand—in the syncopation, which gives it an entirely different color that really changes the color from red to blue.
>
> Now in one of my earliest tunes, *New Orleans Blues*, you can notice the Spanish tinge. In fact, if you can't manage to put tinges of Spanish in your tunes, you will never be able to get the right seasoning, I call it, for jazz.[26]

Later critics refract Morton's aurality. John Storm Roberts hears the hybridization of "La Paloma" into a "ragtime tango"; hybridity, and not just a rhythmic sensibility, makes of Morton's "Spanish tinge" an essential aspect of jazz.[27] Ned Sublette picks up where Morton leaves: "'*Leave the left hand just the same.*' In other words, keep that habanera bass with its bump on the *and* of 2—the same tango bass that was in Gottschalk's 'Ojos Criollos' [1857]. That's a lot of your Spanish tinge, right there."[28] Mention of Gottschalk would push the search for origins further back into the nineteenth century and earlier, when French and Spanish colonial enterprises interacted with nascent U.S. national and imperial ones in eighteenth-century New Orleans.

Morton addresses the immediate temporal relations of local New Orleans; Handy indexes a relatively recent past in Cuba; Sublette would go farther in time: the imperial archive is multi- and poly-temporal and intrinsically linked to listening practices. Listening, remarks David Novak, "is the very crucible of musical innovation."[29] My point is, though, that listening is subject to stagnation too. When Handy's mediation renders the "habanera rhythm" into an index and expression of something negroid in U.S. society, his listening—more precisely the broad network of aurality distributed throughout the society it now informs—also transforms that configuration from Morton's "red to blue" to the "red, white, and blue." Brennan's "demands" capture one aspect of this aural conscription, for Handy doesn't disavow the source of his musical idea but does press aurality in the service of needs internal to the nation and in obedience to the archival command that the space and time of the nation be preserved. That national space is finite seems commonsensical; there are cartographic boundaries, after all. Empire, however, complicates any sense of closed frontiers. Aurality may take place at a national location (e.g., Morton's

New Orleans, Handy's Memphis), but it draws a national space out of a relation with other locations. Other locations have times and histories. People continue to migrate to the United States, bringing their histories. Time and temporality, not space, may be the most challenging dimension of the imperial archive to shelter. The sense that U.S. empire did not depend on territorial annexation only augmented the need to exercise control over time. Music's temporal character only contributed to a complicated, deterritorialized practice of imperial archivization, toward which I turn.

Schizochronias

Following the axiom that "homelands are to their diasporas as the past is to the present and future," jazz has long been held in deep spatiotemporal relation to Africa as ultimate origin.[30] This is in no small part due to global issues of racial pride and solidarity. Against this, the demands of "imperial jazz" that music be "cut off from its sources" result in something like a national will to schizophonia splitting jazz from its foundation.[31] I introduce a supplement: schizochronia. However driven by U.S. society's racial biases, persistent appeals to Africa and to an Afro-diasporic continuum demanded by contemporary U.S. cultural politics produce an altogether singular split: other hemispheric histories and temporalities become blurred, compressed, expanded to the point of transcendence, or even vanished. Although constitutive of the heterogeneous time of empire as well as of the homogeneous time of capitalism, these histories and temporalities appear as ancillary to it, if at all. Corollary to schizochronia is a schizotopic political cartography of the Americas that makes of whatever is not the United States a "hemisphere apart"[32] or, alternatively, reduces the immense complexity of the American continent's entanglement with Africa into a singularity understood solely from an all-encompassing northern perspective of the Black Atlantic. I suggest, furthermore, how, emanating from an empire built on the idea of nonterritorial annexation, the processes become ones of temporal annexation and their means cognitive. But there is a catch: these cognitive means—complex explanations of how the United States is both part of universal history and its producer—yield increasingly contradictory temporal maps. These contradictions are internal to the order of an imperial archive that will remain divided against itself but fully unaware of it (in a word, schizoid).

Schizochronia names the imperial phenomenon of temporal annexation. It too embodies the internal character of imperial subjectivation as emerging relations that actors establish with the times, temporalities, and historiographical operations that co-sign the imperial archive. As a complex temporal assemblage, music serves only too well to shelter the idea that, no matter how undeniable extraterritorial presences may be, the archive will lose none of its power to assuage the nation of its historical autonomy. I offer two examples.

Elsewhere, I have detailed the mid-1940s collaboration between the jazz great Dizzy Gillespie and the Cuban percussionist and composer Chano Pozo.[33] In Pozo, whom Gillespie heard as possessing an unprecedented capacity for rhythmic complexity, Gillespie came into an unexpected moment of negation. Suddenly aware that the rhythmic cognitive sensibility that he thought was his as a U.S. national descendent from African slaves was meager in comparison to that of the Afro-Cuban musician, he reinvented himself by drawing a direct link to Pozo's deep African past, largely bypassing Cuba in the process.

Pozo's rhythmic capacity would reveal the insufficiency of Handy's "negroid character" as an archival category, rendering intelligible a world of rhythm existing outside the United States. If one of the functions of the archive is to shelter and one of its demands that it be sheltered by actors and institutions with the knowledge and authority to do so, this midcentury episode makes an extraordinary demand: the time of blackness must be subsumed as a category internal to empire. If the archive accumulates time and space by remembering to forget, this conjuncture signals the difficult operation of forgetting to forget. I am referring to universalism. Gillespie understood their brief and influential collaboration as the achievement of a universal African musicianship correlative to the universalism of the harmonic rationality of modernist bebop.

Overlapping universalisms emerge: one suspends time in a unified synchrony in order for the U.S. musician to gain access to an archive rich in holdings from a deep past; the other, decidedly diachronic, asserts harmonic complexity as the telos of musical development tout court and attained at the specific time and location of the U.S. musician.[34] These universalisms, of world-cultural geography and of musical autonomy, come together on U.S. soil and under a national logic that elides the recent past of U.S.-Cuba relations. Dialectically, the synthesis of two universalisms necessitates this historical—that is, temporal and territorial—negation.

The momentous encounter between Pozo and Gillespie produces as a paradigmatic example the extraordinary piece "Manteca." But if wonderful music is born, something else is pared down. We have a historical narrative that files the "Cuban influence" under the substyle known as CuBop.[35] And whereas we have rich verbal accounts of Gillespie and other black U.S. musicians' work with Pozo, the latter's part of the exchange is accounted solely by a musicianship entrusted to speak on his behalf. Gillespie's structural advantage is an effect of the discursive power of empire, which, to recall Povinelli, is not evident to itself. Music seems eminently suited for an imperial deafness for which questions of self-evidence may be irrelevant: the music sounds good, and it *feels* even better, the political economy that brings an Afro-Cuban to migrate to New York City be damned, and so be American geopolitics of the first half of the century—end of story.

Music cannot be the totality of Pozo's archive—or anyone else's, for that matter. Yet this is what happens in an analysis where, mobilizing a new set of values promulgated in the late twentieth-century U.S. academy, namely an unquestioned ethical force of improvisation and a transcendent sonic Afrologic out of which cultural variants in the diaspora are born, we are compelled to hear two cultures, Afro-Cuban and Afro-American, coalescing in splendid "interculturality."[36] This coalescence gives historical coherence to an absolute Afro-diasporic temporality.

By recognizing an Afro-Cuban "cultural" contribution, this analysis appears to rectify Gillespie's dialectical negation. No party is excluded from the intercultural encounter and no one endures a sudden coming-into-consciousness of a lack, be it cognitive, cultural, historical, or otherwise. The intercultural narrative presents itself as being decidedly additive and inclusionary. A dialectical subsumption unfurls nonetheless, namely, that the structural asymmetries in the meeting between Pozo and Gillespie could not make of their encounter one among equals. The intercultural model must fabricate *equality* out of the universal African diaspora or else construct *equivalence* among historical actors in order to inscribe the past within an overarching notion of blackness. In fact, both are in play, if one considers the implicit moral law of the intercultural analysis. Morality gives the archive an unquestionable alibi. It too installs a powerful dematerializing force at the heart of empire.

Intercultural equality between Pozo and Gillespie emerges from what Michael Walzer calls "covering-law universalism," here a pivotal event of world history (the forced displacement of African peoples under slavery) rendered as the single principle under which one justice and one understanding addressed to anyone and at anytime who identifies or is identified with it will have been true in perpetuity.[37] The lawlike character of this universalism means that those who ignore it but belong to it will come to learn and obey it in due time, thereby fulfilling the moral imperative of recognizing the equal nature of the diaspora and the equality of its peoples. "Reiterative universalism," by contrast, emphasizes the particular and plural character of peoples, with specific experiences resulting from spatial dispersion. Under covering-law universalism, even those who weren't present in the Middle Passage are represented by and in Afro-diasporicism. Under reiterative universalism, dispersed groups perform the diaspora in their own fashion. Equality in the former reemerges as equivalence in the latter, for, as Walzer notes, "reiterative universalism can always be given a covering-law form."[38] Here, the views of Pozo and of Gillespie as embodying two equivalent cultures are given in the equality that constitutes them before the law of the African diaspora.

Reiterative universalism demands respect for the singularity of any-one's bondage and corollary forms of emancipation, thereby challenging covering-law universalism. In consequence, a perfectly sensible covering-law universalism such as the outraged moral and political response to racial oppression may result in "outcomes that contradict their intention," because "[one] will be overwhelmed by the sheer heterogeneity of human life and surrender all belief in the relevance of our history for anyone else."[39] The intercultural analysis must invoke the logic of reiteration (two distinct Afro-diasporic trajectories yield distinct cultures) in order to uphold the explana-tory power of covering-law designs (they all come together in and through the force of U.S. musico-cultural possibilities and an Afro-logic distinctly developed there). In other words, the militant fidelity to the world-historical mission of explaining Afro-diasporic binds by recourse to interculturality renders silent the fact that this containment and realization of those binds obeys the archival logic of U.S. cultural politics and responds to demands that it accumulates or annexes time.

Schizochronia emerges from relations that historical actors forge with contradictory models of temporality. Intrinsic to the logic of the imperial archive, this contradiction requires and indeed demands forgetting. This forgetting must negate something, and this negation is never temporal (or spatial) in itself. Instead, it must hypostatize imperial time as temporalities. In so doing, it can only remain split and not know it.

Schizochronia does not result from the split of music from an original time that it presumably indexes and/or embodies. To the contrary, a typi-cal schizochronic move involves positing one such original time. Gillespie's case was paradigmatic: for him, Pozo embodied a time no longer available to Afro-descended U.S. musicians. The intercultural analysis draws more obfuscating coordinates, unfurling three temporal logics and three spatial scales. The first level operates under a logic of continuity at the macropoliti-cal level of recognition of all things Afro-diasporic. This comes close to being a double transcendental and transcendent time: transcendental because it operates as the condition of possibility for Afro-diasporic eventality, and transcendent because it is outside of history (i.e., it cannot change, otherwise it might one day cease to be Afro-diasporic or to count as such). Another meso-political level functions within the time-space of the nation-state. Here, the historicity of Afro-diasporic cultural reason reaches a telos on U.S. soil at the same time that this telos reflects the exceptional status of the country as the twentieth-century cultural crossroads. A third level operates partly in a quasi-phenomenological register and partly after the fashion of social interaction models. This is where the face-to-face encounter of two individuals, abetted by their affective and cognitive predisposition toward improvisation, actually makes music, seemingly unconcerned with the fraught politics of the nation-state, its imperial proclivities, and the larger material forces of history that inevitably compel their coincidence in the New World. These are micropolitics and they have the effect of bracketing off the other temporal registers and the overall political economy that made them possible.

Much as one wishes that these levels might address the irreducible social and historical complexity that it seeks to map, positing them as an effect of culture (or interculture) results in the erasure of conflict from history, the simplification of social agonisms and antagonisms, and the refusal to engage with the material conditions of musical production, division of labor, and economic profit. Music is, of course, transformed as it moves through various institutions and is in turn moved by them. Institutions vary. For example, the forces and intensities of immigration and governmental sanction that permit the presence of Pozo in New York City in the 1940s are not the same as the forces and intensities of instituted social norms of racial and/or ethnic difference, or the effective power of that difference to organize practices of encounter and separation within the metropolitan space, or those undergirding the acquisition of musical know-how in Gillespie's 1920s North Carolina or Pozo's 1920s Havana.

We could understand this lack of discernment among institutions as a symptom of music making's broadly distributed and multiply relational character. But how can we account for the reduction of this distribution to a question of interculture? This contradiction between an expansively interrelated world and a reduced culture, I believe, satisfies archival demands that the past be made in the image of the present and that the archive sustains its coherence in spite of or because of its underlying anarchy. This is something for which centralized institutional orders at the meso-political level provide the sole context in which relations between levels take place. The analysis issues from these specific and located political norms (academic as well as social) and their authority to connect, disconnect, or reconnect cultures as needed, provided that they can be *recognized* as discrete cultures. We might regard U.S. academic, neoliberal multiculturalism as a condition of possibility to interculturalism. This in turn transfers privilege to the (liberal) individual as an engine of history, which also accounts for the troubling reversibility between ontology and a quasi-phenomenology (i.e., the being of individuals *is* the being of their experiences and vice versa). Already here, archival demands afford the analysis considerable slippage: we are now at the micro-political level of social interaction among individuals. And it gets better. Rendered as praxis (as intercultural praxis, to be precise), the analysis affirms the meso-reductionist level of a sociology that generates individuals *and* larger social structures from practice.[40] This would transform praxis as individual action into the transcendent and transcendental temporalities of macropolitics. In the end, not only does the intercultural analysis posit a frictionless idea of history, but it also creates a cognitive map to conceive of time and temporality as resistance-free phenomena, phenomena, that is, that can be annexed effortlessly by the all-hearing ear of imperial academic institutions.

I highlight the schizochronic character of these two cases for the way they track a shift from inscription by historical actors to inscription by domestic institutions. The location in the U.S. academy of the latter might seem linked to its critical aura. In reality, academic apparatuses and conceptual dispositives require a flattening of world-political tensions in order to sustain domestic tensions and contestations about race. The crucible of foreign relations, to use Kaplan's expression, remains, now as ever, captive to an imperial aurality that, challenged by the appearance of something or someone not yet consigned to its archival holdings, does not hesitate to fabricate temporalities that might assuage it in its conviction that what happens in the United States stays within its boundless time: it is, after all, the time of the world that its empire in a way *is*. The world, however, is more than that.

File under "Worldly"

"There is a spirit of worldliness in jazz. You can hear how jazz is connected to other musics from around the world."[41] Part of Wynton Marsalis's definition of "what jazz is," this account of worldliness specifically invoked Duke Ellington's pieces from the mid- to late 1960s, exploring musical impressions gathered during his frequent postwar trips overseas.[42] These impressions resulted in the closest thing to concept albums that Ellington would ever record, heartfelt and musically impeccable works titled *Latin American Suite* (a studio project recorded in 1968 and 1970 and released in 1972) and *The Far East Suite* (inspired by 1963 and 1964 tours of Japan and mostly the Middle East, recorded in 1966 and released in 1967). For Marsalis, the suites exemplify a "spirit of worldliness" as a revered master experimented with how elements from "other people's music . . . fit jazz." In "worldliness," the archive gains powerful co-signatories: combined, the music of specific locations and the ecumenical aurality of an acknowledged master—Ellington—affirm for Marsalis the universal character of jazz, America's music. Like Handy and Morton from earlier generations, Ellington and Marsalis readily acknowledge the world.

"Worldliness" stands out among the otherwise rigorously musicological definition of jazz (e.g., swing, call-and-response, blues, etc.). There is good reason: nationally, "worldliness" signals a resistant position. The decidedly nonprovincial outlook of U.S. black jazz musicians counteracts the persistent myth that "regards jazz merely as a product of noble savages—music produced by untutored, unbuttoned semiliterates [*sic*]—for whom jazz history does not exist."[43] This myth originated from the "American prejudices" of early (white) jazz writers. Globally, "worldliness" indexes a universal disposition. Jazz is an "art [that] has had such universal appeal and application that it has changed the conventions of American music as well as those of the world at large."[44] The contributions of black musicians to this universal project are unquestionable.

Jazz is worldly indeed. In contrast with other archival categories (e.g., the intercultural analysis, which seeks to ground Afro-diasporic unity in a hybridization project), "worldliness" stakes a far broader space and asserts a more potent form of American exceptionalism. "Worldliness" designates the movement across an actually existing space separating the United States and the rest of the world. This presupposes the privilege of specific historical actors to traverse this space, both in the sense of affording global travel and the entitlement to freely collect resources that might enrich musical holdings back home. Inseparably from U.S. global hegemony in the postwar era, this privilege is material. "Worldliness," however, is immaterial.

Understood as a creative economy, "worldliness" renders the U.S. jazz musician in his capacity and desire to objectively and materially (i.e., musical form) engage sonic alterity, an index of a valued disposition to embrace difference. Indubitably, subjective transformation is at stake in the practice of musical adaptation as well as an objective and material dimension in the aural and cognitive intervention by which musical matter is handled (i.e., rhythms, harmonies, textures, melodies, etc.).[45] Nonetheless, however much these subjective-objective processes engage the world, the traversal of global space constitutes equally an embrace and an assertion of (musical) difference. As Alejandro Grimson remarks, hegemonic views of difference are not conflict-free; rather, instituted and delimited identitarian categories, as well as forms of action, help stabilize it.[46] Worldliness harbors this tension. Its dialectic of embracing/affirming difference obeys national norms of self-understanding and affirmation (that Americans are worldly), particularly when those norms require being challenged (i.e., by demonstrating that black U.S. musicians are every bit as worldly and so equal to any American). "Worldliness" asserts both jazz's particularism and America's exceptional status in the world. In the end, Ellington's suites do not render jazz any more Latin or Middle Eastern; for Marsalis, jazz becomes "worldly."

But is "worldly jazz" a correlate of "imperial jazz"? Compared to Gillespie's recuperative hybridity or to the self-erasing metanarratives of interculturality, worldliness stands closer to the less appropriational logic of benevolent metropolitan cosmopolitanism. Cosmopolitanism, the blueprint for the idea of a western ecumene, introduces new challenges. First, Marsalis's comment echoes an end-of-century ethos summed up in Paul Rabinow's pithy phrase "we are all cosmopolitans."[47] This is a subject-centered cosmopolitanism, in the fashion of what Pierre-André Taguieff calls "heterophilia" or what Ulf Hannerz identifies as "first of all an orientation, a willingness to engage with the Other . . . an intellectual and aesthetic stance of openness toward diverging cultural experiences."[48] Second, structurally, cosmopolitanism places individuals in the context of large and complex economic, social, and political forces. For some, the late twentieth-century resurgence of cosmopolitanism in metropolitan locations constituted an effort to smuggle the political agenda of world governance and global capitalism under the cloak of a cultural and humanist empathy with Otherness tout court. It was noted that late twentieth-century cosmopolitanism supplanted midcentury international political solidarity.[49] Bruce Robbins considers actually existing cosmopolitanisms to lie at core opportunistic appeals to difference that assert a form of strategic universalism in the waning years of the "American Century," particularly with the fall of the Berlin Wall and the consolidation of globalization.[50] Marsalis, on the other hand, renders midcentury diplomatic jazz tours as a form of cultural empathy.

The question of the affordance of openness that Hannerz praises is important. In place of the enduring Stoic conception of cosmopolitanism as the outward scaling of the individual as she develops loyalties to increasingly larger spheres of family, social group, city, region, country, globe, and indeed the cosmos, Bruno Latour insists instead on the specific capacities a particular location has to connect in a networklike fashion to various locations across the world.[51] This doesn't absolve cosmopolitanism of its inequities, but it makes explicit its dependence on the connections available to someone at a particular place and time but also most fundamentally on the capacity to sustain those links and to extend their number at enormous expense: what he calls "alliances." Latour's impassioned analysis seeks to reveal the attempts at neo-universalization of late modern nations, much in line with what Gustavo Lins Ribeiro identified as the particularism of any cosmopolitan project.[52] These critics insist on the located nature of any cosmopolitanism and warn against its seductive duality as analytical category *and* narrative projection.[53] "Projection" is key, for cosmopolitanism stakes claims on an indefinite future oddly devoid of history and saturated by a paradoxically empty space.

Like cosmopolitanism, "worldliness" is not inherently imperial; it can only become so as an effect of pressures put on the national history of the United States by its constitutive racism. Without denying the worldwide reach and influence of jazz, it is important to understand the force of Marsalis's words in the context of a national particularism that spurs both the claims to cosmopolitanism and the activation of the corollary universalism. Consider universalism. The radical particularism of a U.S. society organized along binary racial lines gives way to an aesthetic universalism that cannot but lapse into a historicism abetted by its national contingencies and at the expense of any others'. Upheld by the wide circulation in the U.S. public sphere and its conceptualization as a universal, the discourse of jazz "worldliness" and its music-cultural ecumenism elides and naturalizes the formidable resources of imperialism, making of transnational power relationships a matter of the neutral predisposition of empathetic and gifted individuals within a musical tradition and as representatives of a race.

Consider history. Although Marsalis reckons explicitly with a hegemonic history of jazz, in what is now a central thread connecting the cases I have discussed, all other histories serve as references outside the United States and enjoy no true co-participatory role in national history. The world, however, may be outside of time, and its space may be an abstract space of "difference," but it is never out of mind. At the conjuncture that finds jazz gaining an unprecedented foothold in the United States, the music requires the world as an unquestionable index of its capacity for self-transformation and innovation, and indeed of its worth. This world functions as an authority and as a silent witness to the fact that prejudices against black U.S. creative endeavors are patently false. Let's call this an uneven but necessary interdependence between the United States and the world. The world has to be available *as* an imperial archive if "worldliness" as consigned and co-signed in the United States is to put pressure on the racist discursive space of the nation-state. This is what I mean by the exclusionary inclusion at the heart of "worldliness," a universalism whose greatest virtue is its capacity for assimilating difference while engaging in imperial practices of sonic extractivism inseparable from state interests. All told, in spite of the recognition that jazz is "worldly" and therefore owes something to extraterritorial resources, the fact is that, for Marsalis, jazz remains the sole possession of the nation where the musical processing takes place: jazz remains "imperial jazz." This jazz is imperial and most powerful by declaring its relation to the outside world. Displacement, not outright denial, or what Brennan identifies as the United States' severance from the world, becomes a capacious archival dispositive.

Let me summarize my analysis of Marsalis.[54] First, a musical practice, jazz, is negated by the mainstream critical (white) tradition as a form of instinctual primitivism. This posits a classic temporal separation between primitive/civilized. Second, Marsalis negates the negation by recourse to the spatial form of "worldliness." "Worldliness" is not a place, however, and so constitutes a spatial negation (nonplace) of a temporal negation (primitive). Embodied in the figure of Ellington cosmopolitanism, jazz emerges as the form overcoming allegations of black primitivism. Its creative labor subsumes as well the capacity of the nation to musically engage the world. This engagement, nonetheless, necessitates positing a center (the United States) to periphery ("world") relation. This relation opens up a set of new tensions. It assumes a flattened world, but it effectively operates within a stratified geopolitical map. The musician may engage the "world" but not necessarily with it. Conceived otherwise, the initial argument of primitivism by mainstream critics is carried out under the assumption that jazz is a particular against which a universal nonprimitivism stands. "Worldliness," then, becomes the negation of particularism and the claim to universalism. But at this point what would have been a national particular—jazz—is given the status of a universal. Marsalis does not merely negate the negation but adopts its very logic, by repeating the gesture of provincializing the world that renders jazz in the United States as a worldly achievement. All told, "the world" does not operate as a negative pole in these dialectical movements. It is effectively a cipher, an empty space out of time, a passive but rich resource unknowingly contributing a necessary piece to the resolution of national antagonisms in the United States.

The relation between the two dialectical poles I have outlined here is one between two claims to the universal, with the synthesis being the combination of these universalisms into a particular U.S. universalism. This U.S. universalism is "intensive," as Balibar might say, gathering under the sign of the nation, as well as "extensive" in its orientation toward overcoming territorial borders.[55] The latter constitutes the passage from universalism into cosmopolitics and the more concrete aspects of imperial affirmation of a particular idea of, say, "freedom," as the norm for a global law of race morality that Paul Gilroy calls "the U.S. racial nomos."[56] This is the stuff of cosmopolitanism's "narrative projections" that Brennan notes. As a projection, imperial cosmopolitanism—a label befitting the notion of jazz's "worldliness"—carries implications beyond Marsalis's present and into an unknown future it seeks to secure.

Back to the Future

The immateriality of "worldliness" and cosmopolitanism took a decidedly material cast when, in the fall of 2011, Jazz at Lincoln Center announced that it was expanding with a club overseas, "as part of a new $1 billion luxury hotel going up in Doha [Qatar] and will be modeled on Dizzy's Club Coca-Cola in Manhattan." In partnership with St. Regis Hotels and Resorts, owned by Starwood Hotels and Resorts Worldwide, the plan includes four more clubs in hotels being built around the world by 2016. The *New York Times* reported Marsalis as stating "that he would initially focus on sending musicians to Doha who are comfortable playing the role of cultural ambassador. The first showcases will have educational themes, he said, highlighting, for instance, important players from New Orleans or different periods in jazz history."[57]

Its worldliness secured at home, the "national treasure" associated with the global brand of Jazz at Lincoln Center is available to suitable bidders. Qatar has the highest per capita index in the world and is of course strategic to U.S. interests in the area, known as a mediating place between "western" concerns and the so-called Arab world.[58] In this sense, the Doha expansion is similar to the State Department–sponsored projects that sent Ellington touring the Americas in the 1950s and 1960s. Showcasing "freedom" and the democratic byways of jazz improvisation in an absolute monarchy like Qatar, however, can hardly be thought of as anything other than the corporatization of the music's "worldliness." If, as Susan Buck-Morss puts it, "universal history does not come to an end. It begins again, somewhere else," it is the case here because those exporting universal history have already attained it, as

I proposed in the dialectical analysis above.[59] But if it can be exported, sold, and so on, it is because it is held as an archival accumulation of time, "tucked away for future use." That future is now: "Today's neo-liberal hegemony," says Buck-Morss, "sets the stage for Universal History."[60]

The archive, however, is never finished. It is not the case that Marsalis would sail into the future of jazz by a territorial expansion based on franchising the Jazz at Lincoln Center brand. Although not untrue, that, in a way, would be too crass. In a rhetorical turn remarkable even for someone as polemically loquacious as Marsalis, he seems to have understood that the archive demanded re-inscription at home. "The 20th century was about communication and the next millennium is going to be about integration," he has said, explaining that

> it's going to go to where jazz started. When Jellyroll [*sic*] Morton described the red light district in New Orleans, he said, "Everybody was there." He was naming all these things that went into jazz—all the Italians and French people and different types of black folks and Creoles. That's the melting pot. Now we have the capability to communicate with each other on a much more global level and once you know you can speak to somebody, then the question becomes, what are you gonna say? And now that we can come closer together with the airplane and the Internet and satellite hookups, we're going to see a much quicker integration. And when that starts to happen, it just means that we'll be where jazz started[,] because jazz was ahead of its time. The expression of jazz had nothing to do with what was going on in the United States of America in 1900. So we're getting ready to see the world step into the world that jazz was born into. All these people like Louis Armstrong and Jellyroll Morton, they were way ahead of their time.[61]

From one perspective, this temporal reversal looks like a severe case of schizochronia, not Marsalis's or Morton's but U.S. society's as a whole, unable to hear, let alone value, the ecumenical reach of jazz musicians. Still, we find the world co-signing the archive, circa 1900, not across the Gulf of Mexico but already in the bustling port of New Orleans. And once again we find the nexus of race and culture as the compelling reason to invoke the world. Marsalis: "The problem is, [*sic*] our culture was not up to the task of absorbing our music. The music was too powerful. It was dealing too much with what is and we were dealing too much with what we wanted to impose on culture, mainly through the vehicle of race but through other things also. I mean, how are you gonna accept Louis Armstrong for who he is when everything that's told you [says] these people ain't shit." The answer might well be "through the imperial archive."

JAZZ AND ITS MUSICIANS created a world at home for themselves and a place in the world to their nation by linking together worlds that were not necessarily linked in the first place. Considered from the much-vaunted perspective of Jacques Attali, turn-of-the-century New Orleans jazz would hold prophetic force, heralding in sound a society yet to come, as Marsalis affirms. But from the perspective developed here, those early, worldly stirrings heralded as well the advent of imperial jazz and with it a society ever ready to call on the world, a society and indeed a nation that, however split at its racial core, is very much of a piece in its position that what grows here must be from here, empire be damned.

The cases explored here reflect the resiliency of imperial demands. These account both for the archival capacity to sustain the fantasy of a self-sufficient aesthetic and creative domus and the maintenance of a racial order where ongoing inequality still rules the day. I have tried to reflect on the conscription of aurality in the service of these contradictory forces. As an expression infused with "something negroid" (Handy), as an occasion for encounters across histories and times (Gillespie), as a gathering force for interculturality, and as the momentous opportunity to showcase the "worldliness" of its notable exponents (Marsalis, Ellington), jazz is paradoxically governed by laws that exceed the nation's racial order. Imperial jazz is heteronomous, but we cannot know it. That, perhaps, is the fate of the justly celebrated coming together of music, race, and empire in the United States.

NOTES

1. Howard Zinn, *A People's History of the United States* (New York: Longman, 1996), 290–91.

2. For diverging accounts of U.S. empire, see Klaus Schwabe, "The Global Role of the United States and Its Imperial Consequences, 1898–1973," in *Imperialism and After: Continuities and Discontinuities,* ed. Wolfgang J. Mommsen and Jürgen Osterhammel, 13–33 (London: Allen and Unwin, 1986), cited in Amy Kaplan, "'Left Alone with America': The Absence of Empire in the Study of American Culture," in *Cultures of United States Imperialism,* ed. Amy Kaplan and Donald E. Pease (Durham: Duke University Press, 1993), 12; George Kennan, *American Diplomacy: 1900–1950* (New York: Penguin, 1952); William Appleman Williams, *The Tragedy of American Diplomacy* (New York: W. W. Norton, 1959); Williams, *Empire as a Way of Life: An Essay on the Causes and*

Character of America's Present Predicament, along with a Few Thoughts about an Alternative (New York: Oxford University Press, 1980); and John Tomlinson, *Cultural Imperialism: A Critical Introduction* (Baltimore, MD: Johns Hopkins University Press, 1991).

3. Timothy Brennan, *Secular Devotion: Afro-Latin Music and Imperial Jazz* (New York: Verso, 2008); Ruth Glasser, *My Music Is My Flag: Puerto Rican Musicians and Their New York Communities, 1917–1940* (Durham: Duke University Press, 1997). On the "contact zone," see Mary Louise Pratt, *Imperial Eyes: Travel Writing and Transculturation* (New York: Routledge, 1992).

4. W. C. Handy, *Father of the Blues: An Autobiography*, ed. Arna Bontemps, with a foreword by Abbe Niles (New York: Macmillan, 1941), 99.

5. For an earlier Cuba–New Orleans link, see John Storm Roberts, *The Latin Tinge: The Impact of Latin American Music on the United States* (New York: Oxford University Press, 1999), 27ff.; Ned Sublette, *Cuba and Its Music: From the First Drums to the Mambo* (Chicago: Chicago Review, 2004), 147–56; Brennan, *Secular Devotion*, 214ff. For a broader trans-Caribbean account, see Ned Sublette, *The World That Made New Orleans: From Spanish Silver to Congo Square* (Chicago: Lawrence Hill, 2008).

6. See Gilbert Chase, *America's Music, from the Pilgrims to the Present*, rev. 3rd ed. (1955; repr., Champaign: University of Illinois Press, 1982); Eileen Southern, *The Music of Black Americans: A History* (New York: W. W. Norton, 1971).

7. See Resolution 57, U.S. House of Representatives, passed September 23, 1987, approved by the U.S. Senate on December 3, 1987. In 1991, Lincoln Center began a department dedicated to jazz, with seed money from the Lila Wallace–*Reader's Digest* Fund ($3.4 million) to support a national performing network for jazz. By 1996, Jazz at Lincoln Center became a full-fledged institution dedicated to the archiving, dissemination, education, and performance of jazz. As of 2012, its annual budget was $41 million.

8. Wynton Marsalis, "What Jazz Is—and Isn't," *New York Times*, July 3, 1988, accessed April 15, 2011, www.nytimes.com/1988/07/31/arts/music-what-jazz-is-and-isn-t.html ?pagewanted=all&src=pm; Robert O'Meally, *The Jazz Cadence of American Culture* (New York: Columbia University Press, 1998). Although widely considered "progressive," O'Meally's volume and its companion, *Uptown Conversation: The New Jazz Studies*, ed. Robert O'Meally, Brent Hayes Edwards, and Farah Jasmine Griffin (New York: Columbia University Press, 2004), are silent about U.S. imperialism's role in jazz.

9. Brennan, *Secular Devotion*, 223. U.S black exceptionalists include James Weldon Johnson, J. Rosamond Johnson, Ralph Ellison, and Richard Wright. U.S. black intellectuals emphasizing "the Caribbean connection" include Claude McKay, Langston Hughes, and, of course, W. E. B. Du Bois (ibid., 224).

10. The expression designates processes of musical exchange between the territorial United States and its citizens and the Hispanophone black Caribbean and the dynamics of dissemination of the musical forms of this exchange, all in the context of nineteenth-century U.S. military interventions. The word "jazz" encompasses a family of popular music genres that Brennan recognizes as emanating from these processes: jazz in its various forms, salsa, disco, and rap, but also ballroom and Broadway music.

11. Ibid., 216–17.

12. See Kaplan, "'Left Alone with America.'" For imperial political experimentation, see Greg Grandin, *Empire's Workshop: Latin America, the United States, and the Rise of the New Imperialism* (New York: Henry Holt, 2007). On cultural imperialism, see Gilbert M. Joseph, Catherine C. Legrand, and Ricardo D. Salvatore, eds., *Close Encounters of Empire: Writing the Cultural History of U.S.-Latin American Relations* (Durham: Duke University Press, 1998). Neither text considers music.

13. Amy Kaplan, *The Anarchy of Empire in the Making of U.S. Culture* (Cambridge: Harvard University Press, 2002), 1.

14. Elizabeth Povinelli, *The Empire of Love: Toward a Theory of Intimacy, Genealogy, and Carnality* (Durham: Duke University Press, 2006), 17. Povinelli paraphrases Du Bois's comments in the encyclical *To the World* from the second Pan-African Congress (London session, 1921).

15. Kaplan, *Anarchy of Empire*, 13–14.

16. Étienne Balibar and Immanuel Wallerstein, *Race, Nation, Class: Ambiguous Identities* (London: Verso, 1991), 53. The point was forcefully made by Du Bois, who wrote of a "rigid racial hierarchy supporting racism at home and colonialism abroad," in *Darkwater: Voices from within the Veil* (New York: Harcourt, Brace, and Howe, 1920), 540, quoted in Kaplan, *Anarchy of Empire*, 240. See also Nikhil Pal Singh, *Black Is a Country: Race and the Unfinished Struggle for Democracy* (Cambridge: Harvard University Press, 2004).

17. Handy, *Father of the Blues*, 99–100. "Maori—a Samoan Dance" (pub. 1908) was a composition by William H. Tyers (1870–1924), a founder-member of ASCAP (the American Society of Composers, Authors, and Publishers). Tyers's exotica also include a 1910 number entitled "Panama—a Characteristic Novelty." Sublette calls "Maori" a habanera (*Cuba and Its Music*, 326), while Roberts hears a syncopated bass "vaguely reminiscent of the rumba" (*The Latin Tinge*, 41).

18. This adapts Foucault's idea of the archive as an active force for ongoing enunciations at any given present, governing the explanatory patterns that confer to this or that statement a historical status. The archive refers to the epistemic force of discursive formations and their accumulated statements, that is, the system of relations between the sayable and the said, the sayable and the unsaid, the unsayable and the said, and the unsayable and the unsaid. Michel Foucault, *The Archaeology of Knowledge*, trans. A. M. Sheridan Smith (New York: Pantheon, 1972).

The archive does not refer to the actual storing of documentation or necessarily to the actually said: "Par archive, j'entends d'abord la masse des choses dites dans une culture, conservées, valorisées, réutilisées, répétées et transformées. Bref toute cette masse verbale qui a été fabriquée par les hommes, investie dans leurs techniques et leurs institutions, et qui est tissée avec leur existence et leur histoire. Cette masse de choses dites, je l'envisage non pas du côté de la langue, du système linguistique qu'elles mettent en œuvre, mais du côté des opérations qui lui donnent naissance. . . . C'est, en un mot, . . . l'analyse des conditions historiques qui rendent compte de ce qu'on dit ou de ce qu'on rejette, ou de ce qu'on transforme dans la masse des choses dites." Michel Foucault, "La naissance d'un monde," in *Dits et écrits, 1954–1988*, vol. 1 (1969; repr., Paris: Gallimard, 1994), 786–87.

19. See also Thomas Richards, *The Imperial Archive: Knowledge and the Fantasy of Empire* (London: Verso, 1998).

20. The concept of archive assembles notions of origination and perpetuity, authenticity and authority, of a static order and preservation subject to often unruly discoveries, along with practices of public institutionalization and private, at times intimate, selection of its holdings. See Jacques Derrida, *Archive Fever: A Freudian Impression*, trans. Eric Prenowitz (Chicago: University of Chicago Press, 1996). The archive both anxiously holds and withholds time. "It is a question of the future, the question of the future itself, the question of a response, of a promise and of a responsibility for tomorrow. The archive: if we want to know what that will have meant, we will only know in times to come," which is to say never (ibid., 36). Remembering and forgetting are shorthand for a constellation that might include denying, ignoring, refusing, disavowing, and being indifferent to.

21. For the archive as "an indefinite accumulation of time," see Michel Foucault, "Of Other Spaces: Utopias and Heterotopias," *diacritics* 16 (Spring 1986): 26. Howard Slater writes of the archive as a system of cultural preferences held in common that may take material form as a dynamic record ("Cannon Blasting for a Living Culture," *Resonance* 8, no. 1 [London Musicians' Collective, 1999]: 4–6). I combine Derrida's principle of ambiguous withholding and deferral, Foucault's notions of indefinite accumulation and epistemic force, and Slater's idea of cultural preferences.

22. John Dewey, *The Public and Its Problems* (New York: Henry Holt, 1927).

23. Igor Kopytoff, "The Cultural Biography of Things: Commoditization as Process," in *The Social Life of Things: Commodities in Cultural Perspective*, ed. Arjun Appadurai (New York: Cambridge University Press, 1986), 64–94.

24. Derrida, *Archive Fever*.

25. The first major "Latin" hit in the United States, "La Paloma" (by the Basque composer Sebastián Yradier, composed in 1859 and published in New York City in 1877) featured the habanera rhythm in the bass.

26. Alan Lomax, *Mister Jelly Roll: The Fortunes of Jelly Roll Morton, New Orleans Creole and Inventor of Jazz* (New York: Universal Library, Grosset and Dunlap, 1950), 62. Available at www.traditionalmusic.co.uk/jelly-roll/ (accessed April 11, 2011).

27. Roberts, *Latin Tinge*, 38–39.

28. Sublette, *Cuba and Its Music*, 326.

29. David Novak, "2.5 x 6 Metres of Space: Japanese Music Coffee Houses and Experimental Practices of Listening," *Popular Music* 27, no. 1 (2008): 15–16.

30. J. Lorand Matory, *Black Atlantic Religion: Tradition, Transnationalism, and Matriarchy in the Afro-Brazilian Candomblé* (Princeton, NJ: Princeton University Press, 2005), 3.

31. Schizophonia "refer[s] to the split between an original sound and its electroacoustic transmission or reproduction"; "originally," he maintains, "all sounds . . . occurred at one time and in one place only." R. Murray Schafer, *The Tuning of the World* (New York: Knopf, 1977), 90. Sonic archives are intrinsically schizophonic: "[since recording and transmission] we have split the sound from the maker of the sound . . . in time as well as in space. A record collection may contain items from widely diverse cultures and historical periods" (ibid.). This influential notion comes to apply to any separation of sound in some original material environment and immaterial culture and it has been explored in popular music studies. See Steven Feld, "From Schizophonia to Schismogenesis: On the Discourses and Commodification and Practices of 'World Music' and 'World

Beat,'" in *Music Grooves: Essays and Dialogues*, ed. Charles Keil and Steven Feld (Chicago: University of Chicago Press, 1994), 257–89. For competing critiques, see Jonathan Sterne, *The Audible Past: Cultural Origins of Sound Reproduction* (Durham: Duke University Press, 2003), 20ff. and 342ff.; and Frances Dyson, *Sounding New Media: Immersion and Embodiment in the Arts and Culture* (Berkeley: University of California Press, 2009), 73ff.

32. John J. Johnson, *A Hemisphere Apart: The Foundations of United States Policy toward Latin America* (Baltimore, MD: Johns Hopkins University Press, 1990).

33. Jairo Moreno, "Bauzá—Gillespie—Latin/Jazz: Difference, Modernity, and the Black Caribbean," *South Atlantic Quarterly* 103, no. 1 (2004): 81–99.

34. Another overarching universalism—the absolute value of complexity as such—makes it possible to posit the first universalism as complexity at the origin and the other as complexity at the destination.

35. The Cuban critic Leonardo Acosta (in *Descarga Cubana: El jazz en Cuba, 1900–1950* [Havana: Ediciones Unión, 2000]) critiques the claims of Gillespie as well as those of the Cuban-born immigrant Mario Bauzá to having initiated the experimentation of jazz and Cuban music.

36. Jason Stanyek, "Transmissions of an Interculture: Pan-African Jazz and Inter-cultural Improvisation," in *The Other Side of Nowhere: Jazz, Improvisation, and Communities in Dialogue*, ed. Daniel Fischlin and Ajay Heble (Middletown, CT: Wesleyan University Press, 2004), 87–130. The author ignores all preexisting formulations of interculturality, which come mainly from Latin American or Latin America–based authors such as Alejandro Grimson, Néstor García Canclini, and Katherine Walsh, to say nothing of Fernando Ortíz's key formulation of transculturation.

37. Michael Walzer, "Two Kinds of Universalism," in *Nation and Universe*, vol. 11 of *Tanner Lectures on Human Values*, ed. Grethe Peterson (Salt Lake City: University of Utah Press, 1990), 509–56.

38. Ibid., 515.

39. Ibid., 516.

40. See Anthony Giddens, *The Constitution of Society* (Berkeley: University of California Press, 1986). For the critique presented here, see Manuel DeLanda, *A New Philosophy of Society: Assemblage Theory and Social Complexity* (London: Continuum, 2006).

41. Marsalis, "What Jazz Is—and Isn't."

42. Ellington's travels abroad were part of the U.S. State Department's cultural diplomacy efforts. See Penny Von Eschen, *Satchmo Blows Up the World: Jazz Ambassadors Play the Cold War* (Cambridge: Harvard University Press, 2006).

43. Marsalis, "What Jazz Is—and Isn't."

44. Ibid.

45. Travis Jackson, in "Tourist Point of View: Ellington's Musical Souvenirs" (unpublished manuscript), proposes that Ellington's "aim was to allow all the experiences he had—musical and nonmusical—to *influence* his way of composing," not to "*imitate* the different musics he heard during the tours." His emphasis. Also cited in Von Eschen, *Satchmo*, 144. Thanks to Professor Jackson for sharing his manuscript with me.

46. *Hegemonía cultural y políticas de la diferencia*, ed. Alejando Grimson and Karina Bidaseca (Buenos Aires: CLACSO, 2013), 11.

47. Paul Rabinow, "Representations Are Social Facts: Modernity and Post-Modernity in Anthropology," in *Writing Cultures: The Poetics and Politics of Ethnography*, ed. James Clifford and George E. Marcus (Berkeley: University of California Press, 1986), 258.

48. Pierre-André Taguieff, *The Force of Prejudice: On Racism and Its Doubles*, trans. and ed. Hassan Melehy (Minneapolis: University of Minnesota Press, 2001); Ulf Hannerz, "Cosmopolitans and Locals in World Culture," in *Global Culture: Nationalism, Globalization and Modernity*, ed. Mike Featherstone (London: Sage, 1990), 239.

49. A comparison can be made between the actual solidarity with African political struggles expressed and acted upon by jazz notables such as Max Roach, among others, and the cosmopolitan vision expressed by Guy Warren upon his return to Ghana from the United States, where, he said, black Americans could not quite comprehend his position. For a thoughtful engagement with cosmopolitanism, see Steven Feld, *Jazz Cosmopolitanism in Accra: Five Musical Years in Ghana* (Durham: Duke University Press, 2012). On jazz solidarity with African causes, see Ingrid Monson, *Freedom Sounds: Civil Rights Call Out to Jazz and Africa* (New York: Oxford University Press, 2007); and Robin D. G. Kelley, *Africa Speaks, America Answers: Modern Jazz in Revolutionary Times* (Cambridge: Harvard University Press, 2012).

50. Bruce Robbins, "Introduction Part I: Actually Existing Cosmopolitanism," in *Cosmopolitics: Thinking and Feeling beyond the Nation*, ed. Pheng Cheah and Bruce Robbins (Minneapolis: University of Minnesota Press, 1998), 1–19.

51. Bruno Latour, "On the Difficulty of Being Glocal," ART-*e*-FACT 4 (2005), accessed March 31, 2015, http://artefact.mi2.hr/_a04/lang_en/theory_latour_en.htm.

52. Gustavo Lins Ribeiro, *Cultural Diversity as a Global Discourse*, Série Antropologia 412 (Brasília: Departamento de Antropologia da Universidade de Brasília, 2007), accessed March 31, 2015, http://repositorio.unb.br/bitstream/10482/17697/1/ARTIGO _DiversidadeCulturalComo.pdf.

53. Timothy Brennan, "Cosmo-Theory," *South Atlantic Quarterly* 100, no. 3 (2001): 659–91.

54. This schematic account benefited from a critique by Stephan Hammel.

55. Étienne Balibar, "'Rights of Man' and 'Rights of the Citizen': The Modern Dialectic of Equality and Freedom," in *Masses, Classes, Ideas: Studies on Politics and Philosophy before and after Marx* (New York: Routledge, 1994), 39–59.

56. Paul Gilroy, *Darker Than Blue: On the Moral Economies of Black Atlantic Culture* (Cambridge: Belknap Press of Harvard University Press, 2010), 176.

57. James C. McKinley Jr., "Jazz at Lincoln Center to Expand, First in Qatar," *New York Times*, November 15, 2011.

58. Qatar was the staging site for the U.S. invasion of Iraq.

59. Susan Buck-Morss, *Hegel, Haiti, and Universal History* (Pittsburgh: University of Pittsburgh Press, 2009), 151.

60. Ibid., 79.

61. Bill Milkowski, "Wynton Marsalis: One Future, Two Views," *Jazz Times* (March 2000), accessed December 13, 2013, http://jazztimes.com/articles/20520-wynton -marsalis-one-future-two-views.

7 · WHERE THEY CAME FROM

Reracializing Music in the Empire of Silence

PHILIP V. BOHLMAN

Rites of Return

March 2012. I again return to Ultadanga, Kolkata, India, and once again I set in motion the ethnographic present of this essay with its complex and considerable historical dimensions. I have been here before, and I shall return again. My return as a scholarly pilgrim privileged to encounter music and religion that are not my own is possible because of a history of empire, a history unavoidable in the everyday that forms the rites of return. Those rites unfold as I write, witnessing the everyday of empire. Each day, outside my bedroom window along a small street in Kolkata, the daily street market awakens. The

FIGURE 7.1. The Ultadanga street market in the early morning.

first arrivals, with their massive bundles of fruits, vegetables, and grains, have already claimed space along the street. They have summoned rickshaw drivers and the elderly men navigating wheelbarrows with a musical language forged for function and efficacy; there is transformation of labor from the fields along the Ganges floodplain to the streets of the neighborhoods along Kolkata's periphery. The Bengali laborers who ply the borders of empire envoice its sonic geography no less today than in the halcyon days of the nineteenth-century Bengal Renaissance or twentieth-century Bengal modernism, the musical and political movements chronicled by the songs (*rabindrasangeet*) of Rabindranath Tagore.[1]

Ultadanga, the neighborhood in which I live during Indian fieldwork, is one of the poorest places in one of the poorest cities of the world. Its poorest residents claim the street with shanties and pallets, illegal but permitted during the many decades of West Bengal's Left Front government. The daily rhythm of my lane in Ultadanga—it is so small that it has no name of its own;

FIGURE 7.2. The Ultadanga street market in the afternoon.

rather it is known only as a street parallel to Bhihandra Road—as a place given presence through labor is evident in the transformation of language, from rural dialects of Bangla, the modern Bengali language, to the sounds of street vendors and vegetable sellers, each shaping a musical language through street-hawking to draw attention to the goods on sale. The street cries I know best are those of the onion and shallot merchants, who appear each morning directly below my window, three meters from where I've been sleeping. Space along the street is at a premium, and the songs of labor enhance the efficiency of presence. By noon, the merchants will bundle up their goods, giving over the street once again to an eerie absence (see figures 7.1 and 7.2).

The spatial transformations formed by labor in Ultadanga contrast dramatically with those on Park Street, fifteen kilometers away, formed by the traces of empire in the center of Kolkata. Flanked by the Asiatic Society, the Geological Survey of India, the Oxford Bookshop, Flury's Viennese Coffee House, and a colonial replica of the Moulin Rouge, Park Street remains the symbolic heart of the Raj.[2] Kolkata is the quintessentially imperial city, founded by the East India Company for British mercantile expansion into Asia in 1693. No one walking the streets of Kolkata (or Calcutta) can avoid the decaying edifice of empire. Kolkata is the epicenter of the songs (rabindrasangeet) and dance of Bengali cultural nationalism no less than Hindustani classical music, the palimpsest of Amitav Ghosh's *Sea of Poppies* no less than Dipesh Chakrabarty's *Provincializing Europe*.[3] The weight of empire in Kolkata is almost unbearable. And, still, the street hawkers of Ultadanga announce that the labors of farmers, transport drivers, vegetable merchants, and street hawkers daily transform its spaces, sounding them again at the edge of empire.

At the center of this essay is the space that forms through the triangulation of music, race, and empire. In the pages that follow I navigate these spaces as they have become a part of my own projects over many years—and in the essay's ethnographic present formed from the rites of return. My use of the metaphor, triangulation, arises from both rhetorical and methodological contexts. "Triangulation"—determining the location of an unknown point by fixing its relation to two known points at sea—developed as a means of navigating the seas to afford new efficiency for the spread of empire. Just as Ultadanga's street-market spaces reveal the triangulated mobility that daily gives new presence to the peripheries of an old empire, so too will the spaces of earlier encounter appear in the course of the following pages. The temporal and temporary mobility of presence will also contrast with conflict and violence at the edge of empire, for it is in many, even most, of these spaces that questions of difference and sameness often fail to yield safe spaces.

Triangulation is and was an inexact science, if indeed it was truly a science at all. Despite or because of its inexactitude, nonetheless, triangulation is inseparable from the paths of return that have historically charted empire. Its inexactitude is as striking today as ever, particularly as we consider the ways in which it has been used to express the growing determination to force racialized peoples from the spaces of modern societies and states. The spaces of the new empires—the European Union or postimmigrant America—seem to those with the power to enforce their size as if they were too small. Absence and presence have become mutually exclusive in the twenty-first-century politics of audible empire. Triangulating "where they came from" has proved to be one of the great illusions of our own day.

Presence/Absence

Every state has the right to decide who may and may not immigrate to it.
—THILO SARRAZIN, *Deutschland schafft sich ab*

Europe cannot close its eyes to illegal camps.
—NICOLAS SARKOZY, September 16, 2010

We're victims of an event we don't want, . . . but maybe if Brazil learns to respect our choice to stay in our homes, the Olympics will be something to celebrate in the end.
—INALVA MENDES BRITO, March 10, 2012

In contrast to the ethnographic opening of this essay the epigraphs that lead into its main body could not ring more ominously.[4] In recent years, always in the name of modernization and globalization, we have witnessed a series of actions against migration throughout the world. The actions against migration are legally sanctioned, and they are carried out with force. They openly employ a language calling for an end to migration, inevitably suggesting that it is migrants themselves who will benefit most from the end of migration. The acts to end migration in the twenty-first century have become so widespread and frequent that the everyday events that constitute them juxtapose the narratives of the past with the ethnographic moments of the present. Each act has a history that is ongoing as I write; each expands its global reach and international significance as the ethnographic present continues. Such is the very presence of migration in a lived-in world.

Migration policy, with its implications of who can become an American citizen, forms one of the longest and most contested narrative threads in the history of the United States. When I first drafted this essay, during a national election campaign in 2012, those narrative threads were unraveling at an ever-increasing rate, above all along the borders of empire and nation. In spring 2010, the state legislature of Arizona had passed S.B. 1070, a law that permitted Arizona police to require any individual to show documentation of the right to reside in the United States. Individuals without proper documentation—immigrant papers, green cards, or legal citizenship—could be immediately deported. The target of the law was clear: migrants from Mexico should not be allowed to live in Arizona. By 2012, thirty-one states had introduced legislation modeled on S.B. 1070, and five states—Alabama, Georgia, Indiana, South Carolina, and Utah—had passed such legislation. Throughout the election year of 2012, the restraint of enforcement remained temporarily in place, awaiting a decision on constitutionality by the United States Supreme Court and legislative action by the U.S. Congress. In 2015, with another American election on the horizon, immigration reform, as it is euphemistically called, still lies far beyond that horizon.

In August 2010, the government of France began to force Roms (Romani people) from the *banlieux* in which they lived and deport them to Eastern Europe, after giving each of them €300. The only Roms officially targeted by the action, aggressively backed by President Nicolas Sarkozy, were those believed to be migratory, especially those who had migrated across the open borders of Europe from Romania and Bulgaria since the implementation of the Schengen Process of 2007. After thousands of Roms had already been deported from their homes, the European Commission officially asked France to stop its deportation of migrants. The question of deporting migrants dominated the summit of EU leaders on September 17, 2010, when France was joined by other EU countries in claiming its right to deport migrants as it saw fit. The practice of cleansing urban neighborhoods and imperial border regions of Romani people forms one of the longest European histories of displacement, so long, indeed, that it has come to define European national and racial identity itself, forming a history of genocidal actions to the spectacle of Romani music in popular culture.[5]

In late August 2010, Thilo Sarrazin, a German economist who had served in the highest commissions to rebuild the economy of a reunified Germany, as finance senator for Berlin, and from 2009 as a member of the board of directors of the German central bank (Deutsche Bundesbank), published a book that called for stopping the future decline of Germany by restricting the presence of Muslims, especially Turkish migrants.[6] That Turkish music had fully entered Germany's urban and national soundscapes, from clubs and music academies in Berlin's Kreuzberg district to the new mosques of Cologne and Hamburg, failed to sound the present for Sarrazin.[7] Instead, he made extensive use of economic statistics to justify his claims, and he mixed these with the pseudo-scientific evidence of genetic traits in Germany's elite class of intellectuals. The old debates in German history about those who belonged and those who did not raged once again. Coupling his statistics with epigraphs from Goethe at the beginning of many chapters, Sarrazin deepened the historical debate about whether the Germany of Goethe and Schiller, Bach, and Beethoven, could ever be home to non-Germans. Soon after publication, Sarrazin's *Germany Dismantles Itself* appeared in translation in many languages (seventeen within the first six months after publication), and Sarrazin had become a public celebrity, championing Germany's role in enforcing austerity in the southern nations of the Eurozone, long sources of migrants for Germany's labor force.[8]

Finally, we return to the immediate ethnographic present and to the destruction of the urban *favelas* of Brazil in preparation for the World Cup in 2014 and the Olympics in 2016. The removal of migrant settlements to make way for progress and the public spectacle of globalization has a long history, formed from the counterpoint of music, empire, and race, and the dissonance between the global-national and the local-racial. That counterpoint could not sustain the history of racial and imperial divide that in Brazil, where the first favelas, called *bairros africanos* (African neighborhoods), began to encircle the imperial city in the eighteenth century. The favelas provided spaces of musical exchange and hybridity, the formation of a sonic mix that shaped and was shaped by the mobility of many generations of migrants. As the Brazilian national identity changed, responding to the migratory movements of Afro-Brazilians, so too did the "favelization" (*favelização*) of the Brazilian metropole. Even though as many as 6 percent of all Brazilians lived in favelas by 2010, and the plight of disenfranchised residents was well known internationally because of films such as Fernando Meirelles and Kátia Lund's *Cidade de Deus* (City of God, 2002), the need to cleanse the favelas and deport their residents to make place for soccer stadiums and Olympic villages (e.g., in the Rio de Janeiro favela of Vila Autodromo) led to police action in 2010. Destruction and deportation were initiated forcefully, but resistance from the favela dwellers followed peacefully in 2012, envoiced through musical acts of public presence. It has not proved easy to accelerate the history of deporting those living at the edges of empire.

The Discourse of Migration and Music: "Where Music Comes From"

A growing understanding that music was spatially malleable and mobile, that it migrated itself no less than it accompanied migration, has been one of the measures of musical modernity and, more recently, musical modernism.

The metaphysics of music's mobility, which received its impetus particularly during the Enlightenment, recognized both the objective and subjective dimensions of music. Music could be moved, *and* it could move. Music's ontology arose from its subjective, human dimensions and from its objective, autonomous dimensions as sound. The metaphysics of music's mobility were crucial to Johann Gottfried Herder's Enlightenment invention of the concept of *Volkslied* (folk song), and we witness this in the very language Herder used to describe folk song in his 1778–79 *Volkslieder* (Folk songs): "Music's rhapsodies do not remain in bookstores or bound to piles of paper, rather in the ear and the heart of living singers and listeners, from which they are gathered, indeed, after they have gathered many different meanings and prejudices before they finally reach us."[9]

In the course of the nineteenth and twentieth centuries, mobility increasingly made music modern, and by extension recognizing music's mobility transformed the ways the modern sciences of music located music in lived-in and changing worlds. The nineteenth-century science of folklore set out to understand how it was that music moved from one place to another. The measure of movement was the way in which oral tradition provided the contexts for folk music's texts, allowed them to be transmitted with fixed identities capable of yielding variations. Folk-music theories affixed principles for the geographical dimensions of movement, famously, for example, in Wilhelm Tappert's theory of *wandernde Melodien* (wandering melodies), which literally could travel across rivers, mountains, and vast expanses of time and place.[10] Tappert's notion of horizontal melodic movement formed a matrix with the vertical model of social movement in song texts proposed by the nestor of German folk-song research, John Meier, who argued that folk song formed as *Kunstlieder im Volksmunde* (art songs in the mouths of the people), that is, through a type of *gesunkenes Kulturgut* (fallen cultural value) appropriated by the people in geographical proximity.[11]

Modern scholarship has long since modified such earlier concepts of mobility, which were closely tied to notions of empire, but the metaphysics of musical mobility have continued to shape the ways in which ethnomusicology and musical folklore locate music in modernity until the present. During the period between the two world wars, comparative musicologists formalized their discipline by establishing the path music followed in global movement. One of the most fundamental questions sought to unravel just why the music of one place was like that of another. Or why it was just a bit different, in certain systemic ways. Among the most significant factors of musical difference produced by mobility were race and empire, which formed the systematic musicology allowing for a new anthropology (*neue Völkerkunde*) in the prisoner-of-war camps intensively studied by European comparativists during World War I.[12]

Following World War II, when the fields of folklore and musical folklore retooled themselves to focus on community, region, nation, and race, the metaphysics of mobility took a turn quite directly toward migration. It is this turn that continues to shape ethnomusicology's position toward music, identity, and migration in the twenty-first century. Fundamental to the turn was the assertion that music was such a powerful marker of identity that it provided a cultural glue, or core, during the migration and displacement that world wars and colonial struggle had created. Scholars in music argued that music was one of the most resilient aspects of migratory and immigrant cultures. It was in song, for example, that ethnic language survived the longest, often long after it had disappeared elsewhere. Music was such a valued marker of identity that migrant groups and exiles took special pains to bring it with them. It was in their music that one immigrant world distinguished itself from others. In the normative migration of a postcolonial world, music was the primary agent of difference.

Notwithstanding the laudable attempt to endow the metaphysics of musical mobility with difference and diversity, the history I have just sketched has been encumbered by its own stasis and telos toward specific goals. History's movement, thus, culminates in the very end of history. The stasis produced by teleological mobility is surely evident in the discourse that represents it. It is for these reasons that a powerful political and financial leader, such as Thilo Sarrazin, can wield such power. The usual language used to describe migration and music privileges a path of aesthetic sameness, in which place is fixed because migration eventually comes to an end. The music of empire and nation remains intact, as German or American, classical or Western. Within the metropole, however, the paths of mobility resist the teleological bounding of space, seeking instead the paths of return to the spaces opened by the workers and inhabitants of the metropole, such as those in Kolkata with which I began this essay.

Encounter and the Silence of Empire

At the beginning of Islam, singing belonged to this discipline. . . . Abû l-Faraj al-Isfahânî wrote a book on songs, the *Kitâb al-Aghânî*. In it, he dealt with the whole of the history, poetry, genealogy, battle days, and ruling dynasties of the Arabs. —IBN KHALDÛN, *The Muqaddimah*, fourteenth century

To this point in the essay, empire has played a rather silent role. It was centrally present even in the spatial peripheries of Ultadanga, the borders crossed by Romani musicians, and the Brazilian favelas once known as bairros africanos.

I now turn to the configuration of space in empire by historically triangulating the silence of encounter—of musical and historical encounter, of colonial and postcolonial encounter. I begin in Basra, Iraq, one of the greatest centers of Muslim theology, philosophy, and aesthetics. Throughout its history Basra has been shaped through imperial encounter. It lay at the borders between Islamic political empires, the Abbasid and the Umayyad. Its schools of learning and theology drew generously from Arabic- and Persian-language traditions and benefited from geographical access to intellectual exchange from the Arabian peninsula, the Persian gulf, the delta formed from the Mesopotamian confluence, and the regions stretching to the northeast across Iran to Central Asia and to the east toward Afghanistan, Pakistan, and India. Local schools of Islamic thought flourished amid Basra's historical multiculturalism. Basra has played a particularly important role in the spread of the British Empire, at historical moments of its earliest expansion and in the twenty-first century for the military exercise of imperial nostalgia. The most modern migrant community of Jews in India, still known as "Baghdadi Jews," was crucial to establishing the British Empire's Calcutta (Kolkata) foothold in South Asia and was intellectually and culturally formed by the Muslim empires intersecting at Basra. In the most recent Iraq War, the British military headquarters were in Basra.

The cultural identity of Basra has long been shaped by the musics and musicians that encountered each other in the cosmopolitan entrepôt and the marshlands stretching from center to periphery. Different histories of encounter began with the British occupations at the beginnings of the twentieth and twenty-first centuries, in which violence and silence were imposed through military encounter. The utter failure of the British to understand the culture of Basra and the succession of military missteps belong to the well-known narrative of the Iraq War. Less well known, perhaps, are the ways in which the military occupation of the British during the first decade of the twenty-first century sustained the aesthetic and political domains that have enriched and troubled Basra, in the past and now again in our present. I turn now to encounter in Basra, beginning with the present, so shaped by the perplexed selfness of the West, but then embarking on the much longer historical excursus to the past, in search of an otherness silenced by encounter.

Basra has been a center for music and music making throughout its history as a cultural center for Islam. Soon after invasion and occupation in the spring of 2003, British and American forces seized on what they perceived as a difference signified by a flourishing musical life in Basra. Music occupied a surprisingly public presence in the city and its environs. Radio stations were vigorously broadcasting, and to the great surprise of the provisional military government, Basra boasted an active concert life, with auditoriums hosting public performances and recording studios producing a wide range of musical styles. Somewhat less familiar but no less distinctive were the private clubs and buildings in which more specialized, semiprivate music making took place. Basra quickly emerged as an emblem of a New Iraq, a Muslim metropole that had not fallen prey to the putative Islamic ban on music. The thriving culture of musical difference served the discourse of early success and justification at the beginning of the Iraq War, and it was added proof that the British, at least, were managing their encounter with Islam in a civilized way. Basra, so such discourse claimed, was assuming a modern place in western civilization.

By 2004, however, the history of a New Basra and a New Iraq radically rerouted itself. Just as local Iraqis turned against the occupying British, so too there was an upsurge in violence directed at private and public music gatherings. In the media, the violence that accompanied music making was blamed on Islam, which, in the language of colonial encounter, had historically banned music and was doing so again. Music clubs and other buildings, in which the people of Basra gathered to listen to music—the modern equivalent of Sufi "houses of samā'"—were no longer safe havens. How could this happen when music in Basra had enjoyed a treasured place in the public sphere, even under Saddam Hussein, when musicians performed publicly and enjoyed the patronage of studios for broadcast and recording? The early 2004 reports from Basra used the threat against music to provide a context for interpreting the growing insurgence against British troops, who, so it seemed only months earlier, had been a beneficent occupying force.

Music might have seemed to many a curious metaphor for understanding the rejection of the West, but news reports coming from Basra as the Iraqi insurgency began to coalesce in 2004 pointed again to Islam's presumed ban on music as a failure of Islam to embrace modernity. The complex metaphysics of music in Islam have long provided one of the most persistent tropes for drawing attention to Islam's irrationality and its failure to embrace the West. The failure to understand Muslim metaphysics of music accompanied the western criticism of the Islamic Revolution in Iran in the late 1970s. How incredible it seemed to many at the time that one of Ayatollah Khomeini's first "official acts" was to "ban music." As part of the post-9/11 crusade against Islam, U.S. commentators pointed to the ban on music by the Taliban as one more reason for ridding Afghanistan of Islamists and by extension launching the so-called global war on terror. In 2014, anxieties about music remain a significant discourse in the construction of Muslim otherness.[13]

As the Iraqi insurgency expanded into civil war, metaphysical discourse gave way to neocolonial discourse on music in Islam. Issues of encounter overwhelmed and silenced issues of being. The music and the music history that had afforded Basra its distinctive identity in Islamic history had been silenced. To understand the historical *longue durée* of Muslim music at the edges of empire, it is necessary to return to Basra in the tenth century of the Common Era. It was in Basra that the community of Islamic scholars known as the *Ikhwān aṣ-Ṣafāʿ* (Brethren of Purity) flourished during the tenth century, a moment of transition from Greek principles of music to those that reflect Islamic concepts of science and the universe. The Ikhwān aṣ-Ṣafāʿ are of special significance in the history of music in Muslim societies because they devoted a treatise, an "epistle," or *Rasaʿil* in a larger encyclopedic work, to music, in which the Pythagorean proportions of pitch and interval structure underwent a process of cultural translation, through which they achieved equivalents in both cosmological and metaphysical proportions. The Pythagorean measurements shifted from the monochord to the ʿūd, following a system established by Abū Yūsuf Yaʿqūb ibn Isḥāq al-Kindī (ca. 801–873 CE). Harmony expressed itself through cosmic measurements and also through the homologous relations of the music of the spheres to the physical proportions of the human body and the healthy functioning of its organs and humors. In Basra, musical canon was to become the musical language of empire through the European Middle Ages well into the sixteenth century.

The Ikhwān aṣ-Ṣafāʿ's *Epistle on Music* (tenth century) was critical for the transmission of a metaphysics of music from one empire to another, from Europe to Asia. It represented the emergence of a canon and of a systematic theory for music that departs in notable ways from Greek music theory and finds a home in the Muslim Middle East. The canonic principles that emerged in tenth-century Basra and Baghdad connected the physical nature of sound to the perception of sound in the physical body, thereby recognizing the distinctiveness of musical production and musical perception. Music assumed meaning at the nexus between sounded proportions in the universe and its re-sounding through the human body, and in this way it historically presages the metaphysics of mobility that I traced through the ethnographic moments with which I began this essay. In the ninth chapter of the *Epistle on Music* the Ikhwān aṣ-Ṣafāʿ summarize the systemic unity of music as a physical journey:

> We now return to the subject which occupies us and we say: if the meanings of the notes and melodies reach the rational faculties of the soul by the route of hearing, and if the signs of the meanings embedded

in the notes and melodies are imprinted on the soul, one can renounce their existence in the air, as one renounces what is written on tablets since the meaning of what is written is contained and retained in the memory. It is the same in the case of the law of the individual soul when it attains perfection, completion and the end of its mission in the body.[14]

The unity of the musical system theorized by the Ikhwān aṣ-Ṣafā' also extended to the materials of sound-producing instruments, the proportions of which lent themselves to representation through ciphers, for example, standing in for the four strings of the 'ūd. Music came into existence through a unity realized via the connections among complex parts, and many of these articulated the spiritual selfness that motivated the Ismaili brotherhood. In tenth-century Basra, it became possible to speak about how music came into being from silence, arguably for the first time, in a Muslim society, itself at the edges of empires spreading into Central and South Asia. In twenty-first-century Basra, the return to silence, following the encounter of the Iraq War, has been deafening.

Empire and the Histories of Silence

The history of imperial encounter is narrated by silence. The colonizer is the agent of silencing, for it is from the power to silence that the power to colonize and to subjugate eventually comes. For the colonized the anxiety of loss, of ending in silence, is overwhelming, even when it enters resistance, far more often as discourse than as action. As we reflect on the themes in this volume, we therefore ask ourselves if we can really refer to a narrative articulated by and through silence as history? Where is the historical evidence? What is the historical record, if it has disappeared or been removed? If the agents of history have been deported to where they came from?

The history of silence is not one of temporal stasis. The temporal telos could not be clearer, for its direction propels it toward the end of things. It is history that is ultimately and finally eschatological. The silence of encounter generates a history that is regressive, that eliminates all that would enter it to envoice difference and all who would choose no longer to be "people without history."[15] Regressive history might, at first glance, seem to make no sense. On one hand, it is anti-Hegelian, and it openly devalues progress and modernity; on the other, when we position it against Hegel's own claims about Africa as a place without history, regressive history paradoxically becomes Hegelian.[16]

The history of silence contains the unvoiced songs of the subaltern. Heard once, they are eliminated from traditional narratives of selfness, and they in turn eliminate tradition. There can be no question that the history of silence should be powerfully ethical, for colonial encounter is justified as moral imperative. Ultimately, as regressive history, the ethical and the moral converge in the eschatological. The great theorist of postcolonial criticism, Aimé Césaire, described the ethical vacuum of encounter in his 1955 *Discours sur le colonialisme* thus:

> I ask the following question: has colonization really *placed civilizations in contact*? Or, if you prefer, of all the ways of *establishing contact*, was it the best?
>
> I answer *no*.
>
> And I say that between *colonization* and *civilization* there is an infinite distance; that out of all the colonial expeditions that have been undertaken, out of all the colonial statutes that have been drawn up, out of all the memoranda that have been dispatched by all the ministries, there could not come a single human value.[17]

Music enters the history of empire as silence, not infrequently as a record of loss and death. In the volumes of folk song that Johann Gottfried Herder published in 1778 and 1779, history accrues at an accelerating pace from the earliest sections to the final sections, which appeared posthumously in print four years after Herder's death in 1803.[18] The teleology of Herder's representation of encounter is powerfully eschatological, by no means surprising, because, as a Lutheran pastor by training and profession, Herder was acutely aware of the need for ethical underpinnings in his thought and in the philosophy of his day. Folk songs—the music of the many parts of the world to which he turned for his examples—were imbued with history and with ethical meaning that reflects moral practice.

Increasingly, as one moves through Herder's collection of world music, with its songs previously gathered at colonial encounter, laments and songs of death proliferate. The laments record sadness and terror, the loss that occurs at moments of encounter. In the posthumously published appendix, the violence of colonial encounter overwhelms Herder's folk songs, particularly in the concluding folio of songs from and about the colonization of Madagascar, eleven songs—vocal commentaries in various genres—that Herder has translated from the French accounts of Count Évariste de Parny. The terror in colonial Madagascar, in the heart of darkness, is that of encounter with the armies and the missionaries of the Europeans, the racialized "whites" whose presence is vilified in the songs. We hear this terror, for example, in the lament, the *Totenklage*, for the fallen son of the king of Madagascar, sung by King Ampanani himself, and in call-and-response by the people of Madagascar:

AMPANANI: My son has fallen in battle! Oh, my friends, weep over the son of your leader. Take his body to the place in which the dead live. A high wall will protect him, for there will be the heads of bulls on that wall, which will be armed with threatening horns. Respect the place in which the dead live. Their sadness is terrible, and their revenge is gruesome. Weep over my son.

THE MEN: Never again will the blood of the enemies turn his arm red.

THE WOMEN: Never again will his lips kiss those of another.

THE MEN: Never again will fruit ripen for him.

THE WOMEN: Never again will his head rest on a tender bosom.

THE MEN: Never again will he sing, resting under a tree thick with leaves.

THE WOMEN: Never again will he whisper new enticements to his beloved.

AMPANANI: Cease, now, with your weeping over my son! Happiness should follow the mourning! Tomorrow, perhaps, we too will follow to the place he has gone.[19]

The history of empire is one of subjugating and resistance to subjugation, yielding violence. Amartya Sen argues that violence results when encounter is between monolithic systems, the self and other as irreconcilably different entities resulting from what Sen calls the "illusion of singular identity."[20] Whereas encounter should bring "civilizations together," it only heightens the gap between them, yielding Césaire's "infinite distance."[21] What we must not avoid as we reflect on silence as a leitmotif running through a volume on the audibility of empire is the reality that violence repeatedly returns to mark the music of encounter. For the Protestant missionary, evangelical hymnody becomes the music of a Christianity going off to war on a global scale. Turkish music enters Europe with the sound of an invading army. Resistance resounds in the music of civil war and insurgency. Where there is violence at encounter, there is also music, audible and inaudible.

Here is where the question of silence of empire becomes particularly historical, for the violence of music at encounter is unidirectional and teleological. It is meant to silence otherness. Silence is possible only after difference is reduced to sameness. Once the colonized and the missionized become the same, once they become mere stereotypes and repetitive images

FIGURE 7.3. Transcription of the Tupinamba melody in de Léry. From Stephen Greenblatt, *Marvelous Possessions: The Wonder of the New World* (Chicago: University of Chicago Press, 1991).

of singularity, it becomes impossible to experience their music as theirs. The mellifluousness of music at encounter signifies the appropriation that makes their music ours. Jean de Léry, the Calvinist missionary writing of the Tupinamba around the Bay of Rio de Janeiro in the mid-sixteenth century, inscribes the music of the other as his own, as chant, sacred but Christian in its melodic aura (see figure 7.3).

We know these ciphers of otherness reduced to sameness in music, for they inhabit the music history of the West, sounding the sonic orientalism of our selfness. It is in this projection of self and other in historical encounter that African bodies make music by always dancing. South Asian music is endowed with a universal spirituality. Exoticism levels the modal richness of East Asia. From perspectives both politically liberal and conservative, Latin American music is always already hybrid. Islam comes to be constituted as radical, fundamentalist, extreme. The history of empire has so brutally violated otherness that it is hardly surprising that silence retains such a lasting heritage. The paradox, nonetheless, remains that, because the violence of encounter refuses to subside, we can and must still listen to the silence of empire.

Imperial Soundings of Similarity

Empire does not only lie at great distance from us, and for this reason I return to geographies and ethnographies of more intimate proximity throughout this essay. It is also for this reason that I turn to music, race, and empire in the United States. Music serves encounter in a multitude of ways, providing those who confront each other with the means of translating words into action. The acts of translation—cultural translation, religious translation, translation of the meaning of life and death—are critical to music's performative power at encounter. The capacity of music to translate the untranslatable and the irreconcilable affords it remarkable power—a horrible potential for violence—at the moments of most extreme encounter. I should now like to turn to a moment of extreme encounter in the space of civil war. In the U.S. Civil War, whose spaces of empire were proximate and intimate, while also expansive and distant (when, for example, Britain sided with the South because of the potential advantages of a slave-holding economy), it is similarity and the reconciliation of its slippage into difference that transform how music engages translation.

The Civil War (1861–65) was a war narrated by music, a war whose history remains shaped by the ways Americans continue to listen to its music. During the first year of the war, publishing and copyright statistics reveal that at least two thousand new compositions were created.[22] Estimates of musical production indicate that no other war produced so much music. Kenneth Bernard has even gone so far as to make the case that more music issued from the Civil War than all other American wars combined.[23] Whether one can properly document such claims or not, there is very little evidence to refute it. Popular songs were produced in massive quantities and in almost every medium, reaching the home, the church, and the army regiment quickly. Sheet music and hymnbooks went quickly into the hands of soldiers, and military bands proliferated for performances that kept the war alive at the home front and the battlefront. Some reports are staggering, for example, one documenting the fifty regimental bands that performed as almost seventy thousand soldiers mustered at Bailey's Cross Roads, Virginia, just outside Washington, DC, on November 20, 1861.[24]

The music of the Civil War was a catalyst in shaping American national identity at the historical moment it was in greatest danger of being destroyed by the violence of encounter. The Civil War transformed the identity of American music. The war narrowed the space between music and the conditions of encounter, not just during the war, but in the mission of engaging with otherness on a global scale that followed the Civil War, not only for decades and generations, but also until the present. I should like to evoke some sense of this transformation and impulse toward encounter that shaped American music, again by triangulating, with three songs, historically located at the eve, during the course, and in the aftermath of the Civil War.

The production of Civil War song proceeded so ferociously that it is hardly surprising that songs for the North and the South were sometimes the same, but more often covers of each other. Thematically, songwriters and publishers needed only to substitute texts or translate meaning. The most stable elements in all Civil War songs were the images of nations charged with sacred mission. Patriotic songs were frequently sacred, and sacred songs

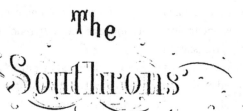

The
Southrons
CHAUNT of DEFIANCE

*"You can never win us back
Never! Never!
Though we perish on the track
Of your endeavor"*

Song or Quartette

Written by a Lady of Kentucky

Music by
A.F. Blackmar.

AUTHOR OF "GOD & OUR RIGHTS."

NEW ORLEANS

Published by A.E. BLACKMAR & BRO. 74. Camp S$\underline{t}$

Charleston.	Mobile.	Memphis	Baton Rouge
H. SIEGLING.	J H. SNOW.	JAS.& Mc CLURE.	C & W. BOGEL.
GEO.F. COLE.	BROWFERG & SON.	E A. BENSON.	GEO.HEROMAN.

Enlered according to Act of Congress AD 1863 by BLACKMAR & C$\underline{o}$ in the Clerk's Off. of the Dist. Court of the East. Dist. of L$\underline{a}$

FIGURE 7.4. A. E. Blackmar, "The Southrons' Chaunt of Defiance."

FIGURE 7.5. Julia Ward Howe, "Battle Hymn of the Republic."

acquired secular texts and functions. Both North and South sent their soldiers to war with hymnbooks, and usually these were the same collections, with the few variants necessary for the appropriate cultural intimacy. The musical space between self and other, therefore, collapsed in upon itself. We witness this in two of the most enduring "anthems" of the Civil War, "The Southrons' Chaunt of Defiance" (1861; see figure 7.4) and the "Battle Hymn of the Republic" (1862; see figure 7.5).

How powerfully these songs sanctify war and sacrifice. From its relatively humble beginnings as a poem in the *Atlantic Monthly*, Julia Ward Howe's "Battle Hymn of the Republic" emerged from the Civil War as an anthem of enormous popularity, which would enter Christian worship in the United States and remain a stalwart reminder of the imperial mission engendered by the war.

FIGURE 7.6. Lowell Mason, "Missionary Hymn."

In the wake of the Civil War, the mission of the United States could not have been clearer in the revival of evangelical Christian hymnody that the national encounter with selfness inspired. Evangelical hymnody truly became the vox populi of a nation charged with the imperative to encounter otherness wherever it was in the world. Hymnbooks and bandbooks alike retranslated the sacred and secular sounds of the Civil War for the war of salvation at home and abroad.[25] The massive production of music after the Civil War transformed antebellum evangelical hymnody to a music of empire. We witness that transformation in Lowell Mason's "Missionary Hymn," an anthem of empire by an American musician of extraordinary influence, appearing in figure 7.6 in the most important publication of evangelical hymns in the nineteenth century, *Gospel Hymns, Nos. 1–6*.[26]

Triangulating Music, Race, and Empire

After the long history of empire and silence, in which the distance between colonizer and colonized was so vast, the site of encounter has undergone a quiet, sometimes silent, triangulation, dependent on and inseparable from our own subject positions. In the course of this essay I have employed case studies to illustrate the extent to which the space of encounter is close at hand, even as we imagine it to be in another part of the world. As we saw with the case study from Basra, the music of Europe is no longer devoid of the presence of a global Islam. Empire is an ongoing social formation. It has been for centuries, but in the twenty-first century, there is no denying it. New conditions accompany the redeployment of imperial encounter, casting it as, at once, both global and local. Violence, real and imagined, is immanent in this era of post-encounter. New forms of silence, and increased nuance in silence, follow the unremitting violence of empire. At the moment of encounter, "hearing" and "listening" have entered a new counterpoint, in which self and other fall apart just as they join again.

The music and race of the new empires are sometimes too close to perceive. Do we hear the *adhān* that envelops our urban neighborhoods, for me in Chicago and Berlin where I live and in Kolkata where I return for fieldwork? Is it even possible to draw nearer to and sound the silence of war and genocide? What kind of imperial counterpoint leads to understanding between the street hawkers gathered below my Ultadanga window? The music of imperial encounter will not fall silent if we embrace our responsibility to listen *and* to hear, to allow the musical sounds of others to draw us together through the triangulation of theories we might bring to the study of music, race, and empire.

NOTES

The title of this essay is adapted from a sign, "Roma Back to India," at the site of the 1994 pipe-bomb murder of four Roms outside of Oberwart, a small city along the Austrian-Hungarian border, one of the most intensively Romani regions of Europe. For a discussion of the aftermath of the murders and the songs that chronicle it, see Ursula Hemetek, *Mosaik der Klänge: Musik der ethnischen und religiösen Minderheiten in Österreich* (Vienna: Böhlau, 2001), CD 1, track 24; and Ursula Hemetek, "Gelem, Gelem Lungone Dromeja—I Have Walked a Long Way: The International Anthem of the 'Travelling People'—Symbol of a Nation?," in *Music in Motion: Diversity and Dialogue in Europe*, ed. Bernd Clausen, Ursula Hemetek, and Eva Sæther (Bielefeld, Germany: Transcript Verlag, 2009), 103–14. All translations are my own, unless otherwise indicated.

1. For recent studies of Tagore and song, see Fakrul Alam and Radha Chakravarty, eds., *The Essential Tagore* (Cambridge: Harvard University Press, 2011); and Lars-Christian Koch, *My Heart Sings: Die Lieder Rabindranath Tagores zwischen Tradition und Moderne* (Münster: LIT Verlag, 2011).

2. For a literary ethnography of the remnants of empire around Park Street, see Amit Chaudhuri, *Calcutta: Two Years in the City* (New York: Knopf, 2013), 22–71.

3. See Alam and Chakravarty, *The Essential Tagore*; Amitav Ghosh, *Sea of Poppies* (London: John Murray, 2008); and Dipesh Chakrabarty, *Provincializing Europe: Postcolonial Thought and Historical Difference* (Princeton, NJ: Princeton University Press, 2000).

4. Thilo Sarazzin, *Deutschland schafft sich ab: Wie wir unser Land aufs Spiel setzen* (Munich: Deutsche Verlags-Anstalt, 2010), 391.

5. See, for example, films such as *Latcho drom*, directed by Tony Gatlif (1993; New York: New Yorker Video, 1998); and *Dom za vešanje* [Time of the Gypsies], directed by Emir Kusturica (1988; Netherlands: Sony Pictures, 2007), both of which use Romani music to connect European history to the everyday of European modernity.

6. Sarazzin, *Deutschland schafft sich ab.*

7. See Martin Greve, *Die Musik der imaginären Türkei: Musik und Musikleben im Kontext der Migration aus der Türkei in Deutschland* (Stuttgart: Metzler, 2003); Philip V. Bohlman, "Music Inside Out: Sounding Public Religion in a Post-Secular Europe," in *Music, Sound and Space: Transformations of Public and Private Experience*, ed. Georgina Born (Cambridge: Cambridge University Press, 2013), 205–23; and Michael O'Toole, "Sonic Citizenship in the New Germany: Music, Migration, and Transnationalism in Berlin's Turkish and Anatolian Diasporas" (PhD diss., University of Chicago, 2014).

8. This argument produced a best-seller, Thilo Sarrazin, *Europa braucht den Euro nicht: Wie uns politisches Wunschdenken in die Krise geführt hat* (Munich: Deutsche Verlags-Anstalt, 2012).

9. Johann Gottfried Herder, *"Stimmen der Völker in Liedern"* and *Volkslieder*, 2 vols. (1778–79; Stuttgart: Reclam, 1975), 168.

10. Wilhelm Tappert, *Wandernde Melodien*, 2nd ed., enlarged (Leipzig: List und Francke, 1890).

11. John Meier, *Kunstlieder im Volksmunde: Materialien und Untersuchungen* (Halle a.S., Germany: M. Niemeyer, 1906).

12. For collections of these songs, with racialized analytical techniques, see Wilhelm Doegen, ed., *Unter fremden Völkern: Eine neue Völkerkunde* (Berlin: Otto Stollberg, Verlag für Politik und Wirtschaft, 1925). See also Philip V. Bohlman, "Erasure: Displacing and Misplacing Race in Twentieth-Century Music Historiography," in *Western Music and Race*, ed. Julie Brown (Cambridge: Cambridge University Press, 2007), 3–23.

13. See John Baily, *Can You Stop the Birds Singing? The Censorship of Music in Afghanistan* (Copenhagen: Freemuse, 2003); and Bronwen Robertson, *Reverberations of Dissent: Identity and Dissent in Iran's Illegal Music Scene* (London: Continuum, 2012).

14. Translated in Amnon Shiloah, ed., *The Epistle on Music of the Ikhwan al-Safa (Bagdad, 10th Century)* (Tel Aviv: Tel-Aviv University, Faculty of Fine Arts, 1978), 41.

15. Eric R. Wolf, *Europe and the People without History* (Berkeley: University of California Press, 1982).

16. See Susan Buck-Morss, *Hegel, Haiti, and Universal History* (Pittsburgh: University of Pittsburgh Press, 2009).

17. Aimé Césaire, *Discourse on Colonialism*, trans. Joan Pinkham (1955; New York: Monthly Review, 1972), 11–12. Emphasis in the published translation.

18. Herder, *"Stimmen der Völker in Liedern."*

19. From Parny, in Herder, *"Stimmen der Völker in Liedern,"* 540–41.

20. Amartya Sen, *Identity and Violence: The Illusion of Destiny* (New York: W. W. Norton, 2006), 175 and passim.

21. Césaire, *Discourse on Colonialism*, 11.

22. Harry S. Stout, *Upon the Altar of the Nation: A Moral History of the Civil War* (New York: Viking, 2006), 110.

23. Kenneth A. Bernard, *Lincoln and the Music of the Civil War* (Caldwell, ID: Caxton, 1966), 45.

24. Ibid.

25. For the classic American bandbook, which appropriated national "airs" from throughout the world, see John Philip Sousa, *National, Patriotic and Typical Airs of All Lands* (Philadelphia: H. Coleman, 1890).

26. Ira D. Sankey, James McGranahan, and George C. Stebbins, comps., *Gospel Hymns, Nos. 1–6* (New York: John Church and Biglow and Main, 1895).

PART III · **CULTURAL POLICIES AND POLITICS IN THE SOUND MARKET**

8 · DI EAGLE AND DI BEAR

Who Gets to Tell the Story of the Cold War?

PENNY VON ESCHEN

Di Eagle an' di Bear have people living in fear
Of the impending nuclear warfare
But as a matter of fact—believe it or not
Plenty people don't care
whether it imminent or not
Or who di first one to attack
or if the human race
Survive or not
—"DI EAGLE AN' DI BEAR" (1984)

At a moment when the western world was preoccupied with the threat of nuclear war, disarmament campaigns, and missile defense, as envisioned by President Ronald Reagan in his "Star Wars" speech of 1983, the Jamaican-born, Britain-based dub poet Linton Kwesi Johnson (LKJ) openly defied the logic of nuclear peril. In his song "Di Eagle an' di Bear" from his 1984 album *Making History*, Johnson warned that the nuclear obsessions of the West were incidental to the seismic shifts in race and empire wrought by the superpower proxy wars of the 1970s and 1980s.[1] While public opinion throughout the West fixated on East-West conflict, the "desperation and despair," in LKJ's words, of third world peoples coping with the violence of super-power proxy wars and covert interventions remained largely invisible. Far from worrying about a nuclear attack, Africans, Asians, and people of color in the Caribbean and Latin America were already dying by the thousands and suffering famine, massacres, and atrocities at the hands of dictatorships propped up by superpowers or because of proxy wars waged by U.S.-trained right-wing militias. In such places as Chile, Angola, El Salvador, Afghanistan, Nicaragua, and Grenada, the violence and chaos of proxy wars, military interventions, and the repressive rule of dictators and military strongmen rendered the nuclear issue irrelevant. Viewing global affairs from the slums of Kingston, Soweto, and Haiti, one was likely to question the validity of cold war justifications for U.S. foreign policy.

"Di Eagle an' di Bear" foregrounded the idea of the bipolar cold war conflict in order to decenter and debunk it. The 1980s, LKJ stated in a May 2011 interview, was "a period of the intensification of the Cold War with Reagan talking about Star Wars and putting missiles in space. For a lot of people in the modern world, the most pressing issue was nuclear [war and] disarmament, the idea that civilization could be annihilated." But, LKJ continued, "if one looks at the third world where the physical proxy wars were being fought on the ground between the Soviet Union and the United States, [the threat of nuclear war] was a non-issue. The pressing issue was food, shelter, and survival." "Di Eagle an' di Bear" points to radically different perceptions of the cold war than those that prevailed in western capitals. From the standpoint of third world peoples in Africa and Latin America, subjected to nightmarish violence and brutality,

> The massacres abound
> Dead bodies all around
> The atrocities abound
> Missing persons can't be found
> Dictators get dethroned
> New clowns are quickly found

One might readily find similar critiques of the violence and disorder wrought by the superpowers' proxy wars in the radical press and in alternative media. But I am particularly interested in the transmission of anti-imperialist, antiracist ideas and formations through popular music. My essay takes LKJ's *Making History* album as a point of departure for a consideration of particular social formations that arose in the 1980s and 1990s at the intersection of music, race, and empire. From the 1980s through the 1990s, in his music and spoken-word poetry as well as his journalism, LKJ bore forceful witness to the intensification of the cold war amid the renewed imperial ambitions of the Margaret Thatcher and Ronald Reagan administrations. The cold war was ignited further by Britain's successful attempt to retain control of its colonial enclaves in the 1982 Falklands War, by the 1983 U.S. invasions of Grenada following the ouster of the leftist New Jewel movement and the murder of Prime Minister Maurice Bishop, and by U.S. support of the anti-Sandinista Contras in Nicaragua and of right-wing militias in El Salvador and ranging proxy wars of Afghanistan; like an exploding supernova, the cold war burned most fiercely at the moment of its demise, with tremendous implication for the future of third world peoples.

With the demise of the Eastern Bloc in 1989 and the collapse of the Soviet Union in 1991, Johnson resisted the prevalent western triumphalism by commenting on these events through the lens of their meanings for black and third world peoples. Despite the detailed scholarly attention to LKJ's early albums, which emerged from his involvement in the anti–police brutality campaigns of London's Black Panther movement, there has been scant attention to particular intersections of art and politics that animated his work in the pivotal decade from 1984 through 1994, a decade that saw not only the collapse of the Soviet Union but also the acceleration of international anti-apartheid movements and multiple challenges to imperial and colonial formations.[2]

LKJ's observations about the striking disparities between dominant western and subaltern third world perceptions of the cold war and his insistence that the decade be understood within a global framework of race and empire raise the question of who gets to tell the story of the cold war. What happens to dominant, bipolar cold war narratives when we view the era from the perspective of LKJ, who is self-consciously rooted in a black radical tradition exemplified by such figures as C. L. R. James and Walter Rodney? How might we view popular culture as a contested field for the production of "commonsense" knowledge about the cold war, in which dub poetry and other forms of popular music challenge the authority of diplomats' papers and memoirs, espionage novels, and films? In other words, what exactly counts as the archive of the cold war?

In this essay I consider LKJ's 1980s and early 1990s dub poetry as the baseline for reading the last decade of the U.S.-Soviet conflict and then its aftermath. I explore LKJ's influential sonic linkage of black struggles in Britain to those of Caribbean and third world peoples *and* to the revolutions of eastern Europe and southern Africa and the anti-apartheid movement. As his 1980s music, poetry, and journalism tracked the "hot wars" in the third world, by the late 1980s and early 1990s, as represented in *Tings an' Times* (1991) and "New World Hawdah" (order), amid celebrations of neoliberalism and globalization, LKJ provided a contrapuntal bass line to the hegemonic global dogma of privatization and to the widespread acceptance of shock therapy, structural adjustment policies, and deregulation. The poems "Mi Revalueshanary Fren" (1989) and "New World Hawdah" explore the links between local black revolutionary struggles in Britain and a global conception of the struggles of the oppressed against totalitarian governments. These poems, occasioned by the seeming watershed events of 1989, hold exhilaration and euphoria at bay to raise searching questions about what kind of world might emerge from the collapse of the Eastern Bloc and what the implications of this change might be for third world peoples.

Much of my discussion draws on an interview with Linton Kwesi Johnson that I conducted in May 2011, along with earlier recorded interviews and close readings of his poetry and live spoken-word performances. I explore the ways in which LKJ produced a sonic contestation of racism and empire, working in the context of a nexus of British, Caribbean, African, and U.S. musicians in the final years of the U.S.-Soviet conflict and the decisive phase of the anti-apartheid struggle. Collectively, these musicians offered powerful critiques and alternative analyses of race, empire, and global politics. While a full consideration of this formation of musicians is beyond the scope of this essay, along with readings of LKJ's work, I consider LKJ in the context of the broader musical and social movement that informed the vibrant U.K. movement of Caribbean and third world perspectives in popular music.

Ronald Radano's conception of music as a performative, textual, and social phenomenon provides a particularly apt framework for considering LKJ's aesthetic interplay of words and sound and its particular place in this formation.[3] In this sense, I regard LKJ's music and that of his fellow musicians and spoken-word artists (including Gil Scott-Heron, Mikey Smith, and Mutabaruka) as a counterhegemonic aural archive of the cold war, a traveling archive of commercially recorded music that crossed oceans and national boundaries and that constituted a social formation of politically charged words and sounds. Far from providing merely a soundtrack of a global movement, in documenting past and present struggles, LKJ and his contemporaries educated successive generations of young people drawn to their sound and called into being a new public, whose lived experiences of self and the movement was anchored, just as LKJ has said in another context of his poetry, "by the one drop beat of reggae with meter measured by the bass line or a drum pattern."[4]

LKJ has described his trajectory as coming to spoken-word performance through the poetry of the Black Arts Movement and Jamaican vernacular poetry and from his introduction to performance poetry through politics. LKJ published books of his poetry before he began performing in musical settings and making records. In 1977, writing in the journal *Race Today*, LKJ described dub lyricism as "a new form of (oral) music-poetry wherein the lyricist overdubs the rhythmic phrases on the rhythmic background of a popular song." LKJ has said that he "wanted to write lines that sounded like a bass-line," exploring the juncture between black vernacular speech and music, in the service of an independent black working-class vision. LKJ's rejection of a hierarchy of lyrics and music, as he "hears music in words" and places already rhythmic "word-music" in relation to the beat of reggae, is critical to the power of his work within this social formation, enabling circuits of listening that moved and inspired beyond what the circulation of written poetry could have achieved, as it expanded the movement by reaching new audiences first drawn to the music.[5]

LKJ was born in Chapletown, Jamaica, in 1952, and moved to Brixton in London at the age of eleven. LKJ was drawn to performance poetry during his involvement in the British Black Panthers, and Jamaican dub music was one of his influences: "I wanted to write poetry that was accessible to those whose experiences I was writing about, namely the black community. I wanted to write oral poetry that could hold the interest of the reader as well as the listener. I heard music in language and I wanted to write word-music, verse anchored by the one-drop beat of reggae with meter measured by the bass-line or a drum pattern; I wanted to write lines that sounded like a bass-line." LKJ's debut album *Dread Beat an' Blood* was released in 1978, followed by *Forces of Victory* in 1979 and *Bass Culture* in 1980. In *Dread Beat an' Blood*, a collaboration with the musical group the Roots, LKJ described the plight of black youth in London, and in such lines as "All wi doin' is defendin' ourselves so get ready for war" he named the street violence and impending 1981 riot as defensive actions taken by black youth after years of systemic police brutality. In 1977, LKJ's mentor Darcus Howe, a journalist, civil liberties activist, and editor of *Race Today* from 1973 to 1985, was arrested for "riot, affray, and assault" and jailed along with eight others as they protested police raids at the Mangrove Restaurant, a gathering place for black radicals, in Notting Hill. In 1977 Howe was again imprisoned for assault following a racially motivated altercation in the London Underground, and LKJ's "Man Free," with the lyrics "Darcus out of jail / *Race Today* cannot fail," pays homage to his activism and was part of the campaign to secure Howe's release. (As we will see, the emphasis on antiblack violence is sustained by LKJ in "Liesense fi Kill" [1991], which recounts the names and stories of those murdered while in police custody, taking on new resonances in the 1990s as it is linked to George H. W. Bush's proclamation of the United States as the world's policeman and to the wars of ethnic cleansing and genocide.)

The title song on the *Making History* album pays homage to black resistance to police brutality, rendered in the Jamaican patois in a manner that seemed to echo C. L. R. James's idea of the revolutionary spontaneity of the black working class: "It is noh mistri / We mekkin histri," acknowledging "Bristal, Toxteh, Brixtan, and Chapletoun" (referring to the town in the rural parish of Clarendon, Jamaica, where LKJ was born), a song that, like others on the album, connected black (including South Asian immigrant) struggles in Britain to global politics. With socialist as well as capitalist regimes in crisis, LKJ not only denounces the racist scapegoating of black peoples, but also rejects the terms of the cold war contest, as the corruption of the ruling classes of both systems have led to the stagnation of both capitalism and the Soviet system.[6]

> From Inglan to Poland
> Every step across di ocean
> The ruling class is dem in a mess, oh yes
> Di capitalist system are regress
> But di Sovjet system nah progress
> So wich one of dem yuh think is best
> When di two of dem work as a contest
> When crisis is di order of di day
> When so much people cryin' out for change nowadays
> . . .
> Nah badda blame it 'pon the black working class, Mr. Racist
> Blame it 'pon the ruling class
> Blame it 'pon your capitalist boss
> We pay the costs, we suffer the loss
> We nah go forget new??
> We nah go forget new plans

Casting a plague on both houses, LKJ draws on the traditions of the British black left, evoking the Trinidad-born intellectual and activist George

Padmore's goal of promoting interracial class solidarity by empowering black workers and radicalizing members of the white working class, a project certainly shared by his colleagues at *Race Today*.

Reflecting his holistic vision of global working-class struggles, LKJ and his band performed in Gdansk, Poland, in 1987 in a concert organized by Poland's Solidarity labor party in support of the anti-apartheid movement. The concert also featured reggae bands from the Caribbean diaspora, including the groups Free Africa and the Twinkle Brothers, whose 1985 album *Anti-Apartheid* LKJ credits with introducing some of the first anti-apartheid songs.[7] The protest music of the Twinkle Brothers anticipated the Sun City album of the same year by Artists United against Apartheid, an international collective of British, American, and South African artists, on which LKJ contributed vocals. Another prominent part of the London/anti-apartheid nexus, Jerry Dammers and the Coventry-based band Special A.K.A., released the single "Free Nelson Mandela" in 1984.

With the 1989 downfall of totalitarian regimes in eastern Europe, some activists were caught up in the changes of Europe while others deepened their focus on connections between southern Africa and worldwide inequalities. In 1990 the Twinkle Brothers released albums entitled *Free Africa* and *Live in Warsaw*, the latter of which included the song "Breaking Down the Barriers."[8] Ostensibly concerned about discord between lovers, the lyrics "break down the barriers between you and I / open the gates and let I in," performed at an anti-apartheid concert in Warsaw, unmistakably referenced global politics. The song's insistence that "if you don't I gonna knock thy walls down" conjured images of the Berlin Wall, as well as the array of physical, social, and legal barriers of apartheid. The Twinkle Brothers' song drew on African diasporic cultural traditions of resistance with the lyric "Joshua sounded the trumpet and break the walls down." During the early to mid-1980s, as members of the Congressional Black Caucus criticized the Reagan administration's anodyne "constructive engagement" policy toward South Africa, and as university students mobilized around demands for economic sanctions against the apartheid regime, the vibrant music scene in South Africa received international exposure. Ladysmith Black Mambazo's extensive international touring, recordings, and radio airplay made them a potent vehicle for the international anti-apartheid movement. Indeed, that group's visibility, and public awareness of the mastery of South African musicians, received a boost with their participation in Paul Simon's critically acclaimed 1986 *Graceland* album, although some anti-apartheid activists criticized Simon for violating the cultural boycott with South Africa. In the heady days after the unbanning of the African National Congress and the release of Nelson Mandela, Walter Sisulu, Govan Mbeki, and others after many years of detention at Robben Island in 1991 and later, on the eve of the Republic of South Africa's first free elections in 1994, the impending demise of apartheid energized the music of the South African bands Stimela, Johnny Clegg and Savuka ("Cruel Crazy Beautiful World" from 1990), and the exiled musician Miriam Makeba ("Eyes on Tomorrow" from 1992), and the vocal ensemble Ladysmith Black Mambazo, who were featured in the anti-apartheid Broadway drama *The Song of Jacob Zulu* (1992).[9] Along with South African musicians, a global array of performing artists seemed to represent an insurgent multicultural spirit of change, from the USA for Africa's star-studded "We Are the World" (1985) song for Ethiopian famine relief, to the consistently trenchant Gil Scott-Heron, whose 1975 song "Johannesburg" brilliantly registered African Americans' struggle to overcome official disinformation and diasporic differences: "Sometimes distance brings misunderstanding / . . . but deep in my heart, I'm demanding" current information about "our brothers over there / . . . defying the man." Black diaspora elders of music, struggle, and political consciousness, including Makeba, Harry Belafonte, Nina Simone, the Mighty Sparrow, Oscar Brown Jr., and Odetta were joined by the singer-songwriter Tracy Chapman, whose "Fast Car" rose on the pop charts after she performed it on a nationally televised tribute to Nelson Mandela in 1988, Labi Siffre ("So Strong," 1988), and the indigenous Australian Archie Roach ("Charcoal Lane," 1990). Their music, or cover versions of it, like that of LKJ and others too numerous to mention here, crisscrossed oceans and continents via radio airplay, was added to copies of mixtape cassettes and the new CD technology, and was shared, swapped, and sometimes blasted through the ubiquitous boombox.

If the popular imagination of the cold war summons in many the memory of video footage of crowds storming and dismantling the Berlin Wall, my alternative history of the era pays tribute to the technologies of the mixtape and boombox both as symbolic and practical technologies of music-sharing sociality and as critical vehicles for understanding the transnational circulations of LKJ's music.[10] Throughout the process of the dissolution of what Michael Denning has called the age of three worlds, and the murky, fraught emergence of "the new world hawdah," music was widely produced, consumed, and circulated across overlapping old and new media of vinyl, tape, and CDs through "mixtapes." Most work on mixtapes, such as Thurston Moore's *Mix-Tape: The Art of Cassette Culture* and Rob Sheffield's *Love Is a Mix-Tape*, has emphasized the technology as a mode of individual self-expression, but the social intimacy presupposed by and enacted through the exchange of mix-tapes was also critical to the formation of political community as it expanded possibilities for circulation and social practices of listening.[11] Importantly, music sharing and social listening didn't require a set location with stereo equipment, but they could happen indoors or preferably in public settings, through the readily available portable boombox. Not only was the boombox critical as a way of contesting, shaping, and owning public space, through its recording function, it also allowed consumers to program and produce mix-tape compilations according to their own aesthetic and political dictates, out-side the strictures of commodification. It was easy to dub a copy of a friend's tape when one couldn't afford a new LP or CD. Both the recording function and portability of the boombox enabled its ubiquitous presence at gatherings of activists, enabling music to function as a resource for the forging of politi-cal community. Like the live performances of dub poets, gatherings around the boombox could serve as a vehicle of consciousness raising and expanding the circle of those committed to movements for social justice.

Of course, not all artists or activists had equal access to the technologies of the reproduction or circulation of music. Linton Kwesi Johnson has re-flected on his location in London rather than Jamaica, and how living in the metropole has facilitated connections to the European and African move-ments. Indeed, reflecting on the particular synergies of this period, LKJ fore-grounded the centrality of Africa and diasporic resonances between Old Testament Exodus stories of escape from bondage and the status of Africans in the Western Hemisphere as understood by Caribbean peoples. According to LKJ, the "African consciousness in Reggae music traced back to the folk music of slavery, and Rastafarian/Abyssinian anti-apartheid struggle, and was prior to the international campaign of the mid-1980s and early 1990s."[12] Recall-ing, for example, that in 1978 sixteen-year-old Hugh Mundell recorded "Africa Must Be Free by 1983," Johnson pointed out that, tragically, 1983 proved to be the year that Mundell was shot to death while sitting in a car with a friend in Kingston, Jamaica, eight years before Nelson Mandela was released from prison and eleven years before the first free election in South Africa elected Mandela president.

Certainly, LKJ's positioning in London afforded advantages for reaching global audiences compared to the limited access to international markets—and different routes of circulation—of LKJ's contemporaries in Jamaica, such as Mutabaruka (formerly Allan Hope), who was born in Rae Town, Kingston, in 1952 (the same year as LKJ's birth), and Michael "Mikey" Smith, born in 1954. These different locations and opportunities among artists and activists throughout the African diaspora have certainly led to frictions. Mutabaruka, the Jamaican-based dub poet, widely considered along with LKJ to be a co-founder of dub poetry, achieved fame with his "It's No Good to Stay inna White Man Country Too Long," an accusatory answer to LKJ's "Inglan Is a Bitch." Documenting the exclusionary racism visited upon nonwhite migrant populations, "Inglan Is a Bitch" argued for the necessity of struggle in Britain: "There's no escapin' it."[13] Seemingly unmindful that LKJ migrated to Britain at the tender age of eleven, Mutabaruka damns him for staying: "So you left Clarendon, to go a Brixtan, and check the King's tools in a Liverpool." And in an unwarranted charge of naïveté, Mutabaruka claims, "but you didn't know that tings could get to blow." It is almost as if Mutabaruka unfairly conflated LKJ with the post-Windrush optimism of Lord Kitchener's early 1950s calypso, "London Is the Place for Me."[14]

Despite such differences, however, through the circulation of his albums and performances first in the United States and then globally, Mutabaruka himself was part and parcel of what Andrew Jones has aptly termed circuit listening.[15] Moreover, the two artists both originally came to dub poetry before becoming reggae musicians. Mutabaruka wrote in Jamaican patois because his primary audience was the Jamaican people; like LKJ, he has reflected extensively on the relation between words and rhythm. Mutabaruka has said, "I'm a poet. I'm a poet first. The words is why reggae is big. It is not the music itself. The music is good, but it's because of what is said in the music." For Mutabaruka, his "intention is really to awaken the conscience and the consciousness of the people."[16] Indeed, although Mutabaruka says of his acclaimed "Dis Poem," described as a collage of all aspects of life and "all aspects of the struggle," that in the final line, "Dis poem will continue in your mind," he is talking to himself, it also suggests his conviction that his poetry may not convince people, but it will make them think. As noted above, LKJ also views himself as a poet first and says, "I wanted to write poetry that was accessible to those whose experiences I was writing about, namely the black community."[17] And while LKJ's hearing "music in language" rejects the hierarchy of lyrics and music, his commitment to accessibility is shared by Mutabaruka.

Yet if Mutabaruka's criticism of LKJ for speaking to English and global audiences rather than Jamaicans seemed oblivious to the different experiences of West Indian migrants from one generation to the next and obscured the two artists' shared access to global circulation and audiences, LKJ's analyses of a global politics of alliance were no doubt facilitated by living in London and touring throughout Europe. Indeed, like an earlier generation of West

Indian writers after World War II, migration from one's island home and mobility in general were a necessity for the twin goals, always blended, of political formation and artistic development. The poet-musician-activist visited Angola as a journalist, during his work for BBC 4's *The Bandung Files*, from 1985 to 1988, sharpening his knowledge of the apartheid regime and liberation struggles of southern Africa. For LKJ, the defeat of the South African defense force by Cuban soldiers and Russian aircraft in support of the People's Armed Forces for the Liberation of Angola's offensive against the National Union for the Total Independence of Angola, which was supported by South Africa, had a profound impact because it marked "the first time that the invincibility of South Africa's defense forces was shattered."

LKJ's experiences in Angola informed his 1989 "Mi Revalueshanary Fren," written as Eastern Bloc regimes toppled and as wars of liberation raged on in southern Africa.[18] LKJ has described the poem as speaking to "the links between black revolutionary struggles and wider struggles against totalitarian governments. These struggles were not isolated and I tried to make the connection, just as 'Wat about the Working Class' made connections between London, Kingston, and Poland."[19] LKJ's critique of the erasure of black and African liberation struggles within a cold war mindset insisted on linking those struggles against empire and racism within a wider, global class struggle against capitalism and totalitarian rule.[20]

Of the late 1980s, LKJ observed that "everything was in flux: the old order had collapsed and a new one had not come into being. That's why the song [referring to a litany of deposed Eastern Bloc dictators, including the German Democratic Republic's Erich Honecker, and Romania's Nicolae Ceausescu] says this one has to go, and that one has to go." Yet for LKJ the emphasis on the overthrow of tyrants and their regimes precluded a new vision of change: "Lots of people were talking about the end of socialism, and while I didn't go for that, it seemed to me like there had to be some new way of thinking." For LKJ, his poetry became a site of reflection on the implications of the wave of anti-authoritarian revolutions for black and African liberation struggles.

"Mi Revalueshanary Fren" begins with a description of the ouster of rulers and collapse of regimes in eastern Europe, emphasizing the critical agency of ordinary people in the process:

> fram di masses shata silence
> staat fi grumble
> fram pawty paramoncy tek a tumble

fram Hungary to Poelan to Romania
fram di cozy cyassle dem staat fi crumble
wen wi buck-up wananada in a reaznin

The song assumes the form of a gentle reproach from LKJ to his friend, a self-styled revolutionary, who seems to be stuck in the moment, content to relive the revolutions of 1989. LKJ suggests a way forward by inserting the ongoing anti-apartheid struggle:

mi fren always en up pan di same ting
dis is di sang im love fi sing:
    [then he leads to the chorus; bracketed names and countries
        are mine]
Kaydar [János Kádár, Hungary]
e ad to go
Zhivkov [Todor Zhivkov, Bulgaria]
e ad to go
Husack [Gustáv Husák, Czechoslovakia]
e ad to go
Honnicka [Erich Honecker, East Germany]
e ad to go
Cauchescu [Nicolae Ceausescu, Romania]
e ad to go
jus like apartied
wi av to go

LKJ's intervention came at a moment when many western commentators loudly proclaimed the triumph of the market; LKJ questioned the spirit of capitalist triumphalism. By the time of the eastern European revolutions and fall of the Berlin Wall in 1989, Ronald Reagan, George H. W. Bush, and a spate of academics and pundits had already established a giddy narrative of the victor's history. Accepting the nomination at the 1988 Republican convention, George H. W. Bush proclaimed a story of simple cause and effect. Suggesting that Soviet actions had prevented change in Afghanistan and southern Africa, and maintaining a discreet silence on U.S. involvement in proxy wars in those regions, Bush characterized the "new relationship" with the Soviet Union: "The INF treaty—the beginning of Soviet withdrawal from Afghanistan—the beginning of the end of the Soviet proxy war in Angola, and with it, the independence of Namibia, and Iran and Iraq are headed toward peace." In his version of events, Bush told the crowd, "It's a watershed. It's no accident. It happened when we acted on the ancient knowledge that strength and clarity lead to peace—weakness and ambivalence lead to war. . . . I will not allow this country to be made weak again, never."[21] Just as significant as Bush's intent to carry a big stick was his propagandized account of global politics. As a former CIA director who certainly knew that the Soviet Union was not the sole cold war actor in southern Africa and Afghanistan, Bush remained silent on U.S. support of white minority governments in southern Africa, CIA actions in Afghanistan (and elsewhere) prior to Soviet intervention, U.S. officials' support of the anti-Soviet Mujahedeen fighters in Afghanistan, and the U.S. alliance with Iraq's Saddam Hussein against the Islamic Republic of Iran after the Shah's overthrow.

Indeed, when Francis Fukuyama proclaimed "the end of history," he reflected the Bush administration's confidence that liberal capitalist democracy had decisively vanquished all possible alternatives for organizing human society.[22] As this view was promulgated throughout western media and academia, it provided a key pillar of the emerging cold war triumphalism. LKJ directly challenged not only this conservative narrative but also its seductive allure for activists and leftists caught up in the euphoria of the moment. What, LKJ pointedly asked, does this supposed triumph of democracy mean for those most affected by the "cold war"? LKJ emphasized an uncertain future, placing the fate of black people's struggles at the heart of his questioning of the consequences and implications of the 1989 revolutions:

awhile agoh mi fren an mi woz taakin
soh mi seh to im:
mi revalueshanary fren is nat di same agen
yu know fram wen?

well mi couldn elabarate
plus it waz gettin kinda late
soh in spite a mi lack af andastandin
bout di meanin a di changes in di eas
fi di wes nonediless
an aldow mi av mi rezavayshans
bout di cansiquenses an implicashans
espehsaally fi black libaraeshan
to bring di reaznin to a canclushan
ah ad woz to agree wid mi fren
hopein dat wen wi meet up wance agen
wi coulda av a more fulla canvahsaeshan

soh mi seh to im, yu know wat?
im seh wat? mi seh:
[chorus]

While the chorus ends resolutely with the last words of "just like apartheid /
has to go," and the apartheid regime would succumb to militant demands for
dissolution over the next two to five years, not only did the white supremacist
regimes maintain their murderous course until the end, but also LKJ's fears
about the fate of formerly colonized peoples in the postsocialist world proved
prescient.

LKJ spoke of the decade after the collapse of the Soviet Union as a time
of deferred dreams: "the 1990s is almost a bit foggy in my head. With all the
talk that socialism was dead, everyone shifted from the right and the left to
the center. [George H. W.] Bush was a neocon and everyone else was neoliberal. This was a depressing period for people who had dedicated their lives
to bringing about revolutionary change."[23] He attributed the retreat from
revolutionary politics during the 1990s in part to the successes of earlier
movements, charting a generational trajectory from a black power movement influenced by America to a mid-1970s move away from racial to class
politics. By the 1990s, a black middle class had begun to emerge and the generation after didn't have to wage the same basic struggles for access and inclusion. The Black People's Day of Action on March 2, 1981, and the April 1981
Brixton Uprising, both responses to racial profiling and police harassment,
had "brought about a paradigm shift" and by the beginning of the 1990s one
could see concrete changes as a result of the struggle.[24] For some, basic goals
of civil liberties and a measure of access to British society had been achieved
and they were no longer interested.

LKJ felt a profound unease with the ascendancy of neoliberalism and a
keen sense of loss over the abandonment of far-reaching goals for justice
and equality. "With the vacuum that had been left after the cold war," he explained, "all was a bit vague."[25] LKJ's *Tings an' Times* contemplated the sense
of betrayal felt by those who had hoped for an alternative to capitalism in
"actually existing socialism" and were dismayed by the repression and au-
thoritarianism of these regimes.

Duped, doped
Demoralized
Dizzied, dozed
Traumatized

Chiding himself for not detecting the deceit of the fallen regimes, he explains a previous lack of understanding that the road to socialism could be derailed by "nepotism and corruption."

> Blinded by resplendent lite of love
> Dazzled by di firmament of freedom
> Im couldn deteck deceit
> All wen it kick im in im teet
>
> Im nevvah know intrigue
> Im nevvah inna dat deh league
> Im nevvah andahstan
> Dat on di road to sawshalism
> Yu could buck-up nepotism

Indeed, after the fall of the Eastern Bloc, even those most critical of the old regimes expressed a disorienting sense of loss. As the East German dissident Jens Reich put it in November 1993: "I can't get rid of this feeling of being an outsider, a sense that all of my life experiences are now irrelevant. It's a strange feeling. It's as if you yourself have disappeared, as if you're a relic of a lost era."[26] LKJ also expressed this sense of being a castaway, exiled from one's own history:

> Now like a fragile fragment af lite
> Trapped inna di belly a di daak nite
> Like a bline man stuicified an dazed
> Last an alone in a mystical maze
>
> Fi days, upan days
> Upan days, upan days
> Watch I'm driffin craus di oweshan of life
> Widoutn ruddah nar hankah nar sail

Yet as he explored the disorienting sense of loss of direction, amid celebrations of neoliberalism and globalization, LKJ also provided a bass-line counterpoint to the hegemonic global lexicons of privatization that were articulated as shock therapy, structural adjustment, and deregulation. His song "Di Good Life," on *Tings an' Times*, examines the aftermath of the demise of Eastern Bloc states, and what these transformations meant for popular aspirations for the good life. LKJ pointedly rejected the view that the failure of authoritarian states was itself an indictment of socialism.

Sowshallism
is a wise ole shephad
im suvvie tru flood
tru drout
tru blizad

Here, LKJ's defense of socialism as a popular ideal and aspiration reminds us that the anti-authoritarian movements of eastern Europe, including the Solidarity movement in Poland, with which LKJ was associated, were emphatically movements to reform socialism and *not* pro-capitalist.[27] LKJ contemplates the seeming triumph of capitalism and the implications of jettisoning socialist ideals as the basis for dreams of the good life for the masses. In a prophetic observation from the standpoint of the twenty-first-century economic crisis and the severity of conservative David Cameron's budget-cutting austerity, LKJ noted that as many abandon socialism, the "other ism" capitalism creeps along with nobody questioning its destructive impact on the life chances of the poor and middle classes:

an wan an two a im flock dem drif a way
while di addah ism dem
jus a watch an a peep
jus a crawl an a creep
an noh baddah ask if dem naw mek fun
fi canfuse an cansume all distray dem

But even as LKJ penned this analysis of global political economy, as western pundits celebrated the triumph of capitalism, many in the former Eastern Bloc experienced dislocation and suffering with the collapse of markets. These victims of the so-called triumph of the market registered deep anxieties amid the fragmentation of states and the disintegration of socialist visions of the good life for the masses.[28] If capitalism had been shielded from critical scrutiny in the West, LKJ anticipated a popular reassessment of "the shepherd and sage of socialism," and, in their collective resistance to market-driven policies of retrenchment, people would demand an emancipatory form of socialism along with their repudiation of despotism and corruption.

but evryting is jus fi a time
soon di flack wi tek a stack an surmise
ow far fram di fole dem a stray
wen dem site ow di pack jus a staak dem
dem wi come back togeddah wance agen

LKJ's insistence that socialism represents a popular vision of the good life may have struck many as naïve in the aftermath of the collapse of the Eastern Bloc:

an shephad di sage to a highah graun
whichpawt di graas is greenah an sweetah
whichpawt di breeze blow is like a balm
whichpawt di stream run quietah an coolah
whichpawt life can pleasant can be calm

But the conviction that the frenetic exploitation of capitalism robbed people of their human potential and happiness is a sentiment that LKJ has sustained in his later work and one that radical critics, activists, and demonstrators have embraced as part of the global Occupy movements. Expressing views also reflected on his album *More Time* (1998), LKJ told the journalist Nancy Rawlinson in 1998 that "there is no reason why we can't work less hours and enjoy our lives more. But if we do get more time," he continued, "we have to organize ourselves to benefit from it. What is life if we can't get some pleasure from friends and family, from relaxation and contemplation? Most people do not have an idea of what their human potential is, we are so used to not having time."[29] Moreover, even in the politically quiescent 1990s, for LKJ, "encouraging developments in South Africa, and revolutions in Venezuela, Brazil and Bolivia gave us hope that the vision of socialism was alive. . . . [There was] hope of challenging the myth that capitalism had defeated communism."[30]

While LKJ maintained hope for "di good life," he persisted in his unrelenting critiques of continuing war and police brutality. In fact, declarations of the end of history and "new world order" during the 1990s were mocked by a subsequent epidemic of state violence, with continuing police brutality in England and throughout Africa and its diaspora , ethnic cleansing in the Balkan wars of independence, and genocide in Rwanda. LKJ's "New World Hawdah" draws attention to Bosnia as well as Kigale in Rwanda; Butare in South Rwanda; Shatila, the Palestinian refugee camp in Beirut, Lebanon, which was the site of an infamous 1982 massacre by the Israeli Defense Force, led by Ariel Sharon; and the ongoing civil war between Christians and Muslims in Lebanon:

di killahs a Kigale [central Rwanda]
mus be sanitary workaz
di butchaz a Butare [South Rwanda]
mus be sanitary workaz

di savijes a Shatila [Palestine]
mus be sanitary workaz
di beasts a Boznia
mus be sanitary workaz
inna di new world hawdah

For LKJ, while violence carried out against those perceived as different is an ancient practice, the so-called new world order had given rise to a new world of organized violence and a new language that naturalized mass atrocities.[31]

An is di same ole cain an able sindrome
Far more hainshent dan di fall of Rome
But in di new world hawdah a atrocity
Is a brand new langwidge a barbarity
Mass murdah
Narmalize
Pogram
Rationalize
Genocide
Sanitize
An di hainshent clan sin
Now name etnic clenzin

For LKJ, the obscenity of these modern technologies of genocide and mass murder was heightened by their being carried out against the backdrop of celebratory claims of the triumph of capitalism and the "end of history, and George H. W. Bush proclaiming that the U.S. was the world's policeman." LKJ's ironic meditation on that quintessential cold war symbol James Bond's license to kill, his 1993 "Liesense fi Kill" documented police brutality and the ongoing deaths of black people in British custody, calling attention to "liesense," the perverse official British epistemology sanctioning state violence, in which questioning far-fetched official rulings of supposedly self-inflicted deaths of black people by self-stabbing or self-suffocation was deemed paranoid and conspiratorial, while law enforcement authorities engaged in covering up deaths in police custody and acting as if they had been granted a license to kill.[32]

"Liesense fi Kill" visually as well as aurally emphasizes lie-sense, explicitly interrogating the contested meaning of conspiracy and what counts as truth, or sense. In the new world order, one *"can't ask"* or can't question highly implausible if not absurd official accounts of deaths of black people in custody, but one *"can ask* the commissioner for the license to kill," repeated with "can ask DDP ... Margaret Thatcher ... John Major [etc.], for the license fi kill." Here, the violence perpetrated against black people is erased from official public knowledge. In LKJ's view, the "James Bond and MI5 and the military" are unaccountable rogue state agents whose *lies* are sanctioned as common *sense* in the *lie-sense to kill*. Here, in LKJ's challenge to official systems of knowledge, power, and violence in the new world order, poetry is the genuine archive of the cold war and the so-called new world order, demystifying the collusion of the mass media and police and military authorities.

The politics of language, structured in this instance by literary and aesthetic legacies of empire, are the subject of LKJ's playful and irreverent declaration of cultural independence "If I wos a tap-natch poet," which he has described as a defense of dub poetry. Published in the 2006 *Mi Revalueshanary Fren* collection, the poem references a litany of modernist poets from Europe, Africa, the United States, and the Caribbean whose work has influenced and inspired LKJ, including Kamau Braithwaite, Jayne Cortez, Amiri Baraka, Nicholas Guillen, T. S. Eliot, and Lorna Goodison:

If I woz a tap-natch poet
like Chris Okigbo
Derek Walcott
ar T.S. Eliot

I would write a poem
soah damn deep
dat it bitta-sweet
like a precious memari
whe mek yu weep
whe mek yu feel incomplete

As we contemplate LKJ's suggestion that the emotional impact of poetry on the reader perhaps renders issues of language incidental, he continues, "inna di meantime," that he is *not* a top-notch poet. Refusing to crave the approval of British establishment critics who look askance at dub poetry, LKJ suggests that to do anything other than write out of his own heritage, history, and his "own sense of time" would be not only derivative but also selling his artistic freedom for a mess of pottage. In language blurring the boundary between words and music, LKJ insists on the dub poet's integral place and role in a vibrant struggle:

wid mi riddim
wid mi rime

wid mi ruff base line
wid mi own sense of time
good poet haffi step in line
caw Bootahlazy mite a gat couple touzan
but Mandela fi him
touzans and touzans and touzans and touzans

Here, referencing a movement that was critical to the downfall of apartheid, LKJ refers to Mangosuthu Buthelezi, the leader of the Zulu-based Inkatha Freedom Party, the opposition party to the nonracialist African National Congress led by Mandela, who would become the first president of postapartheid South Africa. Aspiring poets in search of a personal and independent voice, the poem seems to say, would do well to consider its refrain, contending that history belongs to Mandela's example of political integrity, compared to the insignificance of Buthelezi:

caw Bootahlazy mite a gat couple touzan
but Mandela fi him
touzans and touzans and touzans and touzans

LKJ affirms the complexity of dub poetry and its place in the global struggle against racial hierarchy, cultural imperialism, class oppression, and inequality, a stance elaborated in the poem's closing rejoinder to critics of dub poetry who have accused dub poets of

peddlin . . . purile parchment af etnicity
wid ongle avaig fleetin hint of hawtenticity. . . .
an even worse
a baffling bafoon whe looze im tongue

But to these accusations, LKJ answers:

no sah
nat atall
mi gat mi riddim
mi gat mi rime
mi gat mi riff base line
mi gat me own sense a time

Indeed, dub poetry's rhythm within words and rhythm as the bass line for words—word music—was an integral part of the lived experience and fundamental collective meaning making of the vibrant social movements of the anti-apartheid era. As critics have pointed out, LKJ's dub poetry gives pause to those who would endorse W. H. Auden's claim that "poetry makes nothing happen."[33] But the worldly and embodied poetry of LKJ also invokes William Carlos Williams, who cautioned that "it is difficult to get the news from poems, yet men die miserably every day for lack of what is found there."[34] It *is* hard to get the news from poems, but the transformative impact of LKJ's documentary and inspirational poetry, along with its socially embedded but unique routes of circulation, reminds us that getting the news and then altering the world through music and poetry is not impossible: it is a foundational baseline for social change.

NOTES

1. Linton Kwesi Johnson, *Making History*, produced by Linton Kwesi Johnson and Dennis Bovell, recorded at Studio 80 (1984, Island Records, ILPS 9770).

2. On the earlier period, see Ashley Dawson, "Behind the Mask: Carnival Politics and British Identity in Linton Kwesi Johnson's Dub Poetry," in *Mongrel Nation: Diasporic Culture and the Making of Postcolonial Britain* (Ann Arbor: University of Michigan Press, 2007), 73–94; and L. Franca Junior, "The Arts of Resistance in the Poetry of Linton Kwesi Johnson," accessed May 26, 2014, www.ufsj.edu.br/porta12-repositorio/File /vertentes/v.%2019%20n.%201/Franca_Junior.pdf.

3. Ronald M. Radano, *Lying Up a Nation: Race and Black Music* (Chicago: University of Chicago Press, 2003).

4. Linton Kwesi Johnson, *Mi Revalueshanary Fren* (Keene, NY: Ausable, 2006), iv. The quotation is from the introduction by Russell Banks. The book of poems, which organizes Johnson's work by decade as "Seventies, Eighties, and Nineties Verse," was first published in Europe by Penguin in 2002. Banks is quoting LKJ's *Race Today* article from 1977.

5. Ibid.

6. Johnson, *Making History*.

7. Linton Kwesi Johnson, interviewed by author, May 2011.

8. Since the early 1990s, the Twinkle Brothers "have collaborated regularly with Trebuni-Tutki, fusing reggae and traditional music from the Tatra Mountains." Jeff Todd Titon, ed., *Worlds of Music: An Introduction to the Musics of the World's Peoples*, 5th ed. (Belmont, CA: Schermer Cengage Learning), 249–50.

9. Max Mojapelo, *Beyond Memory: Recording the Moments and Memories of South African Music* (Somerset Erst, South Africa: African Minds, 2008).

10. Ben Sisario, "When the Beat Came in a Box," *New York Times*, October 15, 2010.

11. Thurston Moore, *Mix-Tape: The Art of Cassette Culture* (New York: Universe, 2007); Rob Sheffield, *Love Is a Mix-Tape: Life and Loss, One Song at a Time* (New York: Three River, 2007).

12. Johnson interview.

13. "From Page-Poet to Recording Artist: Mutabaraku interviewed by Eric Doumerc," *Journal of Commonwealth Literature* 44, no. 3 (September 2009): 23–31.

14. I thank Teju Olaniyan for bringing this debate to my attention.

15. See Andrew F. Jones, "Circuit Listening," in this volume.

16. Jonathan Rubell, "Dis Essay," accessed May 26, 2014, http://debate.uvm.edu /dreadlibrary/Rubell.htm.

17. Johnson, *Mi Revalueshanary Fren*, iv.

18. "Mi Revalueshanary Fren" was recorded on Linton Kwesi Johnson's *Tings an' Times*, which was released as an audio cassette and a CD in 1991 on the label Shanashie.

19. Johnson interview.

20. Ibid.

21. George H. W. Bush, speech accepting the Republican Party nomination, August 18, 1988, www.presidency.ucsb.edu/ws/?pid=25955.

22. Mark Hosenball, "Centuries of Boredom in World without War; an American Theory; Spectrum," *Times* (London), September 3, 1989.

23. Johnson interview.

24. Ibid.

25. Ibid.

26. Quoted in Stephen Kinzer, "Prenden Journal: For East German Theme Park, the Bad Old Days," *New York Times*, November 9, 1993.

27. Mary Serotte, *1989: The Struggle to Create a Post Cold War Europe* (Princeton, NJ: Princeton University Press, 2011).

28. For just some of the important scholarship on these multiple and various forms of nostalgia, see Svetlana Boym, *The Future of Nostalgia* (New York: Basic, 2002); Charity Scribner, *Requiem for Communism* (Cambridge: MIT Press, 2003); and Maria Todorova, ed., *Remembering Communism: Genres of Representation* (New York: Social Science Resource Council, 2010).

29. Nancy Rawlinson, "Linton Kwesi Johnson: Dread Beat an' Blood: Inglan Is a Bitch," *Spike*, December 1, 1998, www.spikemagazine.com/1298kwes.php.

30. Johnson interview.

31. "New World Hawdah," in Johnson, *Mi Revalueshanary Fren*, 99–100. The brackets identifying countries are mine.

32. "Liesense fi Kill," in Johnson, *Mi Revalueshanary Fren*, 96–98.

33. W. H. Auden, "In Memory of W. B. Yates," Poets.org, accessed June 1, 2014, www .poets.org/poetsorg/poem/memory-w-b-yeats.

34. William Carlos Williams, "Asphodel, That Greeny Flower," in *Journey to Love* (New York: Random House, 1955), 39.

9 · CURRENTS OF REVOLUTIONARY CONFLUENCE
A View from Cuba's Hip Hop Festival

MARC PERRY

On a muggy August afternoon in front of Havana's stately Capitolio building, I boarded a *máquina*, one of the old, often-ramshackled, pre-1959 American cars that operate as privately run collective taxis, for a twenty-minute ride east to the coastal municipality of Alamar. A sprawling collection of more than two thousand multistoried apartment blocks, the suburb was constructed in the 1970s and 1980s with the assistance of Russian architects and reflects a utilitarian functionalism of Soviet-era design. Built to accommodate influxes of rural workers and young families from Havana's overpopulated center, Alamar has been likened to the Caribbean's largest public housing project.

This semblance carries added resonance when considering Alamar's place in local lore as the birthplace of Cuban hip hop, analogous in this sense to the South Bronx's public housing topography that first gave rise to hip hop's postindustrial urbanism in the 1970s.

It was the summer of 2000 and I was in fact traveling to Alamar that afternoon to attend a sound check for the opening night of the sixth annual Cuban Hip Hop Festival slated for later that evening in the municipality's public amphitheater. Between the colossal Capitolio, the prerevolutionary seat of Cuba's legislature styled after the U.S. Capitol that looms over Havana's skyline, and the antiquated fume-engulfed máquina, I was reminded en route of the everyday intimacies of U.S. imperial legacies and the improvisational nature of their transformation on the island. Might Cuban hip hop, I mused, offer yet another variation on this theme? Or, in hindsight, in what ways might the festival's coming spectacle reveal both convergences and asymmetries of empire and revolution at the millennial turn?

After the ride and an additional fifteen-minute walk down from the main road past rows of high-rise apartment buildings, I arrived at Alamar's amphitheater. Atop descending concrete tiers of empty seats leading to a large stage below, the festival's organizer, Rodolfo Rensoli, was in the control area scrambling to pull together final details for the opening night. While waiting to speak to Rensoli about a promised credential tag affording backstage access during the festival, I joined in on a *cajita* lunch provided to all working the festival prep. Named for the small brown paper boxes stuffed with fried pork, rice, and raw cabbage—long a Havana street staple—these lunches represented a limited, though much appreciated, gesture of governmental support for an otherwise resource-strapped festival.

After a short absence I had recently returned to Havana just prior to the start of Cuba's annual Hip Hop Festival, customarily held during the sweltering month of August. Part of the rationale for the August timing was to schedule the festival during the summer recess when school-age youth, who comprised the bulk of Alamar's hip hop fan base, would be free to attend evening programs that often ran late into the night. Another key consideration was that Black August, a New York–based hip hop collective that collaborated in the two previous festivals, traditionally organized during August in remembrance of the 1971 murder of imprisoned Black Panther George Jackson and of preceding histories of African American resistance dating back to Nat Turner's August 1831 slave rebellion. Through modest donations to Havana's hip hop community and, most significantly, the shepherding of U.S.

hip hop artists to the island for annual performances, Black August had become an integral facet of the festival since 1998.

In step with the rise of Cuban hip hop, the annual festival grew in size and sophistication over the years from one involving a small collection of local *raperos* (rappers or MCs), to a multiday event encompassing a diversity of Cuban groups and an accompanying range of international artists. Hosted in Alamar's amphitheater since 1997, the event was the largest stage and premier occasion for showcasing local hip hop talent. The festival's stature was all the more significant given that scarcities of production resources and commercial markets for hip hop grounded the emerging music scene—like most traditions of Cuban vernacular music—in the intimacies of live performance. Many elements that have come to characterize much of Cuban hip hop were also present from the festival's inception. Central among these were raperos' emphasis on social themes drawn from the lived experiences of a new, largely darker-skinned generation of Cubans as they navigated the daily, often fraught complexities of a Cuba in historical flux: one posed between revolutionary socialism and the rapidly evolving realities of an expanding market economy.

Indeed, while the roots of Cuban hip hop may date back to the mid-1980s, it was not until the economic crisis of the early '90s in the wake of the Soviet collapse and subsequent market-aligned shifts exemplified by the dual currency dollarization of Cuba's economy,[1] that hip hop began to take shape on the island as a self-defined *movimiento* (movement). During this period raperos became increasingly attentive in their music to disparities between long-standing claims of a socially just, racially egalitarian society under state socialism,[2] and the growing everyday inequalities of race and class tied to Cuba's recent market turn.[3] In doing so, many of the pioneering core of Havana's rapero community foreground their identity as *negros* (blacks) as the subjective basis on which their perspectives were critically voiced within an otherwise officially touted "nonracial" Cuba.[4] Yet beyond simply reflecting established ways of being, to what extent might participation within hip hop's global currents in the end offer these artists new social vocabularies of black Cuban selfhood? As an influential interlocutor since 1998, what role might Black August have played in such transnationally expansive conversations? Concurrent with these millennial developments, the Cuban state became increasingly invested in both running the festival and in broader efforts to incorporate hip hop's emergent rise within the regulatory purview of state institutions.[5] For the time being, however, Rensoli and company were still the central organizing force behind the festival's four nights of performances.

While absorbed in my cajita, I listened in as the trio of Reyes de las Calles rehearse during a sound check for their song "El Mundo Va a Acabarse" (The world is coming to an end). The track's instrumental built on a sample riff from the classic 1974 hit "La Habana Joven" (Young Havana) by the immortal Los Van Van, Cuba's premier dance band since the early 1970s. I later found out the track was produced by the pioneering Cuban hip hop producer Pablo Herrera, who often spoke of the need to create an "authentic" Cuban sound behind Cuban MCs rather than relying on U.S.-produced background beats. In marked contrast to the buoyant Van Van original, however, Reyes de las Calles offered a notably different rendering of a "young Havana."

Though deceptively playful in delivery, the song painted a grim portrait of the social hypocrisy of the Cuban everyday. Thick with liturgical allusion, "La Habana Joven" evoked the wrathful coming of a black God to a society riddled with racism and duplicity, taking retribution against racists under whose weight blacks have been perpetually "squeezed." Like many raperos, Reyes employed metaphor and *doble sentido* (double meanings) to veil more overt forms of critique, while further masking the song's bite through a stylized use of humor and satirical play. For further effect, the MCs performed the track accompanied with a small blow-up raft and plastic oars in a thinly guised reference to *los balseros*, the thousands of disillusioned Cubans who fled to the United States in rafts following the onset of the economic crisis, significant numbers of whom were darker and drawn from less privileged urban communities. It was as if the artists were abandoning a torn and sinking Cuba while testifying to its demise. "El Mundo Va a Acabarse," as it turns out, was the opening performance that first night of the festival.

I returned to Alamar that evening with a couple of rapero friends who were slated to perform later in the festival's multiday run. Within a few blocks of the amphitheater we could feel the reverberations of the bass-heavy beats echoing off buildings, ever intensifying as we drew closer. The music was of U.S. rather than Cuban origin, suggesting that the evening's performances, despite our late arrival, had yet to start. The organizers were apparently priming the crowd with recent tracks by Common and the Roots, two local favorites who had or would soon perform in Cuba. As we made our way to the entrance flooded with attendees purchasing tickets at five Cuban *pesos* apiece (roughly $0.25 [USD]), we encountered a few police officers at the doorway who allowed us to pass after viewing our credential tags.

Once inside we were met by a descending sea of roughly three thousand young people milling about in energized anticipation of the festival's first night of music. Surveying the scene, it was a significantly darker-skinned crowd in comparison with the multiracial range of Cuba's broader population, which was commonly the case at hip hop events. Also evident was the apparent youth of those attending, the median age of whom could not have been much beyond seventeen. This was notably a younger following in comparison to those I had encountered at smaller hip hop events throughout Havana where, in line with most artists, the audience generally ranged in age between their early twenties and early thirties. A key factor was that the majority of these youth were drawn locally from Alamar, as the distance and scarcity of reliable night transport for return to Havana made it rather difficult for outsiders to attend. This, however, did not deter the most devoted who managed by one form or another to make it out to each of the festival's four nights of performance.

Amid the gathered crowd many young women could be seen wearing spandex tights along with form-fitting tops, while the men tended toward baggy pants, athletic team jerseys, and a few coveted FUBU and Ecko designer jerseys—the latest in hip hop–affiliated youth apparel from the States. The latter style range and its gendering found inspiration from the dog-eared U.S. rap magazines and videocassettes of recent hip hop videos that often circulated among these youth. This medium, along with much of the associated apparel, often found its way to Cuba by visiting family members, friends, and North American tourists alike. While these commodity streams were tied to recent openings to global capital and a growing culture of consumerism in a once definitely anticonsumerist Cuba, they can also be seen in dialogue with global circuits of style practice linked to cosmopolitan notions of black modernity.[6] Yet draped squarely behind the stage below sat a towering Cuban flag basking in the multicolored stage lighting as if to remind all: "This is Cuba, let there be no confusion."

Once the evening's performances began, all attention was directed to the onstage spectacle below. In addition to Reyes de las Calles, groups performing that opening night included Raperos Crazy de Alamar, Pasión Oscura, and the female trio of Instinto. Waves of call-and-response moved through the crowd, while in classic hip hop fashion a sea of arms bobbed in rhythmic tandem with the beats as energies rose. With performances wrapping up around 1:30 AM the crowd filed out into Alamar's darkened, now quiet streets, heading home in anticipation of the following night's performances.

For some of us, however, the night was far from over. The public buses and *máquinas* that brought many to Alamar from Havana earlier were now nowhere to be found. Sweat-soaked, dehydrated, and exhausted, we dragged ourselves up to the main road to wait for a passing bus carrying early morning commuters, eventually arriving back to Havana by 4 AM, only to do it all again the next night.

The following evening in Alamar had a clearly different energy about it. On approaching the amphitheater one could immediately sense a heightened buzz and nervous tension among the mingling crowd as scores of blue-clad police stood before the entrance overseeing crowd control. Inside, additional stern-faced columns of police were positioned in front and beside the performance stage below. These numbers were in marked contrast to the relatively sparse police presence during the previous night. A key distinction was that, in addition to a list of Cuban groups slated to perform, the hip hop duo of Dead Prez and the DJ-cum-emcee Tony Touch—all from New York City— were topping the bill that night. This was Black August's (aka Augusto Negro's) night at this year's festival.

Upon entering the amphitheater, members of Black August's New York contingent handed out flyers in Spanish introducing the collective. The flyer was adorned with a graphic composite of Afro-clad images of George Jackson beside Assata Shakur, the onetime Black Panther member and Cuba's most renowned African American political exile. The two profiles were framed by a large, five-point, Cuban-style star, and inscribed below in large block letters read the following:

BLACK AUGUST 3RD ANNUAL BENEFIT CONCERT 2000
DEDICATED TO ASSATA SHAKUR AND VIEQUES, PUERTO RICO[7]

The eight-page handout in Spanish opened with the question "¿Por que el agosto negro?" (Why Black August?), followed by a brief history of events: "The Tradition of Black August was established during the '70s in the Californian penal system by men and women of the Black/New Afrikan liberation movement as a way to remember and investigate a heritage of resistance in the Americas." This preface was followed by an outline of the collective's central principles, including the following:

- The global development of hip hop culture as a means of facilitating international interchange between communities of youth with the intention of promoting greater consciousness around social and political issues

- Collective opposition to the criminalization of youth and youth culture
- Organizing against the international prison industrial complex and the escalated incarceration of political prisoners in the U.S.
- Fighting the persistence of white-supremacist propaganda and violations of human rights.

The text closed with this statement: "Through a powerful union of hip hop culture and political information, Black August promotes our own hip hop aesthetic which emphasizes sincere self-expression, creativity, and the sense of responsibility to the community." The remaining six pages were devoted to Spanish translations of song lyrics by Dead Prez and Tony Touch.

As is evident from this material, Black August organized around a set of political commitments in dialogue with recent U.S. histories of black radical thought and practice. Drawing on an earlier prison movement of the same name aimed at political education among African American inmates, Black August formed in the late 1990s in New York City as a project offshoot of the Malcolm X Grassroots Movement (MXGM), a youth-centered activist organization grounded in a black nationalist orientation and human rights advocacy. While in conversation with an earlier moment of black radical organizing, Black August's program reflected cultural priorities of a younger generation of activists who invoked hip hop as a global medium of political engagement and youth outreach. Beyond Cuba, such transnational bearings led to Black August projects involving U.S.-based hip hop artists and activists' tours to South Africa, Brazil, Tanzania, and Venezuela. In the case of South Africa, the 2001 tour was coordinated to coincide with the United Nations' World Conference against Racism in Durban, with artists performing at the adjoining NGO antiracism forum.

Streaming the likes of W. E. B. Du Bois, Paul Robeson, and Richard Wright through ideological currents of Frantz Fanon to Maoism, appeals to revolutionary internationalism have long been formative facets of twentieth-century U.S. black radical traditions.[8] Yet Black August's use of the term "New Afrikan" in reference to African-descendant populations marked alignment with a particular post-1960s vein of black-left nationalism along the lines of the Black Liberation Army and the New Afrikan People's Organization (NAPO), members of which have been imprisoned or, as in the case of a few including Assata Shakur, forced into exile. Black August's support for an older cohort of imprisoned radicals and its broader anti-prison focus grew from intergenerational networks of solidarity with this history. Hip hop in this light is viewed as a temporal bridge through which political sensibilities sought translation into a new era of social activism.

Amid these converging streams of black radicalism, revolutionary internationalism, and hip hop itself, post-'59 Cuba has played its own historical part. Building on legacies of support for African American radicals dating back to Fidel Castro's impromptu 1960 Harlem meeting with Malcolm X, the U.S. black left has shared a long, if at times ambivalent, history of solidarity with revolutionary Cuba.[9] Concurrent with Cuba's anticolonial involvements in Africa, a stream of prominent individuals, including the Black Panthers Eldridge Cleaver and Huey Newton in addition to figures like Stokely Carmichael and Angela Davis, visited or spent time in exile in Cuba during the '60s and '70s. As one of the first African Americans to receive asylum, the radical iconoclast Robert Williams hosted a Havana-based AM radio program, *Radio Free Dixie*, whose 1961–65 broadcast mingling music, news, and political commentary targeted black communities along the southeastern United States. Yet Williams, like a number of subsequent African Americans, left Cuba harboring disillusionment about the perceived shortcomings of the Revolution's antiracist commitments.[10] There have been related suggestions that Cuban support for U.S. black radicals not only served as a proxy challenge to U.S. imperialism, but also offered a popular means of deflecting domestic attention from Cuba's own incongruences of race.[11]

Tensions notwithstanding, such histories have engendered their own structures of feeling and forms of social memory in Cuba. Tapping into a current of this history, I recall my friend Rita reminiscing about her school-age experience singing a popular solidarity song "¡Por Angela!," with its celebratory call for the freeing of Angela Davis during her U.S. imprisonment in the early 1970s.[12] As Rita shared the song, clenched fist raised high, she began to cry as emotionally laden memories of the moment returned to her. Although she was not Afro-Cuban herself, Rita's nostalgias were tied to an affective sense of political solidarity that she, as a child of the Cuban Revolution, shared with African Americans in their labors for social justice.

A more immediate set of conversations began with the arrival of Assata Shakur, who, following a prison escape and a period of underground activity in the United States, was granted political asylum in Cuba in the mid-1980s. A former Panther long active in radical circles in the New York City area, Shakur was also the godmother of the late hip hop artist and global icon Tupac Shakur, an association not lost on many hip hop followers in both the United States and Cuba. Indeed, Assata Shakur's history of activism has attracted popular support among a younger generation of politically minded U.S. hip hop artists and affiliated activists, their ranks composing much of the energy behind a 2005 "Hands Off Assata" campaign organized in response to a U.S. Justice Department's $1 million bounty for her capture.[13] Black August's codedication of the 2000 festival to her reflects these circuits of solidarity.

While Assata Shakur's stature has garnered admiration among Havana-area raperos, a fellow U.S. exile and generational peer, Nehanda Abiodun, has been a more direct and intimately involved figure within Cuba's evolving nexus of black radicalism, revolution, and hip hop. Sharing a similar history of radical organizing, Abiodun has, since her early 1990s Cuban arrival, maintained lines of U.S. engagement among others through membership in Black August's mother organization, MXGM. Building on these networks, Abiodun served as one of the founding members of Black August, helping root Black August's Cuban base from its inception. Now in her early sixties, Abiodun has also played an influential mentoring role within local rapero circles. Through a mix of personal relationships, the hosting of informal class gatherings, and active involvement in numerous hip hop–related events, Abiodun has over the years assumed something of an elder *madrina* (godmother) status within Havana's rapero community.

Black August's engagement with Cuban hip hop and the ongoing lives of African American political exiles is seen as part and parcel of the same project. To these ends Black August hosted a series of annual benefit concerts in New York City with the dual purpose of both raising funds in support of imprisoned African American radicals and their families and providing limited levels of material assistance to Cuba's hip hop community. Cuba in this sense offered an instrumental, if in the end somewhat uneven, confluence of political commitments. With 1998 marking the project's inaugural year and initial Cuban foray, the artists Mos Def (aka Yasiin Bey) and Talib Kweli, then of the duo Black Star, performed alongside the MCs Sticman and M1 of Dead Prez at the hip hop festival under Black August's umbrella. Mergings of music and politics endured the following year as the Chicago-born artist Common interrupted his performance to read a letter of solidarity addressed to the audience from Dr. Mutulu Shakur, a former NAPO member and the stepfather of Tupac Shakur currently imprisoned in the United States. Provoking a stir among Cuban higher-ups, this presentation was prompted by Abiodun, who provided the letter and encouraged its reading.

Common later released the track "A Song for Assata," likely evolving out of his time in Cuba, on his album *Like Water for Chocolate* (2000), recounting Shakur's U.S. imprisonment.

Black August's politics of affinity were not limited to nationalist claims on blackness, however. The collective's 2000 codedication to Vieques, Puerto Rico, underscored a transnational frame of social justice that, reminiscent of internationalist orientations of earlier moments, recognized the often-imbricated linkages between antiracist and anticolonial/anti-imperialist projects. The collective's attention to Vieques also reflected the New York–based membership's sensitivity to histories of Puerto Rican radicalism and labors for national independence, which at the time found expression in the campaign to free the island of Vieques from over sixty years of U.S. military occupation, an effort in which mainland Puerto Ricans played a vocal role.

A number of Nuyorican cultural activists were in fact integral to Black August's formation and inaugural Cuban launching. Key among these was Clyde Valentine, a cofounder and editor of the now defunct hip hop magazine *Stress* and a founding member of Black August. Another sharing long-standing connections with Cuban raperos is Marinieves Alba, a Nuyorican activist, writer, and cultural events producer, who helped organize a 2003 U.S. tour of Havana-based artists that culminated in a concert in Harlem's historic Apollo Theater alongside the Roots. The San Francisco Bay area brothers Kahlil and Eli Jacobs-Fantauzzi are two other enduring Puerto Rican supporters of Havana's hip hop community, with Eli's film *Inventos: Hip Hop Cubano* (2003) representing one of the earliest documentary treatments of Cuban hip hop.

These artistic involvements, once more, built upon legacies of Spanish colonial and U.S. imperial antagonism shared between the islands of Cuba and Puerto Rico. Such communion finds poetic form in the celebrated verse "Cuba y Puerto Rico son de un pájaro las dos alas, reciben flores y balas, sobre el mismo corazón" (Cuba and Puerto Rico are a bird's two wings, receiving flowers and bullets in the same heart), penned in 1863 by the Puerto Rican abolitionist and *independista* poet Lola Rodriguez de Tió and later memorialized in Cuba by Pablo Milanés in his 1978 ballad "Son de Cuba a Puerto Rico." This moment also built on a rich history of Nuyorican participation in hip hop dating back to the mid-1970s. The birth and early development of hip hop are indeed indebted to cultural dialogue and political affinity making among African American, West Indian, and Puerto Rican youth in New York City.[14] Such intimacies, Raquel Rivera argues, arose from shared conditions of racial marginalization and histories of Afro-diasporic belonging forged through overlapping lines of blackness and *latinidad*.[15] Black August's Cuban project can be seen in this light as elaborating on such interwoven affinities of race, diaspora, and hip hop via circulatory solidarities of U.S.-Cuban exchange.

RETURNING TO THAT August festival night, a heightened energy of excitement was ever tangible as the audience milled about in anticipation of the evening's performance. Though both Dead Prez and the Nuyorican DJ-turned-music producer Tony Touch were headlining the bill, it was Dead Prez's Afrocentric duo of M1 and Sticman who clearly set the night's tone. In a buildup to the artists' entrance, their support crew projected images of Nelson Mandela, armed African soldiers, and black shackled fists raised aloft upon two giant screens that framed the Cuban flag at stage rear. When Dead Prez finally arrived, the crowd roared with excitement. The duo opened with their nationalist ode "I'm a African" from their 2000 debut album *Let's Get Free*. The two dreadlocked artists, surrounded by a stoic cordon of Cuban police below, rallied close to three thousand darker-skinned youth in collective unison: "I'm a African, I'm a African / And I know what is happen'in! / You a African, You a African /Do you know what's happen'in?" English proficiency was apparently not necessary for shared intelligibility here, one that seemed to articulate at least in part along lines of racial identification. Directly following Dead Prez's lead, Tony Touch received a notably cooler response from the crowd, this despite his efforts at Nuyorican Spanish and self-billing as Tony Toca (Tony "Touch"). Dead Prez spoke not a word of Spanish, yet they appeared to turn the house out.

I recall my friend Alexey Rodríguez, of the hip hop duo Obsesión, with whom I had traveled to the festival that evening, commenting on how impressed he was with Dead Prez's performance, noting "Su mensaje tenía tremenda fuerza" (Their message had tremendous force). Although Alexey had little fluency in English, he was quite familiar with Dead Prez and the politically charged nature of their music, relying like others on translation assistance from English-speaking friends like myself. He expressed concern, however, about one of the duo's songs that evening, "They Schools," which offered a blistering rejection of the U.S. public education system. Alexey felt Dead Prez's tone of indignation was way over the top, taking particular issue with the line "All my high school teachers can suck my dick, telling me white-ass lies and bullshit," which he felt was excessively irreverent. I shared with him my reading of the song as a critique—one institutional rather than individual in nature—of what was viewed as a corrupt and racist education system, rather than a personal attack on teachers per se. Alexey was not particularly swayed by my interpretation. I wondered at the time if such dissonance of readings might have something to do with long-standing tendencies in revolutionary Cuba to privilege understandings of individual over structural expressions of racism, often obfuscating broader systemic workings of racialized power and privilege. In a more immediate sense it was likely that Alexey, as an Afro-Cuban, simply had difficulty identifying with Dead Prez's level of anger and societal alienation.

This discord reminded me of a distinction that Cuban raperos often made between their music and much of the more commercially oriented hip hop in the United States. Gangsta thuggery, hyper-materialized bling, and virulent misogyny so ubiquitous in corporately promoted U.S. hip hop were conspicuously (and often self-consciously) absent from Cuban hip hop. While mediated and hyperbolic in their seemingly endlessly commercial reproduction, such masculinist tropes nonetheless emerge in dialogue with histories of structural violence painfully endemic to postindustrial U.S. black urban life. Thus while lines of racial affinity may have been in play that evening, Cuba, and by extension Cuban hip hop, was in this sense indeed different.

The disjointedness of Alexey's cultural divide resonated with an experience I later had following a screening of the documentary film *One Dollar: El Precio de la Vida* during the Havana Film Festival in 2002. Directed by the Panamanian American filmmaker Héctor Herrera, *One Dollar* chronicles the aftermath of the 1989 U.S. invasion of Panama on poor working-class Afro-Panamanians in Panama City, depicting in brutal fashion the subsequent intensification of violence, guns, and drug trafficking within these communities. Having attended the screening with a handful of friends, I asked MC Michael Oramas of the hip hop crew Junior Clan about his thoughts on the film. Michael responded incredulously, "Todo lo que presentó no puede ser real—algunos son falsos, fabricados. Era demasiado" (Everything they presented cannot be real—some are false, made up. It was too much). As critically minded and self-declared "underground" as Michael identified as an artist, he found it difficult to imagine such a violently desperate set of circumstances plaguing black folks. While the dollar was also rapidly transforming the lived everyday in Cuba, there were still few if any Caribbean, Latin American, or, for that matter, U.S. cities as relatively free of drugs, guns, and violent crime as Havana. Cuba and its revolutionary history remained (if for the current moment) notably different in this sense, a distinction that defied simple intraracial translation and underscored divergent historical positions vis-à-vis the destructive tendencies of contemporary global capital and legacies of U.S. interventionism.

That said, reflecting on the internationalist dimensions of the festival, Rensoli cited Black August's participation and hip hop as enabling dialogue between Cuban and U.S. MCs by way of diasporic currents of black identification. Regarding such articulations, Rensoli explained:

I used the idea of diaspora to fashion a vision of how blacks in the United States, or blacks in the Caribbean, or blacks in other parts of the Americas are all brothers. Part of our family went here, another part went there, and for a long time we've hardly recognized each other. All these reflections came to me after my own experience with the festival, after the level of communication between North American and Cuban raperos helped me realize that there was a lot more in common between us.[16]

Echoing similar lines, Pablo Herrera, the noted Cuban hip hop producer mentioned earlier, suggested:

When Black August started coming to Cuba we found that that we could identify with them, the same way they could identify with us. It wasn't that they brought the politics to us, that they made us understand what race meant, this is false. . . . That was a beautiful moment to be part of a major moment of Pan-Africanism and solidarity between the people of the United States and Cuba, African Americans and Afro-Cubans. Becoming aware of the resources and the political activism that they were doing in New York and San Francisco gave us tools to try and understand how to deal with the shit here. We need to deal with the shit here in a radical way. So something here that I think is really important to talk about is how cosmopolitan Cuba became through Black August.[17]

While diasporic affinities and appeals to a black cosmopolitanism may indeed have been instrumental during the festival, there appeared to be limitations in their practice. I recall frustrations arising during the 2000 festival over the limited degree of contact between local raperos and Black August's New York entourage. In the case of Dead Prez, the only opportunity most Cuban MCs had to engage the duo was a few fleeting minutes backstage just prior to their festival performance. With the exception of a few well-positioned Cubans who spent time with the artists, handshakes, embraces, and autographs were plentiful, but often not much else. For many in the Black August delegation, the priority of the Cuban trip appeared more centered on connecting with African American political exiles at the expense of any structured time for *intercombio* (exchange) with Havana's hip hop community.

The afternoon following Black August's festival program, I attended a meeting in an Alamar cultural center as part of the festival's *coloquio* (colloquium) series. In a dimly lit room with a handful of metal chairs and small desks, roughly a dozen raperos and a few supporting cast members engaged in a freewheeling discussion around issues, concerns, and grievances affecting the hip hop community. One complaint aired concerned a lack of access to visiting U.S. artists in which a few attendees recalled attempts to visit the Black August delegation in their tourist hotel, only to be denied entrance beyond the lobby by hotel security. I had myself spent time with the Black August circle during the festival, and in most cases these spaces largely conformed to the logics of Cuba's new apartheid economy, which tended to segregate Cubans from dollar-paying foreign tourists and their regulated zones of entitled consumption. Revolutionary appeals to internationalist solidarity notwithstanding, global hierarchies of social difference did not in the end magically dissolve but rather found translated form in Cuba's expanding market workings.

That festival's second night closed with the duo Yosmel Sarrías and Kokino Entenza of Anónimo Consejo (Anonymous advice). Donned in a collage of Vietnamese-styled straw hats, oversized Che Guevara tee-shirts, and baggy jeans with a single pant leg hoisted aloft in au courant hip hop fashion, the duo hit the stage to a ruckus reception. Natives of the neighboring seaside municipality of Cojimar, Anónimo Consejo were among the local favorites and it clearly showed. Working the crowd through a series of call-and-response riffs, the duo had the audience singing in animated harmony with many of their songs. The most exuberant response seemed to arrive with their performance of "Las Apariencias Engañan" (Appearances can deceive). Couched in tones of indignation, the song offered entry into the hardships of black youth navigating the island's new dollarized geographies, and the Cuban state's often racialized efforts to police and regulate these marked spaces of exclusion. In a thinly veiled address to Cuban police, the duo closed the song with the following lines:

Leave me alone, don't squeeze me anymore
Let me live!
This is not to make your skin crawl
This is not to make you fight with me

This is so you can understand once and for all
That not all the young people are garbage
Because the dollar has changed many peoples' way of thinking
And many of those people aren't us,
We are the young Cubans who support
the idea of what revolution is at all moments
Anónimo Consejo, Revolution!
Yosmel and Kokino, Revolution!

Thus amid all its convergences and attending asymmetries of sound and politics that evening, Anónimo Consejo's closing salvo suggests an implicit reckoning along the lines of Michael Hardt and Antonio Negri's work concerning the shifting elusive nature of both empire and revolutionary alterity at the millennial turn.[18] Remixed here, where in their antipodal ends might empire and revolution indeed reside in the current age of neoliberal capital?

NOTES

1. The 1993 legalization of the dollar and the subsequent introduction of a dual U.S. dollar/Cuban peso economy were followed by additional market reforms including the limited sanctioning of privately owned small businesses and cooperatives, establishment of real estate and car markets, openings to foreign investment and joint ventures, and a rapid expansion of foreign tourism.

2. Grounded in the late nineteenth-century ideals of the nationalist intellectual José Martí along with the massive participation of formally enslaved blacks in Cuba's Wars of Independence, and later resuscitated under post-'59 revolutionary efforts to forge a united socialist front, the promise of a nonracial Cuba has been a central facet of Cuban nation building from inception.

3. For discussions of the raced workings of Cuba's new economy, see Alejandro de la Fuente, *A Nation for All: Race, Inequality, and Politics in Twentieth-Century Cuba* (Chapel Hill: University of North Carolina Press, 2001); and Mark Sawyer, *Racial Politics in Post-Revolutionary Cuba* (Cambridge: Cambridge University Press, 2005).

4. See Marc Perry, "Global Black Self-Fashionings: Hip Hop as Diasporic Space," *Identities* 15, no. 6 (December 2008): 635–64; and *Negro Soy Yo: Hip Hop and Raced Citizenship in Neoliberal Cuba* (Durham: Duke University Press, 2015).

5. The Cuban state took full control of the festival's operation the following year, and in 2002 it established the Cuban Rap Agency, which represented a (subsequently diminished) height of state institutionalization efforts.

6. For discussions of global style as a practice of black modernity, see Mark Anderson, *Black and Indigenous: Garifuna Activism and Consumer Culture in Honduras* (Minneapolis: University of Minnesota Press, 2009); Manthia Diawara, *In Search of Africa* (Cambridge: Harvard University Press, 1998); Paul Gilroy, *The Black Atlantic: Modernity and*

Double Consciousness (Cambridge: Harvard University Press, 1993); Michael Hanchard, *Orpheus and Power* (Princeton, NJ: Princeton University Press, 1998); and Robin D. G. Kelley, *Africa Speaks, America Answers: Modern Jazz in Revolutionary Times* (Cambridge: Harvard University Press, 2012).

7. This and all the following excerpts are English translations of the pamphlet's original Spanish text.

8. See Roderick Bush, *The End of White World Supremacy: Black Internationalism and the Problem of the Color Line* (Philadelphia: Temple University Press, 2009); and Robin D. G. Kelley, *Freedom Dreams: The Black Radical Imagination* (New York: Beacon, 2003).

9. See Peniel Joseph, "Where Blackness Is Bright? Cuba, Africa and Black Liberation during the Age of Civil Rights," *New Formations* 45 (2002): 111–24; and Ruth Reitan, *The Rise and Decline of an Alliance: Cuban and African American Leaders in the 1960s* (East Lansing: Michigan State University Press, 1999).

10. See also John Clytus and Jane Rieker, *Black Man in Red Cuba* (Miami: University of Miami Press, 1970).

11. See Carlos Moore, *Castro, the Blacks, and Africa* (Los Angeles: Center for Afro-American Studies, UCLA, 1988).

12. Following the 1971 penning of "¡Por Angela!" by Tania Castellanos, Pablo Milanés later composed "Canción para Angela Davis," of which an iconic version was recorded in 1975 with fellow *nueva trova* artist, Silvio Rodriguez.

13. In 2013 Shakur's U.S. bounty was doubled to $2 million in addition to her rather incongruous placement on the FBI's list of most wanted terrorists.

14. See Jeff Chang, *Can't Stop Won't Stop: A History of the Hip Hop Generation* (New York: St. Martin's, 2005).

15. Raquel Rivera, *New York Ricans from the Hip Hop Zone* (New York: Palgrave, 2003).

16. Rodolfo Rensoli, interview by author, August 1, 1999.

17. Pablo Herrera, interview by author, July 20, 2012.

18. See Michael Hardt and Antonio Negri, *Empire* (Cambridge: Harvard University Press, 2000).

10 · TANGO AS INTANGIBLE CULTURAL HERITAGE

Development, Diversity, and the Values of Music in Buenos Aires

MORGAN JAMES LUKER

In September 2009, the United Nations Educational, Scientific, and Cultural Organization (UNESCO) recognized tango as an "intangible cultural heritage of humanity." UNESCO's declaration, one of the first to acknowledge a genre of popular music and dance with this distinction, had several important consequences within Argentina and Uruguay, the two countries in which tango initially developed as a genre and that jointly applied to UNESCO for tango's recognition as an intangible cultural heritage of humanity. On the one hand, the recognition reinscribed tango within highly prestigious international networks of musical production and consumption while it simultaneously reframed local musical and cultural histories within revisionist narratives of multicultural transnationalism. On the other hand, it gave a significant boost to already robust efforts on the part of local and national governments to promote tango as an engine for economic development via international cultural tourism and the exportation of music and other cultural goods abroad. The declaration also represented a watershed moment in the shifting discourses of institutional engagement and cultural policy making regarding tango specifically and musical culture more broadly, especially within the city government of Buenos Aires, which played a key if contested role in the development of the proposal recognized by UNESCO and was one of its primary beneficiaries.

In this essay, I examine the UNESCO tango declaration and some of the debates surrounding it in order to develop a critical perspective on the cultural politics of musical heritage making within complexly interlocking networks of musical circulation, cultural policy, and global commerce in contemporary Buenos Aires. In doing so, I aim to address broader concerns with how the value and meaning of musical culture have been profoundly reframed in what I call, following George Yúdice, the age of expediency—where music and the arts are called upon and often compelled to address social, political, and economic problems that were previously located outside the cultural domain by theorists and practitioners alike.[1] This phenomenon has arguably gone from being an exceptional curiosity to a near pillar of common sense regarding the role of culture and the arts in social life in Argentina and far beyond, succinctly articulated in the U.S. National Endowment for the Arts' polyvalent motto "art works."[2] The UNESCO declaration fits squarely within this broader trend, which has effectively reshaped the field of cultural production regarding tango specifically and musical culture more generally in Buenos Aires and beyond. Indeed, the UNESCO declaration is emblematic of the new ways musical culture is drawn upon and used in the age of expediency, where previous ambivalences if not outright antagonisms between cultural producers, private enterprise, the state, and so-called third sector or civil society organizations have come to operate as synergistic opportunities for development of all sorts. And while these newly configured relationships are usually not the straightforward "win-win" that many advocates claim, they certainly confound conventional notions of left/right politics—cultural and otherwise—and in that sense present a serious challenge to the critical scholarship of music.

Addressing this challenge requires a critical rethinking of the many "managerial regimes" that have come to define contemporary musical life in Buenos Aires and far beyond. By managerial regime I mean any entity that aims to channel cultural practices into resources for social or economic development. In the case of tango, these regimes include the cultural industries and other media corporations, nonprofit and nongovernmental arts organizations, and, especially, the cultural policies of local and national governments—particularly the city government of Buenos Aires—and their transnational institutional partners such as UNESCO. Indeed, governmental and nongovernmental heritage-making efforts regarding tango are symptomatic of a much broader turn from more traditional conceptions of musical culture that have dominated cultural policy-making efforts in Buenos Aires and elsewhere for many years. Previously, Culture with a capital C—culture as the fine arts and little if anything else—was considered a necessary object of governmental intervention and support because it could articulate a supposedly unified national culture and serve the betterment of what Toby Miller has called an "ethically incomplete" citizenry.[3] The discourse and practice of heritage making, in contrast, frame local cultural forms as natural or renewable resources in need of management like any other, thereby providing both legalistic and ethical frameworks for state intervention in newly audible and differently valuable areas of cultural practice, musical and otherwise. The heritage-making project therefore represents a significant intervention, the consequences of which extend well beyond the parsing of bureaucratic jargon.

I begin with a brief introduction to UNESCO's intangible cultural heritage programs, highlighting some of the challenges they and the broader heritage-making project pose for the critical scholarship of music and the arts. I then discuss the local context in which the UNESCO declaration and other cultural policies regarding tango were developed in Buenos Aires, highlighting some of the musical and historical circumstances that have enabled these projects. Contrary to what one might assume, those who have been interested in preserving tango in Buenos Aires outside of this particular effort have historically been confronted with the reality of long-standing personal and institutional prejudices against tango in Argentina, such that the genre continues to be considered an expression of little or no lasting value (aesthetic or otherwise) in many instances, both official and unofficial, and despite the claims that are represented in the UNESCO declaration. Nevertheless, tango clearly continues to have salience as a potent symbol of Argentine culture within the national imaginary and global representations, not so much a national genre as what one of my interlocutors cited here calls "a national brand." It is precisely this dual trend of detachment and connection that has made tango an exceptionally productive resource for heritage making and other development projects in contemporary Buenos Aires, the values of which clearly extend beyond the aesthetic domain.

I then turn to a more detailed discussion of the UNESCO declaration itself, with particular attention given to how the declaration enacted fundamental transformations in both the aesthetic meaning and economic value of the genre it was designed to preserve and protect. The declaration upended localist formulations that have long posited tango as the exclusive provenance of a uniquely Argentine sentimental and expressive complex, something that was accessible to outsiders only through devotion to widespread mythologies that necessarily framed the genre as artistically isolated and aesthetically self-referential. The UNESCO declaration and the broader heritage-making project, in contrast, frame tango as the rightful heir to cosmopolitan aesthetic ideologies that highlight artistic innovation within a given tradition of musical history as the hallmark of a local popular music's "universal" value. Along with this, the proposal also carefully reframes the historic origins of tango in terms of the "diversity discourses" that are currently in vogue at all levels of cultural policy making. On the one hand, the UNESCO declaration's emphasis on tango as a symbol of cultural (and especially racial) diversity, while historically accurate, represents a fundamental reframing of long-standing hegemonic narratives of both musical and social history in Argentina. On the other hand, these aesthetic and historical interventions bolster a wide variety of economically expedient gestures, which are incorporated throughout the declaration and in fact frame the mission of the UNESCO intangible cultural heritage programs as a whole. Indeed, the UNESCO program is explicitly designed not only to bolster efforts to preserve intangible cultural practices but to more efficiently and creatively harness the new economic potential those practices might have as engines for what UNESCO calls "sustainable development." These features of the program speak to the emergent and multiple values that local cultural differences have begun to take on within new circuits of transnational cultural prestige and economic exchange.

UNESCO's Intangible Cultural Heritage
Program and the New Values of Musical Culture

UNESCO's Convention for the Safeguarding of Intangible Cultural Heritage, adopted in 2003, defines intangible cultural heritage as

> the practices, representations, expressions, knowledge, skills—as well as the instruments, objects, artifacts and cultural spaces associated therewith—that communities, groups and, in some cases, individuals recognize as part of their cultural heritage. This intangible cultural

heritage, transmitted from generation to generation, is constantly re-created by communities and groups in response to their environment, their interaction with nature and their history, and provides them with a sense of identity and continuity, thus promoting respect for cultural diversity and human creativity.[4]

The Convention suggests that intangible cultural heritage is manifest in "(a) oral traditions and expressions, including language as a vehicle of the intangible cultural heritage; (b) performing arts; (c) social practices, rituals and festive events; (d) knowledge and practices concerning nature and the universe; [and] (e) traditional craftsmanship." The stated goal of the 2003 Convention is to "safeguard" exemplary elements of intangible cultural heritage. This is done through "measures aimed at ensuring the viability of the intangible cultural heritage, including the identification, documentation, research, preservation, protection, promotion, enhancement, transmission, particularly through formal and non-formal education, as well as the revitalization of the various aspects of such heritage."[5]

Via the authority of the 2003 Convention, UNESCO encourages member states to develop and implement a range of cultural policies and programs for identifying and safeguarding internal forms of intangible cultural heritage, and it provides some financial assistance for doing so in accordance with international best practices as determined by UNESCO. It also solicits proposals for elements of intangible cultural heritage to be considered for formal inscription on one of two lists, either the "Representative List of the Intangible Cultural Heritage of Humanity" or the "List of Intangible Cultural Heritage in Need of Urgent Safeguarding." The Representative List "aims at contributing to ensuring visibility and awareness of the significance of the intangible cultural heritage and to encouraging dialogue, thus reflecting cultural diversity worldwide and testifying to human creativity"; the Urgent Safeguarding List "aims at taking appropriate safeguarding measures for those intangible cultural heritage expressions or manifestations whose viability—that is whose continuous recreation and transmission—is threatened."[6] A twenty-four-member Intergovernmental Committee for the Safeguarding of the Intangible Cultural Heritage evaluates these proposals, and those selected for inscription on either of the two lists are announced on an annual basis. Crucially, and in accordance with the legalistic authority of the United Nations as a whole, only national governments from States Parties to the Convention (which the United States is not) can present proposals for the consideration of the Intergovernmental Committee, though it is expected that they do so with the formal consent and active participation of the "concerned communities or groups," that is, the actual practitioners of whatever form of intangible cultural heritage is being presented for consideration. As of this writing, 31 elements of intangible cultural heritage from nearly 20 different countries have been inscribed on the Urgent Safeguarding List, while the Representative List includes 257 elements, including tango, from more than 70 different countries.[7]

Returning to the case at hand, it is immediately clear that the very notion of intangible cultural heritage as defined in the 2003 Convention represents a significant departure from previous institutional understandings of music specifically and the performing arts more generally. The idea that intangible cultural heritage is (or should be considered) something of universal value directly undermines the long-standing and widespread privileging of western art music over any and all local musical forms and practices in Buenos Aires and far beyond. This alone is a tremendous intervention, given that the vast majority of elements included in the Representative List come from the nations of the global south, where the public institutionalization of western art music has often been taken as an indicator of modernization efforts if not modernity as such, however contested it might be, going back to the colonial period.[8] The practical and philosophical implications of the heritage-making project should therefore not be underestimated. That said, institutionalization and everything it entails remains very much at the center of these efforts, despite the otherwise profound transformation in how the cultural "content" that is "managed" by these institutions is conceptualized, located, recognized, and valued. It is the emergence of this managerial mode that defines the heritage-making project as much as if not more than the very real cultural diversification these efforts undoubtedly represent within specific national contexts and the transnational public sphere. In that sense, the heritage-making project is clearly congruent with the broader turn toward the use of culture in the age of expediency, where the value and meaning of music and the arts are largely defined by their usability within broader cultural, social, and economic development projects. A key part of this—indeed, the very reason why heritage making has become a compelling paradigm for the public management of culture in recent years—is the fact that heritage making encompasses both the aesthetic and the economic value of intangible cultural practices in equal measure.

Accounting for the politics of this shift can be confounding. Among critics who have directly tackled the UNESCO intangible cultural heritage programs and the larger heritage-making project, some, such as Barbara Kirshenblatt-Gimblett, have anxiously called out the discourse and practice of heritage making as little more than a new and largely cynical wrinkle in the tragic narrative of denial, silencing, and exclusion that is at the heart of modernity itself.[9] Others, such as Anthony Seeger, take a somewhat more celebratory position regarding what they see as the deeply progressive if also complexly problematic impulse to recognize, protect, and promote emblematic features of the world's cultural diversity that partly motivates the UNESCO program.[10] Still others, such as Richard Kurin, fall somewhere in between these positions, exhibiting a pragmatic optimism about the work of UNESCO and the broader heritage-making project while predicting that such efforts may very well leave us with only that many more underfunded and therefore ineffective cultural programs and institutions.[11] Regardless of where we might locate ourselves within these debates, it is important to note that these and other perspectives occupy different points along a continuum between aesthetic and economic prioritizations within the overall heritage-making project rather than entirely different ideological universes. This is a crucial shift, one that represents a striking departure from most critical and practical work on the aesthetic and economic values of culture, intangible and otherwise—from the critical refusals of the Frankfurt School and its followers on the left to the "culture is entertainment" free-trade advocates on the right, both of whom have essentially assumed that the aesthetic and economic aspects of culture are necessarily opposed if not outright antagonistic to one another.

Here, in contrast, we encounter a general reframing of musical values and meanings, with previously ambivalent if not antagonistic practices and relationships—localized practices of cultural heritage and meaning versus globalized networks of recognition and exchange, the "priceless" transcendence of the aesthetic sublime versus the price-tagged products of the commercial cultural industries—becoming productive synergies for development of all sorts. And while the political implications of this new orientation are ambiguous at best, it is crucial to recognize from the outset that both practical and critical engagement with the heritage-making project and the broader expediency of musical culture do not represent a capitulation to the profit motives of the cultural industries or the neoliberal machinations of cultural and other policy makers. Nor do they imply a reactionary defense of capital-letter "Culture" or "the Arts" against those same forces. They do, however, call for renewed ethnographic engagement with the heritage-making project and the larger managerial regimes, which should not be (or not only be) considered static entities within broader narratives of domination and resistance, but dynamic sites of strategic engagement within which various actors can play out their "serious games."[12]

Detachment, Connection, and the
Context of Musical Usability in Buenos Aires

Early in my fieldwork on the culture and politics of contemporary tango music in Buenos Aires, I had the opportunity to interview Enrique Marmonti, a prominent tango film, television, record, and event producer. I met him in the second floor café of the Abasto Hotel, a five-star hotel in Buenos Aires, which had a "tango theme." A modern tower of stone and glass that stands some twenty stories above the surrounding Abasto neighborhood, the hotel is a spectacular testament to both the transnational appeal and productive power of tango today. Included in the cost of any room is a daily group tango lesson taught by bilingual instructors with "extensive international experience." The hotel can also provide guests with private tango lessons catered to their specific needs and levels of experience with the largely improvised and notoriously difficult *salon*, or social, style of tango. The hotel's two "tango suites," their most luxurious accommodations, have small dance floors built into their living rooms where patrons can take private dance lessons or practice their technique on their own. The hotel, in turn, is located across from the Esquina Carlos Gardel, a high-end *cena show* nightclub, named in homage to the legendary tango singer (1890–1935), that presents glossily produced tango floor shows to dining audiences seven nights a week. Each show features a small orchestra of live tango musicians and several pairs of professional dancers who perform in the elaborately choreographed and highly athletic *escenario*, or stage, style of tango.[13] At the time of this writing, a night at the Esquina Carlos Gardel begins at $96 (USD) per person (without dinner) and can go as high as $280, significant sums even for many foreign tourists, who are the Esquina's target audience and primary clientele.

Those who patronized the Esquina Carlos Gardel, the Abasto Hotel, and the innumerable other commercial venues for tango-related performance, dance, accommodation, food, and accessories located throughout the city were part of a much larger boom in foreign tourism that developed following the steep devaluation of the Argentine peso in late 2001.[14] The devaluation made the goods and services of the previously expensive city (on par with New York) jaw-droppingly affordable for those who happened to have U.S. dollars, euros, pounds, reais, or other foreign currencies in their bank accounts, and international tourists flocked to Buenos Aires to take advantage of the highly imbalanced exchange rates. Indeed, by the time I spoke with Marmonti in 2006, the city government was elaborating policies to more deliberately channel the consumption-driven "predatory tourism" that Buenos Aires had gained a reputation for following the devaluation into modes of touristic engagement that officials considered more broadly productive and beneficial for the city and its citizens. Tango was an important resource for these efforts. Unlike the "predatory tourists" who usually made singular trips to Buenos Aires to buy cheap leather jackets by day and binge drink by night, tango tourists would make multiple, sometimes annual, trips to the city and tended to stay longer, for several weeks or even several months at a time. During their stays, tango tourists would have more direct interactions and make more personal connections with local residents who were also active in the tango scene, building ongoing relationships and often genuine friendships over time. These types of interactions between visitors and locals, while clearly shot through with unequal power relationships, were considered qualitatively different from the naked fee-for-service interactions that characterized the more "predatory" tourism industry. In contrast to this, tango tourism was imagined (and lived) as much as a mode of intercultural communication as economic exchange, the benefits of which, according to advocates, would be mutual, multiple, and widely shared.

As Arlene Dávila has shown, the lived experiences of those on both sides of the tango tourism equation do not always measure up to the idealistic formulations of cultural policy makers, especially regarding the long-term prospects for economic stability and mobility on the part of those who labor in the tango tourism industry.[15] But while the nonmaterial cultural benefits of tango tourism are impossible to measure and, frankly, largely debatable, the tremendous economic potential of the sector is simply undeniable: according to a 2007 study produced by the city government's Cultural Industries Observatory, tango-related activity generated the equivalent of $450 million (USD) in Buenos Aires annually, and it did so without significant governmental intervention in the sector up to that point. UNESCO declared tango an intangible cultural heritage of humanity just two years later. Thus the exploding values of tango as both an economic resource and a form of intangible cultural heritage are not contradictory but in fact complementary, with the private accumulation of capital (supposedly) producing broadly shared cultural benefits while the aesthetic value of artistic practice is experienced and articulated via irreducibly economic modes of exchange.

This brings me back to my interview with Marmonti, who articulated precisely this point in response to my somewhat naïve (in hindsight) question about tango tourism in Buenos Aires. I asked him if he thought there was "a conflict between the presence of so many foreign tourists and all the discourse about tango and Argentine identity, tango as *lo nuestro* [our thing], which I have heard so much about?" He replied, somewhat gruffly,

> That's all a lie. Tango is not popular—it is not popular, don't believe that. It is a lie that it is popular. Your problem is that you think about tango, but if you take your recorder and go out walking for two days without thinking about tango you are not going to hear tango anywhere. The only tangos you will hear are tourist tangos, so there is no identity conflict, there is just tango as a national brand.[16]

In saying that tango is "not popular," Marmonti meant not only that tango today operates as a niche genre with a circumscribed, largely specialist audience, which it certainly does, but also that tango was no longer *música popular*, that is, a socially popular form that is understood as coming from and expressing "the people" as a social, cultural, and economic category, which it very much had during previous historical moments.[17] And while Marmonti's claim that "the only tangos you will hear are tourist tangos" is very much a rhetorical overstatement, it nevertheless points to a key fact regarding the contemporary genre culture of tango in Buenos Aires: the dual trend of detachment and connection that, I believe, accounts for much of the truly exceptional value that contemporary tango has come to represent as a resource for cultural, social, and economic development in Buenos Aires. That value is not undermined but in fact bolstered by the fact that the vast majority of Argentines today are indifferent to if not actively disdainful of tango, which they tend to interpret—at best—as a somewhat embarrassing relic of their country's increasingly distant past. This is again not to say that no one in Argentina is genuinely invested in tango today, far from it. Rather, the dual trend of detachment and connection that has defined the genre in recent decades has allowed tango to be coherently incorporated into an ever-widening network of complexly overlapping and often contradictory projects (intangible cultural heritage=economic development) with little if any resistance on the part of individuals and institutions that have famously and at times effectively intervened in past developments that they deemed undesirable for whatever reason.

While the scope and range of what tango is and can be in Buenos Aires today is the product of historical circumstances, it is no coincidence that these processes are focused on a form of expressive culture that is profoundly musical. Tango is valuable in Buenos Aires today not because it somehow inherently embodies and represents "Argentina" or the identification "Argentine," but because it, like all musical culture, is polysemic and polyvalent. That is, it can coherently mean and represent many different things to many different people on many different levels simultaneously.[18] Of course, the scope and range of tango as a zone of practice is shaped if not structured by the messy intersection and circulation of these often-contradictory activities, discourses, and meanings and their uneven accumulation over the course of musical and social history. Nevertheless, I would argue that there is not now and never has been a singularly hegemonic account of what tango is or is about. Instead, there are multiple, contested modes of consensus making that have been variously expansive or restricted for different reasons at different moments in the history of the form. The UNESCO declaration and the broader heritage-making project are therefore not about recognizing tango for what it really is, but about shaping "tango" as a zone of practice and channeling future engagements with it toward what cultural policy makers believe are the most broadly productive ends. The key term in these efforts is "cultural diversity."

Difference, Diversity, Development:
What Intangible Cultural Heritage Gets Done

A core feature of the UNESCO declaration was how it framed the initial codification and development of tango within the heterogeneous social milieu of late nineteenth-century Buenos Aires and Montevideo. Indeed, the declaration presents the racial, ethnic, and economic diversity that characterized the rapid modernization of these cities as a defining feature of the genre:

> Tango is a genre that originally involved dance, music, poetry and singing. Tango expresses a way of conceiving the world and life and it nourishes the cultural imagery of the inhabitants of the capital cities of the Rio de la Plata. . . . Tango was born among the lower urban classes in both cities as an expression originated in the fusion of elements from Argentine and Uruguayan's [sic] African culture, authentic criollos[19] and European immigrants. As the artistic and cultural result of hybridization's processes, Tango is considered nowadays one of the fundamental signs of the Rio de la Plata's identity.[20]

The declaration's interpellation of tango as a product and symbol of a historical experience centered on diversity in general represented a significant intervention in long-standing narratives of musical and social history in Argentina. Most immediately, it validated and reinforced a growing body of recent scholarly, critical, and artistic work that has aimed to more directly acknowledge and recenter the significant historical contributions made by internal minority groups, especially Afro-Argentine residents of the city of Buenos Aires, to Argentine culture and history, in and beyond tango.[21] These contributions have tended to be underemphasized if not entirely denied in many previous accounts of tango and its historical development. This could (and in some cases should) be chalked up to racial prejudice plain and simple, though making a convincing claim in this regard would require a nuanced discussion of racial ideology in Argentina specifically and Latin America more broadly, the details of which are beyond the scope of my discussion here.[22]

Even more important than this historical revisionism, I believe, is the fact that the heritage-making project demands modes of listening, forms of appreciation, and narrative strategies that depart significantly from those that have characterized tango fandom since the late 1950s, following the end of what is known as tango's "golden age." Most immediately, it signals a decisive shift away from the hagiographic orientation of many previous accounts of the genre and its history. These earlier, generally more "popular," efforts tended to focus on the minutiae of a handful of historic styles, performers, or songs, often to the neglect of other artists and stylistic tendencies. This type of focused devotion—while often limitless in its sincerity and enthusiasm—has, over time, resulted in what many observers consider to be a detrimental limitation on the range of tango figures, recorded performances, and musical repertoires that is commonly encountered in Buenos Aires today. Parallel to this celebratory narrowing of the genre's historical scope is a general hostility to "new" musical developments, be they original compositions, nontraditional interpretations or performance practices, or even alternative biographical or historical narratives, especially regarding canonical figures. To those who adhere to these positions, this "popular memory" is, of course, what tango is all about. But to those differently invested in tango and those who are entirely indifferent to the genre—the vast majority—this is also why tango is often considered at best a caricature of itself and at worst an embarrassment to be explained away.

In contrast to this intensely self-referential localism, the heritage-making project begins with what we could call a "universal" vision regarding situated cultural practices, including tango and the more than 250 additional forms that together constitute the intangible cultural heritage of humanity as curated by UNESCO. As we have seen, this perspective performs something of a magic trick, rearranging previously hegemonic aesthetic hierarchies without diminishing the social and aesthetic power of hierarchy as such, substituting, for instance, western art music's canon of "great works" for a canon of "great genres," all of which are taken as simultaneously and self-evidently both equal to and different from one another. The heritage value of these "universally local" genres, moreover, is determined not by their relationship to one another—that is, how a particular example of tango may or may not measure up to a concert of western art music, however those differences might be measured—but by each genre's internal relationship to its own "history" and "tradition." This, in turn, privileges broadly sociological readings of musical history that highlight general conditions—like cultural diversity—over the specific contributions of particular musical figures or styles, which are taken more as exemplary instances of a type rather than singular articulations of artistic excellence. It also calls forth particular types of institutional forms and structures required for the "identification, documentation, research, preservation, protection, promotion, enhancement, transmission, [and] revitalization" of intangible cultural heritage as a category of practice, displacing if not denigrating unofficial engagements with tango as encountered in, say, fan magazines, commercial radio broadcasts, and the informal expertise of record collectors, among many others. When managed "properly," the product of these discourses can operate as the center of gravity for an ever-expanding universe of local cultural practice, transnational appreciation and prestige, and the twin engines of social and economic development.

And we should not lose track of these projects' social goals. Indeed, the emphasis on cultural diversity in the UNESCO declaration reflected and reinforced what were by then long-standing efforts on the part of certain Argentine cultural institutions and policy makers to mobilize culture as a means of addressing the historic legacies and lived experience of social inclusion and exclusion in Argentina, in tango and far beyond. In an interview with Dr. Gustavo López, the former Secretary of Culture for the City Government of Buenos Aires and an intellectual architect of much of the city's cultural policy making following the 2001 economic crisis, he stated:

> We work with the concept of culture as a process of social transformation, something that is in a constant state of evolution, going wherever it goes. . . . The concept we have found for developing this idea

is "cultural diversity," something that does not exacerbate nationalism but instead makes us respect differences.... Today the phenomenon of transculturation is so strong one does not speak of nationalism, one speaks of diversity, of respect for difference, respect for the minority.[23]

It is interesting to note that, when taken to its logical conclusion, Dr. López's conceptualization of cultural diversity would ultimately reject the heritage-making project as such, arguing instead, as he did in my interview with him, that "there should be no national culture" and that the state should work to foster "whatever it is that is there." Given this, it is not just ironic that the city government of Buenos Aires and the national government of Argentina have instead put tremendous efforts into identifying and declaring a wide array of local cultural practices as heritage of the city and the nation if not all of humanity in general.[24] The prioritization of heritage making represents a specific policy move on the part of certain contingents within these governments to shape and restrict the implications of what counts as "diversity."

But even here we need to carefully resist the urge to see Dr. López's invocation of diversity as somehow departing from the larger conflation of economic and cultural interests and values that the heritage-making project is a product of and clearly promotes. The term "cultural diversity," as used by Dr. López and other cultural policy makers, in fact has little or no relationship to how it has been used in struggles over identity politics and institutional inclusion or exclusion in the United States, despite López's emphasis on "respect for difference, respect for the minority."[25] Indeed, the idea of cultural diversity as used here originally emerged from, of all things, debates over the scope and range of free-trade agreements. Most immediately, it is the strategic successor to the previous idea of the "cultural exception," a position championed by France during the 1993 "Uruguay Round" of negotiations on the General Agreement on Tariffs and Trade, a provisional agreement that was replaced by the World Trade Organization in 1994. The cultural exception argued that cultural goods—"tangibles or intangibles conveying cultural content that might take either the form of a good or a service"—should be exempted from the full scope of free-trade agreements because some aspects of those agreements would undermine the cultural specificity of such goods in favor of a more mechanically economic understanding of them.[26] The discourse of "cultural diversity" built on this argument by claiming that the uniquely extra-economic quality of cultural goods and services is not (or not only) accounted for by the specifically cultural or symbolic content of these goods, but by the important role such goods play in society. This is where the issue of national cultural policies—and the heritage-making project as such—reenters the picture, because, as the argument goes, "the free market alone cannot ensure cultural diversity."[27]

As it is understood in these contexts, then, cultural diversity ultimately does not refer to any kind of ethnic, racial, economic, or any other type of social difference but to variety in media content and point of origin. Cultural policy makers posit this type of diversity as a core component of both maintaining viable cultural and national identities in the wake of cultural globalization and helping formulate economically productive cultural development programs within an international milieu that is dominated by a handful of core cultural producers, particularly the United States. From this perspective, the heritage-making project as such has emerged as a priority in Buenos Aires and beyond not because it enables states to reframe historical wrongs, but because heritage can so clearly and coherently address these twin demands for cultural meaning and economic development. Diversity, in other words, is not a virtue in and of itself but a means to multiple, productive ends, not least of which is attaining the recognition of UNESCO and other cultural institutions where the term "diversity" has clearly become a buzzword. Indeed, there are moments in the tango declaration that take this to a nearly comical extreme, though you can't blame the authors for writing to their audience, especially given the end result: "As any long-lasting cultural phenomenon in complex societies, [tango] has enriched itself with a wide variety of contributions. Therefore the need to stress the sense of identity that it proposes, respecting the cultural diversity at its very core. Cultural diversity, in fact, belongs to its origin and is critical for its essence and roots."[28]

While we should probably not make too much of a fuss over this type of institutional grantspeak, I think it does reflect an infatuation with the discourse of diversity that can, at times, eclipse concerns with the history and lived experience of inclusion and exclusion that the heritage-making project and the broader discourse of cultural diversity are at least nominally designed and intended to address. For example, of the ten "concerned community organizations or representatives" cited in the tango declaration, none are directly concerned with representing the cultural life, musical or otherwise, of contemporary Afro-Argentine or Afro-Uruguayan communities, despite the key role those communities played in the initial formation of the genre, at least according to the UNESCO declaration.[29] To be fair, simply asking such organizations to "sign on" to the document when it was in preparation would not necessarily have addressed any of these issues either. Nevertheless, I think the total absence of such groups in the final document indicates how the UNESCO declaration, for all its emphasis on cultural diversity and ethnic, racial, and economic difference, ultimately obscures efforts to acknowledge and address social inequalities in Argentina today.

At the same time, a critique of UNESCO's use of Argentine history, however well deserved, essentially misses the point, because for all its emphasis on the past, the UNESCO declaration and the heritage-making project are ultimately about shaping the future. That future is one in which cultural diversity, as (believed to be) embodied in institutionalized forms of intangible cultural heritage, can serve as the catalyst for multiple and multiplying forms of development, cultural, social, economic, and so on. For example, in compliance with UNESCO's criteria for inscription on the representative list of intangible heritage, the proposal identifies a variety of established "safeguarding measures" for the preservation or promotion of tango, almost all of which operated under the auspices of either the municipal or national governments of the concerned parties. The proposal also outlines the basic objectives and proposed actions of eleven additional safeguarding measures that would be implemented with the support of the UNESCO declaration. These include a tango documentation and record center (essentially a public archive of tango's historic material culture, the first of its kind); a tango dance institute; a training center for the repair, maintenance, and future manufacture of specialty tango instruments; the development and dissemination of tango-themed walking tours; and the creation of tango-themed hostels. The combined budget requested for these safeguarding measures exceeds $2.25 million (USD), a tremendous sum in comparison to previous institutional resources allocated to tango-related projects and policies at the local level. However, that amount is arguably trifling when weighed on a global scale, especially if the projects it would fund in fact accomplish what they claim, that is, provide the institutional infrastructure required to protect, maintain, and promote an intangible cultural practice of universal value and significance. But regardless of such claims, and regardless of the ultimate quantity of funds actually allocated to these projects, these numbers speak to the very tangible consequences of declaring tango an intangible cultural heritage of humanity, especially given that most of the requested support is intended to be used to establish new institutions that are themselves designed to bring in further revenues in the future, both directly and indirectly.

Conclusion: What Diversity Gets Done

Here we can see how the conflicts and contradictions that necessarily underlie the heritage-making project build off one another, accumulating and compounding a multiplicity of values. From the cultural perspective, the declaration's insistence on tango's emblematic status as a marker of ethnic, racial, and economic diversity in Argentina makes a major intervention despite its political shortcomings. This is significant given the continued salience of tango as a potent symbol of the nation both within Argentina and abroad, where the limits and boundaries of the genre have symbolically marked those who are included and those who are excluded from the national imaginary. From the economic perspective, it could be argued that many aspects of the declaration—including its broad aesthetic reevaluation and historical reframing of the genre—represent nothing more than a further entrenchment of a managerial impulse toward economic productivity that has become one of the hallmarks of local, national, and international cultural policy making following the neoliberal turn. This is not necessarily a criticism, especially given the spectacular series of failures on the part of international political-economic ideologies that have successively intended to develop, modernize, integrate, or globalize Latin American economies, political policies, and cultures over the past decades; it is instead a simple recognition of the emergent and multiple values that local cultural differences have begun to take on within new circuits of transnational cultural prestige and economic exchange.

Regarding tango specifically, such processes are, of course, nothing new, in that tango was and is a truly global popular music. Global audiences have been familiar with tango from its circulation in films, television, musical recordings, and other media going back at least to the Parisian tango "craze" of 1913, if not earlier.[30] In these circulatory contexts, tango has served as a conduit for the creative misunderstandings and cross-cultural fantasies that are at the heart of cultural globalization as it is envisioned today.[31] The local milieu in which the genre initially took shape was located in and a product of these broader forms of transnational circulation, such that the UNESCO declaration—itself perhaps the ultimate international validation of situated cultural locality and meaning—in fact stands as little more than a further wrinkle in a narrative of artistic development and exchange that is now more than a century old. Even the ideology of cultural expediency, while perhaps foregrounded to an unprecedented degree here, is not really new to tango. Indeed, tango has been drawn upon and used as a potent symbol of the nation throughout modern Argentine history, contributing at different times to the project of national consolidation, the projection of the nation within global politics and economies, the local rearticulation of musical modernism, and current efforts to promote Argentina as a destination for cultural tourism.[32] What is new is how the discourse of cultural diversity as institutionalized in the UNESCO declaration and elsewhere has reformulated the scope and range of the genre as such. And while I would ultimately argue that this aesthetic reformulation of the genre is more about opening and expanding international consumer markets for tango music than valuing tango as an actually existing cultural practice, it nevertheless has significant implications for the musical efforts of contemporary tango artists, whose experiences and concerns are otherwise largely unaccounted for in these debates.

But even here much of the concern is economic rather than artistic. As we have already seen, the revenue generated in the contemporary cultural economy of tango in Buenos Aires—which the UNESCO declaration is designed to bolster—is unevenly distributed at best, despite the eye-popping numbers supposedly produced by the sector as a whole. The tango guitarist and composer Edgardo González, whose group, 34 puñaladas, is among the most prominent ensembles active in Buenos Aires today, joked with me about this in a casual conversation:

> Our group has been very successful, receiving lots of awards and recognitions from the newspapers and elsewhere. When I read that report about tango generating so much money, I had to laugh and ask: if tango makes so much money, and I make tango, why don't I make money? Awards and recognitions are great, but you can't eat them. If there is so much money in tango, can't I have just a little bit, please?[33]

Is it simply ironic that so many of the musicians, dancers, and other artists who have dedicated their lives to mastering, maintaining, and innovating tango in Argentina—the supposedly priceless cultural heritage of all humanity—in fact live extremely precarious lives and often work in what cannot be described as anything other than abusive conditions? Indeed, and as Matt Sakakeeney has shown in another context, what González described to me is the rule rather than the exception regarding cultural labor in the age of expediency, which more closely resembles the lower rungs of the service economy than any professional policy maker's rosy-glassed vision of venerated "tradition bearers."[34]

Here we arrive at something of a critical impasse. On the one hand, calling out these and other structural inequalities in what Miller calls the "new international division of cultural labor" amounts to little more than a basic observation about the lived experience of contemporary tango musicians and other cultural laborers in the age of expediency.[35] On the other hand, attempting to parse who can or cannot claim tango or any other cultural practice as a supposedly real, genuine, or authentic heritage against those whose claims are somehow construed as fake, artificial, or inauthentic leads us to a critical and political dead end. Either way, the project of critical music scholarship is left in the now well-settled dust of Buenos Aires' cultural/economic revitalization via tango as an intangible cultural heritage of humanity, as well as innumerable other projects that have drawn on and used musical culture in similar ways. The fact that institutions as cumbersome as UNESCO seem to be setting the pace regarding these issues illustrates the real challenge that they pose for academic critics, which extends far beyond the critique or support of any given proposal or project. If, as I argue here, the values and meanings of musical culture and the broader field of cultural production have been fundamentally reframed in the age of expediency, then we need to reframe our questions and broader critical approach to these issues accordingly.

NOTES

1. George Yúdice, *The Expediency of Culture: Uses of Culture in the Global Era* (Durham: Duke University Press, 2003).

2. See www.nea.gov.

3. Toby Miller, *The Well-Tempered Self: Citizenship, Culture, and the Postmodern Subject* (Baltimore, MD: Johns Hopkins University Press, 1993).

4. UNESCO, *Convention for the Safeguarding of the Intangible Cultural Heritage* (Paris: UNESCO, 2003), http://unesdoc.unesco.org/images/0013/001325/132540e.pdf, p. 2.

5. Ibid., pp. 2–3.

6. See UNESCO, "Frequently Asked Questions," www.unesco.org/culture/ich/index.php?pg=00021.

7. See UNESCO, "Lists of Intangible Cultural Heritage and Register of Best Safeguarding Practices," www.unesco.org/culture/ich/index.php?lg=en&pg=00559.

8. See Geoffrey Baker, *Imposing Harmony: Music and Society in Colonial Cuzco* (Durham: Duke University Press, 2008); and Ana María Ochoa, "Sonic Transculturation, Epistemologies of Purification and the Aural Public Sphere in Latin America," *Social Identities* 12, no. 6 (2006): 803–25.

9. Barbara Kirshenblatt-Gimblett, "Intangible Heritage as Metacultural Production," *Museum International* 56, nos. 1–2 (2004): 52–65.

10. Anthony Seeger, "Lessons Learned from the ICTM (NGO) Evaluation of Nomination for the UNESCO Masterpieces of the Oral and Intangible Heritage of Humanity, 2001–2005," in *Intangible Heritage*, ed. Laurajane Smith and Natsuko Akagawa (London: Routledge, 2009), 112–28.

11. Richard Kurin, "Safeguarding the Intangible Cultural Heritage in the 2003 UNESCO Convention: A Critical Appraisal," *Museum International* 56, nos. 1–2 (2004): 66–77.

12. Sherry Ortner, *Anthropology and Social Theory: Culture, Power, and the Acting Subject* (Durham: Duke University Press, 2006).

13. On contemporary tango dance, see Carolyn Merritt, *Tango Nuevo* (Gainesville: University Press of Florida, 2012).

14. The currency devaluation was a component of the devastating Argentine economic crisis of December 2001. See Paul Blustein, *And the Money Kept Rolling In (and Out): Wall Street, the IMF, and the Bankrupting of Argentina* (New York: Public Affairs, 2005).

15. Arlene Dávila, *Culture Works: Space, Value, and Mobility across the Neoliberal Americas* (New York: New York University Press, 2012).

16. Enrique Marmonti, interview by author, Buenos Aires, September 12, 2006.

17. Morgan James Luker, "Contemporary Tango and the Cultural Politics of *Música Popular*," in *Tango Lessons: Music, Sound, Image and Text in Contemporary Practice*, ed. Marilyn G. Miller (Durham: Duke University Press, 2014), 198–219.

18. Steven Feld, "Communication, Music, and Speech about Music," *Yearbook for Traditional Music* 16 (1984): 1–18.

19. This is the wording as it appears in the nomination form. As it appears here, the term "authentic criollos" is used to locate those who are direct descendants of the region's Spanish colonizers. The use (and abuse) of the terms "creole" or "creolization" has a long, complicated history in Latin America, the further exploration of which is beyond the scope of this essay. See Stephan Palmié, "Creolization and Its Discontents," *Annual Review of Anthropology* 35 (2006): 433–56.

20. UNESCO, *Nomination for Inscription on the Representative List in 2009 (Reference No. 00258)* (Paris: UNESCO, 2009), www.unesco.org/culture/ich/index.php?lg=en&pg=00011&RL=00258, p. 2.

21. See George Reid Andrews, *The Afro-Argentines of Buenos Aires, 1800–1900* (Madison: University of Wisconsin Press, 1980); and John Charles Chasteen, *National Rhythms, African Roots: The Deep History of Latin American Popular Dance* (Albuquerque: University Press of New Mexico, 2004).

22. See Peter Wade, *Race and Ethnicity in Latin America*, 2nd ed. (London: Pluto, 2010); and J. Lorand Matory, *Black Atlantic Religion: Tradition, Transnationalism, and Matriarchy in the Afro-Brazilian Candomblé* (Princeton, NJ: Princeton University Press, 2005). Suffice it to say that part of the reason tango came to occupy such a prominent position in the Argentine national imaginary is because it operated as both an active articulation and symbolic representation of a social/political consensus between the ruling, creole elite and the urban "popular" classes in the first half of the twentieth century, both of which were phenotypically "white" in what was, by then, a largely European immigrant population. See Pablo Vila, "Tango to Folk: Hegemony Construction and Popular Identities in Argentina," *Studies in Latin American Popular Culture* 10 (1991): 107–39. While not explicitly "racist" per se, this consensus did amount to a de facto exclusion of nonwhite subjects, both Afro-Argentine and, especially, inhabitants of the interior of the country who displayed mixed indigenous ancestry. It is the latter group that has been historically (and pejoratively) labeled *cabecitas negras* or simply *negros* in Argentina, terms that have racial and ethnic connotations and that also

encompass matters of class difference, geographic displacement, political subjectivity, and cultural citizenship (see Alejandro Grimson, "Ethnic (In)visibility in Neoliberal Argentina," NACLA Report on the Americas 38, no. 4 [2005]: 25–29, 40). Indeed, I would ultimately argue that questions of racial and ethnic inclusion and exclusion in tango would be more productively addressed via considerations of how the rise of this group as an empowered political subject during the first Peronist period (1946–55) challenged some of the core tropes of tango as a national genre rather than considerations of the absence or presence of Afro-Argentines at a quasi-mythological point of origin. See Robert Farris Thompson, *Tango: The Art History of Love* (New York: Vintage, 2006); Juan Carlos Cáceres, *Tango Negro* (Buenos Aires: Planeta, 2010); and Daniel James, *Resistance and Integration: Peronism and the Argentine Working Class, 1946–1976* (Cambridge: Cambridge University Press, 1988).

23. Dr. Gustavo López, interview by author, Buenos Aires, July 12, 2007.

24. As of this writing, one of the seven subunits of the city's Secretary of Culture is dedicated to matters regarding tangible and intangible cultural heritage and the patrimony of the city. See "Patrimonio e instituto histórico," *Buenos Aires Ciudad*, www .buenosaires.gob.ar/areas/cultura/patrimonio_instituto_historico/?menu_id=29468.

25. See Amy Cimini and Jairo Moreno, "On Diversity," *Gamut* 2, no. 1 (2009): 111–96; and George Yúdice, "We Are *Not* the World," *Social Text*, nos. 31/32 (1992): 202–16.

26. UNESCO, *International Flows of Selected Cultural Goods and Services, 1994–2003* (Montreal: UNESCO Institute for Statistics, 2005). See especially the free-trade principle of "national treatment," which stipulates that domestic and imported goods must be treated equally under the law.

27. Pierre Curzi, Jack Stoddart, and Robert Pilon, "Cultural Policy Must Not Be Subject to the Constraints of International Free Trade Agreements," Canadian Coalition for Cultural Diversity, accessed November 16, 2007, www.cdcccd.org/main_pages_en /Publications_en/Paper_CulturalPoliMustnotbeSubjecteng.pdf, p. 5.

28. UNESCO, *Nomination for Inscription*, 3.

29. See George Reed Andrews, *Blackness in the White Nation: A History of Afro-Uruguay* (Chapel Hill: University of North Carolina Press, 2010).

30. Matt K. Matsuda, *The Memory of the Modern* (New York: Oxford University Press, 1996).

31. Anna Tsing, "The Global Situation," *Cultural Anthropology* 15, no. 3 (2000): 327–60.

32. Adriana J. Bergero, *Intersecting Tango: Cultural Geographies of Buenos Aires, 1900–1930* (Pittsburgh: University of Pittsburgh Press, 2008), 369–406; Chris Goertzen and María Susana Azzi, "Globalization and the Tango," *Yearbook for Traditional Music* 31 (1999): 67–76; María Susana Azzi and Simon Collier, *Le Grand Tango: The Life and Music of Astor Piazzolla* (New York: Oxford University Press, 2000).

33. Edgardo González, interview by author, Buenos Aires, August 16, 2007.

34. Matt Sakakeeny, *Roll with It: Brass Bands in the Streets of New Orleans* (Durham: Duke University Press, 2013).

35. Toby Miller, Nitin Govil, John McMurria, Richard Maxwell, and Ting Wang, *Global Hollywood, No. 2* (London: British Film Institute, 2005).

11 · MUSICAL ECONOMIES OF THE ELUSIVE METROPOLIS

GAVIN STEINGO

Central to the shifting relations of global power in the 1970s was the emergence of a novel form of labor. Gradually replacing the "mass worker" of previous decades, a radically new laboring subject came to the fore—or so many analysts at the time believed.[1] Inspired by Marx's much earlier speculations on the increasing importance of collective or social "intelligence" in the production of economic value, a number of activists and scholars began theorizing the contours and parameters of the new "socialized worker," who for them represented an important historical transformation.[2] The precise formulation of this new worker changed repeatedly over the next two decades and found its clearest (and most famous) articulation in the pages of Michael Hardt and Antonio Negri's *Empire*, where postindustrial labor is described as essentially "immaterial" and is characterized by three main aspects: "the communicative labor of industrial production that has newly become linked in informational networks, the interactive labor of symbolic analysis and problem solving, and the labor of production and manipulations of affects."[3] In brief, with immaterial labor (a term that is only useful when forgiven for its shortcomings),[4] the emphasis begins to shift from the production of things to the production of social relations themselves (communicative, informational, interactive, affective).

Although highly oppressive under capitalist conditions, Hardt and Negri argue, immaterial labor also opens the possibility of communism and the triumph of the "multitude" over "empire." Why should this be so? If, with immaterial production, the production of directly social and interpersonal relations becomes hegemonic, then the economic production of value is conflated with the political production of society itself. All that is necessary, under these conditions, is for workers to reappropriate value from capitalists, and then the "way is . . . open for 'absolute democracy,' for the producers directly regulating their social relations without even the detour of democratic [political] representation."[5]

Of course, Hardt and Negri's hypothesis only works if a very particular conceptualization of empire is accepted. And, indeed, along with immaterial production a new theory of empire is the cornerstone of their work. "In contrast to imperialism," they argue, "Empire establishes no territorial center of power and does not rely on fixed boundaries or barriers." Empire "is a *decentered* and *deterritorializing* apparatus of rule," they continue, "that progressively incorporates the entire global realm within its open, expanding frontiers. Empire manages hybrid identities, flexible hierarchies, and plural exchanges through modulating networks of command."[6] I will return to this theorization of empire toward the end of this essay, but for now it is enough to notice that some of empire's primary characteristics (e.g., flexibility and the maintenance of large networks) are similar to those of immaterial labor.

The form of labor that simultaneously produces value and social relations did not emerge suddenly in the 1970s, however. On the contrary, such labor has always existed but has simply occupied a marginal position at earlier "stages" of economic history. Examples of workers who have long performed a type of immaterial labor are numerous and include musicians, dancers, teachers, doctors, and priests—a group that Paolo Virno calls "virtuosi."[7] Musicians and performing artists in particular hold a privileged position in many relevant theorizations. Virno, for example, suggests that music performance anticipated the entire framework of immaterial labor. Similarly, Negri asserts that the "performing arts worker is a person who has prefigured, and now fully enacts, the figure of the intellectual worker," the latter fulfilling a particularly important role in immaterial labor.[8] It was in this intellectual context that Jacques Attali famously challenged the commonly held view that music (as an element of the "superstructure") temporally lagged behind an economic "base."[9] As Fredric Jameson observes in his foreword to *Noise: The Political Economy of Music*, Attali not only challenged this view, but also actually reversed it by suggesting that a superstructure may in fact "*anticipate* historical developments" and "foreshadow new social formations in a prophetic and annunciatory way."[10] For Attali, Jameson observes, "the music of today stands both as promise of a new, liberating mode of production, and as the menace of a dystopian possibility which is that mode of production's baleful mirror image."[11]

The privileged, albeit ambiguous, status granted to music is relevant not only to a diagnosis of economic developments—it also has serious ramifications for the conceptualization and experience of music itself. In this essay, I present the case study of *kwaito*, a genre of South African electronic music that emerged in the early 1990s and has since come to represent the voice of the black youth in the postapartheid period. During my research on kwaito, I have often been told and read about the genre's economic benefits. Particularly in the postindustrial city of Johannesburg, journalists, politicians, and fans have celebrated music and the performing arts for creating employment in a job-shy landscape. With the decline of industrial and extractive industries (such as gold mining) over the past few decades, kwaito musicians in particular come to represent a new form of productive black subjectivity and are often valorized for exemplifying various types of "immaterial" labor associated with communication, information, and affect. But in their celebration of kwaito's labor-producing potential, culture brokers and fans reveal a profound ambiguity surrounding the nature of immaterial production. For, although musicians are often regarded as the earliest and perhaps purest embodiments of immaterial production, music itself is still a marginal aspect of the contemporary economy. As Hardt succinctly explains, it is not so much that "artistic labor is central to the [new] economy," but rather that "the qualities of artistic labor . . . are becoming hegemonic and transforming other labor processes."[12] Hence, the question becomes is kwaito central to South Africa's economy, or are kwaito's "qualities" transforming *other* labor processes that are central to the economy? Furthermore, if kwaito's qualities are transforming these other important labor processes, then could one not say that kwaito is in a sense "central" to the economy?

Unemployment and the Production of Work

South Africa has one of the highest unemployment rates in the world (estimated as high as 40 percent) and one of the highest levels of inequality. Under such conditions, it is not surprising that a large portion of the country's youth has turned to crime. Ironically, crime has given rise to one of South Africa's fastest-growing and largest industries: private security.[13] For millions of young South Africans, the only options available are to "appropriate" private wealth or protect that private wealth against those who intend to appropriate it. Unemployment, and its attendant radical strategies of survival, is predicated upon a new relationship between capital, the laboring body, and the state. During apartheid, black bodies were seen as both "indispensable and expendable."[14] Native life, suggests Achille Mbembe, was seen as excessive and thus "constituted wealth that could be lavishly spent."[15] On the other hand, labor power was necessary for the machinations of the apartheid state, and so black bodies were paradoxically highly valued and reduced to "bare life" (that is to say, laboring bodies without political subjectivity). Unlike the case in settler colonies in Australia and North America, the native inhabitants of South Africa were deliberately kept alive. The white South African settler colonialist lived "on the native as one might live on the fruit of wild trees."[16]

In the postapartheid period, Johannesburg has undergone major transformations. The spatial dynamics of the city have changed, and the meaning of race is far more complex than ever before. Significantly, unemployment rates have risen dramatically, leading to the emergence of nostalgia for any kind of labor, even the exploitative type. As David Coplan suggests, the only thing worse "than a job as a mine migrant is the inability to find one."[17] A new class of expendable and dispensable people has developed, resulting in a mass of superfluity that is impossible to ever fully appropriate.[18] As I explain later, the rise of unemployment in Johannesburg paralleled processes of deindustrialization that occurred in many cities around the world. However, due to South Africa's unusual history of racial capitalism and settler-based capital accumulation, Johannesburg's trajectory also differed in many respects from "global cities" such as New York, London, and Tokyo.[19] Because of the multiplicity of registers at which the city operates, Mbembe and Nuttall refer to Johannesburg as "the elusive metropolis."[20]

Of course, in many cases jobs lost in one place simply means jobs created in another—this is the basic logic of "outsourcing." But mechanization is also an important dynamic. And when labor is mechanized, then the role of humans in the production processes becomes increasingly that of an overseer. Marx already noticed the tendency for labor to move "to the side of the production process instead of being its chief actor."[21] Hardt and Negri assert that Marx's words imply "the fulfillment of a long-standing dream of capital—to present itself as separate from labor, to present a capitalist society that does not look to labor as its dynamic foundation."[22] When a cleft is formed between labor and capital, the fundamental dialect of capitalism is broken.

In this context, goods are still produced—more easily than ever, in fact. But although more and more things are being produced, they "are not given away. . . . So if folks have no work, they won't be able to buy them. That is what is happening in the Third World as is only too obvious."[23] Thus, the era of advanced industrialization exhibits the factual realization of the tendencies described by Marx, but without any emancipating consequences.[24] In other words, the fact that less labor is needed has led not to communism, as Marx predicted, but to a situation that Sylvère Lotringer calls the "communism of capital."[25] This is the *unhappy* success of the proletariat: a success that was ultimately a failure.

The struggle for work results in the production of not material goods or services but production itself. In South Africa, the cultural industries—including music—are a key site for the production of labor. John Comaroff and Jean Comaroff write,

> The sale of culture seems, in part, to be replacing the sale of labor in the Brave Neo South Africa . . . a South Africa whose industrial economy, founded on racial capitalism, is presently undergoing radical reconstruction—the impact of which has included the loss of millions of jobs, an acknowledged unemployment rate of around 40 percent, the casualization of much of the remaining work force, and the privatization of previously public assets.[26]

According to the *Creative Industries Growth Strategy: Final Report* (*CIGS*), a document commissioned by the South African Department of Arts, Culture, Science and Technology in 1998, the "music industry is a key provider of jobs and income revenue in the South African economy."[27] In the words of one of the report's respondents, the music industry "could be the miracle industry of South Africa."[28] Why, we are wont to ask, is an industry that at that time employed only twelve thousand people (by the report's own admission) a "key provider of jobs"? In what ways might it fulfill its potential as a "miracle industry"? According to the report, the music industry is of particular importance because it trades in intellectual property, which is the cornerstone of the new knowledge-based economy. Moreover, the industry is especially open to synergies with other sectors such as law.[29] As such, the report concludes that music is a key site for the production of work in post-apartheid South Africa.

Kwaito musicians often express similar sentiments about music's potential to create work. Arthur Mafokate, the so-called King of Kwaito, put it like this: "For me to really succeed *I had to create my own kind of employment* and by so doing I decided I'm going to have my own genre of music express myself in my own way."[30] According to a national celebrity, DJ Fresh, "that is one of the biggest things kwaito has never been credited for, the employment it has created."[31] The activist and kwaito musician Zola 7 observes that kwaito not only has produced kwaito musicians but also has forged several synergies. "Aside from creating stars," he says, "kwaito, has employed sound engineers, producers, lawyers, secretaries, promoters. . . . It's us kwaito boys who created that employment."[32] According to the 2008 *Creative Economy Report* by the United Nations, although South Africa has a well-established music industry, "there remains a dearth of entertainment lawyers" in the country.[33] For music industry personnel, this gap in the industry signals potential employment opportunities. David Alexander, the vice chair of the National Organization for Reproduction Rights in Music and the chair of South African Music Exports, is vehement that the kind of synergies suggested by Zola 7 is precisely the path that South African cultural workers should take.[34]

In postapartheid South Africa, musicians are valorized for their entrepreneurial abilities. The issue, however, is perhaps not so much that music is the key site for the production of work, but rather that music is a metonym for hegemonic labor under the conditions of contemporary capitalism. Seen this way, when government-commissioned reports suggest that music is a potential "miracle industry," what they really mean is that music is the prototype and archetype of contemporary capitalism. It now makes sense why a neoliberal popular economist like David Fick can use radio station YFM as the prime example of a company that tapped into the "soul of South Africa's exploding youth culture through kwaito music."[35] For, as Fick says elsewhere, South Africans have on many occasions discovered the "secrets of capital, its creation, preservation and expansion."[36] There may be some truth to what Fick says. In fact, as much as 98 percent of music-publishing revenue in Africa is collected by South Africa directly.[37] Perhaps this is what kwaito means in economic terms: not capital itself, or not all that much capital, but rather the secrets of capital and how to create and expand it.

Music, the City, and Capital's Histories

The synergies that people such as Zola 7 and Alexander describe do not only occur *within* a city but also shape the very city within which they occur. Particularly in the last few years, Johannesburg has witnessed a marked increase in joint ventures between informational and culturally oriented corporations. According to Steven Sack, the director of arts, culture, and heritage for the City of Joburg, the lively art scene fueled by resistance to apartheid somewhat subsided after 1994.[38] However, in the early twenty-first century, things "started to stabilize," "because, on the back of a very vibrant economy . . . suddenly there was a lot of opportunity. So you started to see a very different kind of Joburg emerging. You started to see this vibrant city, because [it is] wealthy enough and has a big enough consumer base."[39]

According to the *CIGS* report cited earlier in this essay, convergence is a crucial aspect of any modern economy. "What enables the industry to grow," the report states, "is not so much excellence in a single aspect of the industry but rather highly effective and well-utilized links between its different elements and other industries, the effective communication within the industry and between the music industry and allied industries."[40] In many ways, Johannesburg has achieved what AnnaLee Saxenian calls a "regional advantage," that is to say, an efficient networked economy of agglomeration.[41] About the potentially "miraculous" music industry, the *CIGS* report observes that all major production facilities are located within a thirty-kilometer radius. It continues: "The geographical proximity of the industries allows for easy communication between different parts of the value chain."[42]

There is something troubling, however, about this celebration of music and urban dynamics in the context of a city with high levels of poverty and income inequality, where the majority of the population lives in townships and shantytowns far from the prosperous thirty-kilometer radius described in the report. This raises an important question: to what extent does it makes sense to analyze Johannesburg in terms of formal capital markets? It is certainly no longer possible—if, indeed, it ever was—to conceptualize Johannesburg as a "European city" that simply, by dint of some strange coincidence, happens to be located in Africa. On the other hand, Johannesburg is in a very real sense different from African cities such as Lagos and Douala. To quote Mbembe and Nuttall, "Johannesburg is an elusive metropolis because of the multiplicity of registers in which it is African (or perhaps not at all, or not enough); European (or perhaps not, or no longer); or even American (by virtue of its embeddedness in commodity exchange and its culture of consumption)."[43]

Having recognized the multiple registers, is it appropriate to write the history of Johannesburg in terms of western-derived theories of labor? Surely the history of capitalist development and expansion cannot account (and may even suppress) certain indigenous labor practices and understandings of value? For example, the descriptions of Johannesburg's labor networks offered by Steven Sack (a white South African) and the CIGS report completely omit any mention of the kin- and ethnic-based networks long described by anthropologists of the region. Furthermore, an economic analysis of music may miss aesthetic and cultural aspects that lie outside the economic domain.

It is precisely this issue that Dipesh Chakrabarty addresses in his groundbreaking *Provincializing Europe*.[44] Through a close reading of Marx, Chakrabarty suggests that the history of capitalism is always double. First, there "is the universal and necessary history we associate with capital. It forms the backbone of the usual narratives of transition to the capitalist mode of production."[45] In this history, which he calls "History 1," the past is viewed as a precondition of capitalism and has no real meaning outside of it. But this is only one side of the story. As Chakrabarty emphasizes, History 2 serves to confirm that there existed antecedents to capitalism that have little in common with capitalist logic. And these antecedents, he says, "do not lend themselves to the reproduction of the logic of capital."[46] To clarify this point, Chakrabarty offers an example of how these two histories are related by quoting a rather long passage from Marx's *Grundrisse*:

> What is *productive labour* and what is not, a point very much disputed back and forth since Adam Smith made this distinction, has to emerge from the direction of the various aspects of capital itself. *Productive labour* is only that which produces capital. Is it not crazy, asks e.g . . . Mr Senior, that the piano maker is a *productive worker*, but not the piano player, although obviously the piano would be absurd without the piano player? But this is exactly the case. The piano maker reproduces capital, the pianist only exchanges his labour for revenue. But doesn't the pianist produce music and satisfy our musical ear, does he not even to a certain extent produce the latter? He does indeed: his labour produces something; but that does not make it *productive labour*

in the *economic sense*; no more than the labour of the mad man who produces delusions is productive.[47]

Marx recognizes that the listener derives satisfaction from the piano player. He even suggests that the music performed by the pianist in a way "produces" the ear of the listener. However, he nonetheless dismisses the labor of the pianist as unproductive and it is at this point that Chakrabarty intervenes. Writes Chakrabarty, "In the intimate and mutually productive relationship between one's very particular musical ear and particular forms of music is captured the issue of historical difference, of the ways in which History 1 is always modified by History 2s."[48] His point is that the history of the musical ear is not reducible to the history of piano making under the capitalist mode of production. History 1 and History 2 constantly relate to and modify one another, but neither should be granted primacy over the other, just as neither sublates the other.

Theorists of immaterial labor have often emphasized similar passages from Marx in their analyses but have treated them in a very different way. Virno, in fact, believes that Marx was *correct* in categorizing the labor of pianists as unproductive and sees little point in rescuing some alternative, "cultural" history. But he believes that Marx was only correct in his time. Whereas in the nineteenth century only labor that produces a finished product could be defined as productive labor, Virno argues that in the late twentieth century "activity-without-a-finished-work moves from being a special and problematic case to becoming the prototype of waged labor in general."[49] This is why Virno believes that music—which in Marx's time was not productive in the economic sense—anticipated the entire framework of contemporary labor.

If activity-without-a-finished work is the prototype of contemporary labor, then today the piano manufacturer *and* the piano player can legitimately be considered productive workers. But if this is so, then the ear of the listener is not *merely* satisfied and the piano player does not *simply* exchange his or her labor for revenue. On the contrary, the piano player's performances are resolutely *productive*. In other words, the formerly unproductive (yet social) relationship of the piano player and listener has transformed into a productive-consumptive relationship, which nonetheless continues to be social.

With immaterial labor, as I have suggested, social relationships and economic production are conflated. This conflation implies the collapse of any possible distinction between unproductive and productive labor. From this perspective, the cultural, social, and aesthetic aspects of music in postapartheid South Africa are immediately economic: we do not need to ask whether

History 1 is applicable to the South African context or whether this history elides certain elements of History 2, because in the present conjuncture History 2 is intertwined with History 1 to the extent that the two histories are no longer possible to think of separately.

Immaterial Production, Branding, and Intellectual Property

To a certain extent, the transformations tracked and analyzed by theorists of immaterial labor differ from the labor practices of the 1990s. I would argue, however, that the 1990s witnessed less a departure than an intensification and redefinition of the 1970s model. Ned Rossiter characterizes the 1990s in terms of a shift from cultural to "creative" economy, the latter being a product of the 1995 international agreement on Trade-Related Aspects of International Property Rights (TRIPS).[50] With TRIPS, intellectual property received an international legal framework that transformed the parameters of immaterial labor. Nonetheless, this transformation did not undermine the centrality of culture, information, and "immaterial" commodities in the global economy, but instead provided a more robust system for regulating the late capitalist commodity form.

Kwaito musicians, and music more generally, stand in metonymically for the regime of immaterial production, and they do this in two specific ways: by virtue of branding strategies, on the one hand, and via a relationship to intellectual property (IP), on the other. While branding and IP are certainly interrelated, they are nonetheless distinct. Whereas IP functions by limiting the use of ideas and information, branding thrives on expansion. This tension is perhaps the crucial aporia of economies based on immaterial labor. At least about informational commodities, Sanford Grossman and Joseph Stiglitz argue that efficient markets are literally impossible *within* the framework of neoclassical economics.[51] More cryptically, Slavoj Žižek lists "new forms of apartheid" (i.e., walls and slums) and "the inappropriateness of the notion of *private property* in relation to so-called 'intellectual property'" as two of the four central antagonisms of our day.[52] Intellectual property is thereby a peculiar or even "aporetic" form of ownership, creating obstacles that "undermine the production process" at the very moment that capital is produced.[53]

BRANDING

Arthur Mafokate was forced to forge a relationship with capital in the absence of material resources. As he told me, "Startup capital is always an issue, and because I didn't have money, that's why I took the route I took."[54] From a traditional Marxist perspective, Mafokate's beginnings as a dancer and singer were not, properly speaking, "productive." However, under late capitalist conditions the distinction between unproductive "performance" labor and productive labor disappears. Mafokate was able to capitalize on immaterial affect: although his performances were only activities-without-a-finished-work, they were not—like Marx's piano player—unproductive. Thus, when Mafokate told me that he is "selling an experience," the experience that he sells is not a mere exchange of labor for revenue but a genuine product. Policy makers and culture brokers have fawned over kwaito precisely because its musicians seem to produce value *from nothing*.

Once Mafokate had raised enough money through performances he was able to start his own company, 999 Records, which today produces and manages many of South Africa's most popular artists. Mafokate has chosen to keep 999 Records independent and relatively small in order to maintain organizational flexibility. He contrasts his business (which is close to a post-Fordist model) with major labels (which are closer to a Fordist model): "And even now, I am operating without any major label, but I am still competing with them. Because if I know what people want and I am always spending my time thinking about what people want rather than what is perceived to be the one that works. You rather let the company steal your idea and then when they're busy spending millions go think about something else. That's what I've been doing."

Mafokate emphasizes innovation. Because his company is small and labile, he is able to move on to new projects far quicker than bureaucratically organized companies do. His thoughts also serve as a caution against overly optimistic celebrations of the "death of the music industry" on a global scale. As scholars are slowly beginning to realize, the crisis of the "major" record labels led, in fact, to a relationship between music and capital that is more closely suited to contemporary conditions of capitalism.

Of what is the "experience" that Mafokate sells (through 999 Records) constituted? What exactly is the 999 brand? Here, it is necessary to point out that—contrary to what policy makers and cultural brokers have asserted—Mafokate did not produce the content of the 999 brand ex nihilo. In fact, in many ways his brand is a concatenation of shared or common forms of life. For example, the lyrics of songs produced by 999 Records are often composed of repeated vernacular expressions, dance routines frequently employ "traditional" dance gestures of uncertain (or perhaps collective) ownership, and the sartorial style of artists at 999 Records is typical of township dress (including *spotti* sun hats and canvas sneakers). As such, the 999 brand may be viewed as the congealing of preexisting social relations.

Who, then, are the "laborers" of the brand? It is not enough to say that Mafokate's labor has produced his brand—instead, the production labor invested in brand names is performed by the consumers themselves.[55] On a more general level, it is possible to therefore say that brands are designed by the very people who invest in and purchase those brands. As trendsetters for the rest of the country, youth are of particular interest to brand-management professionals. As Zine Magubane observes, "Market researchers have thus devised a variety of methods, ranging from focus groups to sending young Black account executives to live with Black families in the townships, to get a feel for what young people find appealing so as to better design their ads."[56] The design process is thus completely nonlinear: it is almost as if the youth design their own products, or as if musicians, entertainers, and brand managers simply repackage and mediate consumer desires. Branding under these conditions is less about capitalists "co-opting" subcultural style than the "more immanent process of channeling collective labor (even as cultural labor) into monetary flows and its structuration within capitalist business practices."[57]

But the process of "enclosing" or "structuration" is not entirely immanent: it is embedded, in fact, within the legal framework of IP. It is at this point that the necessity of state intervention becomes clear.

INTELLECTUAL PROPERTY

According to the Comaroffs, *two* aspects mark the contemporary, neoliberal moment. In addition to the emphasis on cultural and informational economies, "the rise of neoliberalism . . . has intensified greatly the reliance on legal ways and means."[58] In contemporary South Africa, politics is often reduced to a juridical process, wherein contestations over land, cultural ownership, and civic rights move from class struggle to "class actions."[59] Although not stated explicitly, the Comaroffs suggest a reflexive, perhaps inherent relationship between "ethno-preneurship" and "lawfare." This relationship is played out most explicitly on the terrain of IP. As Rishab Aiyer Ghosh observes, "Unlike most forms of property, intellectual property is almost unique in requiring state support for its very existence. While it is helpful to have protection for a plot of land, it can also be protected by, for instance, putting a fence around it, and a chair can be protected by sitting on it."[60] This is why Žižek says, in a discussion of IP, that "exploitation in the classical Marxist sense is no longer possible, which is why it has to be enforced more and more by direct legal measures, that is, by non-economic means."[61] Hence, although Žižek emphatically disagrees with the work of Hardt and Negri, he too acknowledges the collapse of any boundary separating the economic and the political under contemporary conditions.

Although crime continues to be one of South Africa's major challenges, the country is internationally revered for its IP laws. In 1998, W. Lesser ranked South Africa highest out of 44 developing countries in terms of IP strength and in 2008 South Africa was rated 22nd out of 115 countries for its IP strength by the Property Rights Alliance.[62] Indeed, the South African state views IP as a key to modernization and liberalization. And, like the International Federation of the Phonographic Industry, South African big business understands "piracy" first and foremost as a threat to *state* sovereignty. In a statement issued by the South African Anti-Piracy Unit, the illegal duplication of CDs and DVDs is connected directly to terrorism:

> In South Africa the reality of organised crime was brought home recently (August 2005) when it was established that the man believed to have co-ordinated the London bombs of July 7th (which left 56 people dead) was found to have made his living selling CDs and DVDs at flea-markets around Johannesburg. This is believed to be just the tip of an iceberg which links the profits made by music pirates to funding terrorist groups and activities and as such has seen the fight against music intensified.[63]

Among ordinary South Africans too, "piracy" is often deemed the work of transnational criminal networks, many of which are believed to be based in China.[64] Indeed, the street slang for fake is "Fong Kong," a term that encompasses "fake" and "Hong Kong." In addition to consistent raids on "piracy rings," the South African police force recently trained an airport sniffer dog to smell out fake DVDs, the only such canine in the world able to do so.

The tensions surrounding the state, black empowerment, music, and IP are most clearly elucidated by the case of Eugene Mthethwa. In the 1980s, Mthethwa performed with the legendary reggae musician Lucky Dube, and in the mid-1990s he made his transition into kwaito, helping to found one of the genre's most successful groups, Trompies. When Trompies members Zynne Sibika and Mandla Mofokeng became codirectors of Kalawa Jazmee, one of the most important black-owned record companies in the early post-apartheid period, Mthethwa turned to politics. In a manifesto titled "Why

I'm Quitting Trompies," he lists several grievances regarding the lack of economic and political empowerment in postapartheid South Africa:

- All Africans [i.e., black South Africans] are systematically excluded from the main economies of the industry even in the latest digital arena, artists are still exploited and reduced to permanent casual workers who have no living wage,
- Distribution channels are physically owned and controlled by multinationals who are major record companies,
- Intellectual property still lies in the hands of the holders who then claim to be the owners whilst the real owners are reduced to beggars.[65]

In order to combat these problems, Mthethwa left Trompies to concentrate his energies on IP, becoming the director of the antipiracy division of the Association of Independent Record Companies (AIRCO) of South Africa.[66] Mthethwa's position was bolstered in 2010, when the recently elected president, Jacob Zuma, appointed him head of the popular presidential hotline, which handles public complaints. Around the same time, in a public response to a private email from Mthethwa, President Zuma vowed to support kwaito music. Zuma wrote, "I would like to assure Eugene and all in the creative industries sector that we remain fully committed to supporting the development of our country's arts and culture."[67]

Multiple Performativities

Music is, in some ways, a prototype and archetype of economics and empowerment in postapartheid South Africa. Clearly, though, there is something amiss since unemployment in South Africa continues to rise. In fact, the primary way that money is transferred to the poor is not through job creation but rather through social grants (Child Support, Old Age, and Disability). Today, almost thirteen million South Africans, approximately a quarter of the country's population and two and a half times the number of those paying income taxes, claim social grants. The situation is exacerbated by the fact that a single social grant is often shared by several people. Hence, the social grant—and not the creation of jobs through music or music-related industries—is the primary mechanism through which wealth is distributed. South African society could not function without these grants, which hold together "what might otherwise be an explosive situation."[68]

But if this is the case, then why do culture brokers continue to emphasize the importance of music for job creation? It is true, on the one hand, that music may function as a cipher for contemporary capitalism and as such the emphasis on music is warranted. On the other hand, however, the loquaciousness surrounding music is itself a specific type of statecraft: it is a performative statecraft. With its repeated advocacy of IP and "artistic labor," the South African state performs its own commitment to neoliberal modernity (or, perhaps, postmodernity). South Africa, as I have mentioned, is ranked very high in terms of its IP strength. If the country hopes to attract international investment and international brands, it has to continually perform its commitment to IP protection. And this it does through a variety of different methods, including training dogs to sniff out fake DVDs. Considering the poverty of much of its population, South Africa has succeeded remarkably in convincing international investors and brands that it can protect copyrights and trademarks with the competency of an advanced capitalist country. South Africa, after all, is the only country in sub-Saharan Africa to have McDonald's. So much for the so-called McDonaldization of the world—the remainder of sub-Saharan Africa is essentially cut off from corporations such as this fast-food giant. According to the McDonald's website, South Africa is one of the most successful markets in the company's international history.[69] A record was set when South Africa opened thirty restaurants in just twenty-three months. In March 2011, the former political activist and union leader Cyril Ramaphosa won a 20-year agreement to run South Africa's 145 McDonald's restaurants. Commenting on his achievement, Ramaphosa said that McDonald's is "giving due recognition to the capability and the capacity of local business people such as myself to run and operate their brand."[70] The ability to adequately regulate international brands is what makes Johannesburg an "elusive" African city and is furthermore what separates Johannesburg from Lagos. At the very least, the South African state would have us believe as much.

Seen this way, the qualities of artistic practice and performance are indeed becoming hegemonic—to the extent that economy itself is resolutely performative.[71] The discourse surrounding "performing artists as exemplary laborers" thus belies a more essential point, namely that the discourses are themselves performative. Stated otherwise, claims about the economic importance of performing artists are most effective when the claims themselves resemble performing art. As such, the terrain of performance extends beyond the sociological object of study—which is presumably music—to the performative utterances *about* music by policy makers, politicians, economists, and scholars. It appears that Hardt was correct: the qualities of artistic labor are, in fact, becoming hegemonic and transforming other labor processes. What Hardt did not imagine, however, is that those "other labor processes" include a meta-discourse about music. Qualities of artistic labor, therefore, transform the way that hegemonic discourses function. But, having done so, those hegemonic discourses only valorize artistic labor itself.

State performance is particularly pertinent in light of South Africa's precarious position in the history of global IP rights. In 2001, the pharmaceutical manufacturers association of South Africa and thirty-nine international pharmaceutical companies took the South African government to court on the grounds that its law breached TRIPS. Because South Africa's HIV epidemic is well known, and because patented antiretrovirals are too expensive for much of the HIV-infected population of the country, the case was eventually dropped after a major PR assault on the pharmaceutical industry. Largely because of this failed case, in November 2001 the World Trade Organization adopted the so-called Doha Declaration, which allowed the circumvention of patents in the case of essential medicines like antiretrovirals. Although this was a major victory for South Africa and much of the Global South, it also put South Africa in a precarious position. After all, this is a country that desperately wants to prove its modernity. Partly because of the Doha affair, the South African government is particularly aggressive about emphasizing its commitment to IP, especially when it comes to so-called nonessential items like music.

Ultimately, what is at stake is the performance of a particular kind of capitalist logic. At stake, in other words, is the commitment to a particular management of economic value and the social relations that sustain it. Musicians perform this commitment, yes, but so too do culture brokers, corporations, and the state. And this "commitment" establishes a particular way of relating to musical and cultural products. It is incumbent upon South Africans—or at least upon the country's economic and political elite—to valorize and spectacularize these manners of relation if they hope to ward off the complete marginalization from capital and if they hope to be part of the "economic-industrial-communicative machine" of "imperial normativity."[72]

Empire is a "machine" that is at once economic, industrial, and communicative. Under its embrace, a poor person is still a "subjugated, exploited figure," but is now—more than ever—"a figure of production."[73] Indeed, as the case of 999 Records shows, even the *unemployed* consumer or listener becomes part of the productive process. "In effect, imperial power can no longer discipline the multitude," write Hardt and Negri. "It can only impose control over their general social and productive capacities."[74] Capitalists, in this context, "enclose" and capture for themselves the value created by the total productive process, a process that extends from manufacturers of musical instruments to performers and listeners.

Empire, then, is indeed audible in kwaito music. But it is not audible in the songs themselves. Instead, empire produces and is produced by a particular arrangement of performance and listening. As the theorist Bill Dietz would say, empire "composes listening."[75] In other words, it structures and organizes the relations through which kwaito becomes audible in the first place. Most intriguingly, those relations are musical or artistic in themselves, or they at least exhibit certain *qualities* (as Hardt puts it) of artistic labor. And as such, empire itself is almost unbearably loquacious. We do not have to strain our ears to hear empire—on the contrary, it is impossible *not* to hear empire, everywhere and always.

NOTES

1. I thank Gabriella Lukacs, Jairo Moreno, Ana María Ochoa, Tejumola Olaniyan, and Ronald Radano for insightful comments and suggestions.

2. An important early text that traces this transformation is Antonio Negri's *Dall'operaio massa all'operaio sociale: Intervista sull'operaismo*, which was first published in 1979. Negri was crucial in the development of so-called autonomous Marxism, which sought to develop a theory and practice of the working class outside of formal organizations such as trade unions. For histories of this movement, see Steve Wright, *Storming Heaven: Class Composition and Struggle in Italian Autonomist Marxism* (London: Pluto, 2002); and Sylvère Lotringer and Christian Marazzi, eds., *Autonomia: Post-Political Politics*, 2nd ed. (Los Angeles: Semiotext[e], 2007). According to Mario Tronti the "*autonomia* movements" of the late 1970s grew out of, but also signaled a departure from, the earlier Italian *operaismo* movement. See Mario Tronti, "Our Operaismo," *New Left Review* 73 (January–February 2012): 119–39.

3. See Michael Hardt and Antonio Negri, *Empire* (Cambridge: Harvard University Press, 2000), 30. Hardt has played an important role in the mediation of Italian autonomous Marxist theory to the Anglophone world and particularly to North America. In addition to the book trilogy coauthored with Negri (*Empire*, *Multitude* [2004], and *Commonwealth* [2009]) he also coedited (with Paolo Virno) the important collection *Radical Thought in Italy* (Minneapolis: University of Minnesota Press, 1996).

4. At a panel on Hardt and Negri's work at the American Anthropological Association in 2010, Hardt said about "immaterial labor," "It's a bad term. It's a bad concept." "Empire, Multitude and Commonwealth: The Anthropology of the Global in the Radical Political Philosophy of Antonio Negri and Michael Hardt," panel presented at the American Anthropological Association, New Orleans, LA, November 17–21, 2010).

Indeed, isn't there something inherently problematic with theorizing our deeply material world in "immaterial" terms? Immaterial labor, it seems to me, is only a helpful term when we do not view it in terms of some bogus "postmodern" theory that valorizes "signs" and semiotics at the expense of real people producing real commodities such as soup, sandals, and toothbrushes. Instead, as Negri observes, "Immaterial labor constructs material products, commodities and communication. It is socially organized through (very material) linguistic, electronic and cooperative networks and through multitudinous movements and associations. This is a fleshy immateriality, that is to say a mobile and flexible materiality, an ensemble of bodies." See Negri, "Metamorphoses," *Radical Philosophy* 149 (May–June 2008): 21–25.

5. This succinct summary is taken from Slavoj Žižek's review of *Empire*, "Blows against the Empire?," Lacan.com, www.lacan.com/zizblow.htm. Note that Žižek fundamentally disagrees with the main arguments of that book. Hardt and Negri speak of a "reappropriation and reorganization" of wealth but find it difficult to specify how this might concretely happen: "Certainly, there must be a moment when reappropriation and self-organization reach a threshold and configure a real event. . . . We do not have any models to offer for this event. Only the multitude through its practical experimentation will offer the models and determine when and how the possible becomes real." See Hardt and Negri, *Empire*, 411.

6. Hardt and Negri, *Empire*, xii–xiii. Emphasis in the original.

7. Paolo Virno, "Virtuosity and Revolution: The Political Theory of Exodus," in Virno and Hardt, *Radical Thought in Italy*, 189–210.

8. Antonio Negri, *Empire and Beyond*, trans. Ed Emory (Cambridge, UK: Polity, 2008), 218. The precise mechanisms through which performing art prefigured "immaterial labor" differ in the work of the theorists mentioned.

9. Jacques Attali, *Noise: The Political Economy of Music*, trans. Brian Massumi (1977; repr., Minneapolis: University of Minnesota Press, 1985).

10. See Fredric Jameson's foreword to Attali, *Noise*, vii–xiv, xi. Emphasis in the original.

11. Ibid.

12. Michael Hardt, "Immaterial Labor and Artistic Production," *Rethinking Marxism* 17, no. 2 (2005): 175–77.

13. Sue Blaine, "Security Training Bodies Team Up," *Business Day*, August 29, 2005.

14. Achille Mbembe, "Aesthetics of Superfluity," in *Johannesburg: The Elusive Metropolis*, ed. Sarah Nuttall and Achille Mbembe (Durham: Duke University Press, 2008), 43.

15. Ibid.

16. Hannah Arendt, *Origins of Totalitarianism* (New York: Harcourt, 1968), 190.

17. David B. Coplan, *In Township Tonight! South Africa's Black City Music and Theatre*, 2nd ed. (Chicago: University of Chicago Press, 2008), 31.

18. It is necessary, however, to heed Michael Denning's warning that "to speak repeatedly of bare life and superfluous life can lead us to imagine that there are really disposable people, not simply that they are disposable in the eyes of state and market." See his "Wageless Life," *New Left Review* 60 (November–December 2010): 80.

19. On global cities, see Saskia Sassen, *The Global City: New York, London, Tokyo* (Princeton, NJ: Princeton University Press, 1991). Sassen expanded her model to include cities of the global south in *Global Networks, Linked Cities* (New York: Routledge, 2002).

20. Achille Mbembe and Sarah Nuttall, "Introduction: Afropolis," in *Johannesburg: The Elusive Metropolis*, ed. Sarah Nuttall and Achille Mbembe (Durham: Duke University Press, 2008).

21. Ibid.

22. Antonio Negri and Michael Hardt, *Labor of Dionysus: A Critique of the State Form* (Minneapolis: University of Minnesota Press, 1994), 226.

23. Jean-François Lyotard, "On Theory: An Interview," in *Driftworks* (1977; repr., New York: Semiotext[e], 1984), 25. Of course, today one could easily say the same about many "folks" from the "first world."

24. See Paolo Virno, *A Grammar of the Multitude*, trans. Isabella Bertoletti, James Cascaito, and Andrea Casson (Los Angeles: Semiotext[e], 2004), 100.

25. Sylvère Lotringer, foreword to Virno, *Grammar of the Multitude*, 17.

26. John Comaroff and Jean Comaroff, *Ethnicity, Inc.* (Chicago: University of Chicago Press, 2009), 11.

27. *Creative Industries Growth Strategy: Final Report* (*CIGS*) (Pretoria: Department of Arts, Culture, Science, and Technology, 1998), 9.

28. Ibid., 11.

29. Ibid., 12.

30. In the DVD documentary *Sharp Sharp! (The Kwaito Story)*, directed by Aryan Kaganof (Johannesburg: Mandala Films, 2003). Emphasis added.

31. Ibid.

32. Ibid.

33. United Nations Conference on Trade and Development, *Creative Economy Report 2008: The Challenge of Assessing the Creative Economy: Towards Informed Policy-Making* (Geneva: United Nations, 2008), 70.

34. David Alexander, interview with author, Johannesburg, 2009.

35. David Fick, *Entrepreneurship in Africa: A Study of Successes* (Westport, CT: Quorum, 2002), 72.

36. Fick, *Africa: Continent of Economic Opportunity* (Johannesburg: STE, 2006), 19.

37. The World Bank and the Policy Sciences Center, "Workshop on the Development of the Music Industry in Africa" (paper presented at the World Bank–Policy Science Center Workshop on the Development of the Music Industry in Africa, July 20–21, 2001, Washington, DC).

38. Steven Sack, quoted in Lara Koseff, "Art and the City: Is Joburg a Cultural Capital?" *ClassicFeel* (October 2009): 36. The name "Joburg" is often used instead of Johannesburg when branding the city.

39. Ibid.

40. *CIGS*, 13.

41. AnnaLee Saxenian, *Regional Advantage: Culture and Competition in Silicon Valley and Route 128* (Cambridge: Harvard University Press, 1996).

42. *CIGS*, 72.

43. Mbembe and Nuttall, "Introduction: Afropolis," 25.

44. Dipesh Chakrabarty, *Provincializing Europe: Postcolonial Thought and Historical Difference* (Princeton, NJ: Princeton University Press, 2000).

45. Ibid., 63.

46. Ibid., 64.

47. Karl Marx, quoted in ibid., 68. Emphasis in the original.

48. Ibid.

49. Virno, "Virtuosity and Revolution," 193.

50. Ned Rossiter, *Organized Networks: Media Theory, Creative Labor, New Institutions* (Rotterdam: NAi, 2006), 24.

51. Sanford Grossman and Joseph Stiglitz, "On the Impossibility of Informationally Efficient Markets," *American Economic Review* 70 (1980): 393–408.

52. Slavoj Žižek, *First as Tragedy, Then as Farce* (London: Verso, 2009), 91. Emphasis in the original. The other two are the threat of ecological catastrophe and techno-scientific developments.

53. Michael Hardt and Antonio Negri, *Commonwealth* (Cambridge: Harvard University Press, 2009), 270.

54. All the quotes from Arthur Mafokate are from an interview with the author conducted in Johannesburg in July 2009.

55. Noam Yuran, *What Money Wants: An Economy of Desire* (Stanford, CA: Stanford University Press, 2014), 159.

56. Zine Magubane, "Globalization and Gangster Rap: Hip Hop in the Post-Apartheid City," in *The Vinyl Ain't Final: Hip Hop and the Globalization of Black Popular Culture*, ed. Dipannita Basu and Sidney J. Lemelle (London: Pluto, 2006), 221.

57. Tiziana Terranova, "Free Labor: Producing Culture for the Digital Economy," *Social Text* 18, no. 2 (2000): 39.

58. Comaroff and Comaroff, *Ethnicity, Inc.*, 53–54.

59. Ibid., 55.

60. Rishab Aiyer Ghosh, "Why Collaboration Is Important (Again)," in CODE: *Collaborative Ownership and the Digital Economy*, ed. Rishab Aiyer Ghosh (Cambridge: MIT Press, 2006), 2.

61. Žižek, *First as Tragedy, Then as Farce*, 145.

62. W. Lesser, "The Effects of TRIPS-Mandated Intellectual Property Rights on Economic Activities in Developing Countries," paper prepared under the World Intellectual Property Organization Special Service Agreement, April 17, 2001, www.wipo.int/export/sites/www/about-ip/en/studies/pdf/ssa_lesser_trips.pdf; Satya Thallam, "International Property Rights Index, 2008 Report," *Property Rights Alliance*, www.libinst.ch/publikationen/LI-2008-IPRI-Report.pdf.

63. Representing the Recording Industry of South Africa, "Piracy and Organised Crime," www.stoppiracy.org.za/?page_id=88.

64. This other economy—which we may call "informal" but which Brian Larkin more subtly terms a "shadow" or "secondary" economy—requires a much fuller analysis than I can provide here. See Larkin, *Signal and Noise: Media, Infrastructure, and Urban Culture in Nigeria* (Durham: Duke University Press, 2008).

65. Eugene Mthethwa, "Why I'm Quitting Trompies," *NewZimbabwe.com*, August 2, 2009, www.newzimbabwe.com/pages/trompies6.19358.html.

66. See Phathu Ratshilumela, "AIRCO Takes a Step Further against Piracy!" *Music Industry Online*, March 23, 2008, www.mio.co.za/article/airco-takes-a-step-further-against-piracy-2007-05-23.

67. "Experts Ask, Can President Zuma Breathe New Life into Kwaito Music?" *Music Industry Online*, June 11, 2009, www.mio.co.za/article/experts-ask-can-president-zuma-breathe-new-life-into-kwaito-music-2009-06-11.

68. James Ferguson, "Formalities of Poverty: Thinking about Social Assistance in Neoliberal South Africa," *African Studies Review* 50, no. 2 (2007): 78.

69. "About Us," McDonald's (South Africa), www.mcdonalds.co.za/aboutus.

70. Penwell Dlamini, "Ramaphosa to Run McDonalds SA," *Sowetan*, March 18, 2011, www.sowetanlive.co.za/news/business/2011/03/18/ramaphosa-to-run-mcdonalds-sa.

71. The notion of the performativity of economics has been most forcefully argued by Michel Callon. His work, however, focuses on economic "devices."

72. Hardt and Negri, *Empire*, 40.

73. Ibid.

74. Ibid., 211.

75. Bill Dietz, "Composing Listening," *Performance Research* 16, no. 3 (2011): 56–61.

PART IV · **ANTICOLONIALISM**

12 · THE SOUND OF ANTICOLONIALISM

BRENT HAYES EDWARDS

In October 1961, Hugh Tracey, the indefatigable English ethnomusicolo-gist who starting in the 1930s made thousands of field recordings through-out eastern, central, and southern Africa, gave a lecture in Johannesburg at the Institute for the Study of Man in Africa in which he reflected in passing on the implications of the "winds of change" then sweeping the continent.[1] Without ever addressing colonial independence directly, Tracey's articles and field notes provide a fascinating record of sidelong glances at what in one editorial he termed "the increasingly disturbed political situation throughout the continent" and the difficulties it posed for his collecting work.[2] In Johannesburg, Tracey reminds his audience that although it is difficult to trace the origins of African music, there is some evidence of its history going back at least to the writings of the first Portuguese explorers to reach the continent in the sixteenth century. He cites a letter by Father Andre Fernandes where the missionary describes the music he heard in southeastern Africa (in what is today Mozambique), explaining that the Chopi "have many songs here, such as 'This is a good man. He gave me this or that, and will give me more.'" Tracey then offers his own rather snide annotation: "How little Africa has changed since 1560. The song to-day, of course, would not read quite like that. It would read something like 'This is a bad colonial. He will get out and will give me everything.'"[3]

Tracey's disdain is not in itself particularly surprising given his overt emphasis on cultural preservationism, the collecting of "authentic African folk music" through ethnographic recording and contextual documentation. For Tracey, the tectonic shifts in the African political landscape in the independence era, like the more gradual forces of labor migration and urbanization, imperiled the supposed authenticity of musical traditions on the continent, breaking the "continuity" of the music's relation to a particular local culture.[4] Tracey's hostility to large-scale societal change was the result of a brand of benevolence, his ultimate ambition of providing an archive of African music that might serve as a "point of reference" or, as he put it elsewhere, "a foundation for future African compositions of worthwhile modern proportions."[5] Nevertheless, the result is an archive developed through a suspicion of the "insidious forces" that were taken to "undermine" African folk tradition, not incidentally including the schemes of "the politically-minded ones who will attempt to use African music as a political rallying cry for nationalism."[6]

In other words, Tracey's orientation is based on a claim that ethnomusicology can somehow remain unsullied by politics even if the work of contextual documentation must attend to the aftertraces of political machination in the music itself. As he puts it in one report from a recording tour in South Africa: "our Library, it will be noted, is not concerned with politics but it must observe and remark upon the social conditions reflected in African songs which may be the outcome of politics."[7] This is to ignore the degree to which ethnomusicological collecting, and indeed the discipline of anthropology more generally, is complicit with the colonial enterprise.[8] On a mundane level, this complicity is legible in Tracey's field notes, with his various acknowledgments of "the kindness of Portuguese friends" in Lourenço Marques (Maputo) and elsewhere, or his gratitude for the lodging and support provided time and time again by a network of district commissioners and colonial administrators.[9] Complicity is not only a matter of logistics, though—the material support that during the colonial era made field recording in remote locations feasible—but also a question of the ethnographic encounter itself: the direct impact of the scene of recording on the material recorded and thereby on the constitution of the archive, despite Tracey's conviction that ethnographic recording yielded access to material "performed entirely for African satisfaction."[10] In his field notes from the Belgian Congo in the early 1950s, Alan Merriam describes hearing a performance of five songs by a group of Bashi girls on a coffee and quinine plantation near Kivu. "These songs were directed at the owner of the plantation," Merriam writes,

> who was acting in the capacity of interpreter and thus could not fail to follow the texts. Because of a recent wage advance he had stopped giving the workers rations of salt and peanut or palm oil. The singers began by indicating the setting, the plantation; they continued with flattery which, by the third song, was in no sense subtle. In the fourth song the question of the cessation of salt and oil rations was introduced, and in the final song the singers threatened to take jobs elsewhere if the rations were not reinstituted. It is clear that the five songs represented a direct warning to the plantation owner of the discontent among his workers. This discontent was unknown to him; while the girls were unwilling to express their doubts directly, they seized this opportunity to inform him of the situation.[11]

Recounting Merriam's description of this episode, Rose Brandel queries bluntly: "Is this a musical strike?"[12] To ask this is to miss the point, which is not that the song suite allows the Bashi girls access to a structural leverage equivalent to that available in the metropolitan workplace—that is, a normative mode of articulating the interests of labor in the face of capital—but instead that the "opportunity" is predicated on the peculiarity of the ethnographic situation. It is a commonplace of African ethnomusicology to argue that, as Merriam phrases it, songs "frequently allow the expression of thoughts which might otherwise be repressed, and at the same time they may express underlying themes or configurations of the culture at hand."[13] But here it is clear that the situation of performing for the ethnomusicologist (and the plantation owner's positioning as the conveyor of meaning) allows the expression of "discontent" in a manner that may not have been otherwise available or heard.

I have opened this essay with Tracey's archive because it has already been revisited by scholars attuned to the very political issues he found so discomfiting. Most notably, Leroy Vail and Landeg White—in one of the most impressive instances of what George Marcus has termed the "restudy of classic works" of anthropology—supplemented Tracey's recordings in Mozambique in the 1940s with their own ethnographic research in the 1970s.[14] Noting that Tracey's annotations on the midcentury recordings "range from the whimsical and patronizing to the completely erroneous," Vail and White review his archive, retranslating song lyrics and providing more careful contextualization of the ways Chopi and Sena-Podzo music represents the nuances of power, migration, and labor under Portuguese colonial rule.[15]

The revisionary scholarship of Vail and White can be read as an example of an approach that might be termed *counterarchival*. What does it mean to read an archive "not concerned with politics" precisely for the political content it nonetheless preserves—that is, for the very songs Tracey jokes about or misreads ("This is a bad colonial")? This is to ask whether an archive devoted to the sedimentation of the "traditional" can be used or abused to trace a history of transformation. In other words, is it possible to excavate from Tracey's archive of African music a counterarchive of anticolonialism in sound?

What Vail and White gain in contextual nuance in their attention to the political implications of public poetry as a medium based on the "actual experience" of Africans in Mozambique, they sacrifice in what is finally the narrow purview in which they allow themselves to ask the question of how one might theorize an African anticolonialism through music. This trade-off is the result of their recognition that the African "point of view" as limned in music is necessarily "more parochial because it varie[s] regionally," and their laudable commitment to the principles of responsible ethnographic scholarship: that is, to read well, one must know the local language(s) and musical traditions, and one must contextualize the performances through onsite field research.[16] It would be a mistake to underestimate the importance of this commitment, particularly with respect to African languages.[17] Vail and White demonstrate with great authority the subtle differences in expression that emerged over time in African communities thrown by labor migration and urbanization into contact not only with the colonial regime but also *with each other*; they note the shifts in tone and critique among the songs of the Lomwe-Chuabo and the Sena-Podzo, for instance, or among the Ngoni, Sena, and Anguru songs on sugar plantations in Mozambique.

But with regard to the currents of musical performance in southern Africa more broadly (much less sub-Saharan Africa in general), this rich regionalism could be characterized as a "retreat from comparison," to use Kofi Agawu's provocative phrase.[18] As Agawu notes, there are good reasons that Africanist ethnomusicologists have long shied away from anything approaching the bold continental assertions that had once been a familiar staple of the field, like A. M. Jones's claim that African music forms "an indivisible whole."[19] Anticolonialist thought, however, is inherently comparative. In the 1950s, it emerges through a process of cross-fertilization, transposition, and translation in which nascent independence struggles are never discrete but emerge crucially in view of and in conversation with one another. Or to adopt the music-derived figure most characteristic of the work of Edward Said, the study of anticolonialism must be "contrapuntal" because it involves an attempt to track a historical phenomenon itself composed of "intertwined and overlapping histories."[20]

Must the archive of anticolonialism in music then be approached through counterpoint as well? Can it be approached not through a single archive, in other words, whether the result of individual fieldwork, the institutionally held collections of ethnomusicologists such as Tracey or Arthur S. Alberts, or state-sponsored research centers such as the Berlin Phonogramm-Archiv or the Institut Français d'Afrique Noire, but instead through a method that reads *across* such collections, striving for what J. H. Nketia calls the "second level of abstraction" in their discrepance?[21] It would also be necessary to consider archives gathered for disparate purposes of dissemination, from organizations such as the Folkways Corporation in the United States and the Office de Cooperation Radiophonique in France, to the various archives assembled for the purposes of radio broadcast in Africa itself. A contrapuntal approach to the archive of anticolonialism in African music would also force us to consider what Christopher Waterman calls the "feedback" between currents of music that are sometimes too quickly presumed to be separate—between rural and urban, folk and professional, traditional and modern—listening for reverberations that may be less a matter of patterns of movement and influence than of similar concerns or predilections, the parallel recourse to related figures in the musical imagining of social change in the broadest sense.[22]

I have been describing Hugh Tracey's recordings as constituting an *archive*, but the application of that term to a body of ethnomusicological field recordings should raise a number of questions about its scope and implications. Even early in his career, Tracey's writing makes it clear that he thought of his work as constituting what he called an "international archive" of African music: the documentation of a broad range of present-day practice that, gathered and preserved in a single institutional home, would prove indispensable for the purposes of future practitioners (that is, African musicians), teachers, and scholars alike. As he argued time and again, "We should collect and treasure as large and representative a selection of authentic African folk music as possible to act as a point of reference for future generations as valid in music as the bronzes of Ife are to the modern sculptures of Nigeria."[23] The repository he eventually founded in South Africa in 1954 was called the International Library of African Music (ILAM), although the term *library* seems less appropriate than *archive*, given the institute's holdings (unique artifacts unavailable elsewhere) and policies (although the ILAM, like Smithsonian Folkways, has made some of its recordings available through commercial releases, the vast majority of Tracey's collection must be consulted onsite).

It is unclear what Tracey envisioned by the phrase "act as a point of reference," especially with regard to future generations of African musicians: did he really expect that a contemporary singer from, say, Kananga in the central Congo would have the resources to make the trip to Grahamstown in South Africa to consult recordings Tracey had made in Kananga in the late 1950s? And given Tracey's commitment to the authenticity of local practice, he does not seem to have taken into account the potential cross-fertilization his continental archive could make possible and the radical implications it could have for musical practice, if isolated pockets of African musicians were actually able to "hear each other" across great distances through the medium of the archive.

In John Miller Chernoff's influential 1979 book on Ghanaian drumming, *African Rhythm and African Sensibility*, there is a brief description of a style of children's music called Atikatika, which is devoted to what Chernoff calls "witty political songs; several times [the children] have been in trouble with local authorities and the national government, and their music is periodically banned."[24] In a footnote, he offers one "example of a typical Atikatika song: the leader sings, 'An airplane has got a punctured tire'; the chorus replies, 'That is the trouble of the people in the sky.' The children are not concerned with the problems of the elite."[25] Even if the figure of the airplane is primarily a representation of "class" division, there seems to be much more implied here, from a subtle juxtaposition of the politics of perspective (that is, you can see the punctured tire only from below), to a poignant reflection on distance as mediated by human transportation technology, to a rather clever joke deflating the pretension to transcendence implied by air travel (the reminder that the flat tire will become a problem when the plane eventually has to land, the "people in the sky" brought literally and figuratively "down to earth").

What would it mean not only to think more carefully about what is "witty" and what is "political" here—and how they are related—but also to place this lyric from a village children's group next to something like Tracey's 1950 recording of the rumba "Meu Amor Era Aviador" (My love was an airman) by the Grupo Manjacaziana, a colonial dance band in Lourenço Marques (Maputo)? Again, Tracey himself has little to say by way of explication ("now that has to be the most handy type of dating imaginable!" he gushes inanely), but the themes clearly at stake here—an implicit understanding of modernity as a condition of *conscription*, one might say, deliberately set in contrast to the "romance of transport" in more than one sense—are not unrelated to the issues being worked through in the Atikatika performance across the distances of language, genre, geography, and time.[26] If we are to take seriously the contention that music is the paradigmatic medium of socialization in Africa, and the concomitant broad-stroke argument that during the colonial era music "remained undisplaced as the regenerative source of the continent's cultural will," then we must be able to read the complex parallels among such examples.[27]

Such a comparative approach also draws our attention to the political implication of opacity in musical performance. Despite the presumption of transparency in so much ethnomusicology of the colonial era, it seems obvious that not every metaphor or allusion would be understood by every listener in any given community, much less outside it. In his recent memoir, *Dreams in a Time of War*, the Kenyan novelist Ngũgĩ wa Thiong'o describes his bewilderment at some of the unexplained references to far-off events in the stories he heard as a child in the 1940s:

> Names of strange people—Mussolini, Hitler, Franco, Stalin, Churchill, and Roosevelt—and places—America, Germany, Italy, and Russia, Japan, Madagascar, and Burma—occasionally cropped up in the story sessions.... These names and places were vague in outline, and . . . were really shadows in a mist.... How did these young men and women, some of them just workers in the nearby Limuru Bata Shoe Company, know such stories and the goings-on in times past and places far away?[28]

C. L. R. James, discussing the impact of Nkrumah's newspaper editorials on the climate in the Gold Coast before independence, insists on the "political education" the articles provided, even when they were not fully understood:

> There is the central idea of being ready to suffer, even to die for the cause. There is the defiance of the overwhelming material power of

imperialism. These are enough to hold the attention and lift not only the hearts but the minds of any people. But in addition there are the following windows to new worlds: fatherland; blood, sweat, and tears; Calvary, Garibaldi, Battle of Britain, campaigns of East Africa, Burma and India, Shakespeare's *Julius Caesar*, "Who is a bondsman that would not . . ."; the day of resurrection, the day of redemption. There is here a mass of ideas, facts, avenues for further exploration. One man reads and the others who do not read listen. Then would come the elucidation of the various points and references. It can last for days.[29]

Opacity, James reminds us, serves a crucial role in anticolonialism, because "every revolution must attempt what by all logic and reason and previous experience is impossible. Like anything creative it extends the boundaries of the known."[30] Or as David Coplan has observed with regard to musical performance, "The singer who desires to shake the nation with a song about his own experience must possess an intuitive seismograph, sensing the fault lines of feeling between social reality and social aspiration."[31]

In 1952 in the Belgian Congo, Hugh Tracey recorded a song called "Kankenene kambula mushete" (The small ant carrying the box). It is tempting to read the lyrics, with their strange figuration of differential perspective (among the first-person singer, the ant, and "the Europeans"), as an oblique and ambivalent allegory for the colonial situation: "I see a small ant carrying the box, and the ant sees the Europeans taking an aeroplane / O small ant, carry the box for me, I see the Europeans taking an aeroplane."[32] As Tracey notes in *Chopi Musicians*, the songs he records often take the form of something like "free association" or "a collection of wholly unrelated observations which are found to be not so unrelated as one might think once the situation has been explained."[33] But it does not occur to him that effects such as indirection, digression, abrupt shifts in register, and juxtapositions of disparate elements might themselves be considered political precisely in the way they evade or exceed straightforward declaration or linear narrative. At the same time, one would need to take into account the politics of musical *form* in a manner that goes beyond the linguistic content of the lyrics, to consider the affective impact of "nonpropositional semiotic domains" including rhythm, harmony, and timbre.[34] As Karin Barber has suggested, these qualities of opacity in music may be related less to strategies of "deliberate concealment" (of what it would be dangerous to express in clear and direct fashion) than to "a way of thinking about politics."[35]

To approach the question of anticolonialism from this angle of emergence is to focus on a quality that cannot necessarily be reduced to nationalism.

Anticolonialism in this sense precedes independence, and it is something only on the way to a practice of "musical nationalism in relation to political nationalist movements and state nationalist projects."[36] This is also the reason that I am focusing here on the so-called classic period of the 1950s leading to the wave of independence struggles across the African continent, rather than the variants of anticolonialism that develop decades later in response to white-settler postcolonialism in Zimbabwe and South Africa. I am interested in the role of music as a mode of thought, of imagining alternative futures— that is, an "outside" or "after" colonialism—through performance, as seemingly oblique and incipient as that mode may be. My sense is that it may be precisely the ephemerality and fragility of musical anticolonialism that may prove central to the eventual constitution of a movement proper. While it may be more a matter of "infrapolitics" than of party politics, anticolonialism here also implies something subtler than terms such as "resistance" and "protest" as they have been deployed in scholarship.[37] Nor can anticolonialism be reduced to some of the features that have often been associated with it: sheer oppositionality, for example, or an obstinate investment in romantic vindicationalism.[38]

The Congolese singer Adou Elenga was arrested by the Belgian authorities in 1957 after he released his song "Ata ndele, mokili ekobaluka," the lyrics of which center around the simple prediction that "the world is going to change." (As Sylvain Bemba explains, the phrase literally means "the world is going to spin on its axis.") Elenga was a musician who, until he was signed that year by the pioneering Ngoma record company, made a name for himself playing informally for free in *matangas* (popular parties to celebrate the end of the mourning period) in Kinshasa, and thus his career could be considered as yet another example in the professionalization of music in the Congo through the emergence of commercial recording in the period.[39] But it is also an example of African anticolonialism in music, not because it is a direct demand for independence, but because it is an incisive intervention—with Elenga for the first time recording on electric rather than acoustic guitar—in "the silent war between colonial ideology and a will to liberation seeking an opening unto a different world."[40] As much as it can involve the call for justice and redress, the demand for the prerogative of self-determination, anticolonialism is also a matter of intuition, the intimation of change: "leaps into the unknown."[41]

GIVEN THE CONSTITUTIVE blind spots in the colonial archive of African music, it is no wonder that the great African diasporic theorists of anticolonialism failed to draw on the materials gathered by ethnomusicologists like

Hugh Tracey as key examples of the struggle against colonialism in the arena of culture. But this would be another way to approach the problem: when black anticolonial theory invokes music, what music does it invoke? One might recall, for instance, that in his magisterial history of the Haitian revolution, *The Black Jacobins* (1938)—a study explicitly "intended to use the San Domingo revolution as a forecast of the future of colonial Africa"[42]—C. L. R. James draws on a musical example in his attempt to describe "the intellectual level" of the slave population in Haiti in the late eighteenth century. As he argues in a forceful passage early in the book:

> But one does not need education or encouragement to cherish a dream of freedom. At their midnight celebrations of Voodoo, their African cult, they danced and sang, usually this favourite song:
>
> > Eh! Eh! Bomba! Heu! Heu!
> > Canga, bafio té!
> > > Canga, mouné de lé!
> > Canga, do ki la!
> > > Canga, li!
>
> "We swear to destroy the whites and all that they possess; let us die rather than fail to keep this vow."
> The colonists knew this song and tried to stamp it out, and the Voodoo cult with which it was linked. In vain. For over two hundred years the slaves sang it at their meetings, as the Jews in Babylon sang of Zion, and the Bantu to-day sing in secret the national anthem of Africa.[43]

I am less concerned with the source of the song (which James neglects to provide) or even the translation (which seems approximate, if not altogether fanciful) than with the use of music as a privileged figure of "intelligence" in the form of "a dream of freedom," one that can be extrapolated by analogy as evidence of a foundational human impulse toward liberation and self-determination. That "intelligence" is first of all a demonstration of autonomy—thinking for oneself, despite those who attempt to "stamp it out"—is a quality equally identifiable in the expanded or contrapuntal archive of African musical anticolonialism I have been sketching here, for instance in the comments by Vail and White on the "Paiva" song (originating in the 1930s but continuing to be sung in the 1970s), which excoriated the Portuguese colonial administration in Mozambique: "The song defines a tiny area in which the labourers and their families have a separate existence, maintaining a small region of the community mind which has refused to capitulate completely. It is in the song that the people's identity is preserved."[44]

If the song in *The Black Jacobins* indicates the slaves' "separate existence," it also marks an area of practice—of what James elsewhere calls "creative activity"—that is indispensable to anticolonialism in that "the process of the revolution is essentially the process of the people finding themselves."[45] This insistence on music as a medium of collective self-discovery is the reason that the Atikatika song reported by Chernoff has something to do with anticolonialism as I am defining it here, even if an allusion to "the people in the sky" suggests a critique of social hierarchy that is loose and imprecise at best, unlike "Paiva" (which criticizes by name a particularly brutal Portuguese colonial administrator). Imaginative flight is central to anticolonialism even when it flies away from historical reference. It is reminiscent of Frederick Douglass's comment in chapter 4 of his 1855 narrative, *My Bondage and My Freedom*, about the impact of standing as a young slave on a plantation in Maryland, watching ships in the distance on Chesapeake Bay. The sloops, Douglass explains, were "wonderous things, full of thoughts and ideas. A child cannot well look at such objects without *thinking*."[46] For Douglass, the ships provoke the first stirrings of his own "dream of freedom."

If one can point to instances of black anticolonial thought where African music comes to signal the specter of reactionary tribalism (ultimately to be superseded by the revolutionary modernism of the nationalist movement), it is nonetheless striking how often music comes to serve, even in vague and amorphous terms, as the preeminent figure of both the precolonial past and a future beyond colonialism.[47] In the literature of the Négritude movement, for instance, this is a prominent effect, whether in the seemingly obligatory "*tam-tams*" that resound through the poems of Léon-Gontran Damas, Aimé Césaire, and David Diop, or in the efflorescence presaged in Paul Niger's "Je n'aime pas l'Afrique"; in Niger's poem, if "Africa is going to speak," it will take the form of "a rhythm / a sound wave in the night through the forests."[48]

It is equally striking, however, given the prominence of arguments about what Amilcar Cabral terms the "dependent and reciprocal relations between the national liberation struggle and culture," how seldom anticolonial thought draws on specific examples from African music.[49] In the "On National Culture" chapter of *The Wretched of the Earth*, Frantz Fanon quotes "African Dawn," a long poem by the Guinean minister of internal affairs Ketia Fodeba, praising its "unquestioned pedagogical value" without discussing its inclusion of parenthetical indications for musical accompaniment or interludes throughout the text: "(Guitar music)," "(Kora music)," "(Balafon)," and so forth.[50] The last section of the chapter is a reprinting of "Fondement réciproque de la culture nationale et des luttes de libération" (Mutual foundations for national culture and liberation struggles), Fanon's speech to the 1959 Rome conference of black writers and intellectuals hosted by the journal *Présence Africaine*.[51] Here Fanon discusses a wide variety of art forms—including not only literature but also oral storytelling, drama, and ceramics—but aside from a few scattered allusions to "popular songs," the main passage devoted to music takes an unexpected detour. As indigenous art is transformed in the service of cultural nationalism, Fanon writes, it is ironic that

> it is the colonialists who become the defenders of indigenous styles. A memorable example, and one that takes on particular significance because it does not quite involve a colonial reality, was the reaction of white jazz fans when after the Second World War new styles such as bebop established themselves. For them jazz could only be the broken, desperate yearning of an old "Negro," five whiskeys under his belt, bemoaning his own misfortune and the racism of the whites. As soon as he understands himself and apprehends the world differently, as soon as he elicits a glimmer of hope and forces the racist world to retreat, it is obvious he will blow his horn to his heart's content and his husky voice will ring out loud and clear. The new jazz styles are not only born out of economic competition. They are one of the definite consequences of the inevitable, though gradual, defeat of the Southern universe in the USA. And it is not unrealistic to think that in fifty years or so the type of jazz lament hiccupped by a poor, miserable "Negro" will be defended by only those whites believing in a frozen image of a certain type of relationship and a certain form of negritude.[52]

It is not clear why the example of jazz would assume "particular significance because it does not quite involve a colonial reality"; Fanon's biographer, David Macey, suggests that this gesture may have more to do with the limitations of Fanon's knowledge of African music than with any substantive point.[53] But especially given the closing link to "negritude," it is worth considering the implications of this contrapuntal impulse, involving the transposition of African American music into a discussion of the African colonial context, and in particular Fanon's ancillary contention in the following paragraph that "well before the political or armed struggle, a careful observer could sense and feel in these arts the pulse of a fresh stimulus and the coming combat. Unusual forms of expression, original themes no longer invested with the power of invocation but the power to rally and mobilize with the approaching conflict in mind."[54] What does it mean to fold jazz into this argument?

This transposition is not particular to Fanon's work, in the end, but instead is a recurrent predilection in African and Caribbean literature of the period, especially but not only in French.[55] For the Senegalese poet and politician Léopold Sédar Senghor, even as early as the 1930s, jazz is the preeminent figure of an African diasporic aesthetic that somehow evades or exceeds western norms.[56] In the Haitian writer Jacques Roumain's scathing poem "Sales nègres," an anticolonial transformation in art is depicted as a matter of New World black music, bands "playing a totally different thing."[57] René Ménil, one of the key collaborators with Aimé and Suzanne Césaire on the journal *Tropiques* in Martinique in the early 1940s, makes recourse to jazz in describing the "situation of poetry in the Antilles" because, as he explains, "the important phenomenon of jazz notably allows us, more certainly than any critical reflection, to conceive of the *historical* character of substance and form within the work"—that is, it offers an aesthetic model based on improvisation ("a technique for creating beauty as you go along") that values innovation without preconception or fixed category, a mode of proceeding, "like an acrobat, on the tightrope of circumstance."[58] Jazz is privileged, in other words, because it is taken to demand invention, the continuing concoction of the new. As Ménil writes, jazz is a "means of purgation and of the recreation in us of a sense of the instant and of transition."[59]

In Fanon, while "new styles" of African American music signaled revolutionary transformation, older forms are associated with that "frozen image of a certain type of relationship and a certain form of negritude" dismissed in "On National Culture." A few years earlier, for example, in "Racism and Culture," his speech at the 1956 *Présence Africaine* conference in Paris, he describes the blues as a "modicum of stylized oppression." The blues, Fanon declares, are simply a reactive encapsulation of racialized suffering, "the slave's response to the challenge of oppression." Thus "the end of racism would sound the knell of great Negro music." Fanon adds that "still today, for many men, even colored, Armstrong's music has a real meaning only in this perspective."[60] By 1960 Fanon describes Louis Armstrong not only as a musical anachronism but also as a "herald" of American neocolonialism.[61] But for other writers, Armstrong in particular remained something close to the personification of the anticolonial force attributed to jazz, as in Paul Niger's "Initiations": "On the judgment day, Armstrong's trumpet will be the interpreter of man's sufferings."[62]

On the one hand, this is a matter of representative black masculinity—Armstrong as a figure for the authority of revolutionary leadership in the era of decolonization. As Senghor writes in "Poème liminaire," "our new nobility is not to dominate our people, / But to be their rhythm and their heart / . . . Not to be the people's head, but their mouth and their trumpet."[63] On the other hand, the figure of Armstrong allows the appropriation of a Judeo-Christian rhetoric of divine retribution, the degree to which an eventual "vengeance and punishment" against "the world's felony" would mean "the sky's eardrum shattered under the fist / of justice."[64] As the historians Penny Von Eschen and Ingrid Monson have reminded us, Armstrong is so consistently invoked in part because he performed in Africa during the period, first on an unofficial tour in the Gold Coast (Ghana) in May 1956 and then on a U.S. State Department tour of twenty-seven cities across the African continent in 1960 and 1961.[65] It is not for nothing that the South African magazine *Drum* proclaimed, in 1956, "Satchmo Blows Up the World."[66] At the same time, the references to Armstrong in Niger's poem from the 1940s or in Léon-Gontran Damas's "Shine" from the 1930s indicate that Pops was an emblematic figure for the transposition of jazz in the burgeoning of African diasporic anticolonial thought long before his visit to the African continent.[67]

THIS ESSAY STAGES a missed encounter. In the awkward discontinuity between the two preceding sections I have attempted to approach the question of the role of African music in anticolonialism by reading contrapuntally against the grain of two discourses—ethnomusicology on the one hand and the theory and literature of anticolonialism on the other—in which the question is foreclosed or sidestepped. I will close with a suggestion about the ways postcolonial literature might be read to supplement the history of anticolonialism precisely by animating the heterogeneous archives of African music.

Ngũgĩ wa Thiong'o's 1980 novel *Caitaani Mũtharaba-inĩ* (*Devil on the Cross*) is perhaps best known as the work that inaugurates the Kenyan writer's deliberate decision, while detained without charge in Kamiti National Security Prison in Nairobi, to write in Gĩkũyũ rather than English.[68] As a broad satire of the hypocrisies of the comprador bourgeoisie in postcolonial Kenya (above all, its acquiescence to the neocolonial stratagems of European and American capital) through a novel that adopts a range of formal features from oral performance, *Devil on the Cross* would seem to follow in the wake of Ngũgĩ's work in the Kamĩrĩĩthũ community theater in the late 1970s, where he collaborated with workers and peasants to develop a mode of populist critique through collective performance in plays such as *Ngaahika Ndeenda* (*I Will Marry When I Want*).[69] In this sense, what Simon Gikandi calls Ngũgĩ's "appropriation of the novel into the oral tradition" in *Devil on the Cross* seems motivated first of all by the writer's espousal of the history of "a patriotic national tradition" that during the colonial era had sprung up "in resistance and opposition to imperialist-sanctioned African culture."[70] Along with its gestures toward proverbs and storytelling—as Gikandi notes, the original Gĩkũyũ edition is framed with a formulaic introduction drawn from Gĩkũyũ folktales (*Uba iitha!*)—the novel frames that anticolonial tradition primarily in terms of Kenyan music.[71]

Kenya provides one of the richest archives of anticolonialism in music, not only through the numerous Gĩkũyũ political songs or *nyimbo* associated with the Mau Mau movement in the early 1950s (which were famously circulated in printed "hymnbooks") but also through protest-song styles, including *Kanyegenyũri* and *Mũthĩrĩgũ*, going back to the 1920s.[72] But the range of music woven into *Devil on the Cross* goes beyond this archive, making it unexpectedly difficult (despite the efforts of some critics) to read it simply as evidence of "a patriotic national tradition" preceding and exceeding the bounds of colonialism.[73] The novel includes Gicaandi songs drawn from Gĩkũyũ orature and also the narcissism of "today's dance song" and bands performing what is described as "Congolese music"; there is a traditional verse-chanting competition, a *Mũthũũngũũci* love song, and a *Mũthuũ* dance song associated with a precircumcision rite from the 1940s.[74] The novel quotes lyrics from a number of Mau Mau songs from the 1950s, and it also includes a Christian hymn and vernacular spirituals ("I shall knock-a-knock the Devil") recast with new words related to the anticolonial struggle ("I shall knock-a-knock the whites").[75]

One key character in *Devil on the Cross*, Gatuĩria, is an aspiring composer who describes himself as a "junior research fellow in African culture."[76] As he laments, the tragedy of the Kenyan postcolonial present is that "everything about our national heritage has been lost to us."[77] His goal is to write what he calls "the music of my dreams," a "national oratorio" that will capture "the soul and the aspirations and the dreams of our nation."[78] But this magnum opus cannot simply involve a return to a "patriotic tradition" in some uncontaminated sense; as Gatuĩria puts it, "The roots of Kenyan national culture can be sought only in the traditions of all the nationalities of Kenya," and so the composition must weave together the variety of strands—the counterpoint of archives, religious and secular, colonial and indigenous, historical and contemporary—into an orchestration that can only be called cosmopolitan.[79]

Gatuĩria completes the composition, and *Devil on the Cross* includes a grandiose sketch of the oratorio's movements, as he describes the composition to his lover, Warĩĩnga.[80] The first performance is planned for their wedding night.[81] But Gatuĩria's explanation of the piece's structure is interrupted when Warĩĩnga becomes distracted, and rather than conclude with the promised apotheosis of a heroic love affair, *Devil on the Cross* ends with the explosive dissolution of their relationship, Warĩĩnga walking away "without once looking back" while a stunned Gatuĩria stands there, "hearing in his mind music that led him nowhere."[82] The counterpoint of musical archives cannot be orchestrated into a triumphant future. We are reminded that, throughout the book, the recourse to tradition serves the forces of domination as much as the forces of liberation. There are the Mau Mau songs sung by the "organization of patriots," yes, but also the songs of the notorious "home guards," Kenyan collaborators with the British colonial authorities.[83]

The closest the novel comes to populist triumph is the scene where the masses gather to confront the compradors and the foreign capitalists. Gatuĩria and Warĩĩnga hear "the people singing a new song" as they march to face the enemy: "Come one and all / And behold the wonderful sight / Of us chasing away the Devil."[84] And the neocolonial gathering does scatter briefly. But then the rebellion is violently put down by the authorities, with its leaders beaten and detained, and we are left with the observation that the situation "does not change much."[85] The novel does not provide a reassuring representation of a future beyond colonialism in a "new song" but instead, through its contrapuntal staging of disparate archives of African performance, attempts to compel the reader into engagement and active participation with the ongoing legacy of musical anticolonialism in a postcolonial African present.[86] What is demanded is not reverence in the shadow of tradition, but instead a spark of innovation that revives that legacy by shattering, re-making, going beyond its prior manifestations: "Change steps, for the song has more than one rhythm!"[87]

NOTES

1. This archive is held at the institution that Tracey founded in 1954, the International Library of African Music at Rhodes University in South Africa. Before his death in 1977, Tracey released 210 LPs of selected recordings from this archive in his "Sound of Africa" series; much of this material is now available on CD compilations released in the past decade. For information on Tracey's work, see the International Library of African Music website (www.ru.ac.za/ilam) and the liner notes by Tracey's son Andrew to the "Sound

of Africa" CD releases. For example, Andrew Tracey, "Hugh Tracey's Recordings," liner notes to *Colonial Dance Bands: Kenya, Tanganyika, Portuguese East Africa, Northern Rhodesia, Belgian Congo, 1950 and 1952* (International Library of African Music SWP 031/HT 020, 2006). For a broader perspective on Tracey in the context of early ethnomusicologists (including A. M. Jones and Klaus Wachsmann) working in southern Africa in the mid-twentieth century, see J. H. Kwabena Nketia, "The Scholarly Study of African Music: A Historical Review," in *The Garland Encyclopedia of World Music, Vol. 1: Africa*, ed. Ruth Stone (New York: Garland, 1998), 51–52. The phrase "winds of change" comes, of course, from Harold Macmillan's speech to the South African Parliament on February 3, 1960, in which the British prime minister famously acknowledged the "fact" of "the growth of national consciousness" in Africa.

2. Hugh Tracey, "Editorial," *African Music* 3, no. 2 (1963): 5.

3. Hugh Tracey, *The Evolution of African Music and Its Function in the Present Day*, Isma Papers no. 3, October 1961 (Johannesburg: Institute for the Study of Man in Africa, 1961), 3.

4. Ibid., 10.

5. Ibid., 21; Hugh Tracey, "African Music within Its Social Setting," *African Music* 2, no. 1 (1958): 57.

6. Tracey, *The Evolution of African Music*, 21.

7. Hugh Tracey, "Basutoland Recording Tour: November 19th to December 3rd, 1959," *African Music* 2, no. 2 (1959): 70.

8. This critique arises first of all *within* the discipline during the very period when Tracey is building his library. Thus Bruno Nettl, among others, has described the disciplinary formation of ethnomusicology as a "tradition of self-critique." See Bruno Nettl, *Nettl's Elephant: On the History of Ethnomusicology* (Urbana: University of Illinois Press, 2010), 54–69. See also Nettl, *The New Grove Dictionary of Music and Musicians*, 2nd ed. (New York: Oxford University Press, 2001), s.v. "Colonialism." For an early critique of the complicity of anthropology in general, see, for example, Michel Leiris, "The Ethnographer Faced with Colonialism," in *Brisées =Broken Branches*, trans. Lydia Davis (San Francisco: North Point, 1989), 112–31.

9. Hugh Tracey, *Chopi Musicians: Their Music, Poetry, and Instruments* (1948; repr., Oxford: Oxford University Press and International African Institute, 1970), vi; Hugh Tracey, "Report on the I.L.A.M. Nyasaland Recording Tour (May 7th to June 30th, 1958)," *African Music* 2, no. 1 (1958): 65.

10. Hugh Tracey, liner notes to *The Columbia World Library of Folk and Primitive Music, Vol. 10: Bantu Music from East Africa*, compiled and edited by Alan Lomax (Columbia 91A 02017).

11. Alan P. Merriam, "African Music," in *Continuity and Change in African Cultures*, ed. William R. Bascom and Melville J. Herskovitz (Chicago: University of Chicago Press, 1958), 55.

12. Rose Brandel, *Music of Central Africa: An Ethnomusicological Study: Former French Equatorial Africa, the Former Belgian Congo, Ruanda-Urundi, Uganda, Tanganyika* (The Hague, Netherlands: Martinus Nijhoff, 1961), 40.

13. Merriam, "African Music," 55.

14. George E. Marcus, "The Once and Future Ethnographic Archive," *History of the Human Sciences* 11, no. 4 (1998): 54.

15. Leroy Vail and Landeg White, "Forms of Resistance: Songs and Perceptions of Power in Colonial Mozambique," *American Historical Review* 88, no. 4 (October 1983): 888. Their revisionary scholarship is gathered in the impressive monographs *Capitalism and Colonialism in Mozambique: A Study of Queliriane District* (London: Heinemann, 1980); and *Power and the Praise Poem: Southern African Voices in History* (Charlottesville: University Press of Virginia, 1991).

16. Vail and White, *Capitalism and Colonialism in Mozambique*, 339.

17. See Kofi Agawu, *Representing African Music: Postcolonial Notes, Queries, Positions* (New York: Routledge, 2003), 40.

18. Ibid., 60.

19. A. M. Jones, *Studies in African Music*, 2 vols. (Oxford: Oxford University Press, 1959), 200.

20. Edward Said, *Culture and Imperialism* (New York: Knopf, 1993), 18. Oddly, given the prominence of this methodological figure—and for a scholar so deeply invested in music—Said's groundbreaking study has very little to say about music itself aside from its analysis of the shadow of empire in works of the European classical tradition such as Verdi's *Aida*.

21. For a sampling of Alberts's recordings from the 1940s, held at the Library of Congress, one might start with *The Arthur S. Alberts Collection: More Tribal, Folk, and Café Music of West Africa*, Library of Congress Endangered Music Project (Rykodisc RCD 10401, 1998). As Nketia puts it, "The ethnographic view is very good in terms of giving you all the details that you need about a culture, but if you have two, three or four ethnographers, then the relationship between the ethnographies becomes the second level of abstraction." See Trevor Wiggins, "An Interview with J. H. Kwabena Nketia: Perspectives on Tradition and Modernity," *Ethnomusicology Forum* 14, no. 1 (June 2005): 65.

22. Christopher Alan Waterman, *Juju: A Social History and Ethnography of an African Popular Music* (Chicago: University of Chicago Press, 1990), 49.

23. Tracey, *The Evolution of African Music*, 21. He calls his recordings an "international archive" in the same speech (22).

24. John Miller Chernoff, *African Rhythm and African Sensibility: Aesthetics and Social Action in African Musical Idioms* (Chicago: University of Chicago Press, 1979), 130.

25. Ibid., 212–13n35.

26. Tracey, field recording notes, *Colonial Dance Bands*. In my cursory comments on the implications of the lyric, I am thinking of David Scott's *Conscripts of Modernity: The Tragedy of Colonial Enlightenment* (Durham: Duke University Press, 2004), 8–9.

27. On the topic of African music as socialization, see Chernoff, *African Rhythm and African Sensibility*, 154. The quotation comes from Wole Soyinka, "The Arts in Africa during the Period of Colonial Rule," in *General History of Africa, Vol. VII: Africa under Colonial Domination, 1880–1935*, ed. A. Adu Boahen (London: Heinemann and UNESCO, 1985), 544. Although I do not have space in which to elaborate this point, my argument here for a contrapuntal approach should be taken as an intervention into recent debates around the very meaning of comparativism in ethnomusicology. For an

introduction to these debates, see Bruno Nettl, "Revisiting Comparison, Comparative Study, and Comparative Methodology," in *Nettl's Elephant*, 70–92.

28. Ngugi wa Thiong'o, *Dreams in a Time of War: A Childhood Memoir* (London: Harvill Secker, 2010), 34–35.

29. C. L. R. James, *Nkrumah and the Ghana Revolution* (Westport, CT: Lawrence Hill, 1977), 123.

30. Ibid., 129.

31. David B. Coplan, *In the Time of Cannibals: The Word Music of South Africa's Basotho Migrants* (Chicago: University of Chicago Press, 1994), 4.

32. Both these examples are taken from Hugh Tracey, *Kanyok and Luba: Southern Belgian Congo, 1952 and 1957* (International Library of African Music SWP 011/HT 05, 1998).

33. Tracey, *Chopi Musicians*, 5.

34. Thomas Turino, *Nationalists, Cosmopolitans, and Popular Music in Zimbabwe* (Chicago: University of Chicago Press, 2000), 174.

35. Karin Barber, "Popular Arts in Africa," *African Studies Review* 30, no. 3 (September 1987): 63.

36. Turino, *Nationalists*, 190.

37. With the term "infrapolitics" I allude to the work of James C. Scott, especially *Domination and the Arts of Resistance: Hidden Transcripts* (New Haven, CT: Yale University Press, 1990).

38. Scott, *Conscripts of Modernity*, 6.

39. Sylvain Bemba, *Cinquante ans de musique du Congo-Zaïre, 1920–1970: De Paul Kamba à Tabu-Ley* (Paris: Présence Africaine, 1984), 79. The recording is available on a number of compilations, including Adou Elenga, "Ata Ndele," *Anthologie de la musique Zaïroise moderne, tome 1* (Bureau du Président de la République du Zaïre BP 3092). On this song, see also Gary Stewart, *Rumba on the River: A History of the Popular Music of the Two Congos* (London: Verso, 2000), 71; John Nimis, "Framing Congolese Music: The Music of Kinshasa and Its 'World,'" in "Literary Listening: Readings in Congolese Popular Music" (PhD diss., New York University, 2010); Charles Didier Gondola Ebonga, "*Ata ndele* . . . et l'indépendance vint: Musique, jeunes et contestation politique dans les capitals congolaises," in *Les Jeunes en Afrique: La politique et la ville*, vol. 2, ed. Hélène d'Almeida-Topor, Odile Goerg, Françoise Guitart, and Catherine Coquery-Vidrovitch (Paris: L'Harmattan, 1992), 463–87.

40. Bemba, *Cinquante ans de musique du Congo-Zaïre, 1920–1970*, 88.

41. James, *Nkrumah and the Ghana Revolution*, 82.

42. C. L. R. James, *The Black Jacobins: Toussaint L'Ouverture and the San Domingo Revolution*, 2nd ed. (New York: Vintage, 1963), 18n12.

43. Ibid., 17.

44. Vail and White, *Capitalism and Colonialism in Mozambique*, 351.

45. James, *Nkrumah and the Ghana Revolution*, 50.

46. Frederick Douglass, *My Bondage and My Freedom* (1855; repr., New York: Barnes and Noble Classics, 2005), 61. I comment on this passage in my introduction to the same edition; see Edwards, "Introduction," xxxiv–xxxv.

47. I am thinking of Richard Wright's *Black Power*, where "the faint sounds of drums beating in the distance, the vibrations coming to my ears like the valved growl of a crouching beast" are emblematic of Wright's alienation in Ghana at the inception of independence. In Wright's narrative, music is part of what instills "the unsettled feeling engendered by the strangeness of a completely different order of life." See Wright, *Black Power: A Record of Reactions in a Land of Pathos* (New York: Harper and Brothers, 1954), 46, 37.

48. Paul Niger, "Je n'aime pas l'Afrique," in *Anthologie de la nouvelle poésie nègre et malgache de langue française*, ed. Léopold Sédar Senghor (1948; repr., Paris: Presses Universitaires de France, 1972), 100. The translation is my own. Among the poems in the same volume (often considered the founding anthology of Négritude poetry) that invoke the drum (*tam-tam*), there are Léon-Gontran Damas, "Ils sont venus ce soir" (6) and David Diop, "Celui qui a tout perdu" (174); see also Aimé Césaire, *Notebook of a Return to the Native Land*, trans. Clayton Eshelman and Annette Smith (Middletown, CT: Wesleyan University Press, 2001), 33.

49. Amilcar Cabral, "National Liberation and Culture" (1970), trans. Maureen Webster, in *Unity and Struggle: Speeches and Writings* (New York: Monthly Review, 1979), 139.

50. Ketia Fodeba, "African Dawn," in Frantz Fanon, *The Wretched of the Earth* (1961), trans. Richard Philcox (New York: Grove, 2004), 163–67.

51. Fanon, *The Wretched of the Earth*, 170–80.

52. Ibid., 175–76.

53. David Macey, *Frantz Fanon: A Biography* (New York: Picador, 2001), 378.

54. Fanon, *The Wretched of the Earth*, 176.

55. One could just as easily turn to the African diasporic literary tradition in English: one thinks for instance of the closing pages of George Lamming's *In the Castle of My Skin* (1953; repr., New York: Schocken, 1983), in which the Barbadian Trumper, who has traveled to the United States as a migrant laborer, says that it was his exposure to African American music—above all the spirituals, and specifically Paul Robeson's recording of "Go Down, Moses"—that taught him racial consciousness: that the Negro is "a different kind o' creature," as he puts it (297).

56. See especially Tsitsi Ella Jaji, "Négritude Musicology: Poetry, Performance, and Statecraft in Senegal," in *Africa in Stereo: Modernism, Music, and Pan-African Solidarity* (New York: Oxford University Press, 2014), 66–110.

57. As it is phrased in the poem: "Surprise / When the rhumba and blues bands / In your clubs / Start playing a totally different thing [*vous jouera tout autre chose*] / That the blasé whoring / Of your gigolos and diamond-studded sluts / Weren't expecting." Jacques Roumain, "Sales nègres" (1945), in *When the Tom-Tom Beats: Selected Prose and Poems*, trans. Joanne Fungaroli and Ronald Sauer (Washington, DC: Azul, 1995), 87–89.

58. René Ménil, "The Situation of Poetry in the Caribbean" (modified), in *Refusal of the Shadow: Surrealism and the Caribbean*, trans. Michael Richardson and Krzysztof Fijalkowski (London: Verso, 1996), 129. The original is Réné Ménil, "Situation de la poésie aux Antilles," *Tropiques* 11 (May 1944), collected in Ménil, *Antilles déjà jadis, précédé de tracées* (Paris: Jean-Michel Place, 1999), 121–22.

59. Ménil, "Situation of Poetry," 129–30. Ménil's allusions to jazz in the Antillean context are jarring. In another essay (framed in a direct address to the reader) he evokes "the natural jazz of life" (*le jazz naturel de la vie*) on the island, as though to shock the Martinican reader out of the complacency of the usual categories. Ménil, "Laissez passer la poésie," *Tropiques* 5 (April 1942): 26. In a later essay he describes this as a deliberate strategy: see Ménil, "Sur un certain effet Ellingtonien dans la créolité," in *Antilles déjà jadis*, 257.

60. Frantz Fanon, "Racism and Culture" (1956), in *Toward the African Revolution: Political Essays*, trans. Haakon Chevalier (New York: Grove, 1969), 37. The original is Fanon, "Racisme et culture," *Présence Africaine* 8–10 (June–November 1956): 126.

61. Frantz Fanon, "This Africa To Come" (1960), in *Toward the African Revolution*, 178.

62. Paul Niger, "Initiation," quoted in Jean-Paul Sartre, "Black Orpheus" (1948), in *"What Is Literature?" and Other Essays*, trans. Bernard Frechtman (Cambridge: Harvard University Press, 1988), 320. The original French version of this essay was published as the preface to Senghor, *Anthologie de la nouvelle poésie nègre*, xxxiv.

63. Senghor, "Liminary Poem" (1948), in *The Collected Poetry*, trans. Melvin Dixon (Charlottesville: University Press of Virginia, 1991), 40, 310.

64. Jacques Roumain, "Bois d'ébène" (1939), in *When the Tom-Tom Beats: Selected Prose and Poems*, trans. Joanne Fungaroli and Ronald Sauer (Washington, DC: Azul, 1995), 77.

65. See Penny M. Von Eschen, *Satchmo Blows Up the World: Jazz Ambassadors Play the Cold War* (Cambridge: Harvard University Press, 2006), 58–73; and Ingrid Monson, *Freedom Sounds: Civil Rights Call Out to Jazz and Africa* (New York: Oxford University Press, 2007), 128–33.

66. "Satchmo Blows Up the World," *Drum* (August 1956), 40, quoted in Von Eschen, *Satchmo Blows Up the World*, 61.

67. Léon-Gontran Damas, "Shine," in *Pigments* (1937; repr., Paris: Présence Africaine, 1962), 66–67. The poem is dedicated "pour Louis Armstrong" (and, of course, is titled after one of his recordings).

68. Ngũgĩ wa Thiong'o, *Devil on the Cross*, trans. Ngugi wa Thiong'o (Oxford: Heinemann, 1982). The Gikuyu original is *Caitaani Mutharaba-ini* (Nairobi: Heinemann, 1980).

69. See Ingrid Björkman, *"Mother, Sing for Me": People's Theatre in Kenya* (London: Zed, 1989). Ngũgĩ writes that his work with the community theater represents an "epistemological break" in his writing; see *Decolonising the Mind: The Politics of Language in African Literature* (London: James Currey, 1986), 44.

70. Simon Gikandi, *Ngugi wa Thiong'o* (Cambridge: Cambridge University Press, 2000), 83; Ngũgĩ wa Thiong'o, *Moving the Centre: The Struggle for Cultural Freedoms* (London: James Currey, 1993), 44.

71. Gikandi, *Ngugi wa Thiong'o*, 211.

72. See Christina Pugliese, *Gikuyu Political Pamphlets and Hymn Books, 1945–1952*, Travaux et Documents 11 (Nairobi, Kenya: Institute Français de Recherche en Afrique, 1993). A recent collection that translates selections of these songs into English is Maina

wa Kinyatti, ed., *Thunder from the Mountains: Poems and Songs from the Mau Mau* (1980; repr., Trenton, NJ: Africa World Press, 1990). But see Pugliese's criticisms (87–89) of the way the songs are presented in the Kinyatti anthology. For a historical background, see Pugliese, *Gikuyu Political Pamphlets*, 82ff.; and Marshall S. Clough, *Mau Mau Memoirs: History, Memory, and Politics* (Boulder, CO: Lynne Rienner, 1998), 105. In *Moving the Centre*, Ngugi comments that "both *Kanyegenyūri* and *Mūthīrīgū* are good examples of the culture of the oral tradition as a theatre of anti-colonial resistance, against colonial oppression" (89).

73. Gitahi Gititi, "Recuperating a 'Disappearing' Art Form: Resonances of 'Gicaandi' in Ngugi wa Thiong'o's *Devil on the Cross*," in *The World of Ngugi wa Thiong'o*, ed. Charles Cantalupo (Trenton, NJ: Africa World Press, 1995), 109–27.

74. For examples, see Ngugi, *Devil on the Cross*: songs from Gikuyu orature, 215; contemporary dance songs, 16; Congolese music, 93, 126; verse-chanting competitions, 128–29; love songs, 240–41; and the Muthuu dance song, 137. On the Muthuu, see Brendon Nicholls, *Ngugi wa Thiong'o, Gender, and the Ethics of Postcolonial Reading* (Burlington, VT: Ashgate, 2010), 171.

75. See Ngũgĩ, *Devil on the Cross*: Mau Mau songs, 39, 54, 198; Christian hymns, 151; vernacular spirituals recast as anticolonial songs, 46, 47. As Pugliese explains, many of the Mau Mau songs grafted new lyrics in Gikuyu onto familiar tunes from the Christian liturgy; because so few English colonials in Kenya spoke Gikuyu, the content of the lyrics went unnoticed. As one English commentator of the time wrote, "If they hear a large, or a small, group singing to the tune of 'Onward Christian Soldiers', 'Abide with Me', or any other well-known hymn, they were hardly likely to suspect that propaganda against themselves was going on under their very noses. They would be more likely to consider that a Christian revival was on its way." See L. S. B. Leakey, *Defeating Mau Mau* (London: Methuen, 1954), 54, quoted in Pugliese, *Gikuyu Political Pamphlets*, 86.

76. Ngũgĩ, *Devil on the Cross*, 58.

77. Ibid., 59.

78. Ibid., 59, 224, 132.

79. Ibid., 59. As Ngũgĩ has been arguing in his recent work, "from its very inception, the colony was the real depository of the cosmopolitan." Ngũgĩ wa Thiong'o, *Globalectics: Theory and the Politics of Knowing* (New York: Columbia University Press, 2012).

80. Ngũgĩ, *Devil on the Cross*, 227–30.

81. Ibid., 226.

82. Ibid., 254.

83. Ibid., 39.

84. Ibid., 200.

85. Ibid., 213–14, 233.

86. See Gikandi, *Ngugi wa Thiong'o*, 214.

87. Ngũgĩ, *Devil on the Cross*, 16. This impulse to jump the tracks of medium, as it were—the paradoxical notion that a novel could somehow compel a solitary reader out into the street and into collective performance—could be called the driving aspiration of Ngũgĩ's later work. The paradigmatic scene of this ambition, to my mind at least, is Ngũgĩ's description of the opening-night performance of the 1976 community theater

production *The Trial of Dedan Kimathi*, where at the end of the show the crowd was inspired to join in on the last song, and they followed the actors in a procession that went out of the theater, still singing and dancing as they walked through Nairobi to one of the real historic sites depicted in the play: "What had been confined to the stage had now spilled out into the open air and there was no longer any distinction between actors and the audience." See Ngũgĩ, "Enactments of Power: The Politics of Performance Space," in *Penpoints, Gunpoints, and Dreams: Towards a Critical Theory of the Arts and the State in Africa* (Oxford: Clarendon, 1998), 50–51.

13 · RAP, RACE, REVOLUTION Post-9/11 Brown and a Hip Hop Critique of Empire

NITASHA SHARMA

In response to the demonization of "the Muslim," rappers are using current technologies to create hip hop music that articulates post-9/11 Brown—an antiracist global political subjectivity that critiques empire. Music has indeed played a central role in empire building, as American popular music flows along global circuits to both advance and resist American racism and imperialism.[1] Black popular culture is a lucrative American commodity that fulfills multiple ideological and material aims. Like jazz, hip hop is the music of African Americans who stake racial claims to national belonging. However, it may also be considered imperial race music that has colonized the minds of the American masses and music charts. While many of rap's messages glorify Blackness, those in power have co-opted dehumanizing images to justify the denigrated position of African Americans.[2] The United States exports these commodified products along with its notions of racism, the free market, and democracy through media outlets that extol the rightness of the American way. And yet around the world, from Algiers to L.A., individuals continue to produce anticolonial hip hop that challenges the conditions of their oppression.[3]

Hip hop emerged in the 1970s as a voice of marginalized Blacks and Puerto Ricans in the Bronx in response to government neglect and increasingly unlivable conditions. In the 1990s large record labels wielded their power to shape the tastes of the mostly White masses by backing depoliticized rap music that appealed to a broader demographic. Never fully co-opted by corporate colonization, however, hip hop registered on multiple levels for American youth. Young *desis*, or South Asians within the United States, were among those who embraced hip hop to express their identities, politics, and alliances. They include Indians, Pakistanis, and Sri Lankans who were born in the 1970s and grew up with hip hop in U.S. cities and suburbs in the 1980s, before its mass commodification. Desi DJs and producers found that rap music's analyses explained their confrontations with racism in their predominantly middle-class White neighborhoods and schools. For those who became MCs, rap music emerged in their working-class neighborhoods where they created hip hop culture with Asian and Black peers. In college, this Black expressive form spoke to some desis' growing racial consciousness and they found rhyme to be cathartic and sonically appealing. Their immigrant parents asked them to focus on education, marriage, and economically stable futures. However, desi artists' desire to understand unnamed forces that affected the lives of those around them and their growing understanding of U.S. racial and economic policies drew them to hip hop culture. While some of the featured artists have created hip hop for two decades, the racial politics of the rap game and the political messages in their rhymes limit their exposure and popularity. Now, however, some have found customized global audiences by using new technologies.

From 9/11 to the Arab Spring, individuals across the globe have combined the resistant messages of early rap music with contemporary technologies.[4] The digital revolution has provided artists a greater modicum of control over production and distribution, and they use the Internet to bypass commercial mainstream outlets. The alternative imaginaries that MCs articulate in rhyme travel across the globe through YouTube videos, for instance, and resonate with other casualties of U.S. empire. This essay focuses on the music of desi rappers who critique repressive responses to 9/11 and concludes with rappers of the Arab Spring whose mobilizing rhymes, called the "soundtrack to the revolutions," were broadcast across the world.[5]

Both desi and Arab rappers critiqued political corruption before 9/11 and the Arab Spring, respectively. These rappers are following historical precedent by engaging cycles of racialization and resistance, as hip hop itself was a response by African Americans to their oppression. The creation of "the Muslim" parallels and is distinct from the construction of Blackness. The orientalized figure of the Muslim is centuries old, and 9/11 justified an ongoing racial project that consolidated disparate groups across races, religions, and nations. Arabs, South Asians, Middle Easterners, and other "Muslim-looking" people, including Latinos and Hindus, are lumped into a religious category of terror that compels imperialism abroad and state repression at home.[6] One response has been the articulation of post-9/11 Brown, a pan-racial, cross-religious, and global identification among those who link racism to empire building.[7] This essay focuses on rappers who use new technologies to illustrate the global orientation and critical outlook of post-9/11 Brown.

Hip Hop as Historical/Cross-Racial/Global Excavation

Desi rappers articulate historical, cross-racial, and transnational links among postcolonial communities. If understanding the myriad ways that the U.S. state wields its power within and outside the boundaries of its nation requires a historical contextualization, hip hop offers a method of critical analysis that links the present to the past. Desi rappers inspect the consequences of British colonization, including the Partition of Pakistan and India. Chee Malabar, a 1.5-generation immigrant from Baroda, India, has been writing rhymes and rapping since the 1980s when he arrived in San Francisco. In "Postcards from Paradise," he upends orientalist fantasies of romantic India with a description of a colonial hangover:

> Follow the stark stench of humans, fume and disease,
> Where my peoples get by simply on ritual beliefs,
> It's steeped deep in what the British did before they flee,
> Left more than just English literature, cricket, whiskey and tea;
> Psychological damage, famines, but we managed . . .

These children of English-speaking, educated post-1965 South Asian immigrants—the "beneficiaries" of British colonization—link British and U.S.

empires.[8] Karmacy, from Oakland, California, is a three-man Indian hip hop group with two albums. Their song "Stop" indicts U.S. presidents whose oppressive capitalist practices succeed British colonialism:

> While multinational conglomerate corporations
> Set up exploitation stations in Third World nations
> With the motivation of leaving mass populations
> Facing the devastation of economic starvation
> This is the result of the Reagan administration
> The next generation of British colonization

Using the grammar of rap music to draw historical connections then leads to their alliances across groups that challenge the divide-and-conquer practices of racism.[9] In "Everything" (2002) by Himalayan Project, Chee Malabar raps, "The first son of some immigrants who ain't learn quicker / This land and all in it ain't for niggas, spics, gooks, kikes and sand niggas." This sentiment of overlapping experiences with oppression is echoed in the track "#Jan.25" (referring to the date in 2011 that the protest in Egypt began), created by several U.S. rappers in solidarity with the demonstrators in Egypt.

Amir Sulaiman, a Black American Muslim and a visiting Harvard Fellow, rhymes "won't just be niggas / won't just be spics / a-rabs, pakis, rednecks, and hicks / the leaders ain't helping them feeding their kids." These artists, like Chee Malabar, draw international links between Black and Brown people as members of diasporas resulting from slavery and indentured servitude: "I stalk the stage, gauge my mood; I came from caged slaves in servitude."[10] And bringing it to the present, MC Freeway raps on "#Jan.25" that "black, white, yellow, it don't matter what race," because "different country same struggle we even."

In their premillennial music, desi rappers targeted the hypocrisy of the stated values of the United States. Their analysis of racism and capitalism unearthed overlapping histories between Blacks and South Asians. Critically, they focus on power and processes rather than on defining identity and defending ethnicity, allowing them to shift and expand allegiances with changing conditions. Today, these conditions include the effects of the Wars on Terror, state suppression at home, and the Arab Spring, all of which these artists see as linked by demonization, exploitation, and imperialism. Central to these processes is what Junaid Rana refers to as the racialization of the Muslim, or the "Islamic peril" through which this religious category comes to allude to phenotypes generally associated with "Arab-Middle Eastern

Muslims."[11] "Brown," including Latinos and "Muslim-looking" people, occupies that formerly unnamed space between people who are "identifiably" "White" or "Black." Populations who fall under this rubric are as varied as multiracial people, Latinos, Middle Easterners, North Africans, southern and eastern Europeans, South Asians, and any other number of individuals (including Blacks and Whites) who are racially ambiguous. These are also the various groups historically constructed as "foreign" to the United States, leading to Rana's interpretation of Islamophobia as a form of anti-immigrant racism. Islamophobia and these myriad historical, global, and cross-racial links that result in the oppression against vulnerable groups then become another target of rappers fighting for social justice.

Some individuals use hip hop to develop a pan-racial, global, and cross-religious lexicon against unfettered power, rather than to advance exclusionary identity politics. Their lyrics explicate the reach of empires over time, space, and race. Their research has led numerous artists to claim that powerful leaders are motivated by capitalist greed to oppress the have-nots and justify their hegemony by using the mass media.

The Hypocrisy of Democracy: Politicians, Religion, Media, and Corporate Profit

And it's a mockery,
To call a system a democracy's hypocrisy
When the people that make up the majority
Don't even have the power to challenge the authority
Of the 5 percent elite wealthy minority
That own a 95 percent monopoly over the world economy
Because they own the land,
which is improperly known as property
and will probably always be, since they also control the policies.
Ya feel me?!
—KB of Karmacy, "Stop"

The California rapper KB wrote these lyrics well before the Occupy Movement began, but they share a class-based critique that links capitalism to the failures of America to live up to its democratic ideals. Democracy is presented to Americans to be the antithesis of empire yet, as the outspoken Indian author and anti-dam activist Arundhati Roy states, "Empire is on the move, and Democracy is its sly new war cry."[12] Desi artists agree that "democracy has become Empire's euphemism for neoliberal capitalism."[13] The Canadian-born Indian and White MC ProfessorD.us, who lives in Madison, Wisconsin, raps,

"We don't live in a democracy that's obviously falsity / our polity is properly known as a plutocracy / ruled by a few by the virtue of money."[14]

Another multiracial rapper, Italian and Indian MC Kabir, is the Boston-based son of the Nobel Prize–winning economist Amartya Sen. Kabir's first album, *Cultural Confusion*, includes the eerie-sounding song "Democracy," which explicates the "obvious falsity" of American democracy evidenced by a number of societal ills:

> Destructive like man and his nuclear plan
> To wipe out humanity, unjustified insanity
> It lacks clarity, guns and nationalities
> Combine to cause casualties, politics and fallacy
> These realities are fake like rap ballads be.
> Murder's a normality, war's a mere formality
> A declaration with circumstantial variations
> Wars over religion, politics and prisons

Other desi artists echo Kabir's sentiments in their analyses of the role of Christian dominance at home and as an arm of U.S. imperialism. These MCs are critical of the broad strokes with which the United States has painted Brown people as Muslim fanatics without looking closely at the hypocrisy of Christian fundamentalism. Religious hegemony is of course part of the U.S. government's agenda for replacing ruling tyrants with secular governments in the name of democracy. Rappers point out the religious aims of U.S. military missions abroad and question the division of church and state at home. ProfessorD.us raps in "Devils in Your Government":

> Iran, Iraq or Vietnam they attack and read a psalm
> take this quote it's from David Rovics
> ask "who would Jesus bomb?"

Like academics and other critical thinkers, political rappers provide alternatives to the mainstream media's hidden messages that maintain the status quo. In her compilation of lectures, *An Ordinary Person's Guide to Empire*, Arundhati Roy relates how George W. Bush Jr. laid bare the workings of the United States not only as a nation, but also as an empire: "He has achieved what writers, activists and scholars have striven to achieve for decades. He has exposed the ducts. He has placed on full public view the working parts, the nuts and bolts of the apocalyptic apparatus of the American Empire."[15] Desis align with Roy's critique of the "free press," including mass media outlets that assist in "manufacturing consent" by appearing to be "unbiased" while contributing to Republican campaigns.[16] "Propaganda," declares Noam Chomsky, "is to a democracy what the bludgeon is to a totalitarian state," and this ideological control is enforced primarily through the mass media.[17] The Staten Island–based Pakistani Muslim duo Abstract Vision and Humanity recorded their first album *politrix* when they were still in their teens. It includes a complex track with a simple title, "Media":

> But the news you are exposed to is so far from real
> Islamic terrorism, now Asian Americans is getting killed
> Due to your misconceptions, corrupted government
> Corrupted government pays the media to be oblivious
> How come you never hear the U.S. confess to seeing American terrorists?
> Go to another country and see who causes terror, kid
> Knowledge is the medicine for the eyes, it clears the blood
> The American pride, CNN should stand for Constant Negligence Noted
> Due to imperialism, no one has voted against the government action
> The media's purpose is to allow Americans to gain pride

Abstract/Vision and Humanity's indictment of the media targets the "moderate" news channel CNN for subduing the masses and shoring up patriotic sentiment that ultimately results in death around the world.

These artists use hip hop not just to critique the existing power structures, but also to air alternatives. Hip hop as an alternative media source allows those without access to mainstream channels a vehicle for their views. Chee Malabar says that his rap music is "like a conversation with media" and its flattened "images of Brown people," including the images of Indians in the television show *Outsourced* or in the racist MetroPCS phone advertisements featuring South Asian buffoons, "Tech and Talk."[18] These representations see "South Asia as an emerging market as opposed to a political identity," Chee Malabar says. His music is "a response also to the grainy pixels" of terrorists projected on the nightly news. Through the alternative media source of independent hip hop, political rappers express the three-dimensional humanity of individuals. Rap music, parts of which have always contested the mass media, is never fully co-opted by commodification despite claims to the contrary. And just as the mass media has turned its attention to "the Muslim world," so too have the analytical gazes of these MCs.

A Hip Hop Critique of Empire

They come to profit
Divide and conquer
Breaking great nations
Sake of the father
Their ways are rotten
Throw us the fire
Constantly plotting
Fuck the Empire!
—Abstract Vision and Humanity, "Empires"

The desi rappers that I have known over the past twenty years have always reflected a critical and historical analysis of power and oppression. Their rhymes narrate the paths and pitfalls of immigrants and American minorities who attempt to make a home in the United States. Their lyrics, like rap music in general, incorporate current events through clever references and unearthed connections. With an eye toward tackling racism and tracing the movements of the wealthy elite, it should come as no surprise that the most explicit arm of the U.S. empire—the Wars on Terror—takes center stage in these rappers' minds and current rhymes. Some artists address the state of the nation by occupying the positionality of the threatening foreigner that they are often assumed to be. Black rappers have traditionally taken the identity of the enemy of the (nation) state, as seen in Ice Cube's 1990 album *Amerikkka's Most Wanted* and in Paris's *Sonic Jihad* (2003). Some desi rappers also identify with the American other, whether they represent the resistant masses or repressive forces, as in Himalayan Project's "Eco Location": "No mas has to be your answer / this monster's Hamas sponsored / I really set off bomb songs in concert." Chee Malabar uses rap music as the fiction to flip the power relation between the police and their stop-and-frisk targets:

> Hip hop's Pol Pot gettin' swoll on your whole block,
> Quick, to stop and search cops at their own spots,
> Fo sho hops, this is,
> Bomb music, like the sounds of scuds whizzin'
> Past an Arab's tunic.

These lyrics also switch common notions of terrorists to reveal the tactics of terror the United States employs upon its own citizens. Desi rappers echo Ice Cube and Paris's rearticulations of America's racist fears, as Ice Cube and Da Lench Mob flipped stereotypes of Blacks-as-primates into *Guerillas in tha Mist* (1992). Desi artists highlight the intersection of religion, looks, and terror as "Muslim-looking peoples" become racialized as dangerous beings—and they play with these discourses by rapping from an antinational subjectivity.[19]

The salience of a specifically Muslim and Middle East–inflected Brown identity (whether or not one is Muslim or Middle Eastern) is the latest in a series of shifting racial positions occupied by South Asians in the United States.[20] In the 1970 Census, Indians were classified as White and were reclassified as Asian a decade later. In the 1990s, the popular media depicted model minority professionals and computer geniuses succeeding in an increasingly specialized economy while generally ignoring working-class cab drivers and other service providers. Now South Asians are conflated with West Asians (or Middle Easterners).

But along with shifting imposed racial categorizations, South Asians actively alter their politics and identifications as well. The desi rappers I studied understood the process of racialization and identified beyond the boundaries of prescribed identities, expanding their allegiances depending on the current context. Many of these artists now identify with the sentiments of protesters in the Middle East and North Africa that are captured by Arab rappers and that parallel the ideas among hip hop desis. This perspective—what I call post-9/11 Brown—expressed in the music of some current rappers reflects a broader phenomenon. The artists' songs reflect the political orientation of people across the globe who are racialized as "Muslims" and who wish to hold leaders accountable, identify the trajectories of power and its unequal impacts on communities, and take part in their political futures.

Chee Malabar, who was in New York during the 2000s, responded to the shifting racialization of South Asians by creating a solo moniker, Oblique Brown, in his post-2000 albums. Oblique Brown, he explains, "meant being lumped in with others and what does it mean to be Brown. A lumped social class and education class. On one level I've been asked to [enter through] the service entry. It's assumed that if I came [to a place], that I'm here to deliver food or drop the mail off." In a song of the same name, "Oblique Brown" (2006), Chee describes the post-9/11 Brown experience of those thought to be Middle Eastern who have become the latest target for repression:

If you Black you sell crack, if you Brown you down buildings,
Timmy McVeigh did the same shit,
Y'all killed him
But you ain't trample the rights of your white civilians
Didn't harass 'em or ask 'em for Passports, Visas,
Didn't freeze their assets, no search no seizures

While Bush is up on stage, quotin' Jesus,
While the sons of the slums cuffed up on trumped charges,
'Cause we look different, talk different, labeled as Jihadists

His songs concern themselves with U.S. racial politics, detailing the experiences of multiple communities of color who are subjected to state-sanctioned violence. He contrasts the "exception" of the White terrorist, Timothy McVeigh, as distinct from the racial lumping that associates all Black and Brown people with racialized crimes (drugs and terrorism, respectively) that are used to justify racial profiling and policing. His understanding of racialization takes into account both phenotypical and cultural markers of difference ("we look different, talk different") and highlights the hypocrisy of the U.S. president's religious fundamentalism ("Bush is up on stage, quotin' Jesus").

Such songs identify a Brown identity distinct from Whites, despite assertions that Asians are (or aspire to be) "honorary" Whites.[21] Brown and Black people's overlapping yet distinct experiences with racism in the United States, detailed in these songs, also challenge scholars' assertions that a Black/non-Black dichotomy has replaced Black/White racial logic.[22] Demographics have changed the racial landscape of America, where "Brownness" refers more often to the increasing numbers of Latinos, particularly Mexicans. Global political events over the past decade concerning "the Muslim world," however, have also changed the contours of Brownness in ways that expand beyond and incorporate Latinos. This shift has implications for how non-Blacks and non-Whites conceive of themselves. Thus, whereas within a Black/White model of U.S. race relations, Blackness signified the strongest minority identity, today many individuals embrace the racial moniker of Brownness. The artists featured in this chapter who analyze the racial politics of the post-9/11 era identify as Brown not in order to choose a circumscribed, biological, or essentialist identification, but in order to be part of an expansive congregation rooted in shared politics rather than a shared identity.

According to Chee Malabar, who first articulated this concept to me, "Being Brown is a very post-9/11 thing. It's political. It's not the same as being Black, it's very distinct. People are embracing this idea of being Brown, [at] an intellectual level, at an artistic level." Racialization is both imposed (the denigration of "Blackness"; the racialization of "the Muslim") and is a process with which individuals can engage (Black racial pride; post-9/11 Brown). Post-9/11 Brown is a global identification expressed by these artists but is representative of a broader constituency that links racism at home to imperialism abroad; it highlights racial and religious markers, it incorporates a critique of global capital (of oil in the Middle East, of militarization) and of dominant and false representations. It is not the case that "Brown is the new Black"—these are distinct, simultaneous, and parallel experiences. Chee explains that with the increasing attention paid to Brown people,

> I think people have forgotten what Black people have been experiencing. It has been swept under the carpet. Coupled with education cuts it affects the inner city. The population I work with is completely underserved; people have forgotten they exist. And there's this idea that Black people are doing okay now 'cause there are a lot more Black people on TV and that's where they get their ideas about Brown and Black youth.

Malabar's expansive notion of "my people" emerges from a global race consciousness, which includes the realization that oppression does not have to happen to one's own group for it to be of concern.[23] "I've always been interested in people at the margins," he said. "I always felt that I was in the margins—not to that extent of living in the rubble, but I've always been left out of the conversation." Thus it came as no surprise to me that he had been working on songs related to recent events in the Middle East.

I was nonetheless struck by the volume of songs with themes about the Arab Spring and Muslims produced by this non-Muslim Indian who just earned his U.S. citizenship. Among the unreleased tracks he sent to me were those titled "Al Jazeera," "Hamas Mix," and "Kandahar Cruise (Sunny Sunday)." "Who are we being interpreted [to be]?," he asked me. "How are people looking at us? I understand that. I get lumped in [as Middle Eastern or Muslim] all the time. [My music is] a political reaction to how I'm looked at, so if I'm being identified as that, I want to have a meaningful dialogue about that. If that's how you're going to look at us, fine, but let me be able to break it down." Interested in historical and U.S. racial politics, rappers like Chee insist upon the continuing significance of race that spills outside national borders. Their orientation is global, and they account for the significant trope of the "Muslim," "Arab," or "Middle Easterner," popularly known as the terror suspect. The artists employ essentialism with strategy, taking on stereotypes in their critique of the state. America's armed relations with "the Muslim World" have stoked fears of vengeful foreigners (some of whom may live among us) that were garnered to support the PATRIOT Act.[24]

In light of such administrative power and mainstream consensus, songs may appear to be an ineffective response; however, cultural productions are an arena of individual agency and creation, and they can reflect the sentiments

FIGURE 13.1.
*Burning Tire
Artisan* album
cover. Image by
Daisy Rock-
well; layout by
Ali Abidi.

of a broader, underrepresented public. For instance, rather than distinguishing themselves from Middle Easterners and clarifying their non-Muslim identities, some desis embrace misrecognition and manipulate racial clues. Malabar, for instance, had worn a beard that read as Muslim when he lived in New York and he faced resultant police scrutiny (see figure 13.1). A recent track of his correspondingly highlights his concern over the plight of Muslims.

Inspired by a *New Yorker* cover revealing how immigrants have turned New York into "New Yorkistan," Malabar details the life of a Muslim immigrant boy who faces harassment from multiple directions in "New Yorkstani":

> A young man's education on love and its obstacles
> on the same block where the brothel is,
> where they shop that shit, fresh off pyrex pots with it
> Mama said, "Nothing's impossible . . .
> son it's better than home,
> 'cause where we come from, the sky's lurked by predator drones."
> Home is a tenement drenched in a curry smell
> where all the neighbors laugh and call it a sleeper cell
> 'cause Mom wears a hijab, Pop rocks a Kufi
> young man? Well, the boys call him dookie

sayin' he smells like shit, even dissed by other coolies till he
knocked a few out, now they fear his arm
appears calm but he worries his dear Mom
playin' 50 [Cent] watchin' clips of Amir Khan when
ICE rushed in, tryna deport his mommy,
he yelled, "This is our home! We NewyorkStani!"

The verse depicts a Muslim boy facing harassment from his fellow working-
class neighbors who target his family's cultural ("curry smell") and religious
practices ("Mom wears a hijab, Pop rocks a Kufi"). Deemed unwelcome, the
boy is nonetheless like other Americans influenced by local and global cultural products, from rapper 50 Cent to the British Asian boxer Amir Khan.
When the ultimate arbitrator of nonbelonging (the U.S. Immigration and
Customs Enforcement) attacks his home, the boy is driven to loudly claim
belonging, revealing as the New Yorker did how immigrants have changed
New York into "New Yorkistan."

These cross-religious and cross-national affiliations, some of which are
rooted in choice, require us to expand theories of diaspora that focus on a
shared homeland and ethnicity. Desi rappers participate in "unlikely encounters" that traverse meaningful differences because of their comprehension
that groups are linked by overlapping racialization. While their premillennial
music analyzed U.S. racial politics within a historical and global framework,
changes over the past decade have revealed the prevalence of this expansive
orientation. Rap music, which these artists used as an alternative news source
to link the repression of communities at home with imperial oppression
abroad, is not coincidentally the chosen vehicle of many youth around the
globe to address their rapidly changing world.

"Rap Is Al Jazeera for Brown Folks":
Hip Hop as an Alternative Media Source

New voices and accounts of histories of imperialism are coming to light by
those with alternative narratives of America's place in the world.[25] These
challenges to American exceptionalism reject the paradigms of assimilation,
colorblind and postracial theories, and attempt to account for international relations. A global military force, the United States has created refugees, shaped
the trajectories of diaspora, and fostered competition among groups. However, the conditions shared by people under domination can also lead to their
unity. Music plays a role in these processes of war and resistance, reflecting

and even encouraging political action. Rappers engaged in consciousness-raising deny interpretations of hip hop's political inefficacy. ProfessorD.us proclaims that "the lethal weapon is the mind so they disarm ya / But real Hip Hop has the power to warn ya."[26] Boston's MC Kabir, who tries "to use hip hop as a social tool," also rhymes to encourage people to participate in formal politics: "Change is the only way to pass inspection / Let your voice be heard, people, vote in the election."[27] The role of hip hop in formal and revolutionary politics is particularly evident in its adoption by young Tunisians, Algerians, Syrians, and Egyptians changing their political futures. "Egypt is revolting against the birds of darkness / The people want the overthrow of the regime," state the Egyptian rap group Arabian Knightz. A Libyan MC, Ibn Thabit, addresses his leader:

> The country next door [i.e., Tunisia] chased its president away!
> He said, "I have understood them" after he insulted them.
> Muammar, you have never served your people.
> Muammar, you'd better give up and repent because,
> Muammar, it's impossible to escape[28]

These rappers use a method central to encouraging democratic political action: producing well-researched texts that advance perspectives not provided in the mainstream media.

Proliferating news accounts of Arab hip hop reveal striking similarities with the themes covered by rappers in the United States, including a critical engagement with the mainstream media and government leaders. Malabar was interested in "all these conversations about Al Jazeera being blacked out in the U.S." and wanted to show "that there are other . . . forms of media that are just as legitimate, and [that] Fox, CNN, and MSNBC aren't the only way to get your news." He states, "If hip hop is the CNN for Black folks, as Chuck D said, then rap is Al Jazeera for Brown folks." And he does his part to bring the news through a track titled "Al Jazeera," which features the writer and scholar Amitava Kumar:

> Still live from Al Jazeera, subtitled, grainy pixeled
> voice of Brown, homegrown yet strangely distant
> they can't reconcile my style, speech and my 'staani-tan
> American passport, face like a Taliban
>
> . . .
>
> we young, Brown, and stressed, long noses-hooded eyelids
> articulate, (yeah) with names on No-Fly Lists

but life is hard, why go at it easy?
for the fruits of my labor, peace to Mohamed Bouazizi.

The Syrian American rapper Omar Offendum also frames Al Jazeera as the network showing what is happening on the streets: "I heard 'em say, The revolution won't be televised / Al Jazeera proved 'em wrong," and new technologies relay information firsthand, despite leaders' attempts to silence the masses: "Twitter has him paralyzed, eighty million strong / And ain't no longer gonna be terrorized." In a striking parallel, both Malabar and Offendum end their verses with mention of the harassed Tunisian fruit vendor Bouazizi, whose self-immolation ignited the revolution that ousted President Ben Ali. These songs capture the important role of revolutionary individuals, the news, and technology (including the Internet and smart phones as alternative news sources) in the current moment. While it is unclear whether or not hip hop has increased the mobilization of political participation, it plays an important role in articulating the mood of the people in the quick time that it takes to record and disseminate lyrics, taking on Roy's "urgent challenge" to "expose the corporate media for the boardroom bulletin that it really is. We need to create a universe of alternate information. We need to support independent media."[29]

Oral and visual subaltern representations of politics, race, and war traverse the globe alongside hegemonic representations that reinforce racism and oppression. Youth in the Middle East and North Africa hear and see Americans living in conditions similar to theirs, and they adopt hip hop to articulate their own discontents and desires. The twin exports of false democracy and everyday resistance complicate interpretations of U.S. cultural exports as either purely positive or entirely imperialistic.

Exporting a Voice of Resistance:
Cultural Imperialism, New Technologies, and the Arab Spring

Time magazine labeled the Tunisian rapper El General's song "Rais Lebled," or "Mister President," "the battle hymn of the Jasmine Revolution."[30]

> Mr. President, your people are dying
> People are eating rubbish
> Look what is happening,
> Miseries everywhere, Mr. President,
> I talk with no fear

Although I know I will get only trouble
I see injustice everywhere.[31]

The current commodities of imperialism are unique to this age of "millennial capitalism" through transnational corporations and the digital revolution.[32] Commercial rap music is one form of American cultural imperialism but its less commodified forms are an import selected by the disenfranchised to articulate their resistance to the standing order. El General, the African-identified Tunisian rapper who penned the song "Rais Lebled" that became a "Facebook sensation," says he was influenced by the African American rapper Tupac Shakur.[33] El General's critique of his leaders led to his incarceration and he faced torture, yet he continued to perform his music. The duality of rap's messages parallels the structure of the mass media and new technologies provided by the Internet. "We are independent artists," says Malabar. "The Internet has stripped away all these markers you needed. . . . The Internet has changed the game."

Youth in the Middle East who have sought change have been described as "the Internet Generation . . . or the Facebook Generation . . . or just call them the Miracle Generation."[34] These are the tools used across the globe to communicate, pointing to the multivalent uses of U.S. influences. Malabar says, "Google, Apple, Myspace, Facebook—these are all American companies. So being an imperial power has changed—it's not steel today. There are still some great ideas coming out of America. . . . I can't think of one foreign-based platform or Internet site that's making the same impacts as the American companies. These are the forms that people in Egypt and Libya are using to call for democracy." Lest we criticize an overly resistant interpretation of new media, Malabar is characteristically ambivalent about the Facebook revolution: "It's subtle and insidious, but it's a privacy thing we give up to use the service. Facebook has more information about people than the FBI or CIA, very personal data. So that's a form of American imperialism, [of] cultural imperialism that we export to other countries and that's very real." But for Arab rappers, access to the Internet—specifically YouTube, Facebook, and Twitter—allows instant exposure, changing the options for artists in the Middle East and North Africa where "for the most part there are no managers, no record labels, and there is no copyright on the music."[35] El General says, "When I wanted to have concerts, or if I wanted to sing somewhere and I'd be on the list to perform, the government would be like, 'No, he has a bad name.' I was prohibited from doing anything. No CDs, no anything. So I just put everything on Facebook. Friends edited my videos. It was very simple."[36]

While quantifying the impact of social media on the revolutions is outside the scope of this essay, it has been central to the discussions of the Arab Spring and the transmission of news on the streets to people around the world.[37] The Egyptian Wael Ghonim created a Facebook page, "Kullena Khaled Said" ("We Are All Khaled Said," liked by more than three hundred thousand people), in honor of his fellow countryman who was murdered by police.[38] In his memoir, *Revolution 2.0*, Ghonim, a Google employee, explains that his intention for the Facebook page was to "mobilize public support for the cause" to create awareness about the circumstances of Said's murder.[39] Egyptian security attempted to stifle his online presence but, like Tunisia's El General, Ghonim's time in custody actually advanced his cause. Malabar says, "Technology is moving so fast that so many older regimes don't know what Twitter and Facebook is. These young people are moving so fast with technology and using them in so many ingenious ways that the status quo doesn't know how to rein them in." Similarly, intellectual property lawyers and record-label owners did not know how to keep up with the rapidly changing technologies of hip hop sampling and reproduction in the 1980s.

While the technologies have changed, many of the questions Arab rappers are asking echo those asked by American rappers decades ago. Hamada Ben Amor, aka El General, who like many desi rappers is not from a poor family, says, "The first song I wrote was called 'Malesh?' or 'Why?' It was a big question about why we were in a situation of corruption, thieves and violence," he says. "I was against the regime, because the corruption was really visible to everyone." His perspective and motivation for writing rhymes mirror those of American desis. He says, "The corruption was so pervasive. You went into the street and saw police disrespecting citizens. You went to court and could be discharged from a case, because you could pay a judge, but poor people got put in jail. . . . My parents both have good jobs, and we aren't poor, but I saw injustice for so many of my friends."[40]

Some of the conditions described by El General and others mirror those experienced by the Black creators of hip hop in the 1970s and '80s. While certainly distinct, in both contexts youth faced joblessness and insecure futures, felt oppressed by their governments, and used the most relevant cutting-edge technologies to produce socially relevant art. Ghonim cites a 40 percent unemployment rate in Egypt, while in the United States the "true jobless rate among noncollege black men was a staggering 42 percent" during the economic "boom" in the 1990s.[41] El General says, "The suffering of the people made me speak. And I chose rap to do this," just as his inspiration, Tupac Shakur, used his music to address "the problems that we [Black men] face in everyday society," including "police brutality, poverty, [and] unemployment."[42]

Hip hop is a constantly changing social formation due to its cutting-edge nature, producers' innovative technological capabilities, and evolving social ills. However, hip hop is not wedded to any particular form of technology for its dissemination; rather, it uses available resources to describe the living conditions of its producers. The use of social networking in the Arab Spring is remarkable, but so are the parallels of the messages found in their music with that of hip hoppers in the United States and elsewhere. The founders of Khalas, an organization formed against Gaddafi, noticed the prominence of hip hop in the revolutions. It released a mixtape of rap music emerging from the protests, featuring songs that analyze politics, history, and power, similar to the lyrics of American desis. The Algerian rapper Lotfi Double Kanon (another inspiration of El General's), who had more than one million hits on a YouTube video, addresses a song to the Algerian president. A Khalas cofounder, Abdullah Darrat, translates the message of Lotfi Double Kanon's song:

> He's saying to him, listen, I'm not here swinging swords, I'm not here bringing you gossip from a newspaper, I'm not here trying to set a new fire. I'm here to give you a message, a message from the youth, and our youth sees their future as bleak, and they see that the people standing in power are there because of nepotism or people who are in those positions have bought into those positions. . . . And if you don't do something about that, you're gonna have problems.[43]

Conclusion

On September the 11th, America under the ash
They hit it in the center, shook it and made it look somber
. . .
The devil, already knew what he's up to
His spokesman must be Sir Colin Powell
The pictures appeared black and white on satellite
Showing the training camps of the Talibans
Here's the ransom: Target Afghanistan
Bombardment in seven days
And the mission is accomplished.
The conclusion: don't ask about the results
To avenge the 3,000,

They killed millions
They didn't stop here, the damage's just started
It's the black power of the American empire.
—Lotfi Double Kanon, "America"

Hip hop relays the pulse of the streets and its producers have been expressing themselves by using the necessary means. Desi rappers were articulating
their experiences with racism in the United States before 9/11, and hip hop
youth in the Middle East and North Africa had addressed their leaders well
before the revolutions.[44] Independent hip hop is an emphatically current and
relevant source for learning about the social realities of individuals who have
little access to mainstream media sources that ignore, misrepresent, or de-
monize them. The rhymes of some rappers across the globe speak back to
hegemonic portrayals to reveal the demands and aspirations of a technologically adroit generation. The digital revolution has enabled a wider and faster
dissemination of individual narratives that counter the top-down stories re-
layed through mainstream networks.

Mainstream media is a form of "controlling images" that relays hegemonic
notions of race, including stereotypes of the inferiority of Blacks and the
danger of Islam. The racialization of "the Muslim" has historical roots, but
this process has sped up over the past decade. In response, people around
the world have created counterimages that engage these fallacious flattened
representations and replace them with three-dimensional ones. Post-9/11
Brown is one such response: a political subjectivity that connects the historical analysis of racism to a critique of empire. This essay featured those who
use hip hop to articulate this global and political orientation.

The revolutions in the Middle East came as a surprise to many, including
those who are focused on corrupt leaders and extremist Islam. Neglected
were the lives of everyday people who are young and unemployed and who
engage Islam routinely rather than radically.[45] They record their own experiences in real time (rather than the delayed time it takes for scholarly
publications), which they disseminate through available technologies. If the
big question is "what's next?" for countries that have recently deposed their
rulers or what issues future generations will tackle, the answer may well be
heard in the music of those everyday cultural workers engaged in the world
around them. We can be sure that it is music that will relay to the world their
future victories and disappointments, and it is through them that hip hop
and social change continue to breathe.

1. See Ronald Radano and Philip Bohlman, eds., *Music and the Racial Imagination* (Chicago: University of Chicago Press, 2000).

2. T. Denean Sharpley-Whiting, *Pimps Up, Ho's Down: Hip Hop's Hold on Young Black Women* (New York: New York University Press, 2007).

3. Tony Mitchell, *Global Noise: Rap and Hip-Hop outside the USA* (Middletown, CT: Wesleyan University Press, 2002); Dipannita Basu and Sidney Lemelle, eds., *The Vinyl Ain't Final: Hip Hop and the Globalization of Black Popular Culture* (London: Pluto, 2006).

4. I would like to thank a number of interlocutors who were (and have always been) generous with their time and ideas: in addition to Ronald Radano and Teju Olaniyan, the conveners of the Music-Race-Empire conference, and my coparticipants, I wish to thank Ana Croegaert, Su'ad Khabeer, Jinah Kim, and Vijay Prashad for their helpful comments.

5. Neil Curry, "Tunisia's Rappers Provide Soundtrack to a Revolution," *CNNworld.com*, March 2, 2011, http://www.cnn.com/2011/WORLD/meast/03/02/tunisia.rappers.balti/index.html; Colin Christopher, "Soundtrack of the Revolution," *Inside Islam: Dialogues and Debates*, February 23, 2011, http://insideislam.wisc.edu/2011/02/soundtrack-of-the-revolution/.

6. Junaid Rana, *Terrifying Muslims: Race and Labor in the South Asian Diaspora* (Durham: Duke University Press, 2011); Sunaina Maira, *Missing: Youth, Citizenship, and Empire after 9/11* (Durham: Duke University Press, 2009).

7. Nitasha Sharma, *Hip Hop Desis: South Asian Americans, Blackness, and a Global Race Consciousness* (Durham: Duke University Press, 2010).

8. Joan Jensen, *Passage from India: Asian Indian Immigrants in North America* (New Haven, CT: Yale University Press, 1988); Bill Ong Hing, *Defining America through Immigration Policy* (Philadelphia: Temple University Press, 2004).

9. Gary Okihiro, *Margins and Mainstreams: Asians in American History and Culture* (Seattle: University of Washington Press, 1994); Vijay Prashad, *Everybody Was Kung Fu Fighting: Afro-Asian Connections and the Myth of Cultural Purity* (Boston: Beacon, 2001).

10. Himalayan Project, "Nuthin Nice."

11. Rana, *Terrifying Muslims*, 7, 48.

12. Arundhati Roy, *An Ordinary Person's Guide to Empire* (New Delhi: Penguin, 2005), 144.

13. Ibid., 155.

14. "Devils in Your Government," *Third World Warriors, Vol. 1*, 2008.

15. Roy, *An Ordinary Person's Guide to Empire*, 134.

16. Ibid., 156.

17. Noam Chomsky, "On Propaganda," *Chomsky.Info*, January 1992, http://www.chomsky.info/interviews/199201—.htm; Edward Herman and Noam Chomsky, *Manufacturing Consent: The Political Economy of the Mass Media* (New York: Pantheon, 2002).

18. Chee Malabar, interview by author, March 14, 2011. All quotations from Malabar in this essay, unless noted as song lyrics, are from this interview.

19. Irum Sheikh, *Detained without Cause: Muslims' Stories of Detention and Deportation in America after 9/11* (New York: Palgrave Macmillan, 2011).

20. Indians have tussled with U.S. racial classifications since their presence in the United States, as seen in the 1923 *United States v. Bhagat Singh Thind* case, which ruled that, contrary to reigning scientific ideas, Indians were indeed non-White and therefore were ineligible for citizenship. See Susan Koshy, *Sexual Naturalization: Asian Americans and Miscegenation* (Stanford, CA: Stanford University Press, 2005).

21. George Yancey, *Who Is White? Latinos, Asians, and the New Black/Non-black Divide* (Boulder, CO: Lynne Rienner, 2003). See Eduardo Bonilla-Silva and David Embrick, "Black, Honorary White, White: The Future of Race in the United States," in *Mixed Messages: Multiracial Identities in the "Color-Blind" Era*, ed. David Brunsma (Boulder, CO: Lynne Rienner, 2006).

22. Jennifer Lee and Frank Bean, "Reinventing the Color Line: Immigration and America's New Racial/Ethnic Hierarchy," *Social Forces* 86, no. 2 (December 2007): 561–86.

23. Sharma, *Hip Hop Desis*.

24. Centre for Contemporary Cultural Studies, *The Empire Strikes Back: Race and Racism in 70s Britain* (London: Routledge, 1982).

25. Brian Edwards and Dilip Gaonkar, eds., *Globalizing American Studies* (Chicago: University of Chicago Press, 2010).

26. "Devils in Your Government."

27. "Just Me," *The Time Is Now*, 2010.

28. Translation from "Ibn Thabit—The Question," *Revolutionary Arab Rap: An Index*, August 27, 2011, http://revolutionaryarabraptheindex.blogspot.com/2011/08/ibn-thabit-question.html. This website also has a list of Arab MCS.

29. Roy, *An Ordinary Person's Guide to Empire*, 168.

30. Bobby Ghosh, "Rage, Rap and Revolution," *Time*, February 17, 2011, 32.

31. For a video with English subtitles, see www.youtube.com/watch?v=IeGlJ7OouRo.

32. Jean Comaroff and John Comaroff, *Millennial Capitalism and the Culture of Neoliberalism* (Durham: Duke University Press, 2001).

33. Christopher Weingarten, "Meet Hamada 'El General' Ben Amor, the Tunisian Rapper Who Changed the World," *Pop Dust*, January 28, 2001, http://popdust.com/2011/01/28/meet-hamada-el-general-ben-amor-the-tunsian-rapper-who-changed-the-world/; Lauren Bohn, "Rapping the Revolution," interview with Hamada Ben Amor, *Middle East Channel*, July 22, 2011, http://mideast.foreignpolicy.com/posts/2011/07/22/rapping_the_revolution.

34. Hassan Nafaa quoted in Ghosh, "Rage, Rap and Revolution," 34.

35. Cordelia Hebblethwaite, "Is Hip Hop Driving the Arab Spring?" *BBC News*, July 24, 2011, www.bbc.co.uk/news/world-middle-east-14146243.

36. Bohn, "Rapping the Revolution."

37. For more on the debate over the role of technology in social change, see Hani Morsi, "Social Media in the Middle East: Is It a Real Tool for (Incremental) Change, or Merely Cathartic Self-expression?," *HaniMorsi.com*, August 2, 2010, www.hanimorsi.com/blog/index.php/archives/2010/08/02/social_media_in_the_middle_east/; and "The Virtualization of Dissent: Social Media as a Catalyst for Social Change (Part One: Why

Gladwell Is Wrong)," *HaniMorsi.com*, February 15, 2011, http://www.hanimorsi.com /blog/index.php/archives/2011/02/15/the-virtualization-of-dissent-social-media-as-a -catalyst-for-social-change-part-one-why-gladwell-is-wrong, his response to Malcolm Gladwell's article in the *New Yorker Magazine*, "Does Egypt Need Twitter?," February 2, 2011, www.newyorker.com/online/blogs/newsdesk/2011/02/does-egypt-need-twitter .html.

38. Wael Ghonim, *Revolution 2.0: The Power of the People Is Greater Than the People in Power: A Memoir* (Boston: Houghton Mifflin Harcourt, 2012).

39. Ibid., 67.

40. Vivienne Walt, "El Général and the Rap Anthem of the Mideast Revolution," *Time*, February 15, 2011www.time.com/time/world/article/0,8599,2049456,00.html.

41. Michelle Alexander, *The New Jim Crow: Mass Incarceration in the Age of Color-blindness* (New York: New Press, 2010), 217.

42. "On the Line with . . . 2Pac Shakur, the Lost Interview," *Davey D's Hip Hop Corner*, February 10, 2012, www.daveyd.com/interview2pacrare.html.

43. Brooke Gladstone, "North Africa's Hip Hop Protest Music," *On the Media from* NPR, February 11, 2011, www.onthemedia.org/transcripts/2011/02/11/02.

44. Regarding Cairo's Arabian Knightz, "'Since the revolution, you will hear a lot of our music and think we wrote it about what is happening. But we had actually written that four years prior, calling for what happened to happen,' said Hesham Abed, who goes by the stage name Sphinx." See Ty McCormick, "Egypt's Revolution Rap Goes Viral," *SFGate*, February 7, 2012, www.sfgate.com/world/article/Egypt-s-revolution-rap -goes-viral-3090061.php.

45. Thomas Soloman, "Hardcore Muslims: Islamic Themes in Turkish Rap between Diaspora and Homeland," in *Muslim Rap, Halal Soaps, and Revolutionary Theater: Artistic Developments in the Muslim World*, ed. Karin van Nieuwkerk (Austin: University of Texas Press, 2011).

14 · ECHO AND ANTHEM Representing Sound, Music, and Difference in Two Colonial Modern Novels

AMANDA WEIDMAN

It is the noise, the noise, the noise, the noise which sucks one into a whirlpool, from which there is no re-emerging. The whole of what one understands by music seems lost forever, or rather seems never to have existed.—E. M. FORSTER

The tongue of the foreigner will not reach there where the rasa of my own language flows.
—RABINDRANATH TAGORE

Whether imagined as a force that threatens one's understanding of and bearing in the world, or constructed as a realm carefully protected from outside influence, the aural is a contested domain in the context of the colonial modern. In this essay I address the ideological work done by aurality in the context of novelistic portrayals of colonial modern India in the first decades of the twentieth century. In discourse and novels of this period, tropes of aurality, as in the above epigraphs, are used to portray unbridgeable gaps between affective/aesthetic orientations toward the world and epistemological understandings of it. Evoking incommensurable difference, these tropes serve as a powerful way to figure racialized distinctions between "India" and "the West" and between colonizer and native.

These tropes are prominently at work in two now-classic novels that chronicle the last days of the British Empire and the emergence of Indian nationalism: E. M. Forster's *A Passage to India*, published in 1924, and Rabindranath Tagore's *The Home and the World*, published in 1919.[1] While both of these novels have elicited many critical readings that probe their complex portrayals of the gendered and raced dynamics of the colonial encounter and the nationalist movement in India, none do justice to what I find to be their most striking characteristics: their consistent use of aural imagery and their evocation of a soundscape through references to noise, music, communication and sound reproduction technologies, and spoken language.[2] Music and sound serve as more than atmospheric detail in these novels; they are the elements that propel the stories and the very ground on which racial difference is established. Both of these authors position themselves as listeners, and it is through this listening to what lies outside or beyond the visual field that they are able to tell their stories. By attending to the soundscape Forster and Tagore create in these novels, I harness the study of literary representation to a broader concern with the act and cultural consequence of listening.[3]

The aim of this essay is to situate ideas about aurality as they emerged and were elaborated within the colonial modern: a late colonial context influenced by nineteenth-century discourses about sound and noise, the technological modernity of the early twentieth century, and the cultural and political context of Indian nationalism. Both Forster and Tagore were writing in a moment that brought together orientalist portrayals of India, colonial institutions and structures of power, and modern technologies of image and sound reproduction—as well as the transformations in visuality and aurality that they enable. As listening subjects, these authors responded to colonialist portrayals of the disordered Orient as a realm in which the aural/oral holds sway, but they were also distinctly part of a twentieth-century discourse network in which new technologies of sound reproduction made it possible to collect, replay, and juxtapose competing sounds.[4] In these novels, Forster and Tagore enable us to hear music and noise alongside each other as mutually constitutive entities that shape and are shaped by the broader dynamics of empire. The realm of the aural here is more than a secondary reflection of social and political dynamics—it is itself a force that has social and political consequences.

Representations of sound, in these novels, are fundamentally about class and race hierarchies and about the clash of whole systems of value, as characters—and authors—make their passage between India and the West. Forster presents the aural as standing for what is uncolonized—indeed, uncolonizable—about India. Sound is out of sync with the visual world; it haunts, rather than accompanies, the visual world of colonial order and colonial desire. Sound—echoing, braying, banging, crooning, thrumming—threatens the effectiveness of the colonial gaze and the integrity of the colonial subject. But it also prevents any sort of collectivization into a national anthem; sound defies the ordering impulses of both colonialism and nationalism. In Tagore's novel, aurality dominates; the absence of visual imagery is striking. There is no third-person narrator to "set the scene" as in Forster; rather the novel is set in the alternating, and competing, first-person voices of the three main characters. Aural imagery, particularly music, is used as an index of inner state; the different subject positions of these three characters are articulated precisely through their different relationships to music. And yet, as in Forster's novel, there are uncanny and unsettling noises that come from outside: from the echoing cries of the anthem "Bande Mataram" from masses of young men who repeat it without realizing its effects, to the mechanical repetition of shrill Calcutta actress voices on the gramophone.

Situating Aurality

Within western modernity, aurality has frequently been positioned in the realm of the premodern or the nonmodern—as that which escapes or somehow lies outside of modernity's visually grounded regimes of knowledge-power. This opposition between visuality and aurality has been naturalized and universalized in a set of seemingly commonsense contrasts that the media theorist Jonathan Sterne has termed the "audio-visual litany": hearing "immerses" us in the world, while vision removes us from it and affords a perspective; hearing is about affect while vision is about intellect. These are often taken as natural, biological facts about the senses.[5] Scholarship showing how these notions developed in particular historical moments has challenged the assertion that such contrasts are universal and transhistorical.[6] However, by remaining largely within the confines of metropolitan locations, such works miss the way in which the audiovisual litany was elaborated in the context of colonial modernity. The mapping of contrasts between visuality and aurality not only onto the modern and the nonmodern, but also onto the West and the non-West, have served as a powerful means of naturalizing these contrasts. It was precisely because the difference between visuality and aurality came to be understood in terms of racial difference that it became so readily available as a way of describing and justifying differences between colonizers and colonized others. As others in this volume suggest, the circulation of racialized ideas of musicality—the notion of natives possessing "natural" musicality or as being especially susceptible to arousal by music—was a pervasive aspect of empire's discursive network of representation. The colony—particularly India—was often perceived as a realm of excessive sensuality, the power of which colonizers sought both to control and appropriate.[7]

In the context of such ideas, it is perhaps not surprising that one of the foundational texts of twentieth-century media theory, Marshall McLuhan's *Understanding Media*, used *A Passage to India* to illustrate what he saw as the incommensurability of the visual and the aural, "a dramatic study of the inability of oral and intuitive oriental culture to meet with the rational, visual European patterns of experience . . . [whose] reasoning powers cannot cope with the total field of resonance that is India."[8] Importantly, McLuhan registered a connection between this experience of being overwhelmed by sound and the nonvisual, and the experience of mass media; he saw in India's orality/aurality not only the past of western culture but also a harbinger of its technologically mediated future, calling *A Passage to India* "a parable of Western man in the electric age."[9]

Colonial Aurality: Sound, Order, and the Other

Colonial constructions of aurality were colored by Victorians' fascination with and repulsion by the power of sound. Sound figured in writings and laws as excessive, something that had to be controlled or confined. In his study of Victorian experiences of aurality, John Picker argues that in the course of the nineteenth century, sound and hearing were transformed from what the Romantics had conceived of as a sublime experience of the wild and intangible into a quantifiable and marketable object or thing. The nineteenth century gave rise to the electric telegraph and the microphone, the telephone and the phonograph, as well as other apparatuses, all of which were "means to make manifest and manipulate formerly intangible, unruly vibrations"—these were the means "by which sound ostensibly was disciplined and made concrete by the end of the century."[10]

Accompanying these technological attempts to discipline and concretize sound was a discourse about noise—what constituted it, who made it, and how to control it. Chronicling the anti–street music laws in 1840s Britain, Picker writes that the street music "noise" problem was linked to the lower classes and often figured as a problem of "foreign infestation" by male writers seeking to shore up their identity as bourgeois subjects. The "soundproof study," which so many of these writers desired, became a figure for bourgeois interiority and privacy that was constantly being threatened by the noise that could invade it from all sides. Street music was represented as a "lawless other" to real music, "a threatening double to the respectable concert or drawing-room recital."[11] By the 1880s, however, following the middle-class exodus to the suburbs, this once-demonized street music—now heard at an appropriate distance—was romanticized, portrayed nostalgically, and appropriated and aestheticized in literary representations.[12] Whether it was demonized or aestheticized, street music remained a potent symbol of class and racial otherness.

Noise as cultural and racial other, as threat to order: these were ideas that operated not only in the metropole but the colonies as well. Colonial order was based on visibility. As Timothy Mitchell has shown in the context of colonial Egypt, colonial regimes at their height relied not on physical force or coercion but on the power of surveillance, the panoptic power of a gaze that was all-seeing while remaining itself invisible.[13] To be ordered, things had first to be made visible and mapped, gridded, exhibited, rendered legible. But sound and music were important as well in the signification of colonial power. The imperial durbars of the late nineteenth and early twentieth centuries—pageants that displayed and celebrated British rule—relied on the "overwhelming buildup of sound, color, and texture" to create a performative spectacle that showcased the ordered and ordering power of the British Empire.[14]

"Noise" as a category was elaborated both in general parlance and in legal discourse in the British Empire. In colonial Ceylon, this led to the Police Ordinance of 1865, which banned the playing of music in Hindu and Buddhist processions outside Muslim places of worship. The ordinance specifically defined the beating of tom-toms, a type of drum played in Buddhist religious processions, as "noise" that would "disturb the sleep of the neighbors" and that was not conducive to proper worship. "Even when the tom-tom was viewed more benignly as part of native exotica, its penetrating and disordering capacities intruded on the British mentality as a symptom of that which was uncultured and ill-disciplined."[15] The control of "noise," therefore, became "an integral dimension of the British regime, as pertinent as the control of crime and disease."[16] In India as well, "noise" came to be defined specifically as any "religious insult"—including music and virulent speech—that threatened the fragile peace between religious communities.[17] The "music before mosques" phenomenon, in which music was both a precipitating factor of Hindu-Muslim riots and a form of political action or violent retaliation in itself, was a widespread phenomenon in India in the nineteenth century and into the first decades of the twentieth century. Through these riots, musical practice became a point of differentiation between Hindu and Muslim communities; it was endowed "with a particular kind of power in terms of how colonial subjects forged consequential political relationships with each other."[18] Music, refigured as "noise" in the British colonial imaginary, was at once associated with disorder and with the irrational religiosity and communal rage of the natives.

The aural more generally was associated with a kind of power that could overwhelm if not checked. Modes of aural and oral communication, with their capacity to evade or circumvent colonial governance, were particularly important in the history of peasant insurgency in colonial India.[19] The drum, the flute, and the horn, as instruments used for the aural transmission of insurgency, "formed a class apart from verbal media in that they . . . acted as a surrogate of human speech, . . . [permitting] the decoding of messages directly rather than through linguistic symbolism."[20] In the second half of the nineteenth century, aural transmission among the natives was treated as a potent form of rebellion, resulting in a generalized ban on the use of musical instruments for gathering people together.[21] Similar to these instruments that produced sound without an identifiable source or author, capable of traveling great distances, Ranajit Guha suggests, was another mode of aural transmission: rumor.[22] Through their intimate but anonymous aural/oral transmission, rumors could grow, combine, and transform with a seemingly uncontrollable force.[23]

Aurality and Technological Modernity

The tropes of aurality in *A Passage to India* and *The Home and the World* should be read in the context of this colonial imaginary, but, as novels written in 1924 and 1919, respectively, they also operate within the context of early twentieth-century technological modernity. Sound recording and radio, as well as the industrialization that occurred in the early twentieth century, produced a host of new noises and new discourses about sound and noise. In the first half of the twentieth century, in many European and North American cities, noise-abatement campaigns arose in response to urban industrialization. The battle against noise was represented in these campaigns as civilization and refinement versus barbarism.[24] Antinoise campaigners suggested that the "visualization" of city life—an increase in visible signs and lights—would decrease the levels of noise.[25] Blaming a host of medical and psychological problems on noise, writers during this period emphasized the vulnerability and fragility of the ear in comparison with the eye.[26] Modernity was imagined as a noisy assault on the writer's sensibility. Noise's imagined ability to penetrate the borders of both the body and the home constituted it as a threat to interiority in both the psychological and the physical senses.[27]

The power of industrial noise and mechanically reproduced sound was not conceived only in negative terms, however; it was also productive of a new literary consciousness. Friedrich Kittler has suggested that technologies of sound recording, by displacing writing's monopoly on memory, transformed ideas about music and literature after 1900. Sound recording made possible a focus on the sonic qualities of language that writing could not register. It produced a new awareness of noise as the constitutive outside of speech and music: the possibility that music and speech might spring from and return to noise, the constant background against which anything "meaningful" must be distinguished.[28] Technologies of sound reproduction also produced a fascination with voices and sounds disembodied from their originary sources.[29] Postphonographic literature explores the possibilities of voices and sounds amplified, multiplied, and circulated by technological means, even, as Ivan Kreilkamp suggests, when these technologies are not an explicit or central subject of the story.[30]

In the second and third decades of the twentieth century, when technologies of sound reproduction were no longer new but had become more established, literary production and colonial discourse began to focus not only on the disorienting possibilities of these technologies, but also on their potential to create new forms of order and new modes of control. Rudolf Mrázek points to the central role that sound reproduction and sound broadcasting played in the late colonial modern context of the Dutch East Indies, where radio was imagined as blocking out the disruptive sounds of local politics and substituting orderly sound and music within the "soundproof walls of the house."[31] The tropes of aurality running through *A Passage to India* and *The Home and the World*, which also spring from this late colonial modern context, can be read as a means of grappling with what sound might mean and to what political projects its power could be harnessed.

Echo

E. M. Forster was fascinated by the power of the aural. Forster himself was deeply interested in music, and he played the piano quite seriously. Music and sound figured prominently both as a theme and a technique of his prose; the composer Benjamin Britten called him "our most musical novelist."[32] Forster was also interested in the possibilities of technological modernity;

between 1929 and 1960, he made regular radio broadcasts on a variety of topics for the BBC.

A short story from 1909, "The Machine Stops," foreshadows Forster's interest in the aural.[33] The story describes a technological dystopia, in which all human life is linked to and made possible by the Machine. The main character, Vashti, like all humans, lives isolated in her room beneath the surface of the earth, and the Machine provides light, darkness, music, lectures, and the images and voices of others at the touch of a button. "Above her, beneath her, and around her, the Machine hummed eternally; she did not notice the noise, for she had been born with it in her ears." When the Machine gradually stops working, noises start interrupting the music and defective rhymes emerge from the poetry machine; Vashti realizes she has lost contact with others since she no longer hears their applause at her lectures, only silence. At the end of the story, the Machine stops providing light and aurality takes over, as Vashti and her son are left crying out for each other in the darkness among the "whispers" and "whimpering groans" of dying fellow humans.

The dystopic aurality of "The Machine Stops" is echoed in Forster's later writings on India. Forster made two trips to India, first in 1912–13, and then again in 1921, when he served as the private secretary to Sir Tukoji Rao III, the Maharaja of Dewas, a princely state in what is now Maharashtra. He recorded his impressions of this time in letters, in which the overwhelming presence of "noise"—singing and the music and clamor associated with Hindu religious festivals—is on almost every page. Forster described the palace in which he lived as a place full of "warped pianos and broken telephones," where instruments meant to discipline and order sound are unusable and silent, in contrast to the constant and overwhelming noise of the festivals outside. Describing the celebration of Gokul Ashtami, the birthday of the god Krishna, in his letters of 1921, Forster wrote, "There are no smells, and . . . no bugs. It is the noise, the noise, the noise, the noise which sucks one into a whirlpool, from which there is no re-emerging. The whole of what one understands by music seems lost forever, or rather seems never to have existed." For Forster, "noise" was a lack of meaning, a failure to communicate; the word itself signified the outside of both music and language. Instead of leading toward meaning, it proliferated only itself: "noise, noise, noise, noise." Noise defied the certainty of representation by sucking the hearer in, by destroying the validity of his categories and his ability to sense things through other channels.[34]

Forster's attention to the audible dimensions of late colonial modernity, in fact, allowed *A Passage to India*, his final and most famous novel, to be perceived as a realistic portrayal of the problems of "the blending of races" in the colonial encounter when it was published in the early 1920s. "More remarkable even than his vision," stated a review from 1924, "is Mr. Forster's power of inner hearing. . . . Dr. Aziz strikes one as less invented than overheard."[35] Alongside this clarity of representation is Forster's interest in probing the point at which representation fails—when vision and communication break down, when voices speak without being visibly attached to speakers, when noise overwhelms music.[36]

Noise is fundamentally at the heart of A Passage to India: a noisy aurality that interferes with both communication and vision. Frustrated vision is a trope that runs throughout the novel, permeating its opening scene, in which Forster describes the "monotonous" quality of everything that "meets the eye" and the lack of perspective afforded to the viewer.[37] Even the sun affords no light by which to see. "The sun was returning to his kingdom with power, but without beauty. . . . Through excess of light, he failed to triumph . . . ; in his yellowy-white overflow not only matter, but brightness itself lay drowned."[38] Adela Quested's repeated expression of her desire to "see the real India" is frustrated not just because of her social situation, but also and more primarily, Forster implies, because the real India is something that cannot be seen. India, rather, is a multiplicity of mouths or voices that whisper, entreat one vaguely and mysteriously to "come," or "fuss and squabble tiresomely."[39]

It is only on their passages out of India that Adela and Fielding experience "clarity," "harmony," and the distinctively visual pleasure of the "joys of form."[40] The description of Mrs. Moore's departure most strikingly evokes the aurality of India and the return to a visual, cartographic perspective accomplished by traveling away from its shores: "thousands of coconut palms appeared all around the anchorage and climbed the hills to wave her farewell. 'So you thought an echo was India; you took the Marabar caves as final?' they laughed. 'What have we in common with them, or they with Asigarh? Goodbye!' Then the steamer rounded Colaba, the continent swung about, and the cliff of the ghats melted into the haze of a tropic sea."[41] The "hundred voices" that are India have the last word in the novel as well, as they proclaim "no, not yet" and "no, not there."[42] The figure of the disembodied voice here evokes an India that is somehow beyond the reach or control of the colonizer, and the multiplicity of these disembodied voices and their capacity to emanate from inanimate things—the caves, the palm trees—evoke the context of technological modernity as well, what Kreilkamp has called "the sound of the mechanistic universe."[43]

In addition to frustrating vision, the aurality Forster depicts powerfully disrupts communication. Indian music, as sung by the enigmatic Professor Godbole early in the novel, embodies such disrupted, or frustrated, communication. It begins with partial comprehension: "His thin voice rose, and gave out one sound after another. At times there seemed rhythm, at times was the illusion of a Western melody." But this almost-understanding gives way to confusion and disorientation: "the ear, baffled repeatedly, soon lost any clue, and wandered in a maze of noises, none harsh or unpleasant, none intelligible. It was the song of an unknown bird. Only the servants understood it. They began to whisper to one another."[44] The music defies structure, notably the visual structure of western notation: "The sounds continued and ceased after a few moments as casually as they had begun—apparently half through a bar, and upon the subdominant."[45] Godbole's explanation of the song's meaning reveals it as a song that is—at least for his western audience—fundamentally *about* frustrated communication: "I say to Shri Krishna, 'Come! come to me only.' The god refuses to come. . . . This is repeated several times. . . . I say to Him, 'Come, come, come, come, come. He neglects to come."[46] Indian music is used here to signify incommensurability, the feeling that Indians and westerners may speak to each other but will never understand each other. There is a sense of language that hangs in the air without reaching its intended recipient. "India calls 'come' through her hundred mouths, through objects ridiculous and august. But come to what? She has never defined. She is not a promise, only an appeal."[47]

Godbole's singing foreshadows a more powerful, and even more disorienting, aurality: the echo of the Marabar caves. The echo, as a means by which one's own utterances are returned in distorted form without being heard, is par excellence a figure of frustrated communication; indeed, the echo *prevents* communication from taking place by substituting another kind of exchange, one that is outside the logic of language, that "does not depend on human speech."[48] The aural here is represented as infinitely more powerful than the visual, for the hills are unbeautiful, "dead and quiet" on the outside. But as soon as one enters their dark "mouth," one is subject to their laws; their reflecting walls produce strange visual effects and an echo so powerful that all sound is reduced to "boum": "whatever is said, the same monotonous noise replies. . . . Hope, politeness, the blowing of a nose, the squeak of a boot, all produce 'boum.'"[49] Meaning, communication, social distinctions: all these are lost in the caves, which reply indiscriminately and condemn all utterances and thought to oblivion. "If one had spoken vileness in that place, or quoted lofty poetry, the reply would have been the same—ou-boum."[50] "'Let there be light' only amounted to 'boum.'"[51] The echo propels the plot forward by changing Mrs. Moore and Adela. Unhinged by the terrifying infinity and meaninglessness the echo presents, Mrs. Moore loses interest in life while Adela becomes disoriented to the point that she convinces herself that Dr. Aziz has assaulted her. The echo continues to haunt her: it "flourished, raging up and down like a nerve in the faculty of her hearing, and the noise in the cave . . . was prolonged over the surface of her life."[52]

Adela's accusation sets the colonial machinery in motion, and a trial ensues—one in which noise is central. The trial is nearly derailed by the crowd of natives chanting the name of Mrs. Moore, who, because she is thought to be friendly to Aziz's cause, has been made into a goddess. Like the indiscriminately repeating echo in the caves, the crowd with its "wide-open mouths" drowns out the proceedings with its echoing, distorted version of Mrs. Moore's name: "esmiss esmoor, esmiss esmoor": "People who did not know what the syllables meant repeated them like a charm."[53] The natives have become a technology of sound reproduction. Language is reduced to mere sound, distorted and repeated as though by mechanical reproduction. The echo is a symbol both of India's ancient mystery and of technological modernity. "Everything echoes now; there's no stopping the echo," thinks Fielding, reflecting on the present. "The original sound may be harmless, but the echo is always evil."[54]

In the final section of the book, Forster makes numerous references to the "throbbing" noise, the "thrum and tumtum," the darkness, rain, and confusion during a Hindu festival. "Music there was, but from so many different sources that the sum-total remained untrammelled. The braying banging crooning melted into a single mass which trailed round the palace before joining the thunder."[55] The European band playing western melodies is drowned out amid such noise. The invisibility of the god among the things used to worship him, and the banners hung where nobody can read them, points to the lack of visual logic. In the midst of this is a small banner that reads, "by an unfortunate slip of the draughtsman," 'God si Love.'" Frustrating communication, noise and the senseless repeating of mantras make a travesty of language itself. Like the instruments of technological modernity (as Kittler argues), the natives reveal language to be only a combination of signs meaningless in themselves, reducing the previously assumed "wholeness and centeredness" of language to a "scatter of differential marks," showing that "all sense making has its frontiers (and therefore its definition) in domains of nonsense and in automatized operations that no longer belong to a subjective authority."[56]

While sound defines "India" in Forster's work, India does not define itself through sound. Sound, figured as noise, as rumor, or as incomprehensible music, is always excessive—it disrupts communication, and, more important, it is portrayed as preventing the establishment of any sense of personal subjectivity or national collectivity. And so, when Aziz sits down toward the end of the novel to compose an anthem for India, he is at a loss. "He longed to compose a new song which should be acclaimed by multitudes and even sung in the fields. In what language shall it be written? And what shall it announce?"[57]

Anthem

Rabindranath Tagore, a Bengali novelist, poet, essayist, musician, artist, and composer of anthems, was a contemporary of Forster's, known for his numerous works of prose and poetry and for a corpus of songs in Bengali that came to be known as *rabindrasangeet*. Tagore participated in a discourse, prevalent in the first decades of the twentieth century, about the essential difference between the "East" and the "West," actively placing himself and his works in the context of ideas about what "Oriental wisdom" could offer to rejuvenate the spiritual life of an overly technologized and materialistic "West."[58] Tagore took seriously his role as a cultural and spiritual ambassador, "carrier of the Eastern Light" to the unhappy West, traveling to Europe and America to lecture numerous times between 1912 and 1930.[59] He translated or assisted with the translation of many of his own Bengali works into English himself (including *The Home and the World*), and he also wrote numerous books and essays in English.[60]

Tagore was also steeped in a nationalist discourse about music that shared the more general assumptions of an opposition between eastern spiritualism and western materialism. In an essay titled "European Music," which Tagore included in his book *My Reminiscences*, Tagore described European music as "intertwined with its material life," while "our tunes . . . transcend the barriers of everyday life . . . their function being to reveal a picture of the inmost inexpressible depths of our being."[61] The performance of an operatic soprano in Brighton, for Tagore, embodied the western materialist focus on the "outward perfection" and embellishment of the voice, a misguided emphasis on the technological perfection of the vehicle rather than on the substance, on the singing voice rather than the song itself. European singing, especially female operatic voices, seemed to him in particular "a misapplication of the human voice," "as good as a circus," and, invoking a technological metaphor, "like the disembodied lament of a forlorn spirit."[62] For Tagore, music was more than simply an example of the incommensurability of East and West; it was the very ground of that incommensurability. "I am convinced that our music and theirs abide in altogether different apartments, and do not gain entry into the heart by the self-same door."[63]

As for Forster, for Tagore music was a prominent part of his prose, thematically and as a technique. Musical terminology and metaphors pervade his writing; his characters describe their feelings in musical terms; nature, love, and woman are all identified in his writings with and through music.[64] Dipesh Chakrabarty has written that for Tagore prose and poetry/music served two very different purposes: while the prose of fiction was seen as intimately connected to questions of political modernity, to portrayals of social injustice and inequality, poetry and music for Tagore were distanced from the political; they "pictured the Bengali home/village as a place blessed with divine grace and beauty."[65] Tagore insisted on keeping the two realms distinct; as he wrote in a letter to a friend who had asked him to write a poem about Africa, "the tongue of the foreigner will not reach there where the rasa of my own language flows."[66] Tagore used both his poetry and his songs to capture what he defined as "the Bengali heart."[67] Music and poetry, for Tagore, took one out of the world, the contemporary here-and-now, into the realm of the eternal, the transcendental. In an analysis of Tagore's prose poem "The Flute" (1932), Chakrabarty argues that Tagore used musical imagery to "pierce the veil of the real": to dissolve the realist gaze and transport readers to another state of mind in which the visual recedes and the song takes over.[68] Although Chakrabarty describes these as two "ways of seeing," a reading of "The Flute" suggests that sight is not privileged in the same way in each mode.[69] The concrete visual detail of the first part of the poem is entirely disrupted by the entry of the sound of the flute, which introduces an altered state of perception that flourishes "where the song is true."[70]

This elaboration of poetry and song in Tagore's imaginary is apparent in *The Home and the World*, a work of prose that is nevertheless filled with references to poetry, music, and sound in general. Originally published serially in the Bengali avant-garde literary journal *Sabuj Patra* in 1915–16 as *Ghaire Baire*, the novel was later translated into English partly by Tagore himself.[71] It was controversial and received criticism from Hindu revivalists who objected to the "adulterous passion" of the heroine, which was thought to be inappropriate for a Hindu housewife; after its English publication, Tagore's critical portrayal of the Swadeshi movement prompted several critics to accuse him of insufficient nationalist sentiment.[72]

The confusion and excitement of Indian nationalist awakening is made audible in Tagore's prose through the profusion of different voices and sounds that play with and against one another. In the novel, Bimala, the wife of a wealthy landowner in rural Bengal, is caught up in a nationalist awakening that eventually destroys her home and forces her to move to Calcutta. She wavers between two men—her husband, Nikhil, cautious, highly educated, and critical of the Swadeshi movement, and his friend, Sandip, a fiery, passionate nationalist—and the novel alternates among their three voices. For all three characters, music provides a metaphor for self. For Bimala, this self is closely bound up with the home. Remembering her mother working in the kitchen, she recalls, "Her service would lose itself in a beauty which passed beyond outward forms. Even in my infancy I could feel its power. It transcended all debates, or doubt, or calculations: it was pure music."[73] Here, music comes to stand for what is traditional, or habitual, untouched by time, history, or change, located in a protected inner realm—a familiar refrain of Indian nationalist discourse.

At the end of the novel, plunged into regret for her actions, Bimala entreats God: "O Lord, sound once again those flute strains which you played for me long ago . . . and let all my complexities become simple and easy. Nothing save the music of your flute can make whole that which has been broken, and pure that which has been sullied. Create my home anew with your music."[74] For what has happened in the interim is that Bimala has been swept away by the "triumphant shouts" of the nationalist movement, embodied in the repetitive cry of the anthem "Bande Mataram" ("Hail Mother" in Bengali) that echoes through the novel.[75] Bimala describes the nationalist awakening as a "flood" of sound that causes her to lose her former self.[76] But although she is captivated by Sandip ("this flesh and blood lute of mine found in him a master player"), she finds herself frustratingly dumb: "Why does not my voice find a word, some audible cry, which would be like a sacred spell to my country?"[77]

The contrast between Nikhil and Sandip is elaborated as the difference between music cultivated as art and music as a release of passion. Late in the novel, as Nikhil sees that things will not be able to remain the same, he invokes western art music as a way of escaping the circumstances: "It had become an absolute necessity for me . . . to feel that this life of mine had been able to strike some real, responsive chord in some other harp of life."[78] But Sandip ridicules Nikhil's interest in western art music and his belief in harmony as a moral concept.[79] "Now that a full flood of music has swept over our country, let Nikhil practice his scales, while we rouse the land with our cracked voices," says Sandip.[80] In Sandip's eyes, passion is the mark of a truly modern subject, and its signifier is music. His voice, deep and husky and "threaten[ing] to be out of tune," is what persuades Bimala to go along with his plans.[81] " 'I want!' Sandip went on one day. This was the primal word at the root of all creation, ... the force which will rush forward with the roar: 'I want!' "—a roar that will clear up what Sandip calls the "hideous confusion" of music that characterizes India.[82]

Amid this world of music, song, and poetry, fleeting images of technological modernity play important roles. Nikhil, in the moment that he becomes disillusioned with Bimala, says, "I could see everything relating to Bimala as if vividly pictured on a camera screen ... and an anthem, inexpressibly sweet, seemed to peal forth from this world, where I, in my freedom, live in the freedom of all else."[83] The camera, a symbol of objective knowledge, stands in for the clarity of emotion, purpose, and allegiance ostensibly invoked by a national anthem. But other images of technological modernity carry a more sinister meaning. As the novel's action rises to a climax, the mounting anticipation and confusion of the atmosphere are evoked through references to aural overload: "Rumour became busy on every side."[84] Bimala, busily working in the kitchen, no longer hears the "music" of her mother's home but is instead distracted by sounds from outside: "Every now and then it seemed to me that there was some noise in the direction of my rooms, upstairs. . . . No, I must not pay heed to those sounds. Let me shut the door."[85] In this atmosphere of anxiety and chaos, the maid interrupts:

> "The Bara Rani mother wants you. . . . Her nephew brought such a wonderful machine from Calcutta. It talks like a man. Do come and hear it!"
>
> I did not know whether to laugh or cry. So, of all things, a gramophone needs must come on the scene at such a time, repeating at every winding the nasal twang of its theatrical songs!
>
> What a fearsome thing results when a machine apes a man.[86]

The gramophone "let[s] loose the shrill treble of the Calcutta actresses all over the place."[87] It *is* Calcutta, the world, modernity, and it shatters the conventions of respectable womanhood and social hierarchy that those categories imply. Ironically, perhaps, it is the Bara Rani, Bimala's sheltered sister-in-law who has never set foot outside the house since she entered it as a child bride, who introduces the gramophone. Making its incongruous appearance just before Bimala and Nikhil are forced to leave for Calcutta, the gramophone powerfully disrupts the world of music and sonic metaphor that Tagore has built up; its music drowns out that other world. As an instrument of domestic musical entertainment, it is the very opposite of the music that Bimala recalls when she thinks of her mother's domestic labors. The gramophone represents the possibility of music from a public, rather than a private, domestic source, and it is also music from an inhuman source; its capacity for repetition is powered by mechanical means rather than by nationalist sentiment. Like rumors, the sounds that issue from the gramophone proliferate without being controlled by a speaking or singing subject.

Conclusion

If Forster's central aural trope is the echo, Tagore's is its apparent opposite, the anthem. While the echo is uncontrolled, unintentional, proliferating without cohering, and subjectless, the anthem is controlled, intentional, collective, and is supposed to articulate both the nation-as-subject and the position of subjects *within* the nation. But both novels play with and disturb these distinctions. For Tagore, the anthem has gone awry, echoing forth from uncontrollable and irrational crowds, while for Forster the "senseless repetition of mantras" seems to give crowds a collective force and direction but one that, crucially, bypasses—and radically undercuts—individual subjectivity. Reading these novels together allows us to see them as part of a larger discourse in which invocations of aurality, in the form of music, sound, noise, or voice, are used to signify both incommensurable difference and a power that always remains out of reach, never reducible to a single political project.

The intertwined tropes of echo and anthem that emerge from auditory readings of these novels draw attention to the agentive aspect of musical circulation within the larger history of empire. Widely read in their time and since, these novels functioned as technologies of circulation, not of music or sound itself but *through* them of ideas and conceptual categories. For it is on the strength of musical and sonic imagery that these novels produce ideas about racial difference, the East and the West, and the human dimensions of the colonial encounter. Investing the aural with a peculiar kind of power to produce competing affects and allegiances, these novels articulate it as a primary site of anxiety and struggle within colonial modernity.

1. E. M. Forster, *A Passage to India* (1924; repr., San Diego, CA: Harcourt, 1985); Rabindranath Tagore, *The Home and the World* (1919; repr., Madras: Macmillan India, 1992).

2. The aural imagery in *A Passage to India*, particularly the echo, has received some attention, if not full focus, in several works of criticism concerned with literary modernism and imperial desire. See, for instance, Timothy Christensen, "Bearing the White Man's Burden: Misrecognition and Cultural Difference in E. M. Forster's *A Passage to India*," *Novel: A Forum on Fiction* 39, no. 2 (2006): 155–78; Gail Fincham, "Arches and Echoes: Framing Devices in *A Passage to India*," *Pretexts* 2 no. 1 (1990): 52–67; Benita Parry, *Delusions and Discoveries: Studies on India in the British Imagination, 1880–1930* (Berkeley: University of California Press, 1972); and Kelly Sultzbach, "Embodied Modernism: The Flesh of the World in E. M. Forster, Virginia Woolf, and W. H. Auden" (PhD diss., University of Oregon, 2008).

3. I thank Ronald Radano and Tejumola Olaniyan for this way of conceptualizing the project I undertake here.

4. Friedrich Kittler, *Discourse Networks 1800/1900*, trans. Michael Metteer with Chris Cullen (Stanford, CA: Stanford University Press, 1990).

5. Jonathan Sterne, *The Audible Past: Cultural Origins of Sound Reproduction* (Durham: Duke University Press, 2003), 15.

6. See Jonathan Crary, *Techniques of the Observer: On Vision and Modernity in the Nineteenth Century* (Cambridge: MIT Press, 1990); and Sterne, *Audible Past*.

7. Tim Barringer, "Sonic Spectacles of Empire: The Audio-Visual Nexus, Delhi-London 1911–12," in *Sensible Objects: Colonialism, Museums, and Material Culture*, ed. E. Edwards, C. Gosden, and R. Phillips (Oxford: Berg, 2006), 172.

8. Marshall McLuhan, *Understanding Media: The Extensions of Man* (New York: McGraw-Hill, 1964), 15.

9. Ibid., 16.

10. John Picker, *Victorian Soundscapes* (New York: Oxford University Press, 2003), 10–11.

11. Ibid., 63.

12. Ibid., 79.

13. Timothy Mitchell, *Colonising Egypt* (Berkeley: University of California Press, 1988).

14. Barringer, "Sonic Spectacles of Empire," 172.

15. Michael Roberts, "The Imperialism of Silence under the British Raj: Arresting the Drum," in *Exploring Confrontation: Sri Lanka: Politics, Culture, and History* (Switzerland: Harwood Academic, 1994), 151.

16. Ibid., 175.

17. Naveeda Khan, "A Particular Genealogy of the Azan," paper presented at the American Anthropological Association meetings, November 2000, San Francisco, 2; Julian Lynch, "Music and Communal Violence in Colonial South Asia," *Ethnomusicology Review* 17 (2012).

18. Lynch, "Music and Communal Violence," 1.

19. Ranajit Guha, *Elementary Aspects of Peasant Insurgency in Colonial India* (Durham: Duke University Press, 1999).

20. Ibid., 228.

21. Ibid., 231.

22. Ibid., 259.

23. Ibid., 261. It is just such a force that is invoked in the title of the Dutch writer Louis Couperus's 1900 novel about the Dutch East Indies, *The Hidden Force*, in which the "hum" and "murmur" of rumor eventually undo the colonial master who fails to hear it. In Couperus's novel, as in the British colonial imaginary, the aural is the realm of the uncontrollable. Louis Couperus, *The Hidden Force*, trans. A. Texeira de Mattos (1900; repr., Amherst: University of Massachusetts Press, 1985).

24. Karin Bijsterveld, "The Diabolical Symphony of the Mechanical Age: Technology and Symbolism of Sound in European and North American Noise Abatement Campaigns, 1900–40," in *The Auditory Culture Reader*, ed. M. Bull and L. Back (Oxford: Berg, 2003).

25. Ibid., 171.

26. Michael Cowan, "Imagining Modernity through the Ear: Rilke's *Die Aufzeichnungen des Malte Laurids Brigge* and the Noise of Modern Life," *Arcadia* 41, no. 1 (2006): 131.

27. Ibid., 138–39.

28. Kittler, *Discourse Networks*.

29. Ivan Kreilkamp, *Voice and the Victorian Storyteller* (Cambridge: Cambridge University Press, 2005), 182–83.

30. Ibid., 184.

31. Rudolf Mrázek, *Engineers of a Happy Land: Technology and Nationalism in a Colony* (Princeton, NJ: Princeton University Press, 2002), 163–70.

32. Nicola Beauman writes that Forster "spent many hours playing [the piano]. . . . He went to concerts whenever he could. In his later years he listened to the gramophone. And he incorporated music into his novels, to such an extent that he was to be called by his future friend Benjamin Britten 'our most musical novelist': from the opera scene in *Where Angels Fear to Tread* to the description of Beethoven's Fifth Symphony in *Howards End* to the more subtle musical imagery of the trial scene in *A Passage to India*, in all three and in the other novels music, as Morgan himself put it, would be 'deep beneath the arts' and beneath his life." See Beauman, *Morgan: A Biography of E. M. Forster* (London: Hodder and Stoughton, 1993), 162.

33. E. M. Forster, *"The Machine Stops" and Other Stories* (1947; repr., London: Andre Deutsch, 1997).

34. E. M. Forster, *The Hill of Devi* (New York: Harcourt, Brace, 1953), 114, 163.

35. "*A Passage to India* by E. M. Forster," *Guardian*, June 20, 1924, accessed July 28, 2013, www.guardian.co.uk/books/1924/jun/20/classics.

36. For more on the failure of representation in Forster, see Christensen, "Bearing the White Man's Burden."

37. Forster, *A Passage to India*, 3–4.

38. Ibid., 124.

39. Ibid., 12, 150, 239.

40. Ibid., 314.

41. Ibid., 253.

42. Ibid., 362.

43. Kreilkamp, *Voice and the Victorian Storyteller*, 203.

44. Forster, *A Passage to India*, 84.

45. Ibid., 85.

46. Ibid.

47. Ibid., 150.

48. Ibid., 137.

49. Ibid., 163.

50. Ibid., 165.

51. Ibid., 166.

52. Ibid., 215.

53. Ibid., 250.

54. Ibid., 307.

55. Ibid., 318–19.

56. David Wellerby in Kittler, *Discourse Networks*, xxx, xxxix.

57. Forster, *A Passage to India*, 298.

58. Nabaneeta Sen, "The 'Foreign Reincarnation' of Rabindranath Tagore," *Journal of Asian Studies* 25, no. 2 (1966): 281.

59. Stephen Hay, "Rabindranath Tagore in America," *American Quarterly* 14, no. 3 (1962): 439.

60. Sen, "The 'Foreign Reincarnation,'" 284.

61. Rabindranath Tagore, *My Reminiscences* (New York: Macmillan, 1917), 191.

62. Ibid., 190.

63. Ibid., 191.

64. Sitansu Ray, "Tagore on Music and Musical Aesthetics," *Sangeet Natak Akademi* 56 (1980): 20, 34.

65. Dipesh Chakrabarty, *Provincializing Europe: Postcolonial Thought and Historical Difference* (Princeton, NJ: Princeton University Press, 2000), 152–55.

66. Quoted in ibid., 161.

67. Ibid., 153.

68. Ibid., 150–51, 166.

69. Ibid., 149–50.

70. Tagore, quoted in ibid., 167.

71. *Sabuj Patra* (Green leaves) was an avant-garde literary journal that sought to "jolt" or "shock" its readers. Tagore contributed many short stories to the journal, which, like the journal more generally, focused on women's choices and desires. See Pradip Kumar Datta, "Introduction," in *Rabindranath Tagore's "The Home and the World": A Critical Companion* (London: Anthem, 2005), 8–9.

72. Jayanti Chattopadhyay, "Ghaire Baire and Its Readings," in *Rabindranath Tagore's "The Home and the World*," 187–204; Sumit Sakar, "Ghaire Baire in Its Times," in *Rabindranath Tagore's "The Home and The World*," 143–73.

73. Tagore, *The Home and the World*, 10.

74. Ibid., 254.

75. "Bande Mataram" is the opening of a poem composed by Bankimchandra Chatterjee, the Bengali poet and novelist and figurehead of the nationalist movement, in 1875. It became the rallying cry of the Swadeshi movement in 1905, as a protest against the British partition of Bengal and against British economic domination and exploitation of India. The poem was set to music by Rabindranath Tagore. Tagore sang it at the 1896 convention of the Indian National Congress. Bose Records/Pathé recorded Tagore singing it in 1907. See Suresh Chandvankar, "Vande Mataram: A Most Popular and Evergreen Indian Song," *Musical Traditions* 195 (2003), accessed September 11, 2013, www.mustrad.org.uk/articles/mataram.htm.

76. Tagore, *The Home and the World*, 56.

77. Ibid., 82, 92.

78. Ibid., 267.

79. Ibid., 169.

80. Ibid., 118.

81. Ibid., 214.

82. Ibid., 96–97, 101–2.

83. Ibid., 142–43.

84. Ibid., 250.

85. Ibid., 251.

86. Ibid.

87. Ibid., 252.

15 · TONALITY AS A COLONIZING FORCE IN AFRICA

KOFI AGAWU

The modern musical world is not really imaginable without the musical results of colonialism. —BRUNO NETTL

Colonial administrators and their allies, the European missionaries, condemned everything African in culture—African names, music, dance, art, religion, marriage, the system of inheritance. —ADU BOAHEN

Colonial education was a series of limitations inside other limitations. —WALTER RODNEY

[The] ideological premises [of colonial education] obliged its agents to have recourse to texts, images, and other modes of discourse and representation that devalue the humanity of their dark-skinned wards, as parts of the effort to establish the cultural and moral authority of the colonizing race. —ABIOLA IRELE

Tonality, understood as a hierarchically organized system of pitch relations animated by semitonal desire, accompanied Europe's ostensibly civilizing mission to Africa from the 1840s onward.[1] Stabilized earlier in the works of composers like Corelli, Bach, Handel, Vivaldi, and their contemporaries, tonality is typically expressed by a key-defining impulse. When we speak of a symphony "in G minor" or a sonata "in F major" or a concerto in "B-flat major," we are acknowledging the existence of a ruling tonic-dominant polarity as well as degrees of relatedness with and among the remaining members of the work's triadic universe. Different theorists explain the process differently. The expression of a sense of key may involve cadential punctuation of varying strengths, temporary departures from "home" for purposes of contrast and also to enhance—or indeed intensify—the desire for return, or a multileveled unfolding of the tonic triad as both linear and vertical configurations. These differences notwithstanding, many would be inclined to agree with Brian Hyer that "tonality is perhaps best conceptualized as a *tertium quid* that integrates melody, harmony and metre into a single nexus."[2] It remains the most influential system of pitch organization in western Europe since the early eighteenth century.[3]

That such a central and resilient resource played a role in the network of exchanges and impositions that defined European colonialism in Africa should come as no surprise. Church music, choral anthems, and light music for dancing and entertainment, all of them tonal, enhanced, or even defined civic and religious life in communities in Sierra Leone, Ghana, Togo, Nigeria, Uganda, Kenya, Zambia, Tanzania, Malawi, and South Africa, among other places. A ready example and perhaps *the* iconic marker of the kind of tonal thinking exported to Africa is the Protestant Christian hymn. Figures 15.1 and 15.2 show the familiar hymn "My Jesus I Love Thee, I Know Thou Art Mine" along with its importation into the Ewe hymnal ("Nye Yesu Melɔa Wo, Be Tɔnye Nenye").[4] The extraordinary popularity of hymns like this and hymn-based compositions throughout Africa stems from both their message and music. Hymns carry messages about Christian living; they comfort those in distress, reinforce ties with an all-powerful God, and offer enticing glimpses of the better life that awaits the faithful in the hereafter. Vehicles for delivery of these messages include simple poetic forms (typically quatrains featuring end rhymes), vivid imagery, and memorable or quotable lines. Hymn tunes are conveniently placed within the normal registers of male and female voices so that they can be easily learned and remembered by congregations. Typically diatonic, hymn phrases are arranged with a clear expressive profile (*aaba* in the case of "My Jesus I Love Thee," where *a* is a presentational phrase that returns to perform a recapitulatory and closing function, and *b* is the contrasting and at the same time intensifying phrase). They are harmonized using the primary chords of the tonal system (tonics, dominants, and subdominants, or their functional substitutes), cadence frequently, and thus display only modest trajectories of tonal thought.

Leaving aside the religious message, this collection of attributes frequently entails a series of reversals from indigenous African expression, musical as well as linguistic. Hymns introduced by Protestant missionaries in the nineteenth

FIGURE 15.1. A. J. Gordon, "My Jesus I Love Thee."

century typically came in a standardized four-part texture (SATB) that no African group had ever used before. They were clothed in a prosody that few Africans would have recognized, including poetic meters with syllabic counts like 8.7.8.7 (as in the lyrics "The king of love my shepherd is" or "Love Divine, all loves excelling") and 11.11.11.11 (as in the lyrics "My Jesus I love Thee, I know Thou art mine" or "Immortal, invisible God only wise"), and they displayed a rhyme scheme that is difficult to achieve in indigenous tone languages. Finally, in domesticating hymns whose texts were originally in German or English for local consumption, melodies often disregarded the natural declamation of indigenous singing, imposed a regime of regular and symmetrical periodicity, and rode roughshod over the intonational contours prescribed by speech tones.[5]

FIGURE 15.2. "Nye Yesu Melɔa Wo," the Ewe version of figure 15.1.

All of this amounts to musical violence of a very high order, a violence whose psychic and psychological impacts remain to be properly explored. To be sure, the collective practices associated with the African reception of the Protestant hymn served both colonizer (the encountering society) and colonized (the encountered society) alike. For the colonizer, they were a means of exerting power and control over native populations by making them speak a tonal language that they had no chance of mastering. (The European tonal language of which hymns were a part underwent various forms of chromatic enrichment in the course of the nineteenth century, but few of these "progressive" developments reached African musicians operating within a hymn economy.) Limited and limiting, the language of hymns, with its reassuring cadences and refusal of tonal adventure, would prove alluring, have a sedative effect, and keep Africans trapped in a prisonhouse of diatonic tonality. For the colonized, on the other hand, hymn singing was a passport to a new and better life; it was a way of "speaking" a new language, one that was moreover introduced by self-announced enlightened Europeans; it promised access to some precious accoutrements of modernity and eventually a place in heaven.

Hymn-based tonality has by now spread throughout Africa, encompassing a wide variety of musical forms and genres. In urban popular music from highlife to hiplife, afrobeat to *soukouss*, and *mbaqanga* to *benga*, chord progressions are often anchored by a tonic-dominant polarity.[6] In the realm of art music, itself another (direct) response to the European heritage, and one in which tonal experimentation is normal, black African composers have generally preferred the relative security of closed tonal forms to the uncertainties and insecurities of post-tonal expression.[7]

Understanding the *why* of these developments would entail looking into a complex of factors: some of them material and economic, some political, some educational, and all mediated by the movement of global capital, for it appears that tonality has always followed the movement of global capital.[8] Indeed, as Nettl notes in one of the epigraphs to this essay, one can hardly imagine the modern musical world "without the musical results of colonialism." But the exportation and importation of tonality are topics too big to be dealt with adequately in a short essay like this. What I would like to do, instead, is paint a stark portrait of African tonal thinking before and after contact with Europe as a step toward future theorization of the dynamics of musical colonization. We know that colonial assaults on Africa through spoken language (French, English, and Portuguese, principally) and religious expression (Islam and Christianity, principally) have already claimed tens of millions of casualties. Relatively little has been said about parallel developments in the area of musical colonization, however. One reason is ontological: the variety of music's modes of existence, including its essence as a performed art, the centrality of its aesthetic function, and the complex trajectories of transmission, influence, and ownership all present challenges to arguments suggesting a denial of sovereignty or the domination of individual or group consciousness in the sonic realm.

Another reason is institutional: the discipline that traditionally houses research on African music is ethnomusicology, but ethnomusicology itself is a child of colonialism, a discipline rich in colonial filiation and affiliation. As one of its leading practitioners concedes, "Colonialism and its cultural outcroppings have been a major and, indeed, indispensable factor in the development of ethnomusicology (at least as practiced in North America and Western Europe)."[9] Another warns that "where ethnomusicology loses sight of its complex and thorny historical complicity with colonialism, it reproduces its myths."[10] Ethnomusicology's richly diverse research programs are yet to give pride of place to a systematic interrogation of the effects on African psyches of having to speak a foreign or European tonal language. Embrace of such projects would demand both a practical and political commitment; it would also entail an honest critique of the very foundations of the discipline. This is not to suggest that no voices have ever been raised in opposition to western tonal influence in Africa. A. M. Jones, himself a missionary, devoted a chapter to what he called neofolk elements in his groundbreaking book *Studies in African Music*, while Michelle Kisliuk has recently sided with the BaAka pygmies against the missionary efforts of the Grace Brethren Church in the Central African Republic.[11] And the literature on southern African music (by Veit Erlmann, Christine Lucia, and Martin Scherzinger, among many others) includes helpful discussions of Africans' consumption of western tonal products and systems, including the diatonically biased learning system associated with tonic solfa.[12] It is fair to say, however, that there is simply no equivalent in Africanist ethnomusicology to Frantz Fanon's *Black Skin, White Masks*; Albert Memmi's *The Colonizer and the Colonized*; or Walter Rodney's *How Europe Underdeveloped Africa*—all works that address the forms, content, and, especially, psychological impact of colonial-imperial influence in Africa.[13] Indeed, nowadays, the sometimes uncritical appropriation of tropes of hybridity—uncritical insofar as they pass over in silence the losses, indignities, and humiliation suffered by people who are forced to speak other people's musical languages instead of their own—together with a principled resistance to essentialism have effectively muted discussion of *transformations in consciousness* wrought by the tonal forms exported to Africa.[14]

I have assembled a few recorded performances in order to lay bare the sonic environments that might support the argument that tonality has functioned as a colonizing force in Africa. I will address these in three stages. First, by means of a simple show-and-tell strategy, I acknowledge a few obvious traces of tonality (citing examples from South Africa and Ghana). Second, stepping back from the present, I draw attention to salient features of the (imagined) sound of precolonial Africa, the African soundscape before tonality arrived (these examples are from Gabon, Ghana, the Central African Republic and the Republic of Benin). Third, returning to the present, I consider three imaginative responses to European tonality, attempting—indirectly— to answer the question, What does it mean to compose under a tonal regime?

(These last examples are from Nigeria and Ghana.) It should be emphasized that for every one of the aural texts cited here, there are literally hundreds of others that essay similar tonal courses. So, although geocultural reference is, for the sake of convenience, limited to six African countries (Nigeria, the Central African Republic, South Africa, Gabon, Benin, and Ghana), a much larger set of examples could easily have been cited from both live performances and recordings.

Finally, I recognize that colonialism is too complex and profound a historical phenomenon to be reduced to a few local signs, and it cannot be analyzed by means of hasty or knee-jerk reactions. Nevertheless, if—as I believe—we are a long way from restoring sovereignty to Africans in the spheres of politics, language, religion, and music, then there may be some point to making a programmatic and symbolic argument.

Traces of Tonality in African Music

Ladysmith Black Mambazo, an all-male a capella group from South Africa, has over the years produced a popular repertory that labors under tonal rule. Collectively, Ladysmith's tonal experience is wide and varied, ranging from hymnlike original compositions through the folk-inflected harmonies of Paul Simon's *Graceland* to the sometimes chromatic harmonies of Mozart's "Ave verum corpus."[15] The beginning of their song "Paulina" will serve as an example.[16] Here are the opening lines, each of which finishes on tonic harmony:

> Paulina, Paulina, somebody's crying for you.
> You, Paulina, somebody's crying for you.
> Paulina, why did you leave him alone?
> Now, he asked me to call you
> I looked for you all over.
> You were nowhere to be found.
> Please, Pauline, come back to him
> He loves you, he wants to marry you
> Get away from those who want to touch-touch and kiss-kiss
> Thereafter they leave you alone.

What kind of tonal thinking is on display here? We never leave the home key; the sound of the tonic predominates, and the interstices are weighted toward the subdominant rather than the dominant. The absence of half cadences, important agents for the arousal of tonal desire, confers on the song as a whole a somewhat flat trajectory. Indeed, repeating harmonic cycles (I-IV-I) are made to bear various semantic weights in the expression of text. The same tonic freight accompanies questions ("Why did you leave him alone?"), statements ("You were nowhere to be found"), entreaties ("Please, Paulina, come back to him"), and warnings ("Get away from those who want to touch-touch and kiss-kiss"). This apparent lack of alignment between semantic sense and tonal meaning is, however, not an exception but rather the rule in the global aesthetics of song. Ladysmith's way of enriching the tonal palette is to invoke a not-so-distant pentatonic horizon and to hint at the microtonal realm through the use of glissandi on phrases like "*call* you" and "he *loves* you." There are no large trajectories of tonal thought here, just repetitions of a single progression. What keeps listeners engaged, however, is the asymmetry that results from the additive patterning of harmonic cycles. This pedal-like function serves to channel a Christian-tinged message about what boys do to girls. A simple diatonic base rules throughout.[17]

A second example of the reception of tonal harmony comes from the brass-band tradition found throughout the continent and also in diasporic communities in Bolivia, Peru, Suriname, and Jamaica. Brass bands are associated with Protestant churches, police and military bands, and various community entertainment groups. A good example is a "highlife hymn" recorded by the Peace Brass Band from Ghana.[18]

The harmonic palette here is a little more varied than Ladysmith's. Within a basic diatonic framework, the Peace Brass Band incorporates deceptive as well as perfect cadences; the phrase discourse proceeds in two- and four-bar blocks. What may sound like infelicities in voice leading result from the use of both the flattened and natural-seventh scale degree in the approach to the final cadence. The former is used as part of a descending line, while the natural seventh occurs within an ascending motion. These cross-relations are not aberrations, however; they are uninflected elements in the song's polyphonic system.

The influence of foreign musical procedures is most evident in the realm of voice leading. Each member of the Peace Brass Band has presumably grown up speaking a musical language in which parallelism rules in multipart expression. Here, however, under the constraints of a hymnlike texture, they attempt to speak a harmonic language that not only forbids certain parallels (like seconds, fourths, and fifths) but also abandons even permitted parallels (like thirds) in the approach to cadences. And so the musicians find themselves caught between opposing impulses. The situation is perhaps analogous to the kinds of error we make when speaking a foreign language. But whereas in linguistic grammar they are simply called errors, in musical language they are endowed with poetry or are said to be "interesting" or—worse—"different." Aestheticizing other people's errors is apparently a favorite colonialist pastime.

This highlife hymn is ontologically conceivable only since the early 1900s, only as a product of colonial-missionary influence in West Africa (Ghana, Sierra Leone, Togo, Côte d'Ivoire, Nigeria). Although bands of wind instruments played throughout the precolonial era—we will encounter an example from the Central African Republic later on—none of them utilized functional harmony, or the kind of cadential phraseology we heard in the Peace Brass Band's performance, or indeed a consistently hierarchic separation between a treble and a functional bass voice and two inner voices (SATB). What is of interest from the point of view of a postcolonial critique is the apparent ease with which African musicians seem to surrender aspects of their native musical languages; it would seem that as soon as they were offered a taste of hymnlike cadences and phraseology, they were prepared to give up a part of their tonal-harmonic birthright. (The question *why* African musicians seem uneager to resist in the tonal-harmonic realm but not apparently—or at least not to the same extent—in the area of rhythmic behavior is an interesting one. Some would say that indigenous harmonic systems are not as strong as the invading European ones, but that argument is weakened by the fact that the imposition of tonal rule was always accompanied by various forms of material, political, and religious control.)

These are only two brief examples of tonal production enabled by colonialism. I could have cited many more: national anthems of various countries; scores of compositions produced under the rule of tonic solfa; music designed for praise in charismatic churches; arrangements of folk music for voice and piano; original choral anthems and masses for school and church choirs, and so on. But the point is made, I think, namely, that certain forms of tonal imagining and expressing became possible only after exposure to European tonal harmony. To the Bible and the gun (again following Basil Davidson), we can now add diatonic tonality as an instrument of colonial domination.

The question surely arises: what were Africans doing (tonally or harmonically) before the Europeans came along?

African Tonal Thinking in the Pre-European Era
It should come as no surprise that African tonal thinking took many forms before Europeans arrived. We catch a glimpse of this plurality in A. M. Jones's *Studies of African Music* (1959), one of the key texts in the history of anal-

ysis of African music. On the basis of field research in Zambia and close listening to then-available recordings, Jones was able to partition a large portion of the continent according to the intervals preferred by individual ethnic groups in polyphonic performance. A fold-out, color-coded map inserted into the second of his two-volume treatise differentiates between groups according to whether they sing in parallel thirds, sixths, fourths, fifths, unisons, or octaves. The so-called 8-5-4 groups, for example, are the pentatonic groups, while those that use thirds and sixths belong to a heptatonic category. Although Jones's early taxonomy now stands in need of a sizeable supplement to take account of research done in the last half century, it was possible, already in 1959, to observe the heterogeneous nature of African polyphonic choices. More recently, Gerhard Kubik has assembled a conspectus of African polyphonic behaviors, with emphasis on eastern, central, and southern parts of the continent. He quotes from various written accounts, studies the procedures used especially by the San and the pygmies (who are noted for their distinctive polyphonic style of singing), and describes some of the most important techniques, emphasizing the existence of different sound ideals and especially of the ingenuity with which parts are negotiated.[19] A brisk review of these resources and associated procedures is impossible given the size of the corpus, so I will simply highlight one particular resource, the so-called anhemitonic pentatonic scale (roughly equivalent to the black keys of the piano), one of the most characteristic and widespread tonal constructs found on the African continent. I will later add a piece of drumming to complete the account of tonal expression originating in the pre-European era.[20]

A five-voice performance by Bibayak pygmies from Gabon provides a good example of pentatonic usage.[21] Each singer has internalized the pentatonic horizon and sings her individual part against that horizon, assured that articulating one or two notes—that is, a subset of the five-note collection—is enough to guarantee the integrity of the resultant pentatonic texture. There are no long-term trajectories in this mode of play, no phrase-generated expectations, no authentic cadences, no archetypal urges of managed desire and its fulfillment. There is only presentness, the repetition of notes and groups of notes into patterns organized around a palpable pulse. The form emerges additively from an accumulation of nows, a kind of moment form. The aesthetic is minimalistic, and the tonal resource is accepted and treated with reverence, not manipulated with the dubious ethics associated with individual cleverness. If modern artistic production were being guided by this pentatonic practice, it would explore the openness of resultant sounds; give priority to intervals of seconds, fourths, and fifths; embrace a nonteleological temporality; and prefer an egalitarian texture to a hierarchic one. This is, of course, not a prescription for what composers *should* do but a thought experiment about what they *would* do if they were following certain cultural or communal imperatives.

Pygmies are not the only exponents of pentatonicism in Africa. Closer to my own home are the southern Ewe of Ghana, some of whose vocal music is based on this scale. A good source is a recording of music from Dzodze made by the American ethnomusicologist James Burns.[22] The verbal message in one song is directed at a beautiful young woman: "Do not bluff, young woman, do not bluff, beautiful one; the day you die, termites will be in the ground." As in the Bibayak pygmy example, the pentatonic serves throughout as a source of pitches, but the Anlo-Ewe style is different. For one thing, the initial call-response pattern signals a kind of hierarchic organization that the more egalitarian pygmies generally avoid. Each melodic part avails itself of the scale or part thereof, but the voices do not proceed mechanically in parallel. From the singers' point of view, this southern Ewe performing practice privileges linearity over verticality. Sonorities are incidental except at ends of phrases (where they attain purity in the form of unisons or octaves), and they are based on the purposeful *melodic* use of the pentatonic, although the polyphonic outcome is known in advance given the referential collection. In other words, if each singer stays within the pentatonic orbit, then every two-note, three-note, four-note, or five-note resultant will conform to the source set. The pentatonic thus constitutes a kind of sound field, a *complexe sonore* subjected to various forms of articulation—syllable-based articulation by the pygmies (who use vocables but not words) and word-based articulation by the Anlo-Ewe.

The pentatonic is not, of course, manifest solely in vocal repertories; instrumental music for horns, trumpets, and xylophones often features a pentatonic referent. A vivid example may be cited from the repertory of a horn orchestra from the Banda ethnic group of the Central African Republic, recorded (and later analyzed) by Simha Arom.[23] Incidentally, this is one of the African repertoires that fascinated György Ligeti in the early 1980s and about which he writes in the preface to the English translation of Arom's magnum opus, *African Polyphony and Polyrhythm*.[24]

The recording features eighteen horns, each playing a single note. The whole is based on an anhemitonic pentatonic scale (in descending order): G-E-D-C-A-(G). The hocket technique so beloved of such ensembles is on display here. No individual part is meaningful without the others, and this is because only the resultant produces the desired Ur-melody. Strictly speaking, there is no hierarchy here, no treble versus bass. Although the instruments are assigned different registers such that the total ensemble range encompasses two and a half octaves, contrapuntal priority does not reside in any pair of parts. Again, this is music of precolonial origins, owing nothing to Europe and everything to black Africa.

Consider, finally, a snippet from a different kind of music of pre-European origins: *dùndún* drumming from among the Yoruba of Benin.[25] These so-called hourglass drums are noted for their ability to mimic the inflections of spoken language and, in the process, explore a wide tonal spectrum. The dùndún both talks and mimics talking, that is, a given drummer may drum in the speech mode without actually saying anything. While some parts of the musical utterance are oriented toward indefinite rather than definite pitch, we can just about infer a distant pentatonic horizon in this recording. Although nowadays the dùndún, in the hands of an expert such as the Yoruba master drummer Adebisi Adeleke, sings everything from "Amazing Grace" to "God Save the Queen," its tonal potential is more closely aligned with the complex tonality of (in this case) spoken Yoruba. Such a language-based or language-derived tonality offers a rich resource for African composers, one that boasts an expressive and historical depth different from that available from the imported hymn-based tonality associated with Ladysmith or the Peace Brass Band.

We would obviously need more than five brief examples to characterize precolonial African tonal thinking comprehensively, but I believe that these examples are paradigmatic and thus adequate to the task of introducing the imagined sound of precolonial Africa. (I speak of them as "imagined" because the specific recordings cited here were made in the last half century, so they postdate the actual precolonial period, but this says nothing about the stability of the traditional institutions that sponsor these performing practices and repertories.) It should perhaps be emphasized that the techniques and scalar resources enshrined in these excerpts are not necessarily unique to Africa—pentatonicism, for example, may well be universal, occurring as it does in Africa, Asia, Indonesia, and in various corners of Europe—but that they were in use in Africa until functional harmony came along and decisively transformed the musical soundscape. Now, functional harmony did not cover every inch of musical surface on the continent, only some of it, notably the coastal regions, urban locations, places with schools (including mission schools), and, of course, churches. But quantity may be deceptive here, for these are privileged symbolic sites for interpreting African modernity.

Composing under a Tonal Regime

What, finally, did colonization make possible, and how has the challenge of postcolonial creativity been handled in specific reference to tonal thinking? Once again, there are dozens of models on which one might frame an answer, but I will confine discussion to two categories of music: art music by the Nigerian composer Joshua Uzoigwe (1946–2005), and popular or neotraditional music by Wulomei, a 1970s Ghanaian band.

The peculiar alchemy of an indigenous complex of tonal, rhythmic, and timbral resources inflected or transformed by functional tonality has not lent itself to straightforward theoretical formulation. Regarding compositional practice and aesthetic choice, two options seem to have been favored. First is a simple grafting of one tonal system on to another; the effect here is one of strategic indifference to the foreign source, a mode of coexistence (sometimes peaceful, sometimes fraught). Second is an inflection or transformation of the traditional African input, or its translation into a modern, postcolonial economy, drawing on consciously crafted procedures, some of them borrowed from Europe, others abstracted from indigenous idioms; the whole, however, is arranged in conformity with the ethical and aesthetical imperatives of indigenous creativity. Although these strategies—separate existence versus interpenetration (and there are several others, of course, as well as differing degrees of enactment)—are not always localized in a single work, they nevertheless offer useful vantage points for critical interpretation.[26]

Among Uzoigwe's works is a set of four Igbo songs for voice and piano, composed in 1973.[27] Although the melodies originate from folk song, they have been done up in ways that distance them from those origins—"defamiliarized," we might say after the Russian formalists. The first of the set, "Eriri Ngeringe" (meaning "a riddle") is based on the following text composed by Uzoigwe himself (the original is in Igbo):

> Let it be, let it be
> Let be the thin thread
> The thin thread
> That lengthened the snake's tail
> The thin thread
> That caused the bird to balance in the air.

Shown in figure 15.3 is a harmonic ostinato that supports the singer's narrative. It is heard both at this pitch level and in transposition up a fourth. In light of the tonic solfa placed above the staff notation in his original manu-

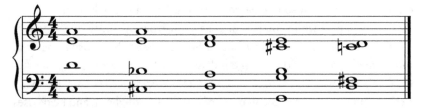

FIGURE 15.3. Harmonic ostinato in Uzoigwe's "Eriri Ngeringe."

script, Uzoigwe apparently heard this progression in D minor (ending with a tierce de Picardy). Such melodic-harmonic cycles are common in the traditional music that the composer knew, so he may simply have been "speaking" naturally. At the same time, the careful arrangement of parts in this five-chord cycle betrays a European influence, perhaps the influence of hymn playing at the keyboard.

It is legitimate, I believe, to speak of a transformation of whatever Uzoigwe borrowed from Europe, because he has not allowed himself to be submerged entirely in that tonal world. The specific act of tonal resistance is the simple one of anchoring the expression in folk material, material with its own modal center, which Uzoigwe enriches without violating. The sung melody (not shown in the figure) is familiar and yet has been made strange in this nontraditional arrangement for voice and piano. And the singer's style is beholden to the presentational forms of the lied or even opera. The harmonic progression is framed by dissonances; indeed, the closing D7 sonority, although normatively unstable, is deployed in a terminal position, thus endowing the ostinato with a more mobile feel. Because the top voice in the figure is entirely diatonic, it contrasts with the other voices, each of which contains at least one chromatic pitch. Some listeners will moreover hear something of the sound of drums in the percussive style of piano playing. This music too is not conceivable except as a product of the colonial-missionary encounter, but unlike the more or less passive acquiescence that we might read into the music of Ladysmith or the Peace Brass Band, Uzoigwe's "Eriri Ngeringe" displays an element of struggle and thus announces an ideological stance. The hybridity of Uzoigwe's song is marked; it is an earned hybridity, perhaps a hard-won one, not a default outcome or one that represents a flabby coexistence of antithetical elements.

Composing under a tonal regime may be further illustrated by the third of Uzoigwe's "Talking Drums," a set of piano pieces composed in 1991.[28] Modeled on a traditional Igbo dance, "Egwu Amala," this composition immediately creates a vibrant atmosphere based on forward-driving rhythms and a tonal arrangement that, while not diatonic, charts an evolving centricity.[29] Uzoigwe anchors the work in an African sound field by using the unusual meter of 19/8, a meter that is said to be the indigenously felt meter by performers of the original dance. He invokes a communal performance style by deploying a call-response gesture in the manner of a refrain throughout, and he devises an approach to pitch organization in which pentatonic elements are incorporated into a more complex chromatic texture.

Tonal thinking in "Egwu Amala" is more sophisticated than that which we heard in Ladysmith's "Paulina" or in the highlife hymn. There is more obvious compositional labor here than anything the pygmies do. Uzoigwe's harmonies are paper harmonies, harmonies conceived through acts of inscription. They are, at least for this composer, a most productive site for resisting tonality's colonizing tendencies. Notable is the fact that Uzoigwe, perhaps unusually among composers of his generation, was never a passive recipient of a European tonal legacy; rather, he sought to reinscribe everything under an African sign. At least that seemed to be the intention.

My final musical example is from the repertoire of a Ghanaian band active in the 1970s known as Wulomei ("priests" in the Ga language). Theirs is popular music; some would describe it as neotraditional (analogous to neoclassic or neofolk). The song "Soyama" (meaning boat or ship) is a fine example of Wulomei's style.[30] Immediately noticeable from the first sounds is the animating dance beat. This is at once functional music and an invitation to contemplative behavior. Featured are a guitar, various bells and drums, and two female lead voices. The main narrative is presented in the introduction and the first two melodic verses. In the introduction, a *clave* timeline underlies the solo guitar's rhythmic paraphrase of the melody that is about to be sung. The first verse features the two singers in alternation (four bars each); then, in the second, the voices proceed in a mixture of parallel thirds and fifths (four bars each). There is a critical moment at the end of each verse, where a cadence on B-flat is sounded. In some ways, this is the linchpin of the song, the key to understanding the colonial element inscribed in "Soyama."

The bundle of attributes that conveys the African essence of "Soyama" includes a self-satisfied, almost flirtatious beat that both invites and at the same time discourages dancing, a series of bell ejaculations that regularly punctuate the otherwise untroubled duple meter, the linguistic message ("He is waving a hand at me," says she about her lover), and the drum commentary in speech mode that seems to emanate uncannily from a subterranean world. This last advances the rhythmic narrative, expands the registral limits by opening up the lowest registers, and assumes a meta-musical function in directing the performance as a whole. Regarding the tonal imagination on display, the chantlike melody itself is modal, and the collection of pitch classes and their intervallic disposition suggest the Phrygian mode. In its initial chantlike appearance, where it is heard in a gentle rhythmic elaboration by the guitar, the mode is clear and the melody proceeds almost exclusively in parallel thirds. When the singers give up the guitarist's rubato and perform the melody in a relatively strict rhythm (verse 1), we hear a series of short-long dominant-chord punctuations played by the guitar. These seem blissfully oblivious to anything else that might be going on. Their persistence sets up an expectation for resolution. (In semiotic terms, we might say that they are charged indexical signs.) Confirmation of their meaning comes at the end of the eight-bar verse where they acquire their object in the form of an I chord. Talk about "desire" as a defining feature of tonality.

Notable in "Soyama" are the ways in which the composers (the songwriter Saka Acquaye and the lead drummer Nii Ashitey) have managed, as it were, to resist the colonizing force of tonality by using it and at the same time undermining it—placing it under erasure, we might say. A large-scale dominant-to-tonic progression is present, but it no longer has the uncontested status of a controlling background. To the extent that there is a background, it is a more complex configuration that incorporates the Phrygian elements as well as the pitched but nontonal sounds of bells and drums. Put in stark binary terms for rhetorical purposes, we might say that the guitar comes from the outside but plays insider-inflected music. Singing in parallel thirds and fifths comes partly from the inside: this is the traditional African way, but whereas singing in thirds dovetails with the European way, Europeans typically interrupt the stream of thirds in order to cadence satisfactorily. Singing in parallel fifths is *not* the European way, at least not according to the specific tonal models exported to Africa in the nineteenth century. The net effect of the tonal procedures of "Soyama" is of an imaginative recasting of African and European elements. The colonizing force is contained. Semitone tonality (as heard in hymns) is acknowledged but it does not rule; it is incorporated as one element in a constellation. All told, this is African music of some imagination, a music that, as critique perhaps, signals what it might mean to relativize and contextualize the primitive tonal resources with which European missionaries and colonial administrators colonized African consciousness. Relatively simple and transparent, Wulomei's "Soyama" is nevertheless significant and productively paradoxical music whose structure inscribes affirmation as well as resistance.

Conclusion

Historians of Africa have not been restrained in their assessments of the colonial period. Basil Davidson described "the arrival of Europeans [since the early sixteenth century]" as "the greatest calamity in [Africa's] history."[31] For Adu Boahen, "the colonial era [1880–1970] will go down in history as a period of wasted opportunities, of ruthless exploitation of the resources of Africa, and on balance of the underdevelopment and humiliation of the peoples of Africa."[32] And Walter Rodney saw in colonial education only "a series of limitations inside other limitations."[33] Similar sentiments have been expressed by political and social theorists, linguists, and language planners. An analogous critique by scholars of African music has, however, not been as audible. Are musicologists perhaps too enamored of the aesthetic, reveling in the ostensible otherworldliness or "nonlinguisticity" of music to confront the political and ideological work it does? Is daily practice in Africanist ethnomusicology long on description and short on evaluation? If so, a reordering of priorities would be in order, for I believe we can affirm one aspect of the historians' claim on the basis of our own reflections on tonal routines: Europe underdeveloped Africa tonally by creating the conditions of possibility for inaction (or limited action) in the realms of creation (or *poiesis*) and reception (or *esthesis*).

There is reason to be skeptical of the argument presented here, however. It could be said, for example, that the churches, schools, community centers, and dance halls in which tonality animates music making are so firmly established as sites of African modernity that any claim that the musical forms they sponsor are derivative, or that they betray a colonization of consciousness, seems entirely beside the point. So what if the national anthems that channel pride—symbolically speaking—in many independent African nations are deeply marked by European harmony and phraseology? Why does it matter that many popular songs use a musical language beholden to the primary chords of European tonality, and who cares if vast portions of music in Christian worship are riffs on the limited tonal trajectories enshrined in nineteenth-century European hymns? Even if they were produced in the course of culture contact, have they not been assimilated as naturalized *African* modes of expression?

Assimilated without losses? In the rush to embrace a borderless global aesthetics, or to celebrate hybridity and pluralism, we may have turned a blind eye to the violence that attends certain forms of sanctioned coexistence. We may have ignored the deficits that have accrued to those who have been forced to give up their native musical languages and speak others'. Tonality, let us not forget, is a complex resource, a nexus of freighted options presented to various African communities under a number of political, economic, and religious imperatives. If the analogy with language is valid, if composing is akin to speaking a language, then, for some Africans, composing tonally at certain historical moments was like speaking a foreign language—complete with new regimes of syntax, grammar, and intonation—distinct from their (musical) mother-tongue. Even in instances where the colonized attained a measure of fluency in using the colonizer's language, an immediate and practical outcome was almost always the gradual loss of a heritage language.

More tragically perhaps, we have overlooked or undervalued the creative potential of a number of musical resources, resources that have been consigned to the margins at various schools of music since tonality took center stage as the desired modern language. Various uses of nontempered scales, the possibilities opened up by overtone singing, echo-chamber effects associated with water drumming, subtle explorations of the boundaries between speech and song (in funeral laments and dirges, and in weeping songs and epic recitation), and the achievement of closure not through stepwise motion or a juvenile slowing down but by the use of melodic leaps and the injection of rhythmic life all constitute a rich set of stylistic opportunities for the modern composer. We await an African-originated resistance to the easy victories that tonal harmony has won on the continent since the 1840s.

NOTES

This essay was first presented as the inaugural Peter le Huray Lecture for the Royal Musical Association at the Tonality in Perspective conference held at King's College London in March 2008, and it subsequently was given at the fifty-third annual conference of the Society for Ethnomusicology in Middletown, Connecticut, in October 2008. It has also been read at colloquia at Indiana University, Peabody Institute, Oxford University, the University of Michigan, Royal Holloway University of London, Southampton University, the Royal Museum for Central Africa in Tervuren, University of Cape Coast, and Boston University. It formed the basis of a keynote address to the Music-Race-Empire conference held at the University of Wisconsin–Madison, April 28–30, 2011. I thank Ron Radano and Tejumola Olaniyan for their valuable feedback on earlier versions of this essay.

The epigraphs for this chapter are from the following sources: Bruno Nettl, "Colonialism," *Grove Music Online*, accessed December 6, 2013; A. Adu Boahen, *African Perspectives on Colonialism* (Baltimore, MD: Johns Hopkins University Press, 1987), 107; Walter Rodney, *How Europe Underdeveloped Africa* (London: Bogle-L'Ouverture, 1972), 264; and Abiola Irele, *The African Imagination: Literature in Africa and the Black Diaspora* (Oxford: Oxford University Press, 2001), viii.

1. I extend here the discussion "Tonal Harmony as Colonizing Force," begun on pages 8–10 of my book *Representing African Music: Postcolonial Notes, Queries, Positions* (New York: Routledge, 2003). In keeping with its origins as a talk, the argument here is partly inscribed in the recorded examples cited in this essay and listed in the discography. Readers are encouraged to consult the recordings while reading the text.

2. Brian Hyer, "Tonality," in *The Cambridge History of Western Music Theory*, ed. Thomas Christensen (Cambridge: Cambridge University Press, 2006), 735.

3. For a recent study of tonality's enabling mechanisms seen through geometrical lenses and exemplified in a wide range of repertory, see Dmitri Tymoczko, *A Geometry of Music: Harmony and Counterpoint in the Extended Common Practice* (New York: Oxford University Press, 2011).

4. This hymn was composed in 1876 by the American Baptist preacher Adoniram Judson Gordon (1836–95) to words by William Ralph Robertson. For a recording, see *More Than 50 Most Loved Hymns* (Hollywood, CA: Liberty Records, 2004), CD 1, track 16. It appears as #409 in the Ewe hymnbook *Nyanyui Hame Hadzigbalẽ Gã*, 5th ed. (Maharashtra, India: Evangelical Presbyterian Church, Ghana and Eglise Evangélique Presbytérienne du Togo, 2002), 484.

5. For a valuable introduction to hymns—their history, texts, religious function, reception, and aesthetics—see *An Annotated Anthology of Hymns*, ed. J. R. Watson (Oxford: Oxford University Press, 2002). An early discussion of African hymnody appears in A. M. Jones, *African Hymnody in Christian Worship: A Contribution to the History of Its Development*, Mambo Occasional Papers (Gwelo, Rhodesia: Mambo, 1976); and in Lazarus Ekwueme, "African Music in Christian Liturgy: The Igbo Experiment," *African Music* 5 (1973–74): 12–33. See also Roberta King, Jean Ngoya Kidula, James R. Krabill, and Thomas A. Oduro, *Music in the Life of the African Church* (Waco, TX: Baylor University Press, 2008). For an important recent study of the mission-based reception of European tone systems in Africa, including modal as well as tonal usages, see Anna Maria Busse Berger, "Spreading the Gospel of *Singbewegung*: An Ethnomusicologist Missionary in Tanganyika of the 1930s," *Journal of the American Musicological Society* 66, no. 2 (2013): 475–522.

6. For helpful insights into the reception of tonal harmony by highlife musicians, see David Coplan, "Go to My Town, Cape Coast! The Social History of Ghanaian Highlife," in *Eight Urban Musical Cultures*, ed. Bruno Nettl (Urbana: University of Illinois Press, 1978), 96–114. In refining the claim that I-IV-V progressions rule in African popular music, one might note the use of modality and pentatonicism in repertories such as "King" Sunny Ade's jùjú and Fela Kuti's afrobeat.

7. By "European heritage" I mean, essentially, Handel and a bit of Bach; some Mozart, Beethoven, Chopin, and Mendelssohn; a little Brahms; and plenty of Gilbert and Sullivan. The preference for tonality is mainly statistical, however. A few composers— Akin Euba, Joshua Uzoigwe, Bode Omojola, and Gyimah Labi—have experimented with atonal or post-tonal resources.

8. I owe this observation to the music theorist Brian Hyer, whose remark in the course of a roundtable discussion during the Tonality in Perspective conference at King's College London in March 2008 I am recalling here. See also Hyer, "Tonality."

9. Nettl, "Colonialism."

10. Martin Stokes, "John Blacking and Ethnomusicology," in *The Queen's Thinkers: Essays on the Intellectual Heritage of a University*, ed. David N. Livingstone and Alvin Jackson (Belfast: Blackstaff, 2008), 168–69.

11. A. M. Jones, *Studies in African Music*, 2 vols. (Oxford: Oxford University Press, 1959); Michelle Kisliuk, *Seize the Dance! BaAka Musical Life and the Ethnography of Performance* (New York: Oxford University Press, 1998).

12. See Veit Erlmann, *Music, Modernity and the Global Imagination: South Africa and the West* (Oxford: Oxford University Press, 1999); Christine Lucia, "Back to the Future? Idioms of 'Displaced Time' in South African Composition," in *Composing Apartheid: Music for and against Apartheid*, ed. Grant Olwage (Johannesburg: Wits University Press, 2008), 11–34; and Martin Scherzinger, "Negotiating the Music Theory/African Music Nexus: A Political Critique of Ethnomusicological Anti-Formalism and a Strategic Analysis of the Harmonic Patterning of the Shona Mbira Song 'Nyamaropa,'" *Perspectives of New Music* 39 (2001): 5–118. On tonic solfa specifically, see Robin Stevens and Eric Akrofi, "Tonic Sol-fa in South Africa—A Case of Endogenous Musical Practice," in *Australian Association for Research in Music Education: Proceedings of the XXVIth Annual Conference, 25–28 September 2004*, Southern Cross University, Tweed-Gold Coast Campus, New South Wales, Australia, September 25–28, 2004 (Clayton, Victoria: Australian Association for Research in Music Education, 2004), 301–14.

13. See Frantz Fanon, *Black Skin: White Masks*, trans. Charles Lam Markmann (1952; repr., London: MacGibbon and Kee, 1968); Albert Memmi, *The Colonizer and the Colonized*, trans. Howard Greenfield (Boston: Beacon, 1965); and Rodney, *How Europe Underdeveloped Africa*. The literature on the effects of colonialism in Africa is obviously too large to be meaningfully referenced in a single note. Among writings with a philosophical orientation, I might mention Paulin Hountondji, *African Philosophy: Myth and Reality*, trans. Henry Evans with Jonathan Rée (Bloomington: Indiana University Press, 1996); Kwasi Wiredu, *Cultural Particulars and Universals: An African Perspective* (Bloomington: Indiana University Press, 1996); V. Y. Mudimbe, *The Invention of Africa: Gnosis, Philosophy, and the Order of Knowledge* (Bloomington: Indiana University Press, 1988); and Olufemi Taiwo, *How Colonialism Preempted Modernity in Africa* (Bloomington: Indiana University Press, 2010). Several of the essays gathered in *A Companion to African Philosophy*, ed. Kwasi Wiredu (Oxford: Blackwell, 2004), deal with the colonial influence. From the perspective of social theory, see Achille Mbembe's *On the Postcolony* (Berkeley: University of California Press, 2001). For a variety of literary perspectives, see Olakunle George, *Relocating Agency: Modernity and African Letters* (Albany: State University of New York Press, 2003); Irele, *The African Imagination*; and Gaurav Desai, *Subject to Colonialism: African Self-fashioning and the Colonial Library* (Durham: Duke University Press, 2001).

14. On the colonization of consciousness, see Jean Comaroff and John Comaroff, *Of Revelation and Revolution: Christianity, Colonialism and Consciousness in South Africa* (Chicago: University of Chicago Press, 1991).

15. For a sampling of Ladysmith's tonal experiences, see the CD *No Boundaries: Ladysmith with the English Chamber Orchestra* (Cleveland, OH: Heads Up International, 2004).

16. *Best of Ladysmith Black Mambazo* (Shanachie/SHA-43098, 1992), track 14.

17. A comprehensive study of Ladysmith is included in Veit Erlmann's study of *isicathamiya* in *Nightsong: Performance, Power and Practice in South Africa* (Chicago: University of Chicago Press, 1996). See also his *Music, Modernity and the Global Imagination*. In a lively review of this book, Martin Scherzinger takes issue with some of Erlmann's analytical claims pertaining to tonal orientation in ways that are pertinent to the discussion of tonal understanding in this essay. See Scherzinger, "Review of *Music, Modernity and the Global Imagination: South Africa and the West*," *Journal of the Royal Musical Association* 126 (2001): 117–41.

18. See the CD *Frozen Brass: Africa and Latin America* (PAN, 1993), track 2.

19. Gerhard Kubik, "Multipart Singing in Sub-Saharan Africa: Remote and Recent Histories Unravelled," in *Papers Presented at the Symposium on Ethnomusicology: Number 13 University of Zululand 1995 and at the Symposium Number 14 Rhodes University 1996*, ed. Andrew Tracey (Grahamstown, South Africa: International Library of African Music, 1997), 85–97. See also his earlier essay, "African Tone Systems: A Reassessment," *Yearbook for Traditional Music* 17 (1985): 31–63.

20. One point of clarification regarding methodology: I'm not trying to construct a genealogical argument here, a literal "before-and-after" scenario. In other words, I do not, for example, trace a single ethnic group's tonal thinking from its precolonial state to its colonial and postcolonial phases. This periodization is, in any case, the colonizer's, and it almost certainly subtends interests, values, and desires that are antithetical to those of the colonized. I'm depending rather on strategically displaced attributions in order to enhance the potential for cross-ethnic generalization. The disadvantage in proceeding in this manner is that what might have been a temporally intact historical narrative dissolves into a series of speculations and affiliations. The advantage, however, is that it allows readers with different African referents to plug their particular variables into the framework outlined here. This "contrapuntal" approach is not yet normative for Africanist ethnomusicology, but it seems to me more promising than approaches that accept the strictures of conventional history and ethnography and thus decline the invitation to indulge in certain kinds of intertextual imagining. For a cogent advocacy and exemplification of contrapuntal reading, see Brent Hayes Edwards, in this volume.

21. Recorded on the CD *Gabon: Music of the Bibayak Pygmies: Epic Cantors* (OCORA, 2001), track 2.

22. See the CD *Ewe Drumming from Ghana: The Soup Which Is Sweet Draws the Chairs Closer* (Topic Records, 2005).

23. Excerpted on the CD accompanying Monique Brandily's *Introduction aux musiques africaines* (Paris: Cité de la Musique; Arles: Actes Sud, 1997), track 21.

24. Simha Arom, *African Polyphony and Polyrhythm: Musical Structure and Methodology*, trans. Martin Thom, Barbara Tuckett, and Raymond Boyd (1985; repr., Cambridge: Cambridge University Press, 1991). For a thorough exposition of Ligeti's African affinities, see Martin Scherzinger, "György Ligeti and the Aka Pygmies Project," *Contemporary Music Review* 25 (2006): 227–62. In listening to the Bibayak pygmy excerpt, please take account of a margin of tolerance in the relational tuning of the horns so that the core pentatonic collection C-D-E-G-A is not replaced by a chromatic variant.

25. *Yoruba Drums from Benin, West Africa* (Washington, DC: Smithsonian/Folkways, 1996), track 12, "Esikesi." Two major scholarly studies of the dynamics of Yoruba drumming are Akin Euba, *Yoruba Drumming: The Dùndún Tradition* (Beirut, Lebanon: African Studies Series, 1990); and Amanda Villepastour, *Ancient Text Messages of the Yorùbá Bàtá Drum: Cracking the Code*, soas Musicology Series (Surrey, UK: Ashgate, 2010).

26. The Nigerian composer and scholar Akin Euba has given a great deal of thought to the creative choices available to the modern African composer. See, for example, *Essays on Music in Africa 2: Intercultural Perspective* (Beirut, Lebanon: Elékóto Music Centre, 1989). Also of interest is Geoffrey Poole, "Black-White-Rainbow: A Personal View on What African Music Means to the Contemporary Western Composer," in *Composing the Music of Africa: Composition, Interpretation and Realisation*, ed. Malcolm Floyd (Aldershot, UK: Ashgate, 1999), 295–334.

27. For a concise introduction to Uzoigwe's music, see Godwin Sadoh, "Intercultural Creativity in Joshua Uzoigwe's Music," *Africa: Journal of the International African Institute* 74 (2004): 633–61.

28. All three are recorded on the cd *Senku: Piano Music by Composers of African Descent* (msr Classics, 2003). The published score of "Egwu Amala" is included in *Piano Music of Africa and the African Diaspora*, ed. William Chapman Nyaho (New York: Oxford University Press, 2009). For an appraisal of this first-ever anthology of piano music by black composers, see my "The Challenge of African Art Music," *Circuit, Musiques Contemporaines* 21, no. 2 (2011): 55–72.

29. For an ethnographic study, see Sister Marie Agatha Ozah, "*Égwú Àmàlà*: Women in Traditional Performing Arts in Ogbaruland" (PhD diss., University of Pittsburgh, 2008).

30. See the cd *Legendary Wulomei* (Sam Records, 2000), track 14. Already in 1978, David Coplan drew attention to Wulomei's artistry in an essay on highlife music, "Go to My Town, Cape Coast!" A comprehensive recent study of Wulomei is Gavin Webb, "The Wulomei Ga Folk Group: A Contribution towards Urban Ethnomusicology" (PhD diss., University of Ghana, Legon, 2012).

31. Basil Davidson, *Africa: A Voyage of Discovery* [video recording], Program 5: "The Bible and the Gun" (Chicago: Home Vision Select, 1984).

32. Boahen, *African Perspectives on Colonialism*, 109.

33. Rodney, *How Europe Underdeveloped Africa*, 264.

DISCOGRAPHY

Abstract Vision and Humanity. "Empires." *Politrix*. Self-released, n.d.

——. "Media." *Politrix*. Self-released, n.d.

Adou Elenga. "Ata Ndele." *Anthologie de la musique Zaïroise moderne, tome 1*. Bureau du Président de la République du Zaïre BP 3092, 1974. Vinyl.

Arabian Knightz. "Rebel." Arab League Records, 2011.

Araújo, Emanoel. *A Feminilidade do Canto*. São Paulo: Atração Fonográfica, 2003. CD.

The Arthur S. Alberts Collection: More Tribal, Folk, and Café Music of West Africa. Produced by Mickey Hart. Library of Congress Endangered Music Project, Rykodisc RCD 10401, 1998. CD.

Brandily, Monique. *Introduction aux musiques africaines*. Paris: Cité de la Musique; Arles: Actes Sud, 1997. CD.

Chee Malabar. "Hamas Mix." Unreleased.

——. "Kandahar Cruise." *Burning Tire Artisan*. Red Bench Records, 2011. CD.

——. "Live from Al-Jazeera." *Burning Tire Artisan*. Red Bench Records, 2011. CD.

——. "Oblique Brown." *Oblique Brown*. Red Bench Records, 2006. CD.

The Columbia World Library of Folk and Primitive Music, Vol. 10: Bantu Music from East Africa. Compiled and edited by Alan Lomax. Columbia 91A 02017. CD.

Da Lench Mob. *Guerillas in tha Mist*. Atco, 1992. CD.

"Dundun Ensemble from Adjarra, Benin, 'Esikesi' (for Wedding)." *Yoruba Drums from Benin, West Africa*. Vol. 8: The World's Musical Traditions. Smithsonian/Folkways/SWF 40440, 1996. CD.

Elsie Houston Sings Brazilian Songs. RCA Victor, 1954.

Etta Moten Barnett's Return to the United States. WMAQ Radio, 1955. New York Public Library, Schomburg Branch, Recorded Sound Division.

Ewe Drumming from Ghana: The Soup Which Is Sweet Draws the Chairs Closer. Topic Records, 2005. CD.

Gabon: Music of the Bibayak Pygmies: Epic Cantors. OCORA, 2001. CD.

Himalayan Project. "Eco Location." *The Middle Passage.* Himalayan Project, 2002.

———. "Everything." *The Middle Passage.* Himalayan Project, 2002.

———. "Nuthin Nice." *The Middle Passage.* Himalayan Project, 2002.

———. "Postcards from Paradise." *Wince at the Sun.* Red Bench Records, 2001.

Houdini, Wilmoth. *Poor but Ambitious: Calypso Classics from Trinidad, 1928–1940.* Arhoolie Folkloric/ARHCD-7010, 1993. CD and liner notes.

Ibn Thabit. "The Question." 2011. www.youtube.com/watch?v=c_9pBiwS21I.

Ice Cube. *Amerikkka's Most Wanted.* Priority Records, 1990. CD.

Johnson, Linton Kwesi. *Dread Beat an' Blood.* Produced by Vivian Weather and Linton Kwesi Johnson. Front Line Records/FL1017, 1978. Vinyl.

———. *Making History.* Produced by Linton Kwesi Johnson and Dennis Bovell. Island Records ILPS 9770, 1984. CD.

———. *Tings an' Times.* Shanashie/B000000DX8, 1991. CD.

Kabir. "Democracy." *Cultural Confusion.* Uncle Trouble Music, 2003. CD.

———. "Just Me." *The Time Is Now.* CDBY, 2010. CD.

Karmacy. "Stop." *Wooden Bling.* Karmacy, 2008. CD.

Ladysmith Black Mambazo. *No Boundaries: Ladysmith with the English Chamber Orchestra.* Cleveland, OH: Heads Up International, 2004. CD.

———. "Pauline." *Best of Ladysmith Black Mambazo.* Shanachie/SHA-43098, 1992. CD.

"La Paloma." Composed by Sebastián Yradier in 1859. Published in 1877.

Lotfi Double Kanon. "America (Remix)." *Mixtape.* Dounia, 2013. CD.

The Mexican Revolution; Corridos about the Heroes and Events, 1910–1920 and Beyond. Edited by Guillermo E. Hernández. Arhoolie Folkoric/ARHCD 7041–7044, 1998. Four CDs and booklet.

"My Jesus I Love Thee." *More Than 50 Most Loved Hymns.* Liberty Records, 2004. CD 1, track 16.

Omar Offendum, Ayah, the Narcicyst, Freeway, and Amir Sulaiman. "#Jan25." Produced by Sami Matar. July 2, 2011.

Paris. *Sonic Jihad.* Guerrilla Funk, 2003. CD.

Peace Brass Band. "Highlife Hymn." *Frozen Brass: Africa and Latin America.* Anthology of Brass Band Music #2, PAN, 1993. CD.

ProfessorD.us and the Dope Poet Society. "Devils in Your Government." *Third World Warriors, Vol. 1.* JustusLeagueRecords.com, 2008. CD.

Spottswood, Dick. "Who Was Butler?" *The Classic Calypso Collective, West Indian Rhythm: Trinidad Calypsos on World and Local Events Featuring the Censored Recordings 1938–1940.* Bear Family Records/BCD 16623 JM, 2006. CD.

Tracey, Hugh. *Colonial Dance Bands: Kenya, Tanganyika, Portuguese East Africa, Northern Rhodesia, Belgian Congo, 1950 and 1952.* International Library of African Music, SWP 031/HT 020, 2006. Liner notes.

———. *Kanyok and Luba: Southern Belgian Congo, 1952 and 1957.* International Library of African Music, SWP 011/HT 05, 1998. CD.

Uzoigwe, Joshua. "Four Igbo Songs #1: Eriri Ngeringe." Unpublished recording.
———. "Talking Drums (for Piano): Egwu Amala." *Senku: Piano Music by Composers of African Descent*. MSR Classics, 2003. CD.
Wulomei. "Soyama." *Legendary Wulomei*. Sam Records, 2000. CD.

BIBLIOGRAPHY

Acosta, Leonardo. *Descarga Cubana: El jazz en Cuba, 1900–1950*. Havana: Ediciones Unión, 2000.

Adorno, Theodor. *Essays on Music*. Edited by Richard Leppert. Translated by Susan H. Gillespie. Berkeley and Los Angeles: University of California Press, 2002.

———. *Otra vision de la música popular cubana*. Havana: Letras Cubanas, 2004.

Agawu, Kofi. "The Challenge of African Art Music." *Circuit, Musiques Contemporaines* 21, no. 2 (2011): 55–72.

———. *Representing African Music: Postcolonial Notes, Queries, Positions*. New York: Routledge, 2003.

Ahmed, Sara. "Affective Economies." *Social Text* 79, no. 2 (Summer 2004): 117–39.

Alam, Fakrul, and Radha Chakravarty, eds. *The Essential Tagore*. Cambridge: Harvard University Press, 2011.

Alatas, Syed Hussein. *The Myth of the Lazy Native*. London: Frank Cass, 1979.

Alexander, Michelle. *The New Jim Crow: Mass Incarceration in the Age of Colorblindness*. New York: New Press, 2010.

Amaral, Aracy A. *Blaise Cendrars no Brasil e os modernistas*. Rio de Janeiro: Livraria Martins Editora, 1970.

———. *Tarsila: Sua vida, sua obra*. São Paulo: Perspectiva, 1975.

Ames, Eric. "The Sound of Evolution." *Modernism/Modernity* 10, no. 2 (2003): 297–325.

Anderson, Mark. *Black and Indigenous: Garifuna Activism and Consumer Culture in Honduras*. Minneapolis: University of Minnesota Press, 2009.

Andrews, George Reid. *Blackness in the White Nation: A History of Afro-Uruguay*. Chapel Hill: University of North Carolina Press, 2010.

Arboleda, Dario Blanco. "Los bailes sonideros: Identitidad y resistencia de los grupos populares Mexicanos ante los embates de la modernidad." In *Sonideros en las Aceras, Véngase la Gozadera*, coordinated by El Proyecto Sonidero, 53–82. Creative Commons: Tumbona, 2012.

Arendt, Hannah. *Origins of Totalitarianism*. New York: Harcourt, 1968.

Arom, Simha. *African Polyphony and Polyrhythm: Musical Structure and Methodology*. Translated by Martin Thom, Barbara Tuckett, and Raymond Boyd. 1985. Reprint, Cambridge: Cambridge University Press, 1991.

Askew, Kelly M. *Performing the Nation: Swahili Music and Cultural Politics in Tanzania*. Chicago: University of Chicago Press, 2002.

Atkins, E. Taylor. *Blue Nippon: Authenticating Jazz in Japan*. Durham: Duke University Press, 2001.

Attali, Jacques. *Noise: The Political Economy of Music*. Translated by Brian Massumi. 1977. Reprint, Minneapolis: University of Minnesota Press, 1985.

Auden, W. H. "In Memory of W. B. Yates." Poets.org. www.poets.org/poetsorg/poem /memory-w-b-yeats.

Ayimpamle, Théophile. "Ata ndele, mokili ekobaluka." *Le Climat Tempéré*, July 7, 2010. www.leclimat.cd/News/Details/Tribune%20du%20cinquantenaire/ata-ndele-mokili -ekobaluka.

Azzi, María Susana, and Simon Collier. *Le Grand Tango: The Life and Music of Astor Piazzolla*. New York: Oxford University Press, 2000.

Baily, John. *Can You Stop the Birds Singing? The Censorship of Music in Afghanistan*. Copenhagen: Freemuse, 2003.

Baker, Geoffrey. *Imposing Harmony: Music and Society in Colonial Cuzco*. Durham: Duke University Press, 2008.

Balibar, Étienne. "Racism as Universalism." In *Masses, Classes, Ideas: Studies on Politics and Philosophy before and after Marx*, 191–204. New York: Routledge, 1994.

———. "'Rights of Man' and 'Rights of the Citizen': The Modern Dialectic of Equality and Freedom." In *Masses, Classes, Ideas: Studies on Politics and Philosophy before and after Marx*, 39–59. New York: Routledge, 1994.

Balibar, Étienne, and Immanuel Wallerstein. *Race, Nation, Class: Ambiguous Identities*. London: Verso, 1991.

Barber, Karin. "Popular Arts in Africa." *African Studies Review* 30, no. 3 (September 1987): 1–78.

Barringer, Tim. "Sonic Spectacles of Empire: The Audio-Visual Nexus, Delhi–London 1911–12." In *Sensible Objects: Colonialism, Museums, and Material Culture*, edited by E. Edwards, C. Gosden, and R. Phillips, 169–96. Oxford: Berg, 2006.

Bartók, Béla. "Gypsy Music or Hungarian Music?" *Musical Quarterly* 33, no. 2 (1947): 240–57.

Baskaran, S. Theodore. *The Message Bearers: The Nationalist Politics and the Entertainment Media in South India 1880–1945*. Madras, India: Cre-A, 1981.

Bastide, Roger. *Les Ameriques noires: Les civilisations africaines dans le nouveau monde*. Paris: Payot, 1967.

Basu, Dipannita, and Sidney Lemelle, eds. *The Vinyl Ain't Final: Hip Hop and the Globalization of Black Popular Culture*. London: Pluto, 2006.

Beauman, Nicola. *Morgan: A Biography of E. M. Forster*. London: Hodder and Stoughton, 1993.

Becker, Judith. "One Perspective on Gamelan in America." *Asian Music* 15, no. 1 (1983): 82–89.

Bemba, Sylvain. *Cinquante ans de musique du Congo-Zaïre, 1920–1970: De Paul Kamba à Tabu-Ley*. Paris: Présence Africaine, 1984.

Benedict, Carol. *Golden Silk Smoke: A History of Tobacco in China, 1550–2010*. Berkeley: University of California Press, 2011.

Berger, Anna Maria Busse. "Spreading the Gospel of *Singbewegung*: An Ethnomusicologist Missionary in Tanganyika of the 1930s." *Journal of the American Musicological Society* 66, no. 2 (2013): 475–522.

Bergero, Adriana J. *Intersecting Tango: Cultural Geographies of Buenos Aires, 1900–1930*. Pittsburgh: University of Pittsburgh Press, 2008.

Berland, Jody. *North of Empire: Essays on the Cultural Technologies of Space*. Durham: Duke University Press, 2009.

Berlioz, Hector. "Moeurs musicales de la Chine (Musical Customs of China)." In *The Art of Music and Other Essays*, translated by Elizabeth Csicsery-Rónay, 176–79. Bloomington: Indiana University Press, 1994.

Bernard, Kenneth A. *Lincoln and the Music of the Civil War*. Caldwell, ID: Caxton, 1966.

Bijsterveld, Karin. "The Diabolical Symphony of the Mechanical Age: Technology and Symbolism of Sound in European and North American Noise Abatement Campaigns, 1900–40." In *The Auditory Culture Reader*, edited by M. Bull and L. Back, 165–89. Oxford: Berg, 2003.

Björkman, Ingrid. *"Mother, Sing for Me": People's Theatre in Kenya*. London: Zed, 1989.

Blaine, Sue. "Security Training Bodies Team Up." *Business Day*, August 29, 2005.

Blake, Jody. *Le tumulte noir: Modernist Art and Popular Entertainment in Jazz-Age Paris, 1900–1930*. University Park: Pennsylvania State University Press, 1999.

Blustein, Paul. *And the Money Kept Rolling In (and Out): Wall Street, the IMF, and the Bankrupting of Argentina*. New York: Public Affairs, 2005.

Boahen, A. Adu. *African Perspectives on Colonialism*. Baltimore, MD: Johns Hopkins University Press, 1987.

Bohlman, Philip V. "Erasure: Displacing and Misplacing Race in Twentieth-Century Music Historiography." In *Western Music and Race*, edited by Julie Brown, 3–23. Cambridge: Cambridge University Press, 2007.

———. "Ethnomusicology's Challenge to the Canon; the Canon's Challenge to Ethnomusicology." In *Disciplining Music: Musicology and Its Canons*, edited by Katherine Bergeron and Philip V. Bohlman, 116–36. Chicago: University of Chicago Press, 1992.

———. "Music Inside Out: Sounding Public Religion in a Post-Secular Europe." In *Music, Sound and Space: Transformations of Public and Private Experience*, edited by Georgina Born, 205–23. Cambridge: Cambridge University Press, 2013.

Bohn, Lauren. "Rapping the Revolution." Interview by Hamada Ben Amor. *Middle East Channel*. July 22, 2011. http://mideast.foreignpolicy.com/posts/ 2011/07/22 /rapping_the_revolution.

Bonilla-Silva, Eduardo, and David Embrick. "Black, Honorary White, White: The Future of Race in the United States." In *Mixed Messages: Multiracial Identities in the "Color-Blind" Era*, edited by David Brunsma. Boulder, CO: Lynne Rienner, 2006.

Borneman, Ernest. "Creole Echoes." *Jazz Review* 2, no. 8 (1959): 13–15.

———. "Creole Echoes: Part II." *Jazz Review* 2, no. 10 (1959): 26–27.

Bourriaud, Nicolas. *Postproduction: Culture as Screenplay: How Art Reprograms the World*. New York: Lukas and Sternberg, 2002.

Bowles, Paul. *Without Stopping: An Autobiography*. New York: Ecco, 1985.

Boym, Svetlana. *The Future of Nostalgia*. New York: Basic, 2002.

Brandel, Rose. *Music of Central Africa: An Ethnomusicological Study: Former French Equatorial Africa, the Former Belgian Congo, Ruanda-Urundi, Uganda, Tanganyika*. The Hague, Netherlands: Martinus Nijhoff, 1961.

Brandily, Monique. *Introduction aux musiques africaines*. Paris: Cité de la Musique; Arles: Actes Sud, 1997.

Brennan, Timothy. "Cosmo-Theory." *South Atlantic Quarterly* 100, no. 3 (2001): 659–91.

———. *Secular Devotion: Afro-Latin Music and Imperial Jazz*. London: Verso, 2008.

Brito, Mário da Silva. *História do modernismo Brasileiro*. Vol. 4 of *Antecendentes da semana de arte moderna*. 6th ed. 1978. Reprint, Rio de Janeiro: Civilização Brasileira, 1997.

Brown, Julie, ed. *Western Music and Race*. Cambridge: Cambridge University Press, 2007.

Brown, Wendy. *Walled States, Waning Sovereignty*. New York: Zone, 2010.

Buck-Morss, Susan. *Hegel, Haiti, and Universal History*. Pittsburgh: University of Pittsburgh Press, 2009.

Burkholder, James Peter. *Charles Ives and His World*. Princeton, NJ: Princeton University Press, 1996.

Bush, Roderick. *The End of White World Supremacy: Black Internationalism and the Problem of the Color Line*. Philadelphia: Temple University Press, 2009.

Butler, Judith. *Bodies That Matter: On the Discursive Limits of "Sex."* New York: Routledge, 1993.

———. *Gender Trouble: Feminism and the Subversion of Identity*. New York: Routledge, 1990.

———. "Imitation and Gender Insubordination." In *The Lesbian and Gay Studies Reader*, edited by Henry Abelove, Michèle Aina Barale, and David M. Halperin, 307–20. New York: Routledge, 1993.

Cabral, Amilcar. "National Liberation and Culture." In *Unity and Struggle: Speeches and Writings*. 1970. Reprint, New York: Monthly Review, 1979.

Cáceres, Juan Carlos. *Tango Negro*. Buenos Aires: Planeta, 2010.

"Calypso and Cha Cha." [In Chinese.] *Nanguo* 3 (October 1958).

"Calypso Enjoys Worldwide Popularity." [In Chinese.] *International Screen* 23 (September 1957).

Camacho, Alicia R. Schmidt. *Migrant Imaginaries: Latino Cultural Politics in the U.S.-Mexico Borderlands*. New York: New York University Press, 2008.

Cançado, Tania Mara Lopes. "An Investigation of West African and Haitian Rhythms on the Development of Syncopation in Cuban Habanera, Brazilian Tango/Choro and American Ragtime (1791–1900)." PhD dissertation, Shenandoah University, 1999.

Cantalupo, Charles, ed. *The World of Ngugi wa Thiong'o*. Trenton, NJ: Africa World Press, 1995.

Carl Van Vechten Collection, Library of Congress Prints and Photographs Division.

Castro, Gustavo López. *El Río Bravo es charco: Cancionero del migrante*. Zamora: Colegio de Michoacán, 1995.

Caws, Mary Ann. "Péret's 'Amour sublime'—just Another 'Amour fou'?" *French Review* 40, no. 2 (November 1966): 204–12.

Cendrars, Blaise. *Etc., etc., . . . um livro 100% Brasileiro*. São Paulo: Editora Perspectiva, 1976.

———. *Histoires Vraies*. Paris: Bernard Grasset, 1927.

Centre for Contemporary Cultural Studies. *The Empire Strikes Back: Race and Racism in 70s Britain*. London: Routledge, 1982.

Césaire, Aimé. *Discourse on Colonialism*. Translated by Joan Pinkham. 1955. Reprint, New York: Monthly Review, 1972.

———. *Notebook of a Return to the Native Land*. Translated by Clayton Eshelman and Annette Smith. Middletown, CT: Wesleyan University Press, 2001.

Chakrabarty, Dipesh. *Provincializing Europe: Postcolonial Thought and Historical Difference*. Princeton, NJ: Princeton University Press, 2000.

Chandvankar, Suresh. "Vande Mataram: A Most Popular and Evergreen Indian Song." *Musical Traditions* 195 (2003). http://www.mustrad.org.uk/articles/mataram.htm.

Chang, Jeff. *Can't Stop Won't Stop: A History of the Hip Hop Generation*. New York: St. Martin's, 2005.

Chao, Y. R. *New Poetic Song Collection*. [In Chinese.] Shanghai: Commercial Press, 1928.

Chase, Gilbert. *America's Music, from the Pilgrims to the Present*. Rev. 3rd ed. 1955. Reprint, Champaign: University of Illinois Press, 1982.

Chasteen, John Charles. *National Rhythms, African Roots: The Deep History of Latin American Popular Dance*. Albuquerque: University Press of New Mexico, 2004.

Chaudhuri, Amit. *Calcutta: Two Years in the City*. New York: Knopf, 2013.

Chénieux-Gendron, Jacqueline. "Surrealists in Exile: Another Kind of Resistance." *Poetics Today* 17, no. 3 (Fall 1996): 437–51.

Chernoff, John Miller. *African Rhythm and African Sensibility: Aesthetics and Social Action in African Musical Idioms*. Chicago: University of Chicago Press, 1979.

Chiu, Wan-Ting. *Formosan Baritone King: Hong Yifeng's Journey of Discovery*. [In Chinese.] Taipei: Tonsan, 2013.

Chomsky, Noam. "On Propaganda." January 1992. www.chomsky.info/interviews/199201.html.

Christensen, Dieter. "Berlin Phonogramm-Archiv: The First 100 Years." In *Music Archiving in the World: Papers Presented at the Conference on the Occasion of the 100th Anniversary of the Berlin Phonogramm-Archiv*, edited by Gabriele Berlin and Artur Simon, 19–31. Berlin: Verlag für Wissenschaft und Bildung, 2002.

Christensen, Timothy. "Bearing the White Man's Burden: Misrecognition and Cultural Difference in E. M. Forster's *A Passage to India*." *Novel: A Forum on Fiction* 39, no. 2 (2006): 155–78.

Christopher, Colin. "Soundtrack of the Revolution." *Inside Islam: Dialogues and Debates*, February 23, 2011. http://insideislam.wisc.edu/2011/02/soundtrack-of-the-revolution/.

Cidade de Deus (City of God). Directed by Fernando Meireilles and Kátia Lund. Burbank, CA: Buena Vista, 2002.

Cimini, Amy, and Jairo Moreno. "On Diversity." *Gamut* 2, no. 1 (2009): 111–96.

Classen, Constance. "Sweet Colors, Fragrant Songs: Sensory Models of the Andes and the Amazon." *American Ethnologist* 17, no. 4 (November 1990): 722–35.

Clayton, Buck. *Buck Clayton's Jazz World*. Assisted by Nancy Miller Elliott. New York: Oxford University Press, 1987.

Clayton, Martin. "Rock to Raga: The Many Lives of the Indian Guitar." In *Guitar Cultures*, edited by Andy Bennett and Kevin Dawe, 179–208. Oxford: Berg, 2001.

Clough, Marshall S. *Mau Mau Memoirs: History, Memory, and Politics*. Boulder, CO: Lynne Rienner, 1998.

Clytus, John, and Jane Rieker. *Black Man in Red Cuba*. Miami: University of Miami Press, 1970.

Cochran, Sherman. *Big Business in China: Sino-Foreign Rivalry in the Cigarette Industry, 1890–1930*. Cambridge: Harvard University Press, 1980.

Comaroff, John, and Jean Comaroff. *Ethnicity, Inc.* Chicago: University of Chicago Press, 2009.

———. *Millennial Capitalism and the Culture of Neoliberalism*. Durham: Duke University Press, 2001.

———. *Of Revelation and Revolution: Christianity, Colonialism and Consciousness in South Africa*. Chicago: University of Chicago Press, 1991.

Cook, Susan. "Passionless Dancing and Passionate Reform: Respectability, Modernism, and the Social Dancing of Irene and Vernon Castle." In *The Passion of Music and Dance: Body, Gender and Sexuality*, edited by William Washbaugh. New York: Berg, 1998.

Cooper, Frederick. *Colonialism in Question: Theory, Knowledge, History*. Berkeley: University of California Press, 2005.

Coplan, David. "Go to My Town, Cape Coast! The Social History of Ghanaian Highlife." In *Eight Urban Musical Cultures*, edited by Bruno Nettl, 96–114. Urbana: University of Illinois Press, 1978.

———. *In the Time of Cannibals: The Word Music of South Africa's Basotho Migrants*. Chicago: University of Chicago Press, 1994.

———. *In Township Tonight! South Africa's Black City Music and Theatre*. 2nd ed. Chicago: University of Chicago Press, 2008.

Corbin, Alain. *Village Bells: Sound and Meaning in the 19th-Century French Countryside*. Translated by Martin Thom. New York: Columbia University Press, 1998.

Cornejo, Marco Ramirez. "Entre luces, cables, y bocinas: El movimiento sonidero." In *Sonideros en las Aceras, Véngase la Gozadera*, coordinated by El Proyecto Sonidero, 99–132. Creative Commons: Tumbona, 2012.

Cottrell, Stephen. "Smoking and All That Jazz." In *Smoke: A Global History of Smoking*, edited by Sander L. Gilman and Zhou Xun, 154–59. London: Reaktion, 2004.

Couperus, Louis. *The Hidden Force*. Translated by A. Texeira de Mattos. 1900. Reprint, Amherst: University of Massachusetts Press, 1985.

Cowan, Michael. "Imagining Modernity through the Ear: Rilke's *Die Aufzeichnungen des Malte Laurids Brigge* and the Noise of Modern Life." *Arcadia* 41, no. 1 (2006): 124–46.

Cox, Jim. *Music Radio: The Great Performers and Programs of the 1920s through Early 1960s*. Jefferson, NC: McFarland and Company, 2005.

Cramer, Gisela. "How to Do Things with Waves." In *Media, Sound and Culture in Latin America and the Caribbean*, edited by Alejandra Bronfman and Andrew Grant Wood, 37–54. Pittsburgh: University of Pittsburgh Press, 2012.

Crary, Jonathan. *Techniques of the Observer: On Vision and Modernity in the Nineteenth Century*. Cambridge: MIT Press, 1990.

Creative Industries Growth Strategy: Final Report (CIGS). Pretoria: Department of Arts, Culture, Science, and Technology, 1998.

Crowley, Daniel J. "Towards a Definition of the Calypso." *Ethnomusicology* 3, no. 2 (1959): 57–66.

Curry, Neil. "Tunisia's Rappers Provide Soundtrack to a Revolution." *CNNworld.com*, March 2, 2011. http://articles.cnn.com/2011-03-02/world/tunisia.rappers.balti_1 _- tunisian-people-rappers-sfax?_s=PM:WORLD.

Curzi, Pierre, Jack Stoddart, and Robert Pilon. "Cultural Policy Must Not Be Subject to the Constraints of International Free Trade Agreements." Canadian Coalition for Cultural Diversity Position Paper, 2001. www.cdcccd.org/main_pages_en /Publications_en/Paper_CulturalPoliMustnotbeSubjecteng.pdf.

Dalton, Karen C. C., and Henry Louis Gates Jr. "Josephine Baker and Paul Colin: African American Dance Seen through Parisian Eyes." *Critical Inquiry* 24, no. 4 (Summer 1998): 903–34.

Damas, Léon-Gontran. "Shine." *Pigments*. 1937. Reprint, Paris: Présence Africaine, 1962.

Danielson, Virginia. *The Voice of Egypt: Umm Kulthūm, Arabic Song, and Egyptian Society in the Twentieth Century*. Chicago: University of Chicago Press, 1997.

Datta, Pradip Kumar, ed. *Rabindranath Tagore's "The Home and the World": A Critical Companion*. London: Anthem, 2005.

Dávila, Arlene. *Culture Works: Space, Value, and Mobility across the Neoliberal Americas*. New York: New York University Press, 2012.

Dawson, Ashley. *Mongrel Nation: Diasporic Culture and the Making of Postcolonial Britain*. Ann Arbor: University of Michigan Press, 2007.

de Genova, Nicholas. "The Deportation Regime: Sovereignty, Space, and the Freedom of Movement." In *The Deportation Regime: Sovereignty, Space, and the Freedom of Movement*, edited by Nicholas de Genova and Nathalie Peutz, 33–68. Durham: Duke University Press, 2010.

de la Fuente, Alejandro. *A Nation for All: Race, Inequality, and Politics in Twentieth-Century Cuba*. Chapel Hill: University of North Carolina Press, 2001.

de Léry, Jean. *Histoire d'un voyage faict en la terre du Bresil.* La Rochelle: Antoine Chuppin, 1578.

de Menezes Bastos, Rafael José. "Brazil in France, 1922: An Anthropological Study of the Congenital International Nexus of Popular Music." *Latin American Music Review* 29, no. 1 (2008): 1–28.

Demos, T. J. *The Migrant Image: The Art and Politics of Documentary during Global Crisis.* Durham: Duke University Press, 2013.

Denning, Michael. "Wageless Life." *New Left Review* 60 (November–December 2010). http://newleftreview.org/II/66/michael-denning-wageless-life.

Derrick, Jonathan. *Africa's "Agitators": Militant Anti-Colonialism in Africa and the West, 1918–1939.* New York: Columbia University Press, 2008.

Derrida, Jacques. *Archive Fever: A Freudian Impression.* Translated by Eric Prenowitz. Chicago: University of Chicago Press, 1996.

Desai, Gaurav. *Subject to Colonialism: African Self-fashioning and the Colonial Library.* Durham: Duke University Press, 2001.

Dewey, John. *The Public and Its Problems.* New York: Henry Holt, 1927.

Dewitte, Philippe. *Les mouvements nègres en France pendant les entre-deux-guerres.* Paris: Harmattan, 1985.

Dexter, Dave. *Playback: A Newsman-Record Producer's Hits and Misses from the Thirties to the Seventies.* New York: Billboard, 1976.

Diawara, Manthia. *In Search of Africa.* Cambridge: Harvard University Press, 1998.

Dietz, Bill. "Composing Listening." *Performance Research* 16, no. 3 (2011): 56–61.

Dlamini, Penwell. "Ramaphosa to Run McDonalds SA." *Sowetan*, March 18, 2011. www .sowetanlive.co.za/news/business/2011/03/18/ramaphosa-to-run-mcdonalds-sa.

Doegen, Wilhelm, ed. *Unter fremden Völkern: Eine neue Völkerkunde.* Berlin: Otto Stollberg, Verlag für Politik und Wirtschaft, 1925.

Doheny, John. "The Spanish Tinge Hypothesis: Afro-Caribbean Characteristics in Early New Orleans Jazz Drumming." *Jazz Archivist* 19 (2006): 8–15.

Dolan, Emily I. *The Orchestral Revolution: Haydn and the Technologies of Timbre.* Cambridge: Cambridge University Press, 2013.

Dom za vešanje. Directed by Emir Kusturica. 1988. Netherlands: Sony Pictures, 2007.

Douglass, Frederick. *My Bondage and My Freedom.* 1855. Reprint, New York: Barnes and Noble Classics, 2005.

Doumerc, Eric. "From Page-Poet to Recording Artist: Mutabaraku interviewed by Eric Doumerc." *Journal of Commonwealth Literature* 44, no. 3 (September 2009): 23–31.

Dregni, Michael. *Django: The Life and Music of a Gypsy Legend.* New York: Oxford University Press, 2004.

Du Bois, W. E. B. *Darkwater: Voices from within the Veil.* New York: Harcourt, Brace, and Howe, 1920.

Dumm, Thomas. *Loneliness as a Way of Life.* Cambridge: Harvard University Press, 2008.

Dyson, Frances. *Sounding New Media: Immersion and Embodiment in the Arts and Culture.* Berkeley: University of California Press, 2009.

Eberly, Philip K. *Music in the Air: America's Changing Tastes in Popular Music, 1920–1980*. New York: Hastings House, 1982.

Ebonga, Charles Didier Gondola. "*Ata ndele* . . . et l'indépendance vint: Musique, jeunes et contestation politique dans les capitals congolaises." In *Les Jeunes en Afrique: La politique et la ville*, vol. 2, edited by Hélène d'Almeida-Topor, Odile Goerg, Françoise Guitart, and Catherine Coquery-Vidrovitch, 463–87. Paris: L'Harmattan, 1992.

"Editorial." *African Music* 3, no. 2 (1963): 5.

Edwards, Brent Hayes. *The Practice of Diaspora: Literature, Translation, and the Rise of Black Internationalism*. Cambridge: Harvard University Press, 2003.

Edwards, Brian, and Dilip Gaonkar, eds. *Globalizing American Studies*. Chicago: University of Chicago Press, 2010.

Ekwueme, Lazarus. "African Music in Christian Liturgy: The Igbo Experiment." *African Music* 5 (1973–74): 12–33.

Erlmann, Veit. *Music, Modernity and the Global Imagination: South Africa and the West*. Oxford: Oxford University Press, 1999.

———. *Nightsong: Performance, Power and Practice in South Africa*. Chicago: University of Chicago Press, 1996.

———. *Reason and Resonance: A History of Modern Aurality*. London: Zone, 2010.

Euba, Akin. *Essays on Music in Africa 2: Intercultural Perspective*. Beirut, Lebanon: Elékóto Music Centre, 1989.

———. *Yoruba Drumming: The Dùndún Tradition*. Beirut, Lebanon: African Studies Series, 1990.

"Experts Ask, Can President Zuma Breathe New Life into Kwaito Music?" *Music Industry Online*, June 11, 2009. www.mio.co.za/article/experts-ask-can-president -zuma-breathe-new-life-into-kwaito-music-2009-06-11.

Fabre, Michel. *From Harlem to Paris: Black American Writers in France, 1840–1980*. Urbana: University of Illinois Press, 1991.

Fair, Laura. *Pastimes and Politics: Culture, Community, and Identity in Post-Abolition Urban Zanzibar, 1890–1945*. Athens: Ohio University Press, 2001.

Fanon, Frantz. *Black Skin, White Masks*. Translated by Charles Lam Markmann. 1952. Reprint, London: MacGibbon and Kee, 1968.

———. *A Dying Colonialism*. New York: Grove, 1967.

———. *Toward the African Revolution: Political Essays*. Translated by Haakon Chevalier. New York: Grove, 1967.

———. *The Wretched of the Earth*. Translated by Richard Philcox. 1961. Reprint, New York: Grove, 2004.

Featherstone, David, Richard Phillips, and Johanna Waters. "Introduction: Spatialities of Transnational Networks." *Global Networks* 7, no. 4 (2007): 383–91.

Feld, Steven. "Communication, Music, and Speech about Music." *Yearbook for Traditional Music* 16 (1984): 1–18.

———. "From Schizophonia to Schismogenesis: On the Discourses and Commodification and Practices of 'World Music' and 'World Beat.'" In *Music Grooves: Essays and Dialogues*, edited by Charles Keil and Steven Feld, 257–89. Chicago: University of Chicago Press, 1994.

———. *Jazz Cosmopolitanism in Accra: Five Musical Years in Ghana*. Durham: Duke University Press, 2012.

Ferguson, James. "Formalities of Poverty: Thinking about Social Assistance in Neoliberal South Africa." *African Studies Review* 50, no. 2 (2007): 71–86.

Fick, David. *Africa: Continent of Economic Opportunity*. Johannesburg: STE, 2006.

———. *Entrepreneurship in Africa: A Study of Successes*. Westport, CT: Quorum, 2002.

Fiehrer, Thomas. "From Quadrille to Stomp: The Creole Origins of Jazz." *Popular Music* 10, no. 1 (1991): 21–38.

Field, Andrew David. *Shanghai's Dancing World: Cabaret Culture and Urban Politics, 1919–1954*. Hong Kong: Chinese University Press, 2010.

Fincham, Gail. "Arches and Echoes: Framing Devices in *A Passage to India*." *Pretexts* 2, no. 1 (1990): 52–67.

Forster, E. M. *The Hill of Devi*. New York: Harcourt, Brace, 1953.

———. *"The Machine Stops" and Other Stories*. 1947. Reprint, London: Andre Deutsch, 1997.

———. *A Passage to India*. 1924. Reprint, San Diego, CA: Harcourt, 1985.

Foucault, Michel. *The Archaeology of Knowledge*. Translated by A. M. Sheridan Smith. New York: Pantheon, 1972.

———. "La naissance d'un monde." In *Dits et écrits, 1954–1988*, vol. 1. 1969. Reprint, Paris: Gallimard, 1994.

———. "Of Other Spaces: Utopias and Heterotopias." *diacritics* 16 (Spring 1986): 22–27.

Franca, L., Jr. "The Arts of Resistance in the Poetry of Linton Kwesi Johnson." www.ufsj .edu.br/porta12-repositorio/File/vertentes/v.%2019%20n.%201/Franca_Junior.pdf.

Frank Canaday Papers. Yenching Library, Harvard University.

Frazier, David. "Kupa Big Band: That Old Style Hoklo Swing." *Fountain: Arts and Living*, vol. 4 (2010).

Fu, Poshek. "Modernity, Diasporic Capital, and 1950s Hong Kong Mandarin Cinema." *Jump Cut*, no. 49 (Spring 2007). www.ejumpcut.org/archive/jc49.2007/Poshek/text .html.

Funk, Ray, and Donald R. Hill. "'Will Calypso Doom Rock 'n' Roll?': The U.S. Calypso Craze of 1957." In *Trinidad Carnival: The Cultural Politics of a Transnational Festival*, edited by Garth L. Green and Philip W. Scher, 178–97. Bloomington: Indiana University Press, 2007.

Galeano, Eduardo. *Open Veins of Latin America*. Translated by Cedric Belfrage. 1971. Reprint, New York: Monthly Review, 1973.

Gamio, Manuel. *Mexican Immigration to the United States: A Study of Human Migration and Adjustment*. Mineola, NY: Dover, 1971.

Gandhi, Mohandas K. *An Autobiography: The Story of My Experiments with Truth*. Boston: Beacon, 1993.

George, Olakunle. *Relocating Agency: Modernity and African Letters*. Albany: State University of New York Press, 2003.

Ghonim, Wael. *Revolution 2.0: The Power of the People Is Greater Than the People in Power: A Memoir*. Boston: Houghton Mifflin Harcourt, 2012.

Ghosh, Amitav. *Sea of Poppies*. London: John Murray, 2008.

Ghosh, Bobby. "Rage, Rap and Revolution." *Time*, February 17, 2011.

Ghosh, Rishab Aiyer. "Why Collaboration Is Important (Again)." In CODE: *Collaborative Ownership and the Digital Economy*, edited by Rishab Aiyer Ghosh, 1–7. Cambridge: MIT Press, 2006.

Gibbs, Jason. "Spoken Theater, La Scène Tonkinoise, and the First Modern Vietnamese Songs." *Asian Music* 31, no. 2 (2000): 1–34.

———. "The West's Songs, Our Songs: The Introduction and Adaptation of Western Popular Song in Vietnam before 1940." *Asian Music* 35, no. 1 (Autumn 2003/Winter 2004): 57–83.

Giddens, Anthony. *The Constitution of Society*. Berkeley: University of California Press, 1986.

Gikandi, Simon. *Ngugi wa Thiong'o*. Cambridge: Cambridge University Press, 2000.

Gilroy, Paul. *The Black Atlantic: Modernity and Double Consciousness*. Cambridge: Harvard University Press, 1993.

———. *Darker Than Blue: On the Moral Economies of Black Atlantic Culture*. Cambridge: Belknap Press of Harvard University Press, 2010.

Ginway, M. Elizabeth. "Surrealist Benjamin Péret and Brazilian Modernism." *Hispania* 75, no. 3 (September 1992): 543–53.

Gladstone, Brooke. "North Africa's Hip Hop Protest Music." *On the Media from* NPR, February 11, 2011. www.onthemedia.org/transcripts/2011/02/11/02.

Glasser, Ruth. *My Music Is My Flag: Puerto Rican Musicians and Their New York Communities, 1917–1940*. Durham: Duke University Press, 1997.

Glissant, Édouard. *Caribbean Discourse: Selected Essays*. Charlottesville: University Press of Virginia, 1989.

Goertzen, Chris, and María Susana Azzi. "Globalization and the Tango." *Yearbook for Traditional Music* 31 (1999): 67–76.

Goodman, Steve. *Sonic Warfare: Sound, Affect, and the Ecology of Fear*. Cambridge: MIT Press, 2012.

Gottschild, Brenda Dixon. *The Black Dancing Body: A Geography from Coon to Cool*. New York: Palgrave Macmillan, 2005.

Grandin, Greg. *Empire's Workshop: Latin America, the United States, and the Rise of the New Imperialism*. New York: Henry Holt, 2007.

Greenblatt, Stephen. *Marvelous Possessions: The Wonder of the New World*. Chicago: University of Chicago Press, 1991.

Gregg, Melissa, and Gregory J. Seigworth, eds. *The Affect Studies Reader*. Durham: Duke University Press, 2010.

Grein, Paul. *Capitol Records: Fiftieth Anniversary, 1942–1992*. Hollywood, CA: Capitol Records, 1992.

Greve, Martin. *Die Musik der imaginären Türkei: Musik und Musikleben im Kontext der Migration aus der Türkei in Deutschland*. Stuttgart: Metzler, 2003.

Grimson, Alejandro. "Ethnic (In)visibility in Neoliberal Argentina." NACLA *Report on the Americas* 38, no. 4 (2005): 25–29, 40.

Grimson, Alejandro, and Karina Bidaseca, eds. *Hegemonía cultural y políticas de la diferencia*. Buenos Aires: CLACSO, 2013.

Grossman, Sanford, and Joseph Stiglitz. "On the Impossibility of Informationally Efficient Markets." *American Economic Review* 70 (1980): 393–408.

Guha, Ranajit. *Elementary Aspects of Peasant Insurgency in Colonial India.* Durham: Duke University Press, 1999.

Guo, Shu. "The Silver River Rolls On and On: A Historical Gallery of Chinese Film Stars." [In Chinese.] *Dianying Huakan,* no. 4 (2004): 58–59.

Hanchard, Michael. *Orpheus and Power.* Princeton, NJ: Princeton University Press, 1998.

Handy, Roger, Maureen Erbe, Aileen Antonier, and Henry Blackham. *Made in Japan: Transistor Radios of the 1950s and 1960s.* San Francisco: Chronicle, 1993.

Handy, W. C. *Father of the Blues: An Autobiography.* Edited by Arna Bontemps, with a foreword by Abbe Niles. New York: Macmillan, 1941.

Hannerz, Ulf. "Cosmopolitans and Locals in World Culture." In *Global Culture: Nationalism, Globalization and Modernity,* edited by Mike Featherstone, 237–52. London: Sage, 1990.

Hansen, Miriam Bratu. "The Mass Production of the Senses: Classical Cinema as Vernacular Modernism." *Modernism/Modernity* 6, no. 2 (1999): 59–77.

———. "Vernacular Modernism: Tracking Cinema on a Global Scale." In *World Cinemas, Transnational Perspectives,* edited by Nataša Durovicová and Kathleen Newman. London: Routledge, 2007.

Hardt, Michael. "Empire, Multitude and Commonwealth: The Anthropology of the Global in the Radical Political Philosophy of Antonio Negri and Michael Hardt." Panel presented at the American Anthropological Association, New Orleans, LA, November 17–21, 2010.

———. "Immaterial Labor and Artistic Production." *Rethinking Marxism* 17, no. 2 (2005): 175–77.

Hardt, Michael, and Antonio Negri. *Commonwealth.* Cambridge: Harvard University Press, 2009.

———. *Empire.* Cambridge: Harvard University Press, 2000.

———. *Labor of Dionysus: A Critique of the State Form.* Minneapolis: University of Minnesota Press, 1994.

———. *Multitude: War and Democracy in the Age of Empire Hardcover.* New York: Penguin, 2004.

Hay, Stephen. "Rabindranath Tagore in America." *American Quarterly* 14, no. 3 (1962): 439–63.

He, Fan. "Taiwan's Fake Label Records." [In Chinese.] *Lianhe Bao,* October 27, 1965.

Hebblethwaite, Cordelia. "Is Hip Hop Driving the Arab Spring?" *BBC News,* July 24, 2011. www.bbc.co.uk/news/world-middle-east-14146243.

Hellwig, David J., ed. *African-American Reflections on Brazil's Racial Paradise.* Philadelphia: Temple University Press, 1992.

Hemetek, Ursula. "Gelem, Gelem Lungone Dromeja—I Have Walked a Long Way: The International Anthem of the 'Travelling People'—Symbol of a Nation?" In *Music in Motion: Diversity and Dialogue in Europe,* edited by Bernd Clausen, Ursula Hemetek, and Eva Sæther, 103–14. Bielefeld, Germany: Transcript Verlag, 2009.

———. *Mosaik der Klänge: Musik der ethnischen und religiösen Minderheiten in Öster-reich*. Vienna: Böhlau, 2001.

Henriques, Julian. "Situating Sound: The Space and Time of the Dancehall Session." In *Sonic Interventions*, edited by Sylvia Mieszkowski, Joy Smith, and Marijke de Valck, 287–310. New York: Rodopi, 2007.

———. *Sonic Bodies: Reggae Sound Systems, Performance Techniques, and Ways of Knowing*. London: Continuum, 2011.

———. "Sonic Dominance and the Reggae Sound System Session." In *Auditory Culture Reader*, edited by M. Bull and L. Back, 451–80. Oxford: Berg, 2003.

Herder, Johann Gottfried. *"Stimmen der Völker in Liedern"* and *Volkslieder*. 2 vols. Leipzig: Weygandsche Buchhandlung, 1778–79. Reprint, Stuttgart: Reclam, 1975.

Herman, Edward, and Noam Chomsky. *Manufacturing Consent: The Political Economy of the Mass Media*. New York: Pantheon, 2002.

Herskovits, Melville J. "African Gods and Catholic Saints in New World Negro Belief." *American Anthropologist* 39 (1937): 635–43.

Hilton, Matthew. *Smoking in British Popular Culture 1880–2000*. Manchester, UK: Manchester University Press, 2000.

Hong, Guo-Juin. *Taiwan Cinema: A Contested Nation Onscreen*. New York: Palgrave Macmillan, 2011.

"Hong Kong's Grace Chang Warmly Received in the US." [In Chinese.] *Lianhe Bao*, May 2, 1961.

Horkheimer, Max, and Theodor W. Adorno. *Dialectic of Enlightenment: Philosophical Fragments*. Edited by Gunzelin Schmid Noerr. Translated by Edmund Jephcott. 1947. Reprint, Stanford, CA: Stanford University Press, 2002.

Hosenball, Mark. "Centuries of Boredom in World without War; an American Theory; Spectrum." *Times* (London), September 3, 1989.

Hountondji, Paulin. *African Philosophy: Myth and Reality*. Translated by Henry Evans with Jonathan Rée. Bloomington: Indiana University Press, 1996.

Houston, Elsie. *Chants Populaires du Brésil*. 1st ed. Paris: Librairie Orientaliste Paul Geuthner, 1930.

———. "La musique, la danse et les cérémonies populaires du Brésil." In *Art populaire: Travaux artistiques et scientifiques du 1er Congrès int'l des arts populaires, Prague, 1928*, 162–64. Paris: Duchartre, 1931.

Hu, Brian. "Star Discourse and the Cosmopolitan Chinese: Linda Lin Dai Takes on the World." *Journal of Chinese Cinemas* 4, no. 3 (November 2010): 183–209.

Hughes, Langston. *I Wonder as I Wander: An Autobiographical Journey*. New York: Rinehart, 1956.

Hui. "Paramount Distributes Its First Mambo Movie." [In Chinese.] *Lianhe Fukan*, May 10, 1955, 6.

Hutchinson, James Lafayette. *China Hand*. Boston: Lothrop, Lee and Shepard, 1936.

Hyer, Brian. "Tonality." In *The Cambridge History of Western Music Theory*, edited by Thomas Christensen, 726–52. Cambridge: Cambridge University Press, 2006.

Imada, Adria. *Aloha America: Hula Circuits through the U.S. Empire*. Durham: Duke University Press, 2012.

International Library of African Music. Rhodes University. www.ru.ac.za/ilam/.

Irele, Abiola. *The African Imagination: Literature in Africa and the Black Diaspora.* Oxford: Oxford University Press, 2001.

Irwin S. Smith Oral History, July 28, 1982. East Carolina Manuscript Collection, J. Y. Joyner Library, East Carolina University.

Jackson, K. David. "Alienation and Ideology in *A Famosa Revista* (1945)." *Hispania* 74, no. 2 (May 1991): 298–304.

"Jaime Ovalle." *Dicionário Cravo Albin da Música Popular Brasileira.* Rio de Janeiro: Instituto Cultural Cravo Albin, 2002–2011. www.dicionariompb.com.br/jaime-ovalle.

Jaji, Tsitsi Ella. "Négritude Musicology: Poetry, Performance, and Statecraft in Senegal." In *Africa in Stereo: Modernism, Music, and Pan-African Solidarity,* 66–110. New York: Oxford University Press, 2014.

James, C. L. R. *The Black Jacobins: Toussaint L'Ouverture and the San Domingo Revolution.* 1938. 2nd ed., New York: Vintage, 1963.

———. *Nkrumah and the Ghana Revolution.* Westport, CT: Lawrence Hill, 1977.

James, Daniel. *Resistance and Integration: Peronism and the Argentine Working Class, 1946–1976.* Cambridge: Cambridge University Press, 1988.

James N. Joyner Papers. Special Collections Department, J. Y. Joyner Library, East Carolina University.

Jensen, Joan. *Passage from India: Asian Indian Immigrants in North America.* New Haven, CT: Yale University Press, 1988.

Johnson, John J. *A Hemisphere Apart: The Foundations of United States Policy toward Latin America.* Baltimore, MD: Johns Hopkins University Press, 1990.

Johnson, Linton Kwesi. *Mi Revalueshanary Fren.* Keene, NY: Ausable, 2006.

Jones, A. M. *African Hymnody in Christian Worship: A Contribution to the History of Its Development.* Mambo Occasional Papers. Gwelo, Rhodesia: Mambo, 1976.

———. *Studies in African Music.* 2 volumes. Oxford: Oxford University Press, 1959.

Jones, Andrew F. *Yellow Music: Media Culture and Colonial Modernity in the Chinese Jazz Age.* Durham: Duke University Press, 2001.

Joseph, Gilbert M., Catherine C. Legrand, and Ricardo D. Salvatore, eds. *Close Encounters of Empire: Writing the Cultural History of U.S.-Latin American Relations.* Durham: Duke University Press, 1998.

Joseph, Peniel. "Where Blackness Is Bright? Cuba, Africa and Black Liberation during the Age of Civil Rights." *New Formations* 45 (2002): 111–24.

Kaplan, Amy. *The Anarchy of Empire in the Making of U.S. Culture.* Cambridge: Harvard University Press, 2002.

———. " 'Left Alone with America': The Absence of Empire in the Study of American Culture." In *Cultures of United States Imperialism,* edited by Amy Kaplan and Donald E. Pease, 3–21. Durham: Duke University Press, 1993.

Kawash, Samira. "*The Autobiography of an Ex-Coloured Man*: (Passing for) Black Passing for White." In *Passing and the Fictions of Identity,* edited by Elaine K. Ginsberg, 59–74. Durham: Duke University Press, 1996.

Kelley, Robin D. G. *Africa Speaks, America Answers: Modern Jazz in Revolutionary Times.* Cambridge: Harvard University Press, 2012.

——. *Freedom Dreams: The Black Radical Imagination.* New York: Beacon, 2003.

——. "A Poetics of Anticolonialism." *Monthly Review* (November 1999). www .monthlyreview.org/1199kell.htm.

Kennan, George. *American Diplomacy: 1900–1950.* New York: Penguin, 1952.

Khaldûn, Ibn. *The Muqaddimah: An Introduction to History.* Translated by Franz Rosenthal. Edited and abridged by N. J. Dawood. Princeton, NJ: Princeton University Press, 1967.

Khan, Naveeda. "A Particular Genealogy of the Azan." Paper presented at the American Anthropological Association meeting, November 2000, San Francisco.

King, Roberta, Jean Ngoya Kidula, James R. Krabill, and Thomas Oduro. *Music in the Life of the African Church.* Waco, TX: Baylor University Press, 2008.

Kinyatti, Maina wa, ed. *Thunder from the Mountains: Poems and Songs from the Mau Mau.* 1980. Reprint, Trenton, NJ: Africa World Press, 1990.

Kinzer, Stephen. "Prenden Journal: For East German Theme Park, the Bad Old Days." *New York Times,* November 9, 1993.

Kirshenblatt-Gimblett, Barbara. "Intangible Heritage as Metacultural Production." *Museum International* 56, nos. 1–2 (2004): 52–65.

Kisliuk, Michelle. *Seize the Dance! BaAka Musical Life and the Ethnography of Performance.* New York: Oxford University Press, 1998.

Kittler, Friedrich. *Discourse Networks 1800/1900.* Translated by Michael Metteer with Chris Cullen. Stanford, CA: Stanford University Press, 1990.

——. *Gramophone-Film-Typewriter.* Translated by Geoffrey Winthrop-Young and Michael Wutz. 1986. Reprint, Stanford, CA: Stanford University Press, 1999.

Koch, Lars-Christian. "Images of Sound: Erich M. von Hornbostel and the Berlin Phonogram Archive." In *The Cambridge History of World Music,* edited by Philip V. Bohlman, 475–97. Cambridge: Cambridge University Press, 2013.

——. *My Heart Sings: Die Lieder Rabindranath Tagores zwischen Tradition und Moderne.* Münster: LIT Verlag, 2011.

Kopytoff, Igor. "The Cultural Biography of Things: Commoditization as Process." In *The Social Life of Things: Commodities in Cultural Perspective,* edited by Arjun Appadurai, 64–94. New York: Cambridge University Press, 1986.

Koseff, Lara. "Art and the City: Is Joburg a Cultural Capital?" *ClassicFeel* (October 2009).

Koshy, Susan. *Sexual Naturalization: Asian Americans and Miscegenation.* Stanford, CA: Stanford University Press, 2005.

Kreilkamp, Ivan. *Voice and the Victorian Storyteller.* Cambridge: Cambridge University Press, 2005.

Kubik, Gerhard. *Africa and the Blues.* Jackson: University Press of Mississippi, 1999.

——. "African Tone Systems: A Reassessment." *Yearbook for Traditional Music* 17 (1985): 31–63.

——. "Multipart Singing in Sub-Saharan Africa: Remote and Recent Histories Unravelled." In *Papers Presented at the Symposium on Ethnomusicology: Number 13 University of Zululand 1995 and at the Symposium Number 14 Rhodes University*

1996, edited by Andrew Tracey, 85–97. Grahamstown, South Africa: International Library of African Music, 1997.

Kun, Josh. "Arts of Contraband: On Julio Cesar Morales' Contrabando at Frey Norris." In *Contrabando: Julio Cesar Morales*, April 2–May 28, 2011, 3–4. San Francisco: Wendy Norris Gallery, 2011.

———. "Death Rattle." *American Prospect.* January 5, 2012, http://prospect.org/article/death-rattle.

Kurin, Richard. "Safeguarding the Intangible Cultural Heritage in the 2003 UNESCO Convention: A Critical Appraisal." *Museum International* 56, nos. 1–2 (2004): 66–77.

LaFeber, Walter. *The New Empire: An Interpretation of American Expansion, 1860–1898.* Ithaca, NY: Cornell University Press, 1963.

Lahiri, Tripti. "Under the Musical Spell of the Sonidero." *New York Times*, November 22, 2003.

Lamming, George. *In the Castle of My Skin.* 1953. Reprint, New York: Schocken, 1983.

Larkin, Brian. *Signal and Noise: Media, Infrastructure, and Urban Culture in Nigeria.* Durham: Duke University Press, 2008.

Latcho drom. Directed by Tony Gatlif. 1993. New York: New Yorker Video, 1998.

Latour, Bruno. "On the Difficulty of Being Glocal," ART-*e*-FACT 4 (2005), accessed March 31, 2015, http://artefact.mi2.hr/_a04/lang_en/theory_latour_en.htm.

Lee, Jennifer, and Frank Bean. "Reinventing the Color Line: Immigration and America's New Racial/Ethnic Hierarchy." *Social Forces* 86, no. 2 (December 2007): 561–86.

Leiris, Michel. "The Ethnographer Faced with Colonialism." In *Brisées =Broken Branches*, translated by Lydia Davis, 112–31. San Francisco: North Point, 1989.

Lesser, W. "The Effects of TRIPS-Mandated Intellectual Property Rights on Economic Activities in Developing Countries." Paper prepared under the World Intellectual Property Organization Special Service Agreement, April 17, 2001. www.wipo.int/export/sites/www/about-ip/en/studies/pdf/ssa_lesser_trips.pdf.

Lethbridge, H. J. *All About Shanghai: A Standard Guidebook.* 1935. Reprint, Hong Kong: Oxford University Press, 1983.

Leymarie, Isabelle. *Cuban Fire: The Story of Salsa and Latin Jazz.* 1997. Reprint, New York: Continuum, 2002.

L'Hoeste, Héctor Fernández, and Pablo Vila, eds. *Cumbia! Scenes of a Migrant Latin American Music Genre.* Durham: Duke University Press, 2013.

Lim, Kay Tong, and Tiong Chai Yiu. *Cathay: 55 Years of Cinema.* Singapore: Landmark, 1991.

Lionnet, Françoise, and Shu-mei Shih, eds. *Minor Transnationalism.* Durham: Duke University Press, 2005.

Lomax, Alan. "Folk Song Style." *American Anthropologist* 61 (1959): 927–54.

———. *Mister Jelly Roll: The Fortunes of Jelly Roll Morton, New Orleans Creole and Inventor of Jazz.* New York: Universal Library, Grosset and Dunlap, 1950. www.traditionalmusic.co.uk/jelly-roll/.

Lomnitz, Claudio. *Death and the Idea of Mexico.* Cambridge: MIT Press, 2005.

Lotringer, Sylvère, and Christian Marazzi, eds. *Autonomia: Post-Political Politics*. 2nd ed. Los Angeles: Semiotext(e), 2007.

Lucia, Christine. "Back to the Future? Idioms of 'Displaced Time' in South African Composition." In *Composing Apartheid: Music for and against Apartheid*, edited by Grant Olwage, 11–34. Johannesburg: Wits University Press, 2008.

Lugo, Alejandro. *Fragmented Lives, Assembled Parts: Culture, Capitalism and Conquest at the U.S.-Mexico Border*. Austin: University of Texas Press, 2008.

Luker, Morgan James. "Contemporary Tango and the Cultural Politics of *Música Popular*." In *Tango Lessons: Music, Sound, Image and Text in Contemporary Practice*, edited by Marilyn G. Miller, 198–219. Durham: Duke University Press, 2014.

Lynch, Julian. "Music and Communal Violence in Colonial South Asia." *Ethnomusicology Review* 17 (2012).

Lyotard, Jean-François. "On Theory: An Interview." In *Driftworks*, 19–33. 1977. Reprint, New York: Semiotext(e), 1984.

Macdonald, Hugh. *Berlioz's Orchestration Treatise: A Translation and Commentary*. Cambridge: Cambridge University Press, 2002.

Macey, David. *Frantz Fanon: A Biography*. New York: Picador, 2001.

Macmillan, Harold. "Speech to the South African Parliament." February 3, 1960. Online video. Apartheid in South Africa. BBC. www.bbc.co.uk/archive/apartheid /7203.shtml.

Magubane, Zine. "Globalization and Gangster Rap: Hip Hop in the Post-Apartheid City." In *The Vinyl Ain't Final: Hip Hop and the Globalization of Black Popular Culture*, edited by Dipannita Basu and Sidney J. Lemelle, 208–29. London: Pluto, 2006.

Maira, Sunaina. *Missing: Youth, Citizenship, and Empire after 9/11*. Durham: Duke University Press, 2009.

Marchini, Jorge. *El tango en la economía de la ciudad de Buenos Aires*. Buenos Aires: Observatorio de Industrias Culturales, Subsecretaría de Industrias Culturales, Secretaría de Producción, Gobierno de la Ciudad de Buenos Aires, 2007.

Marcus, George E. "The Once and Future Ethnographic Archive." *History of the Human Sciences* 11, no. 4 (1998): 49–63.

Marsalis, Wynton. "What Jazz Is—and Isn't." *New York Times*, July 3, 1988. www.nytimes .com/1988/07/31/arts/music-what-jazz-is-and-isn-t.html?pagewanted=all&src=pm.

Martins, Wilson. *O Modernismo (1916–1945)*. Vol. 6 of *A Literatura Brasileira*, 4th ed. São Paulo: Editora Cultrix, 1973.

Marx, Karl. *Grundrisse: Foundations of the Critique of Political Economy*. Translated by Martin Nicolaus. 1939. Reprint, London: Penguin, 1993.

Matory, J. Lorand. *Black Atlantic Religion: Tradition, Transnationalism, and Matriarchy in the Afro-Brazilian Candomblé*. Princeton, NJ: Princeton University Press, 2005.

Matsuda, Matt K. *The Memory of the Modern*. New York: Oxford University Press, 1996.

Mbembe, Achille. "Aesthetics of Superfluity." In *Johannesburg: The Elusive Metropolis*, edited by Sarah Nuttall and Achille Mbembe, 37–67. Durham: Duke University Press, 2008.

———. "Necropolitics." In *The Unhomely: Phantom Scenes in Global Society*, edited by Okwui Enwezor, 32–51. Barcelona: Biacs, 2006.

———. *On the Postcolony*. Berkeley: University of California Press, 2001.

Mbembe, Achille, and Sarah Nuttall. "Introduction: Afropolis." In *Johannesburg: The Elusive Metropolis*, edited by Sarah Nuttall and Achille Mbembe, 1–36. Durham: Duke University Press, 2008.

McAllester, David. "The Astonished Ethno-muse." *Ethnomusicology* 23, no. 2 (May 1979): 179–89.

McHugh, Kathleen. "South Korean Film Melodrama: State, Nation, Woman, and the Transnational Familiar." In *South Korean Golden Age Melodrama: Gender, Genre, and National Cinema*, edited by Kathleen McHugh and Nancy Abelmann, 17–42. Detroit, MI: Wayne State University Press, 2005.

McKinley, James C., Jr. "Jazz at Lincoln Center to Expand, First in Qatar." *New York Times*, November 15, 2011.

McLuhan, Marshall. *Understanding Media: The Extensions of Man*. New York: McGraw-Hill, 1964.

Meier, John. *Kunstlieder im Volksmunde: Materialien und Untersuchungen*. Halle a.S., Germany: M. Niemeyer, 1906.

Memmi, Albert. *The Colonizer and the Colonized*. Translated by Howard Greenfield. Boston: Beacon, 1965.

Ménil, René. "Laissez passer la poésie." *Tropiques* 5 (April 1942): 21–28.

———. "The Situation of Poetry in the Caribbean." In *Refusal of the Shadow: Surrealism and the Caribbean*, translated by Michael Richardson and Krzysztof Fijalkowski, 129. 1944. Reprint, London: Verso, 1996.

———. "Sur un certain effet Ellingtonien dans la créolité." In *Antilles déjà jadis: précédé de tracées*. Paris: Jean-Michel Place, 1999.

Merriam, Alan P. "African Music." In *Continuity and Change in African Cultures*, edited by William R. Bascom and Melville J. Herskovitz, 49–86. Chicago: University of Chicago Press, 1958.

———. *The Anthropology of Music*. Evanston, IL: Northwestern University Press, 1964.

———. *Ethnomusicology of the Flathead Indians*. Chicago: Aldine, 1967.

Merritt, Carolyn. *Tango Nuevo*. Gainesville: University Press of Florida, 2012.

Middleton, Richard. *Voicing the Popular: On the Subjects of Popular Music*. London: Routledge, 2006.

Milhaud, Darius. *Notes without Music*. 1952. Reprint, New York: Knopf, 1953.

Milkowski, Bill. "Wynton Marsalis: One Future, Two Views." *Jazz Times* (March 2000). http://jazztimes.com/articles/20520-wynton-marsalis-one-future-two-views.

Miller, Toby. *The Well-Tempered Self: Citizenship, Culture, and the Postmodern Subject*. Baltimore, MD: Johns Hopkins University Press, 1993.

Miller, Toby, Nitin Govil, John McMurria, Richard Maxwell, and Ting Wang. *Global Hollywood, No. 2*. London: British Film Institute, 2005.

Mitchell, Timothy. *Colonising Egypt*. Berkeley: University of California Press, 1988.

Mitchell, Tony. *Global Noise: Rap and Hip-Hop outside the USA*. Middletown, CT: Wesleyan University Press, 2002.

Mojapelo, Max. *Beyond Memory: Recording the Moments and Memories of South African Music*. Somerset Erst, South Africa: African Minds, 2008.

Monson, Ingrid. *Freedom Sounds: Civil Rights Call Out to Jazz and Africa*. New York: Oxford University Press, 2007.

Moore, Carlos. *Castro, the Blacks, and Africa*. Los Angeles: Center for Afro-American Studies, UCLA, 1988.

Moore, Robin. "The Danzón and Musical Influence on Early Jazz." In *Danzón: Circum-Caribbean Dialogues in Music and Dance*, coauthored with Alejandro Madrid. New York: Oxford University Press, forthcoming.

Moore, Thurston. *Mix-Tape: The Art of Cassette Culture*. New York: Universe, 2007.

Morales, Helmer G. "Sonideros, sobreviventes del desdén." *El Universal*, February 20, 2008.

Moreno, Jairo. "Bauzá—Gillespie—Latin/Jazz: Difference, Modernity, and the Black Caribbean." *South Atlantic Quarterly* 103, no. 1 (2004): 81–99.

Moreno, Jairo, and Gavin Steingo. "Rancière's Equal Music." *Contemporary Music Review* 31, nos. 5–6 (2012): 487–505.

Morsi, Hani. "Social Media in the Middle East: Is It a Real Tool for (Incremental) Change, or Merely Cathartic Self-expression?" *HaniMorsi.com*, August 2, 2010. www.hanimorsi.com/blog/index.php/archives/2010/08/02/social_media_in_the_middle_east/.

———. "The Virtualization of Dissent: Social Media as a Catalyst for Social Change (Part One: Why Gladwell Is Wrong)." *HaniMorsi.com*, February 15, 2011. www.hanimorsi.com/blog/index.php/archives/2011/02/15/the-virtualization-of-dissent-social-media-as-a-catalyst-for-social-change-part-one-why-gladwell-is-wrong/.

Mrázek, Rudolf. *Engineers of a Happy Land: Technology and Nationalism in a Colony*. Princeton, NJ: Princeton University Press, 2002.

Mthethwa, Eugene. "Why I'm Quitting Trompies." *NewZimbabwe.com*, August 2, 2009. www.newzimbabwe.com/pages/trompies6.19358.html.

Mu, Shiying. "Craven A." In *Mu Shiying dai biao zuo* [Mu Shiying's representative work]. Beijing: Huaxia chubanshe, 1998.

Mudimbe, V. Y. *The Invention of Africa: Gnosis, Philosophy, and the Order of Knowledge*. Bloomington: Indiana University Press, 1988.

Mullen, Harryette. "Optic White: Blackness and the Production of Whiteness." *diacritics* 24, nos. 2–3 (1994): 74–89.

Muñoz, José. *Cruising Utopia: The Then and There of Queer Futurity*. New York: New York University Press, 2009.

"Music: Mambo-San." *Time*, July 25, 1955.

Myatt, Carl. "Pirates Capturing Business." *Billboard*, August 31, 1963, 30.

———. "Tito Puente Dates Boost Latin Music." *Billboard*, November 7, 1962, 33.

Myers, Helen. *The New Grove Dictionary of Music and Musicians*, 2nd ed., s.v. "Ethnomusicology." Oxford: Oxford University Press, 2001.

Needell, Jeffrey D. *A Tropical Belle Epoque: The Elite Culture of Turn-of-the-Century Rio de Janeiro*. New York: Cambridge University Press, 1987.

Negri, Antonio. *Empire and Beyond*. Translated by Ed Emory. Cambridge, UK: Polity, 2008.

———. "Metamorphoses." *Radical Philosophy* 149 (May–June 2008): 21–25.

Nettl, Bruno. *Nettl's Elephant: On the History of Ethnomusicology*. Urbana: University of Illinois Press, 2010.

Nicholls, Brendon. *Ngugi wa Thiong'o, Gender, and the Ethics of Postcolonial Reading*. Burlington, VT: Ashgate, 2010.

Nimis, John. "Literary Listening: Readings in Congolese Popular Music." PhD dissertation, New York University, 2010.

Nketia, J. H. Kwabena. "The Scholarly Study of African Music: A Historical Review." In *The Garland Encyclopedia of World Music, Vol. 1: Africa*, edited by Ruth Stone, 51–52. New York: Garland, 1998.

Novak, David. "2.5 x 6 Metres of Space: Japanese Music Coffee Houses and Experimental Practices of Listening." *Popular Music* 27, no. 1 (2008): 15–34.

Nuttall, Sarah, and Achille Mbembe, eds. *Johannesburg: The Elusive Metropolis*. Special issue of *Public Culture*. Durham: Duke University Press, 2004.

Nyaho, William Chapman, ed. *Piano Music of Africa and the African Diaspora*. New York: Oxford University Press, 2009.

Nyanyui Hame Hadzigbalẽ Gã. 5th ed. Maharashtra, India: Evangelical Presbyterian Church, Ghana and Eglise Evangélique Presbytérienne du Togo, 2002.

Ochoa Gautier, Ana María. "Sonic Transculturation, Epistemologies of Purification and the Aural Public Sphere in Latin America." *Social Identities* 12, no. 6 (2006): 803–25.

Oehlkers, Peter (Robert Porter). *The Annotated "Ends Her Life: Elsie Houston."* http://home.comcast.net/~gullcity/elsiehouston/Houston.html.

———. "Paul Bowles and Elsie Houston." *Robert's Basement*, November 9, 2005. http://robertsbasement.blogspot.com/2005/11/paul-bowles-and-elsie-houston.html.

Okihiro, Gary. *Margins and Mainstreams: Asians in American History and Culture*. Seattle: University of Washington Press, 1994.

O'Meally, Robert. *The Jazz Cadence of American Culture*. New York: Columbia University Press, 1998.

O'Meally, Robert, Brent Hayes Edwards, and Farah Jasmine Griffin, eds. *Uptown Conversation: The New Jazz Studies*. New York: Columbia University Press, 2004.

"On the Line with . . . 2Pac Shakur, the Lost Interview." *Davey D's Hip Hop Corner*, February 10, 2012. www.daveyd.com/interview2pacrare.html.

Ong Hing, Bill. *Defining America through Immigration Policy*. Philadelphia: Temple University Press, 2004.

Orovio, Helio. *Cuban Music from A to Z*. Durham: Duke University Press, 2004.

Ortner, Sherry. *Anthropology and Social Theory: Culture, Power, and the Acting Subject*. Durham: Duke University Press, 2006.

O'Toole, Michael. "Sonic Citizenship in the New Germany: Music, Migration, and Transnationalism in Berlin's Turkish and Anatolian Diasporas." PhD dissertation, University of Chicago, 2014.

Ozah, Sister Marie Agatha. "*Égwú Àmàlà*: Women in Traditional Performing Arts in Ogbaruland." PhD dissertation, University of Pittsburgh, 2008.

Palmié, Stephan. "Creolization and Its Discontents." *Annual Review of Anthropology* 35 (2006): 433–56.

Parry, Benita. *Delusions and Discoveries: Studies on India in the British Imagination, 1880–1930.* Berkeley: University of California Press, 1972.

"*A Passage to India* by E. M. Forster." *Guardian*, June 20, 1924. www.guardian.co.uk /books/1924/jun/20/classics.

"Pathé Records Nets MP&GI's Flock of Stars." [In Chinese.] *International Screen* 33 (July 1958): 50–51.

Pemberton, John. "Musical Politics in Central Java (or How Not to Listen to Javanese Gamelan)." *Indonesia* 44 (October 1987): 17–29.

Pérez Firmat, Gustavo. *Life on the Hyphen: The Cuban-American Way.* Austin: University of Texas Press, 1994.

Perry, Elizabeth J. *Shanghai on Strike: The Politics of Chinese Labor.* Stanford, CA: Stanford University Press, 1993.

Perry, Marc. "Global Black Self-Fashionings: Hip Hop as Diasporic Space." *Identities* 15, no. 6 (December 2008): 635–64.

———. *Negro Soy Yo: Hip Hop and Raced Citizenship in Neoliberal Cuba.* Durham: Duke University Press, 2015.

Picker, John. *Victorian Soundscapes.* New York: Oxford University Press, 2003.

Pollock, Sheldon. "Cosmopolitan and Vernacular in History." *Public Culture* 12, no. 3 (2000): 591–625.

———. "The Cosmopolitan Vernacular." *Journal of Asian Studies* 57, no. 1 (February 1998): 6–37.

Poole, Geoffrey. "Black-White-Rainbow: A Personal View on What African Music Means to the Contemporary Western Composer." In *Composing the Music of Africa: Composition, Interpretation and Realisation*, edited by Malcolm Floyd. Aldershot, UK: Ashgate, 1999.

Portes, Alejandro, Luis E. Guarnizo, and Patricia Landolt. "The Study of Transnationalism: Pitfalls and Promise of an Emergent Research Field." *Ethnic and Racial Studies* 22, no. 2 (1999): 217–37.

Povinelli, Elizabeth. *The Empire of Love: Toward a Theory of Intimacy, Genealogy, and Carnality.* Durham: Duke University Press, 2006.

Prashad, Vijay. *Everybody Was Kung Fu Fighting: Afro-Asian Connections and the Myth of Cultural Purity.* Boston: Beacon, 2001.

Pratt, Mary Louise. *Imperial Eyes: Travel Writing and Transculturation.* New York: Routledge, 1992.

———. "Why the Virgin of Zapopan Went to Los Angeles: Reflections on Mobility and Globality." Keynote address presented at the Third Annual Encuentro of the Hemispheric Institute, Lima, Peru, July 8, 2002. http://hemi.nyu.edu/eng/seminar /peru/call/mlpratt.shtml.

Pugliese, Christina. *Gikuyu Political Pamphlets and Hymn Books, 1945–1952.* Travaux et Documents 11. Nairobi, Kenya: Institute Français de Recherche en Afrique, 1993.

Rabinow, Paul. "Representations Are Social Facts: Modernity and Post-Modernity in Anthropology." In *Writing Cultures: The Poetics and Politics of Ethnography*, edited by James Clifford and George E. Marcus, 234–61. Berkeley: University of California Press, 1986.

Radano, Ronald. "Introduction." *Musical Quarterly* 89, no. 4 (Winter 2006): 452–58.

———. *Lying Up a Nation: Race and Black Music.* Chicago: University of Chicago Press, 2003.

Radano, Ronald, and Philip Bohlman, eds. *Music and the Racial Imagination.* Chicago: University of Chicago Press, 2000.

Radwanski, Livia. "Cultura Sonidera." http://liviaradwanski.com/site/archives /portfolio/cultura-sonidera.

Ragland, Cathy. "Communicating the Collective Imagination: The Sociospatial World of the Mexican Sonidero in Puebla, New York, and New Jersey." In *Cumbia! Scenes of a Migrant Latin American Music Genre,* edited by Héctor Fernández L'Hoeste and Pablo Vila, 119–37. Durham: Duke University Press, 2013.

———. "Mexican Deejays and the Transnational Space of Youth Dances in New York and New Jersey." *Ethnomusicology* 47, no. 3 (Autumn 2003): 338–54.

Rana, Junaid. *Terrifying Muslims: Race and Labor in the South Asian Diaspora.* Durham: Duke University Press, 2011.

Ratshilumela, Phathu. "AIRCO Takes a Step Further against Piracy!" *Music Industry Online,* March 23, 2008. www.mio.co.za/article/airco-takes-a-step-further-against -piracy-2007–05–23.

Rawlinson, Nancy. "Linton Kwesi Johnson: Dread Beat an' Blood: Inglan Is a Bitch." *Spike,* December 1, 1998. www.spikemagazine.com/1298kwes.php.

Ray, Sitansu. "Tagore on Music and Musical Aesthetics." *Sangeet Natak Akademi* 56 (1980): 17–43.

Reitan, Ruth. *The Rise and Decline of an Alliance: Cuban and African American Leaders in the 1960s.* East Lansing: Michigan State University Press, 1999.

Representing the Recording Industry of South Africa. "Piracy and Organised Crime." www.stoppiracy.org.za/?page_id=88.

Ribeiro, Gustavo Lins. *Cultural Diversity as a Global Discourse.* Série Antropologia 412. Brasília: Departamento de Antropologia da Universidade de Brasília, 2007.

Richards, Thomas. *The Imperial Archive: Knowledge and the Fantasy of Empire.* London: Verso, 1998.

Ritter, Jonathan, and J. Martin Daughtry, eds. *Music in the Post-9/11 World.* New York: Routledge, 2007.

Rivera, Raquel. *New York Ricans from the Hip Hop Zone.* New York: Palgrave, 2003.

Robbins, Bruce. "Introduction Part I: Actually Existing Cosmopolitanism." In *Cosmopolitics: Thinking and Feeling beyond the Nation,* edited by Pheng Cheah and Bruce Robbins, 1–19. Minneapolis: University of Minnesota Press, 1998.

Roberts, John Storm. *The Latin Tinge: The Impact of Latin American Music on the United States.* New York: Oxford University Press, 1999.

Roberts, Michael. "The Imperialism of Silence under the British Raj: Arresting the Drum." In *Exploring Confrontation: Sri Lanka: Politics, Culture, and History,* 149–82. Switzerland: Harwood Academic, 1994.

Robertson, Bronwen. *Reverberations of Dissent: Identity and Dissent in Iran's Illegal Music Scene.* London: Continuum, 2012.

Rodney, Walter. *How Europe Underdeveloped Africa.* London: Bogle-L'Ouverture, 1972.

Rohter, Larry. "Music Dialogue beyond Embargoes." *New York Times,* March 25, 2011. www.nytimes.com/2011/03/25/arts/music/cuban-music-renaissance-in-new-york .html?_r=1&scp=1&sq=ned%20sublette&st=cse.

Romero, Simon. "People Power Thwarts the Olympics." *Sydney Morning Herald,* March 10, 2012. www.smh.com.au/world/people-power-thwarts-olympic-planners -20120309-1upqy.html.

Rossiter, Ned. *Organized Networks: Media Theory, Creative Labor, New Institutions.* Rotterdam: NAi, 2006.

Roumain, Jacques. *When the Tom-Tom Beats: Selected Prose and Poems.* Translated by Joanne Fungaroli and Ronald Sauer. Azul's Caribfest Series 2. Washington, DC: Azul, 1995.

Roy, Arundhati. *An Ordinary Person's Guide to Empire.* New Delhi: Penguin, 2005.

Rubell, Jonathan. "Dis Essay." http://debate.uvm.edu/dreadlibrary/Rubell.htm.

Sadoh, Godwin. "Intercultural Creativity in Joshua Uzoigwe's Music." *Africa: Journal of the International African Institute* 74 (2004): 633–61.

Said, Edward. *Culture and Imperialism.* New York: Knopf, 1993.

Sakakeeny, Matt. *Roll with It: Brass Bands in the Streets of New Orleans.* Durham: Duke University Press, 2013.

Sankey, Ira D., James McGranahan, and George C. Stebbins, comps. *Gospel Hymns, Nos. 1–6.* New York: John Church and Biglow and Main, 1895.

Sarazzin, Thilo. *Deutschland schafft sich ab: Wie wir unser Land aufs Spiel setzen.* Munich: Deutsche Verlags-Anstalt, 2010.

———. *Europa braucht den Euro nicht: Wie uns politisches Wunschdenken in die Krise geführt hat.* Munich: Deutsche Verlags-Anstalt, 2012.

Sartre, Jean-Paul. *"What Is Literature?" and Other Essays.* Translated by Bernard Frechtman. Cambridge: Harvard University Press, 1988.

Sassen, Saskia. *The Global City: New York, London, Tokyo.* Princeton, NJ: Princeton University Press, 1991.

———. *Global Networks, Linked Cities.* New York: Routledge, 2002.

———. "Weaponized Fences and Novel Borderings: The Beginnings of a New History." In *Beyond la Frontera: The History of U.S.-Mexico Migration,* edited by Mark Overmeyer-Velázquez. New York: Oxford University Press, 2011.

Sawyer, Mark. *Racial Politics in Post-Revolutionary Cuba.* Cambridge: Cambridge University Press, 2005.

Saxenian, AnnaLee. *Regional Advantage: Culture and Competition in Silicon Valley and Route 128.* Cambridge: Harvard University Press, 1996.

Scales, Rebecca P. "Subversive Sound: Transnational Radio, Arabic Recordings, and the Dangers of Listening in French Colonial Algeria, 1934–1939." *Comparative Studies in Society and History* 52, no. 2 (2010): 384–417.

Schafer, R. Murray. *The Tuning of the World.* New York: Knopf, 1977.

Schenker, Frederick. "Navigating Musical Latitudes: Hearing Empire in the Global Circuits of Early Twentieth-Century Popular Music." Paper presented at the International Association of the Study of Popular Music, Chapel Hill, NC, March 13–16, 2014.

Scherzinger, Martin. "György Ligeti and the Aka Pygmies Project." *Contemporary Music Review* 25 (2006): 227–62.

———. "Negotiating the Music Theory/African Music Nexus: A Political Critique of Ethnomusicological Anti-Formalism and a Strategic Analysis of the Harmonic Patterning of the Shona Mbira Song 'Nyamaropa.'" *Perspectives of New Music* 39 (2001): 5–118.

———. "Review of *Music, Modernity and the Global Imagination: South Africa and the West* [by Veit Erlmann]." *Journal of the Royal Musical Association* 126 (2001): 117–41.

Schiffer, Michael B. *The Portable Radio in American Life.* Tucson: University of Arizona Press, 1992.

Scott, David. *Conscripts of Modernity: The Tragedy of Colonial Enlightenment.* Durham: Duke University Press, 2004.

Scott, James C. *Domination and the Arts of Resistance: Hidden Transcripts.* New Haven, CT: Yale University Press, 1990.

Scribner, Charity. *Requiem for Communism.* Cambridge: MIT Press, 2003.

Seeger, Anthony. "Lessons Learned from the ICTM (NGO) Evaluation of Nomination for the UNESCO Masterpieces of the Oral and Intangible Heritage of Humanity, 2001–2005." In *Intangible Heritage,* edited by Laurajane Smith and Natsuko Akagawa, 112–28. London: Routledge, 2009.

Seigel, Micol. "Beyond Compare: Historical Method after the Transnational Turn." *Radical History Review* 91 (Winter 2005): 62–90.

———. "The Disappearing Dance: Maxixe's Imperial Erasure." *Black Music Research Journal* 25, nos. 1/2 (Spring/Fall 2005): 93–117.

———. *Uneven Encounters: Making Race and Nation in Brazil and the United States.* Durham: Duke University Press, 2009.

Sen, Amartya. *Identity and Violence: The Illusion of Destiny.* New York: W. W. Norton, 2006.

Sen, Nabaneeta. "The 'Foreign Reincarnation' of Rabindranath Tagore." *Journal of Asian Studies* 25, no. 2 (1966): 275–86.

Senghor, Léopold Sédar, ed. *Anthologie de la nouvelle poésie nègre et malgache de langue française.* 1948. Reprint, Paris: Presses Universitaires de France, 1972.

———. "Liminary Poem." In *The Collected Poetry,* translated by Melvin Dixon. Charlottesville: University Press of Virginia, 1991.

Serotte, Mary. *1989: The Struggle to Create a Post Cold War Europe.* Princeton, NJ: Princeton University Press, 2011.

Shank, Barry. *The Political Force of Musical Beauty.* Durham: Duke University Press, 2014.

Shanley, John B. "Bayanihan Troupe." *New York Times,* October 26, 1959, 59.

Shanyue, Gao. "The Other Agenda of *Air Hostess.*" [In Chinese.] *Ta Kung Pao,* June 10, 1959, 6.

Sharma, Nitasha. *Hip Hop Desis: South Asian Americans, Blackness, and a Global Race Consciousness.* Durham: Duke University Press, 2010.

Sharp Sharp! (The Kwaito Story). Directed by Aryan Kaganof. Johannesburg: Mandala Films, 2003.

Sharpley-Whiting, T. Denean. *Pimps Up, Ho's Down: Hip Hop's Hold on Young Black Women*. New York: New York University Press, 2007.

Sheffield, Rob. *Love Is a Mix-Tape: Life and Loss, One Song at a Time*. New York: Three River, 2007.

Sheikh, Irum. *Detained without Cause: Muslims' Stories of Detention and Deportation in America after 9/11*. New York: Palgrave Macmillan, 2011.

Shelton, Marie-Denise. "Le monde noir dans la littérature dadaiste et surréaliste." *French Review* 57, no. 3 (February 1984): 320–28.

Shi, Shu-mei. *The Lure of the Modern: Writing Modernism in Semicolonial China, 1917–1937*. Berkeley: University of California Press, 2001.

Shifman, Limor. *Memes in Digital Culture*. Cambridge: MIT Press, 2014.

Shih, C. S. Stone. "Taiwan Ballads as a Form of Mainstream Popular Music: Shanghai and Other Mixed-blood Influences in Musical Taipei, 1930–1960." [In Chinese.] *Taiwan Shehui Xuekan* 47 (September 2011): 94–141.

Shiloah, Amnon, ed. *The Epistle on Music of the Ikhwan al-Safa (Bagdad, 10th Century)*. Tel Aviv: Tel-Aviv University, Faculty of Fine Arts, 1978.

Shope, Bradley. "They Treat Us White Folks Fine." *South Asian Popular Culture* 5, no. 2 (2007): 97–116.

Simmel, Georg, "The Metropolis and Mental Life." In *The Sociology of Georg Simmel*, translated by Kurt H. Wolff, 409–424. 1902–3. Reprint, Glencoe, IL: Free Press, 1950.

Singh, Nikhil Pal. *Black Is a Country: Race and the Unfinished Struggle for Democracy*. Cambridge: Harvard University Press, 2004.

Sisario, Ben. "When the Beat Came in a Box." *New York Times,* October 15, 2010.

Slater, Howard. "Cannon Blasting for a Living Culture." *Resonance* 8, no. 1 (1999). www.1-m-c.org.uk/.

Smith, Mark M. *Sensing the Past: Seeing, Hearing, Smelling, Tasting, and Touching in History*. Berkeley: University of California Press, 2007.

Smith, Pamela J. "Caribbean Influences on Early New Orleans Jazz." Masters thesis, Tulane University, 1986.

Smith, Susan J. "Beyond Geography's Visible Worlds: A Cultural Politics of Music." *Progress in Human Geography* 21, no. 4 (August 1997): 502–29.

Soloman, Thomas. "Hardcore Muslims: Islamic Themes in Turkish Rap between Diaspora and Homeland." In *Muslim Rap, Halal Soaps, and Revolutionary Theater: Artistic Developments in the Muslim World*, edited by Karin van Nieuwkerk, 27–55. Austin: University of Texas Press, 2011.

Sousa, John Philip. *National, Patriotic and Typical Airs of All Lands*. Philadelphia: H. Coleman, 1890.

Southern, Eileen. *The Music of Black Americans: A History*. New York: W. W. Norton, 1971.

Soyinka, Wole. "The Arts in Africa during the Period of Colonial Rule." In *General History of Africa, Vol. VII: Africa under Colonial Domination, 1880–1935*, edited by A. Adu Boahen, 539–63. London: Heinemann and UNESCO, 1985.

St. John, Graham. "Outback Vibes: Sound Systems on the Road to Legitimacy." *Post-colonial Studies* 8, no. 3 (2005); 321–36.

Staley, S. James. "Is It True What They Say about China?" *Metronome* (December 1936).

Stanyek, Jason. "Transmissions of an Interculture: Pan-African Jazz and Intercultural Improvisation." In *The Other Side of Nowhere: Jazz, Improvisation, and Communities in Dialogue*, edited by Daniel Fischlin and Ajay Heble, 87–130. Middletown, CT: Wesleyan University Press, 2004.

Statistisches Reichsamt, ed. *Monatliche Nachweise über den auswärtigen Handel Deutschlands / Herausgegeben vom Statistischen Reichsamt* 1 (December 1925).

———. *Monatliche Nachweise über den auswärtigen Handel Deutschlands / Herausgegeben vom Statistischen Reichsamt* 2 (December 1929).

Stearns, Marshall. *The Story of Jazz.* Oxford: Oxford University Press, 1956.

Sterne, Jonathan. *The Audible Past: Cultural Origins of Sound Reproduction.* Durham: Duke University Press, 2003.

———. *MP3: The Meaning of a Format.* Durham: Duke University Press, 2012.

Stevens, Robin, and Eric Akrofi. "Tonic Sol-fa in South Africa—A Case of Endogenous Musical Practice." In *Australian Association for Research in Music Education: Proceedings of the XXVIth Annual Conference, 25–28 September 2004.* Southern Cross University, Tweed-Gold Coast Campus, New South Wales, Australia, September 25–28, 2004, 301–14. Clayton, Victoria: Australian Association for Research in Music Education, 2004.

Stewart, Gary. *Rumba on the River: A History of the Popular Music of the Two Congos.* London: Verso, 2000.

Stewart, Kathleen. *Ordinary Affects.* Durham: Duke University Press, 2007.

Stich, Sidra. *Anxious Visions: Surrealist Art.* New York: University Art Museum; Abbeville, 1990.

Stokes, Martin. "John Blacking and Ethnomusicology." In *The Queen's Thinkers: Essays on the Intellectual Heritage of a University*, edited by David N. Livingstone and Alvin Jackson, 159–70. Belfast: Blackstaff, 2008.

Stout, Harry S. *Upon the Altar of the Nation: A Moral History of the Civil War.* New York: Viking, 2006.

Stovall, Tyler. *Paris Noir: African Americans in the City of Light.* Boston: Houghton Mifflin, 1996.

Sublette, Ned. *Cuba and Its Music: From the First Drums to the Mambo.* Chicago: Chicago Review, 2004.

———. *The World That Made New Orleans: From Spanish Silver to Congo Square.* Chicago: Lawrence Hill, 2008.

Suisman, David. *Selling Sounds: The Commercial Revolution in American Music.* Cambridge: Harvard University Press, 2009.

Sultzbach, Kelly. "Embodied Modernism: The Flesh of the World in E. M. Forster, Virginia Woolf, and W. H. Auden." PhD dissertation, University of Oregon, 2008.

Sumera, Matthew. "War's Audiovisions: Music, Affect, and the Representation of Contemporary Conflict." PhD dissertation, University of Wisconsin, 2013.

Szendy, Peter. *Hits: Philosophy in the Jukebox.* Translated by Will Bishop. 2008. Reprint, New York: Fordham University Press, 2012.

Tagore, Rabindranath. *The Home and the World.* 1919. Reprint, Madras: Macmillan India, 1992.

———. *My Reminiscences.* New York: Macmillan, 1917.

Taguieff, Pierre-André. *The Force of Prejudice: On Racism and Its Doubles.* Translated and edited by Hassan Melehy. Minneapolis: University of Minnesota Press, 2001.

Taiwo, Olufemi. *How Colonialism Preempted Modernity in Africa.* Bloomington: Indiana University Press, 2010.

Tappert, Wilhelm. *Wandernde Melodien.* 2nd ed., enlarged. Leipzig: List und Francke, 1890.

Tate, Claudia. *Cigarette Wars: The Triumph of "the Little White Slaver."* New York: Oxford University Press, 1999.

Taylor, Diana. "Save as . . . Knowledge and Transmission in the Age of Digital Technologies." In *Foreseeable Futures #10: Position Papers from Imagining America,* 2–20. Imagining America, 2011. http://imaginingamerica.org/wp-content/uploads/2011/05 /Foreseeable-Futures-10-Taylor.pdf.

Taylor, Jeremy. "From Transnationalism to Nativism? The Rise, Decline, and Reinvention of a Regional Hokkien Entertainment Industry." *Inter-Asian Cultural Studies* 9, no. 1 (2008): 62–81.

———. *Rethinking Transnational Chinese Cinemas: The Amoy-Dialect Film Industry in Cold War Asia.* London: Routledge, 2011.

Taylor, Timothy. *Beyond Exoticism: Western Music and the World.* Durham: Duke University Press, 2007.

Terranova, Tiziana. "Free Labor: Producing Culture for the Digital Economy." *Social Text* 18, no. 2 (2000): 33–58.

Thallam, Satya. "International Property Rights Index, 2008 Report." *Property Rights Alliance.* http://www.libinst.ch/publikationen/LI-2008-IPRI-Report.pdf.

Thiong'o, Ngũgĩ wa. *Decolonising the Mind: The Politics of Language in African Literature.* London: James Currey, 1986.

———. *Devil on the Cross.* Translated by Ngũgĩ wa Thiong'o. Oxford: Heinemann, 1982.

———. *Dreams in a Time of War: A Childhood Memoir.* London: Harvill Secker, 2010.

———. "Enactments of Power: The Politics of Performance Space." In *Penpoints, Gunpoints, and Dreams: Towards a Critical Theory of the Arts and the State in Africa,* 37–70. Oxford: Clarendon, 1998.

———. *Globalectics: Theory and the Politics of Knowing.* New York: Columbia University Press, 2012.

———. *Moving the Centre: The Struggle for Cultural Freedoms.* London: James Currey, 1993.

Thompson, Robert Farris. *Tango: The Art History of Love.* New York: Vintage, 2006.

Tinhorão, José Ramos. *O samba agora vai . . . a farsa da música popular no exterior.* Rio de Janeiro: JCM Editôres, 1969.

Titon, Jeff Todd, ed. *Worlds of Music: An Introduction to the Musics of the World's Peoples.* 5th ed. Belmont, CA: Schermer Cengage Learning.

Todorova, Maria, ed. *Remembering Communism: Genres of Representation.* New York: Social Science Resource Council, 2010.

Tomlinson, John. *Cultural Imperialism: A Critical Introduction.* Baltimore, MD: Johns Hopkins University Press, 1991.

Tommasini, Anthony. *Virgil Thomson: Composer on the Aisle.* New York: W. W. Norton, 1997.

Torgovnick, Mariana. *Gone Primitive: Savage Intellects, Modern Lives.* Chicago: University of Chicago Press, 1990.

Tota, Antônio Pedro. *O imperialismo sedutor: A americanização do Brasil na época da segunda guerra.* São Paulo: Companhia das Letras, 2000.

Tracey, Hugh. "African Music within Its Social Setting." *African Music* 2, no. 1 (1958): 56–58.

———. "Basutoland Recording Tour: November 19th to December 3rd, 1959." *African Music* 2, no. 2 (1959): 69–76.

———. *Chopi Musicians: Their Music, Poetry, and Instruments.* 1948. Reprint, Oxford: Oxford University Press and International African Institute, 1970.

———. *The Evolution of African Music and Its Function in the Present Day.* Isma Papers no. 3. Johannesburg: Institute for the Study of Man in Africa, 1961.

———. "Report on the I.L.A.M. Nyasaland Recording Tour (May 7th to June 30th, 1958)." *African Music* 2, no. 1 (1958): 65–68.

Tronti, Mario. "Our Operaismo." *New Left Review* 73 (January–February 2012): 119–39.

Tsing, Anna. "The Global Situation." *Cultural Anthropology* 15, no. 3 (2000): 327–60.

Turino, Thomas. *Nationalists, Cosmopolitans, and Popular Music in Zimbabwe.* Chicago: University of Chicago Press, 2000.

Tymoczko, Dmitri. *A Geometry of Music: Harmony and Counterpoint in the Extended Common Practice.* New York: Oxford University Press, 2011.

UNESCO. *Convention for the Safeguarding of the Intangible Cultural Heritage.* Paris: UNESCO, 2003. http://unesdoc.unesco.org/images/0013/001325/132540e.pdf.

———. *Nomination for Inscription on the Representative List in 2009 (Reference No. 00258).* Paris: UNESCO, 2009. www.unesco.org/culture/ich/index.php?lg=en&pg=00011&RL=00258.

United Kingdom Statistical Office of the Customs and Excise Department. *Annual Statement of the Trade of the United Kingdom with Foreign Countries and British Countries 1929 Compared with the Years 1925–1928.* Vol. 3. London: His Majesty's Stationery Office, 1930.

United Nations Conference on Trade and Development. *Creative Economy Report 2008: The Challenge of Assessing the Creative Economy: Towards Informed Policy-Making.* Geneva: United Nations, 2008.

Vail, Leroy, and Landeg White. *Capitalism and Colonialism in Mozambique: A Study of Queliriane District.* London: Heinemann, 1980.

———. "Forms of Resistance: Songs and Perceptions of Power in Colonial Mozambique." *American Historical Review* 88, no. 4 (October 1983): 838–919.

———. *Power and the Praise Poem: Southern African Voices in History*. Charlottesville: University Press of Virginia, 1991.

Verán, Cristina. "¡Viva la rap revolución!" *Source*, no. 100 (January 1998): 132–35.

Verger, Pierre. "Book Review of Alfred Metraux, *Voodoo in Haiti*." *Man* 60 (July 1960): 111–12.

Vila, Pablo. "Tango to Folk: Hegemony Construction and Popular Identities in Argentina." *Studies in Latin American Popular Culture* 10 (1991): 107–39.

Villa-Franca, Gregóire de, and Maria Lucia Montes, eds. *Elsie Houston/A Feminilidade do Canto*. São Paulo: Grupo Takano, 2003.

Villepastour, Amanda. *Ancient Text Messages of the Yorùbá Bàtá Drum: Cracking the Code*. SOAS Musicology Series. Surrey, UK: Ashgate, 2010.

Virno, Paolo. *A Grammar of the Multitude*. Translated by Isabella Bertoletti, James Cascaito, and Andrea Casson. Los Angeles: Semiotext(e), 2004.

Virno, Paolo, and Michael Hardt, eds. *Radical Thought in Italy: A Potential Politics*. Minneapolis: University of Minnesota Press, 1996.

Vogel, Shane. *The Scene of Harlem Cabaret: Race, Sexuality, Performance*. Chicago: University of Chicago Press, 2009.

Volcler, Juliette. *Extremely Loud: Sound as a Weapon*. Translated by Carol Volk. 2011. Reprint, New York: New Press, 2013.

Von Eschen, Penny M. *Satchmo Blows Up the World: Jazz Ambassadors Play the Cold War*. Cambridge: Harvard University Press, 2006.

Wade, Peter. *Race and Ethnicity in Latin America*. 2nd ed. London: Pluto, 2010.

Walt, Vivienne. "El Général and the Rap Anthem of the Mideast Revolution." *Time*, February 15, 2011. www.time.com/time/world/article/0,8599,2049456,00.html.

Walzer, Michael. "Two Kinds of Universalism." In *Nation and Universe*. Vol. 11 of *Tanner Lectures on Human Values*, edited by Grethe Peterson, 509–56. Salt Lake City: University of Utah Press, 1990.

Washburne, Christopher. "The Clave of Jazz: A Caribbean Contribution to the Rhythmic Foundation of an African American Music." *Black Music Research Journal* 17, no. 1 (1997): 59–80.

Waterman, Christopher Alan. *Juju: A Social History and Ethnography of an African Popular Music*. Chicago: University of Chicago Press, 1990.

Watkins, Lee. "Minstrelsy and Mimesis in the South China Sea: Filipino Migrant Musicians, Chinese Hosts, and the Disciplining of Relations in Hong Kong." *Asian Music* 40, no. 2 (2009): 72–99.

Watson, J. R., ed. *An Annotated Anthology of Hymns*. Oxford: Oxford University Press, 2002.

Webb, Gavin. "The Wulomei Ga Folk Group: A Contribution towards Urban Ethnomusicology." PhD dissertation, University of Ghana, Legon, 2012.

Weingarten, Christopher. "Meet Hamada 'El General' Ben Amor, the Tunisian Rapper Who Changed the World." *Pop Dust*, January 28, 2001. http://popdust.com/2011/01/28/meet-hamada-el-general-ben-amor-the-tunsian-rapper-who-changed-the-world/.

Wiggins, Trevor. "An Interview with J. H. Kwabena Nketia: Perspectives on Tradition and Modernity." *Ethnomusicology Forum* 14, no. 1 (June 2005): 57–81.

Williams, Juliet A. "On the Popular Vote." *Political Research Quarterly* 58, no. 4 (December 2005): 637–46.

Williams, William Appleman. *Empire as a Way of Life: An Essay on the Causes and Character of America's Present Predicament, along with a Few Thoughts about an Alternative.* New York: Oxford University Press, 1980.

———. *The Tragedy of American Diplomacy.* New York: W. W. Norton, 1959.

Williams, William Carlos. "Asphodel, That Greeny Flower." In *Journey to Love.* New York: Random House, 1955.

Wiredu, Kwasi, ed. *A Companion to African Philosophy.* Oxford: Blackwell, 2004.

———. *Cultural Particulars and Universals: An African Perspective.* Bloomington: Indiana University Press, 1996.

Wolf, Eric R. *Europe and the People without History.* Berkeley: University of California Press, 1982.

Wolfe, Charles K., and Ted Olson, eds. *The Bristol Sessions: Writings about the Big Bang of Country Music.* Jefferson, NC: McFarland and Company, 2005.

Wong, Ain-ling, ed. *The Cathay Story.* Hong Kong: Hong Kong Film Archive, 1992.

The World Bank and the Policy Sciences Center. "Workshop on the Development of the Music Industry in Africa." Paper presented at the World Bank–Policy Science Center Workshop on the Development of the Music Industry in Africa, July 20–21, 2001, Washington, DC.

Wright, Richard. *Black Power: A Record of Reactions in a Land of Pathos.* New York: Harper and Brothers, 1954.

Wright, Steve. *Storming Heaven: Class Composition and Struggle in Italian Autonomist Marxism.* London: Pluto, 2002.

Yancey, George. *Who Is White? Latinos, Asians, and the New Black/Non-black Divide.* Boulder, CO: Lynne Rienner, 2003.

Ye, Longyan. *Remembering the Taiwanese Recording Industry, 1895–1999.* [In Chinese.] Luzhou: Boyang Wenhua, 2001.

Yúdice, George. *The Expediency of Culture: Uses of Culture in the Global Era.* Durham: Duke University Press, 2003.

———. "We Are *Not* the World." *Social Text*, nos. 31/32 (1992): 202–16.

Yuran, Noam. *What Money Wants: An Economy of Desire.* Stanford, CA: Stanford University Press, 2014.

Za, Albin J., III. *The Poetics of Rock: Cutting Tracks, Making Records.* Berkeley: University of California Press, 2001.

Zavella, Patricia. *I'm Neither Here nor There: Mexicans' Quotidian Struggles with Mexican Migration and Poverty.* Durham: Duke University Press, 2011.

Zinn, Howard. *A People's History of the United States.* New York: Longman, 1996.

Žižek, Slavoj. "Blows against the Empire?" 2007. www.lacan.com/zizblow.htm.

———. *First as Tragedy, Then as Farce.* London: Verso, 2009.

Zon, Bennett. *Representing Non-Western Music in Nineteenth-Century Britain.* Rochester, NY: University of Rochester Press, 2007.

CONTRIBUTORS

KOFI AGAWU · is professor of music at Princeton University. His books include *Playing with Signs* (1991), *African Rhythm* (1995), *Representing African Music* (2003), and *Music as Discourse* (2008). A corresponding fellow of the British Academy since 2010, he was music theorist in residence for the Dutch-Flemish Music Theory Society in 2008–9 and George Eastman Visiting Professor at Oxford University in 2012–13. His introductory text, *The African Imagination in Music*, is forthcoming.

PHILIP V. BOHLMAN · is Mary Werkman Distinguished Service Professor of Music and the Humanities at the University of Chicago, where he is artistic director of the cabaret, the New Budapest Orpheum Society. Bohlman is also Honorarprofessor at the Hochschule für Musik, Theater und Medien Hannover. He was a recipient of a Guggenheim Fellowship in 2013. Among his recent books are *Focus: Music, Nationalism, and the Making of the New Europe* (2011), *Hanns Eisler—In der Musik ist es anders* (with Andrea F. Bohlman, 2012), *Revival and Reconciliation: Sacred Music in the Making of European Modernity* (2013), *Wie sängen wir seinen Gesang auf dem Boden der Fremde!* (2016), and the edited volume, *The Cambridge History of World Music* (2013). His most recent CD with the New Budapest Orpheum Society, *As Dreams Fall Apart: The Golden Age of Jewish Stage and Film Music, 1925–1955* (Cedille

Records), was released in 2014. With Ronald Radano, Bohlman is coeditor of the new monograph series, Big Issues in Music.

MICHAEL DENNING · is the William R. Kenan Jr. Professor of American Studies at Yale University, and codirector of the Initiative on Labor and Culture. His books include *Noise Uprising: The Audiopolitics of a World Musical Revolution*, *Culture in the Age of Three Worlds*, and *The Cultural Front: The Laboring of American Culture in the Twentieth Century*. He also coordinates the Working Group on Globalization and Culture, whose collective works include "Going into Debt," published online in *Social Text: Periscope*, and "Spaces and Times of Occupation," published in *Transforming Anthropology*.

BRENT HAYES EDWARDS · is a professor in the Department of English and Comparative Literature and the Center for Jazz Studies at Columbia University. His books include *The Practice of Diaspora: Literature, Translation, and the Rise of Black Internationalism* (2003) and *Uptown Conversation: The New Jazz Studies* (2004). His new book, *Epistrophies: Jazz and the Literary Imagination*, will be published in 2016, as will his translation of Michel Leiris's *Phantom Africa*. His current projects include the restoration of *Sweet Willie Rollbar's Orientation* (an experimental film made by Julius Hemphill and members of the Black Artists Group in 1972), and a book project on "loft jazz" in downtown Manhattan in the 1970s.

NAN ENSTAD · is professor of history at the University of Wisconsin and is a cultural historian of capitalism, race, and gender. She is the author of *Ladies of Labor, Girls of Adventure: Popular Culture and Labor Politics at the Turn of the Twentieth Century* (1999), and is currently completing a manuscript on the transnational cigarette industry titled, "The Jim Crow Cigarette: Following Tobacco Road from North Carolina to China and Back."

ANDREW F. JONES · teaches modern Chinese literature and media culture at the University of California, Berkeley. He is the author of *Like a Knife: Ideology and Genre in Contemporary Chinese Popular Music*, *Yellow Music: Media Culture and Colonial Modernity in the Chinese Jazz Age*, and *Developmental Fairy Tales: Evolutionary Thinking and Modern Chinese Culture*.

JOSH KUN · is associate professor in the USC Annenberg School for Communication and Journalism. He is the author of *Audiotopia* (2005), *And You Shall Know Us By the Trail of Our Vinyl* (with Roger Bennett, 2008), *Songs in the Key of Los Angeles* (2013), and *To Live and Dine in L.A.: Menus and the Making of the Modern City* (2015), and coeditor of the volumes *Sound*

Clash (2012), *Tijuana Dreaming* (2013), and *Black and Brown Los Angeles* (2013). He coedits, with Ronald Radano, the book series Refiguring American Music.

MORGAN JAMES LUKER · is assistant professor of music at Reed College. His studies focus on music and cultural policy in Buenos Aires with a special interest in the cultural politics of contemporary tango music. His book, *The Tango Machine: Musical Culture in the Age of Expediency*, is forthcoming.

JAIRO MORENO · teaches at the University of Pennsylvania in the Department of Music. He is the author of *Musical Representations, Subjects, and Objects* (2004) and coeditor, with Gavin Steingo, of a *boundary 2* issue on Sound and Value.

TEJUMOLA OLANIYAN · is Louise Durham Mead Professor of English, African, and African Diaspora literatures and cultural studies at the University of Wisconsin–Madison. He is the author of *Arrest the Music! Fela and His Rebel Art and Politics* (2004; revised edition, 2009), which was nominated for Best Research in World Music by the Association for Recorded Sound Collections in 2005. His other publications include *Scars of Conquest/Masks of Resistance: The Invention of Cultural Identities in African, African American, and Caribbean Drama* (1995). He is also coeditor of *African Literature: An Anthology of Criticism and Theory* (with Ato Quayson, 2010), *African Diaspora and the Disciplines* (with James H. Sweet, 2010), and *African Drama and Performance* (with John Conteh-Morgan, 2004).

MARC PERRY · is a visiting professor of anthropology and the humanities at Bard Early Colleges New Orleans. His research centers on the convergence of critical race studies and black expressive culture with a comparative focus on the circum-Caribbean, Latin America, and broader Afro-Atlantic region. Perry is the author of *Negro Soy Yo: Hip Hop and Racial Citizenship in New Liberal Cuba* (2015). His current project explores the post-Katrina racial and classed remapping of New Orleans by ways of market capital, tourism, and structural violence, and the ways working-class African Americans mediate theses currents through local music making and Carnival masking traditions.

RONALD RADANO · is professor of music at the University of Wisconsin–Madison, where he is presently Senior Fellow at the Institute for Research in the Humanities and teaches courses in cultural music studies and the transnational circulation of U.S. black music. Radano is the author of two award-winning books, *New Musical Figurations: Anthony Braxton's Cultural Critique* and *Lying up a Nation: Race and Black Music*. He is coeditor, with Philip V. Bohlman, of *Music and the Racial Imagination*. He is presently completing a new monograph on the historical formation of value in U.S. black music.

MICOL SEIGEL · is associate professor of American studies and history at Indiana University, Bloomington. Her work on policing, prisons, and race in the Americas has appeared in such venues as *Transition, Social Justice, Social Text, Journal of American History, Journal of Transnational American Studies, Hispanic American Historical Review*, and *Radical History Review*. Her book, *Uneven Encounters: Making Race and Nation in Brazil and the United States* (2009), received a finalist mention for the Lora Romero First Book Publication Prize of the American Studies Association. Seigel's research has been supported by the American Council of Learned Societies, the Cornell Society of Fellows in the Humanities, David C. Driskell Center for the Study of the African Diaspora at University of Maryland, the Institute of International Education, the National Endowment for the Humanities, and the Rockefeller Foundation. In 2014, Seigel was a visiting scholar at the University of Sydney's United States Studies Centre, drafting a manuscript on the transnational circulation of policing policy and practice during the Cold War tentatively titled "Beyond the Beat: Cold War Cops and the Nature of State Power."

NITASHA SHARMA · is the Charles Deering McCormick Professor of Teaching Excellence and associate professor of African American studies and Asian American studies at Northwestern University. Her work analyzes interminority relations in the United States in order to retheorize race and develop models of antiracism. Her publications include *Hip Hop Desis: South Asian Americans, Blackness, and a Global Race Consciousness* (2010) and "Pacific Revisions of Race: Blacks Address Race and Belonging in Hawai'i" (*Amerasia Journal*, 2011). She is currently working on an edited volume on race in Hawai'i and is writing the first ethnography on Black people in Hawai'i.

GAVIN STEINGO · is assistant professor of music at the University of Pittsburgh. He has published articles in journals such as *African Music, African Identities, Black Music Research Journal, Contemporary Music Review, Review of Disability Studies, The World of Music*, and *Cultural Critique* (forthcoming). His book, *Kwaito's Promise: Music and the Aesthetics of Freedom in South Africa*, is forthcoming. He has received grants and fellowships from a range of agencies and institutions, including the Andrew W. Mellon Foundation, the American Musicological Society, the Heyman Center for the Humanities, Akademie Schloss Solitude (Stuttgart), National Gugak Center (Seoul), Merck Pharmaceuticals, and, most recently, the Alzheimer's Association. In addition to his academic pursuits, he regularly consults with popular media outlets such as Afropop Worldwide and MTV Iggy and performance venues such as the Apollo Theater and Carnegie Hall.

PENNY VON ESCHEN · is professor of U.S. cultural and foreign policy history at Cornell University. Her books include *Satchmo Blows Up the World: Jazz Ambassadors Play the Cold War* and *Race against Empire: Black Americans and Anticolonialism*. She is currently writing a manuscript titled "Rebooting the Cold War: A Cultural History of Triumphalism and Nostalgia in the post-1989 World."

AMANDA WEIDMAN · is associate professor of anthropology at Bryn Mawr College. She is a cultural anthropologist with interests in music, sound, performance, technological mediation, gender, and postcoloniality. She has conducted research in Tamil-speaking South India since the mid-1990s. She is currently at work on a project on playback singing in relation to the cultural politics of gender in South India from post-Independence to the post-liberalization. Her publications include the book *Singing the Classical, Voicing the Modern: The Postcolonial Politics of Music in South India* (2006), several journal articles on performance, embodiment, and technological mediation in relation to South Indian classical music, film songs, and historic South Indian sound recordings, and a review article on voice for the *Annual Review of Anthropology*.

INDEX

aviation industry: Chinese musical film as promotion of, 76; in Taiwan, 81, 85–87

Chicago Defender newspaper, 58

China: cabaret culture and entrepreneurship in, 56–63; cigarette-sponsored radio shows in, 52; diasporic (Nayang) cultural circuit and, 76–77; emergence of multinational corporations in, 46; musical production in, 66–88; piracy networks and, 258–59

Chinese music, early recordings, 28, 34

Chomsky, Noam, 298

Chopi music, recordings of, 269–72, 276

Chopi Musicians (Tracey), 276

Christian fundamentalism, desi rap critique of, 297–98

Cidade de Deus (film), 167

cigarette industry: African American musicians and, 60–63; cigarettes as barter items in Shanghai, 55–56; in interwar Shanghai, 45–63

circuit listening: imperial archive and, 140–43; migration politics and, 196–207; world music and, 72–74, 89n13

circulation of things, 47, 140–43

Civil Disobedience Movement, 33

Clark, Ernest (Slick), 59

Classen, Constance, 3

class mobility: cold war politics and, 199–207; Cuban hip hop and, 210–23; desi rap and, 296–98; Houston's performances and, 124–28; literature about India and, 315–29; in postwar China, 70–74; tango culture and, 236–43, 244n22

Clayton, Buck, 57–63

Cleaver, Eldridge, 216

Clooney, Rosemary, 78

Coelho, Olga, 124

cold war politics: ethnomusicology and, 11; imperialism and, 187–207; neoliberalism and globalization and, 200–207

Cole, Nat "King," 136

Colombia, *sonidos* culture from, 97–104

colonialism: anticolonial music and, 35–42; aurality and, 317–19; cold war politics and, 199–200; cultural creativity under, 346–49; desi rap music and, 294–96; ethnomusicology and, 269–84; in Forester's *Passage to India*, 321–25; geographic boundaries and, 48; histories of silence and, 173–76; in literature about India, 314–29; military

bands and, 6, 136–38; sound production and, 2–13; tonality as colonizing force, 334–51; transnational exchange and, 56–63; vernacular phonograph music and, 25–42; visibility of, 318

The Colonizer and the Colonized (Memmi), 339

Columbia records, 27

Comaroff, Jean, 250, 257

Comaroff, John, 250, 257

Comité de Défense de la Race Nègre, 29

commodification of music, 13–19; colonial music and, 37; cultural imperialism and, 306–10

Common (rap artist), 212, 217–18

Common Era in Basra, 172–73

Communism, anticolonialism and, 29

"communism of capital," 250

Compagnie Gramophone du Française, 28

Congressional Black Caucus, 193

contrabando aesthetics, 112

contrapuntal approach to anticolonial music, 273–74, 286n27, 354n30

Cook, James, 2–3

Cooper, Frederick, 38

Coplan, David, 249, 276

Corbin, Alain, 2

Corelli, Archangelo, 334

corporate colonization: cabaret culture in Shanghai and, 53–56; desi rap and, 296–98; music and, 18–19; segregation of foreign settlements in Shanghai and, 59–60

corridos (Mexican popular songs), 26; migrant politics and, 105–7

Cortez, Jayne, 205

cosmopolitanism, in jazz, 148–53

Cotton Club, 29

counterarchival approach, ethnomusicology and, 272–84

country music: in Chinese musical production, 68; early recordings of, 27

Couperus, Louis, 331n23

covering-law universaling, intercultural equality and, 145–46

"Craven A" (Mu Shiying), 51

Crawford, Kate, 4

Creative Economy Report (United Nations), 251

Creative Industries Growth Strategy: Final Report (CIGS), 250–53 criminalization of movement, *sonidero* culture and, 103–4

"criollos," tango culture and, 235, 244n19

crossborder cultural production: Afro-Brazilian music and, 125–30; Chinese musical films and, 75–76, 81, 87; examples of, 16–17; imperial aurality and, 135–37; racialization of music and, 161–70, 181–82; *sonideros* and, 96–113

crossfading, *sonideros'* use of, 102–4

Cuba: African American exiles in, 214–16; Afro-Cuban culture and music of, 144–48, 211–23; apartheid economy in, 221–23; blues and music of, 136; Hip Hop Festival in, 17, 209–23; international exposure of music from, 29–30, 40; jazz and music from, 144–45, 159n35; market reforms in, 223n1; neglect of music from, 11; nonracial ideology in, 211, 221–22, 223n2; social structure in, 220–23; son sexteto in, 25–26; state institutionalization in, 223n5; Taiwan and music from, 80–81; vaudeville influences in music of, 37

Cuban Rap Agency, 223n5

CuBop, 144

cultural activity: in American Civil War, 177–81; Arab Spring and, 306–10; Chinese musical films and, 66–88; colonialism and, 338–51, 346–49; cultural diversity discourse and, 235–43; decolonization and, 30–42; as immaterial production, 255–59; imperialism and, 137–38; in Iraq, 170–73; job creation in South Africa through, 252–55, 259–62; music as, 9–10; in postwar Europe, 121–22; social transformation through, 10; *sonidos* as, 97–104; tango music as, 225–43

Cultural Confusion (album), 297

cultural exception, globalization and, 238–39

cumbia sonidera: migrant politics and, 105–7; *sonidos* culture and, 97–104

d'Alembert, Jacques, 7

Da Lench Mob (rap group), 299

Damas, Léon-Gontran, 282

Dammers, Jerry, 193

dance music: African American musicians and, 59–63; African popular music and,

348–49; Asian dance on U.S. television, 70–74; in Asian jazz circuit, 57–58; cigarettes and jazz and, 47–51; corporate culture and, 54–56; *sonideros* and, 96–104; tango culture and, 225–43. See also *bailes*

Dào Nha, 27

Darrat, Abdullah, 309

Davidson, Basil, 342, 350

Dávila, Arlene, 233–34

Davis, Angela, 216

Dead Prez hip hop group, 214–15, 217, 219–23

death, in migrant discourse, 107–10, 114n28

Debussy, Claude, 12

decolonization, 22n29; vernacular phonograph music and, 25–42

Decolonizing the Mind (Thiongo), 30

"Degenerate Art" of Nazi Germany, 9

de L'Autre Côté (From the Other Side) (documentary), 107–10

Delfino, Ollie, 78, 90n30

Del Monte cabaret (Shanghai), 55–56

democracy, desi rap critique of, 296–98

"Democracy" (desi rap song), 297

Demos, T. J., 102–3

Denning, Michael, 15, 25–42, 194, 263n18

Densmore, Francis, 41

De Paisano a Paisano (album), 105

deportation: of Romani migrants, 166–67; *sonidos* culture and, 103–7

"Deportee" (song), 106

Derrida, Jacques, 141–43, 158n21

desi rap music, 18, 293–94; critique of politics, religion and media in, 296–98; empire critiqued in, 299–304; transnational links in, 294–96

Destour, 29

"Devils in Your Government" (rap song), 297–98

Dexter, Dave, 71–72

"Di Eagle an' di Bear" (song), 187–207

Dietz, Bill, 262

digital technology: Arab Spring and, 306–10; aurality and, 317–19; hip hop music and, 293–94; *sonideros'* use of, 101–2, 113n11

"Di Good Life" (LKJ), 201–2

Dinah Shore Show, 70–74, 81

Dion, Celine, 6

ethnomusicology: colonialism and, 338–51, 354n20; cultural preservation and, 269–71; evolution of, 9–13; self-critique in, 285n8

Etoile Nord-Africain, 29

"European Music" (Tagore), 325

Euro-western music: ethnomusicology and, 10; imperialism and, 7–13; Ladysmith Black Mambazo and influence of, 340–41; Tagore's discussion of, 325–29; tango culture and, 236–43; tonality in, 334–35, 352n7

"Everything" (desi rap), 295

Ewe culture, music of, 335, 344–45

exoticism: in Houston's performances, 123–28; imperialist culture and, 29–30

expediency, tango culture and age of, 226

export of music, phonograph industry and, 32–33

Facebook, Arab Spring and, 307–10

Falklands War, 189

Fanon, Frantz, 30, 31–32, 39, 215, 279–81, 339

Far East Suite (Ellington), 149

"Fast Car" (song), 194

Feld, Steven, 12, 14, 89n13

A Feminilidade do Canto (The Femininity of Song) (album), 128–30

Fernandes, Father Andre, 270

Fétis, François-Joseph, 7–8

Fick, David, 251–52

Field, David, 54–56

50 Cent (rap artist), 304

Filipino music, 37; cigarettes and jazz and, 51; in Taiwan, 81

Finkelstein, Sidney, 9

"The Flute" (Tagore), 326

Flying Down to Rio (film), 127

Fodeba, Ketia, 279–80

folk music: in Africa, 339; African American musicians and, 119–21, 127–28; African compositions based on, 346–49; ethnographic study of, 41; histories of silence and, 174–76; mobility of, 168–69

Folkways Corporation, 273–74

Forces of Victory (album), 191

Fordist economic model, immaterial production and, 256–59

foreign investment, music in South Africa and, 260–62

foreign settlements in Shanghai: segregation in, 58–61; smoking and jazz and, 47–63

"Formosa Mambo" (song), 81

Forster, E. M., 18, 314–29, 331n32

Foucault, Michel, 157n18

France, anti-immigrant legislation in, 166–67

Frankfurt School, 231–32

Free Africa group, 193

"Free Nelson Mandela" (song), 193

French Revolution, music in, 9

frequency research, decontextualization of music and, 3

Fukuyama, Francis, 199

futurism, 122

Galeano, Eduardo, 2

Gallet, Luciano, 121

Gallo, Eric, 29

Gallop, Rodney, 32

gamelan music, 11–12, 21n22

Gamio, Manuel, 105

Gandhi, Mohandas K., 29, 30, 33, 36–37, 39

Gardel, Carlos, 26, 232

Garvey, Marcus, 40

Ge Lan. See Chang, Grace

gender: in Houston's performance persona, 124, 128–30; in literature of empire, 315–29; smoking and, 51–52

genocide, in music, 203–7

genre in music: Chinese musical films and, 67–68, 78; tango tourism and, 234–35

geopolitics: ethnomusicology and, 11–13; schizochronia and, 145–48; soundings of imperialism and, 176–81; U.S. imperialism and, 135–38

German record industry, exports from, 33

Germany, Turkish migrants in, 166–67

Germany Dismantles Itself (Sarrazin), 167

Gershwin, George, 118

gesunkenes Kulturgut (fallen cultural value), 168

"Getting to Know You" (song), 71

Ghanaian drumming, 274

Ghonim, Wael, 308–9

Ghosh, Amitav, 164

Ghosh, Rishab Aiyer, 257–58

intangible cultural heritage: diversity and development and legacy of, 228, 235–43; UNESCO convention regarding, 228–32

intellectual property: immaterial production and, 255–59; South African protections for, 259–62

interculturalism, schizochronia and, 145–48

Intergovernmental Committee for the Safeguarding of the Intangible Cultural Heritage (UNESCO), 229–32

International Federation of the Phonographic Industry, 258

International Library of African Music (ILAM), 274, 284n1

International Screen (Guoji Dianying) magazine, 70, 79

International Settlement of Shanghai, 61–63

international stereotypes, in Chinese musical films, 75

Internet: hip hop music and, 293–94, 307–10; *sonideros* on, 96

interwar cultural production: mobility of music and, 168–69; in Shanghai, 45–63

In the Castle of My Skin (Lamming), 288n55

Inventos: Hip Hop Cubano (film), 218

Iraq: cold war politics and, 198–99; cultural identity in, 170–73

Irelem, Abiola, 334

I Remember When (radio show), 116–21

Isḥāq al-Kindī, Abū Yūsuf Yacqūb ibn, 172–73

Islamic Revolution in Iran, 171–73

Islamophobia, hip hop music and, 295–96

Israeli Defense Force, 203–4

"It's No Goood to Stay inna White Man Country Too Long" (Mutabaruka), 196

Ives, Charles, 6

"I Want to Fly in the Blue Sky" (Wo yao feishang qingtian) (song), 76

Jack Carter Band, 57–58

Jackson, George, 210, 214

Jacobs-Fantauzzi, Kahlil and Eli, 218

Jamaican music: cold war politics and, 187, 192–207; sound systems and, 98–99; vernacular poetry and, 191, 195–97

James, C. L. R., 39, 189, 275–76, 278–79

Jameson, Fredric, 248

Janissary bands of Ottoman Empire, 5

Japan: Shanghai cabaret culture and performers from, 51, 55–56, 60; Taiwanese popular culture and, 82–83; transistor radios and, 88n6

jazz: in Africa, 89n13, 143–48, 160n49; anticolonialism and, 31–32, 280–82, 289n59; Asian jazz circuit, 57–63; Cuban music and, 144–45, 159n35; ethnomusicology and, 11–13; European reception of, 40; global branding of, 153–55; Houston's discussion of, 126; hybridity in, 143; imperialism and, 136–38; in interwar Shanghai, 45–63; musical exchange and origins of, 156n10; phonograph recordings of, 26; politics of, 9; schizochonia in, 143–48; in Taiwanese musical film, 85; U.S. imperialism and, 16–19; vernacular music and, 38–39; worldliness of, 148–53

Jazz at Lincoln Center, 153–54, 156n7

Jewish culture, in India, 170

Jim Crow segregation, African American jazz musicians and, 58–59

Johannesburg, South Africa, economic and cultural joint ventures in, 252–55

"Johannesburg" (song), 194

Johnny Clegg band, 194

Johnson, Happy, 58–59

Johnson, Linton Kwesi. *See* LKJ (Linton Kwesi Johnson)

Jones, A. M., 273, 339, 342–45

Jones, Andrew F., 15, 28, 66–88, 196; on anticolonial music, 34; on jazz in Shanghai, 48–49

Jones, Reginald, 59

Joyner, James N., 54, 60

Julio de Caro, 26

Junior Clan (hip hop crew), 220

Kabir (rap artist), 297, 305

Kalama's Quartet, 27, 40, 41

Kalawa Jazmee record company, 258–59

Kamīrīīthū community theater (Kenya), 282–83

"Kandahar Cruise (Sunny Sunday)" (rap song), 302

"Kankenene kambula mushete" (The small ant carrying the box) (song), 276

Kanyegenyūri songs, 283

Kaplan, Amy, 137, 139–43

CPSIA information can be obtained
at www.ICGtesting.com
Printed in the USA
LVHW052142261120
672778LV00013B/2008